A NORMAL PERSON DOING NORMAL THINGS

AN UNCOMFORTABLE MEMOIR

JAY COLBURN

BAWLER MEDIA

Published by Bawler Media

18117 Biscayne BLVD

Suite 2018

Miami, FL 36160

Library of Congress Control Number:

2022917704

Paperback ISBN: 9798985955002

Hardback ISBN: 9798985955019

Ebook ISBN: 9798985955026

Printed in the United States of America

This is a work of creative nonfiction. The events are portrayed to the best of the
author's memory. While the events of the book are true, those involving alcohol may
be less reliable. Some events have been compressed and some names and identifying
details have been changed to protect the privacy of people involved. Dialogue has
been recreated with the intention of maintaining the essence and emotional impact
of the original conversation.

CONTENTS

1

SPIT ME OUT TO GEORGIA

I'm almost 100% certain that I wasn't really born in the backwoods of the Deep South, but rather spat out by them. It's like Alabama ate something that disagreed with it and purged it after nine months of negotiations.

After my older sister arrived, quickly following our older twin brothers, my parents took measures to eliminate the possibility of more children. I showed up (from somewhere) anyway, proving the futility of their efforts or the overriding determination of my destiny. Either way, I became a slowly awakening disappointment. God had given my parents a surprise seed, and instead of a weeping willow, an oak, or a masculine rose bush, a reluctant dandelion peeked through the soil of their lovemaking. Soon, it became obvious that Alabama was no place for a dandelion; it had probably been trying to spit me out to Georgia the entire time.

For the first ten years of my life, we were poor and Pentecostal. The one benefit of this combination was that it was against our religion to do anything fun, but it didn't bother us because we couldn't afford it anyway. It also meant that God didn't allow my mom to work. This contributed significantly to our perpetual commitment to staying miles below the poverty line. Occasionally, she would sneak off to work at her sister's gas station to make extra money while my dad toiled away at the tractor implements factory. Afterwards, she would rush home, wash out all the cigarette odor, and complete her housewife duties. If my dad smelled a hint of cigarette smoke, he would ask questions and that would eventually lead to an argument. He was also not a huge fan of my aunt Evie, probably because she chain-smoked and actively practiced non-Pentecostalism. She also cursed, wore jeans and makeup, drank wine coolers, and owned multiple televisions. I thought she was awesome.

The bad thing about being poor and Pentecostal, besides everything, was there was really nothing else to do but survive, pray, and go to church. Imagine the Amish, but with electricity, cars, and less money. Three times a week, the women, wearing long skirts and barefaced with their uncut hair in a bun, and the men in simple outfits of light-colored, button-up shirts and belted trousers, would show up to praise Jesus and sing songs to the Lord.

Depending on how the preacher gauged the spiritual state of the world that week, the church service would range from subdued to very dramatic. Subdued services didn't make much of an impression, so I think I only remember one. The preacher probably had the flu or had eaten some bad barbecue that week. Or, maybe he was experiencing another weakness of flesh; I once witnessed him rubbing the leg of another man's wife, so maybe his fear of being struck by lightning for being a hypocrite in God's house would restrain his tongue. Some days, he would calmly talk about fishes and loaves rather than getting worked up about single mothers being more likely to give birth to the Antichrist. But, that was rare.

Since the world remained in an increasingly hopeless state of fucked-up, the service most weeks leaned towards the dramatic. It usually started with a few hymns and then crescendoed into a cadenced fire and brimstone sermon that pulsed and pulled you into its primal rhythm. This rhythm plucked disjointedly at people throughout the church as if they were instruments, and each pull of their spiritual string elicited an "amen" or a "hallelujah." Soon, congregants would speak in tongues and stand at their pews with arms raised.

For reasons lost to the years, one service was particularly emotional. Everyone in church was walking around with tears in their eyes, hugging each other. Except me. As the preacher's wife moved towards me, wet-bloused and open-armed, I panicked and froze in place. She pulled me into her ample bosom and I wondered if not crying would get me sent to hell.

Years later, I realized that it wasn't my dry eyes that were going to get me assigned to the down escalator at death.

I learned everyone is going to hell, especially the Baptists, because they were fake Christians, and the homosexuals (whoever they were), because they were abominations. Catholics were also going to hell, but there weren't many in our neck of the woods so they were rarely mentioned. Only good Pentecostal people would be saved from spending an eternity being tortured by the worst roommate ever, Satan.

I also learned that the world was going to end at any minute, and that the Communists or Russians (used interchangeably) were going to shoot me in the head in front of my family unless I took the mark of the beast on my arm. So, I could either have 666 tattooed onto my arm or get a bullet in the head. There were no good options. If I chose the tattoo, it meant an eternity in hell and probably having to watch the rest of my family get their heads blown off. Since they were much better Christians than me, they would have taken bullets for sure. I would be an orphaned 666 boy, wandering the planet alone until Satan eventually picked me up off the side of the road. I imagined myself sitting quietly in the passenger seat as he drove me to hell, singing AC/DC in his woefully seductive voice. My bloodstained pajamas (stained with the blood of my family and evidence of their true faith) would turn black with heat before gradually catching flame and engulfing me into my eternal burning.

I never learned when or how the Russians would get to us, but I knew the Four Horsemen were already close. So, I thought, maybe the Four Horsemen were the Russians... and if four of them could conquer us on horseback, then they must be pretty powerful. We were screwed.

Since the world was always going to end soon, my dad remained completely disinterested in improving himself or the lives of his family. He didn't worry that we never had enough food. It didn't seem to bother him that the walls of the bedroom I shared with my sister and two brothers glistened with frost on cold winter nights. He would sit in the living room, a tobacco-less pipe dangling from his lips (Pentacostals aren't allowed to smoke, but my dad still liked his pipe), reading and waiting for it all to be over. I don't think he was a bad person. He probably would've just been much happier living in the 1800s or possibly in a cave.

My father stood around six feet tall. Not skinny or overweight, just average. His light blue eyes and slightly larger nose distinguished him from others, and his head of white hair made him easy to pick out at church.

He and I were not close. I always assumed that he was the quiet type until I realized that I was the only one he wasn't talking to. Considering that they named me after him, you would think it would have connected us. That was far from the case. In fact, we both kind of gave up on the name Thomas after a while. Everyone called me by my middle name or some derivative of it, like Jay, Bluejay, or Jaybird. He had that head of white hair all of his life, so everyone called him Cotton.

I think he might have tried to hang out with me once or twice, but it didn't take him long to realize that I wasn't good at it. Plus, he preferred activities that usually involved killing something, while my favorite activities were coloring, behaving, and picking flowers for Mama. My dad had my twin brothers, David and Daniel, to kill stuff with, so I just gradually faded into his background. Thankfully, my sister was already there (in the background), so she and I started hanging out more. Rachel never asked me to kill anything and she had better toys.

While my father was relatively plain, my mother was beautiful (a description potentially biased by distributed affection levels). Hers wasn't an aggressive beauty; it lingered softly around her. Her long, thick black hair extended to slightly beyond her lower back. Since God wouldn't let her cut it or go to the beauty salon, she usually pulled it back and held it in place with bobby pins and Aqua Net. Other than the fact that she was only slightly shorter than my father, my mom stood in complete contrast to him—with her olive-tinged skin and dark brown eyes.

She would always ask me "If I left your daddy, would you go with me?" My answer was always yes. I wasn't sure if that would make me an accomplice to her mortal sin, but I knew I would follow her anywhere, even to hell. Though, there was the part of me that didn't believe this scenario would actually ever play out, because in our world divorce was an almost unimaginable sin.

My mom brought it up to my father a few times over the years. He would respond by clutching his chest, falling to the floor, and faking a heart attack. An ambulance would pull into the driveway, sirens blaring and lights flashing and take him away. A bit later, my mom would load her four kids into the car and drive us to the hospital to retrieve him. He would return home feeling much better, and my mom would let it go.

Our home was the color of key lime pie that had been sitting in the display case too long. While there was no heating or air conditioning, there was a fireplace, but it was only ever strong enough to heat one room. During the cold months, my mother would get up every morning, start a fire, and make our breakfast. I would stay in bed with my brothers, covering my head for warmth until the fire had been lit and was beginning to heat the living room. Then we would all scamper across the cold floors of the house and sit under a blanket on the couch waiting for Mom to finish breakfast.

Fortunately, when my mom left my dad it was summertime. Otherwise I might have just kept my head under the covers forever.

Because of the ever-deepening trench of poverty surrounding us, my dad eventually allowed my mom to get a job. I can only assume that he based his new position less on newly adopted feminism and more on the steady flow of hospital bills arriving in our mailbox. He insisted he would find the job for her, and it would be the only acceptable job for a Pentecostal woman: cleaning houses.

So, three times a week, while we were at school, my mom would leave our house and go to another man's house to clean. These small doses of freedom began to infiltrate our existence. and quickly developed into an addiction for my mom. She soon brought home a controversial gift: a black-and-white TV. Normally, my dad didn't take to sinful gestures such as this. My aunt Evie once set up a Christmas tree in our living room while we were at church. Underneath it, she had placed a box of food. As we pulled into the driveway, the multicolored lights blinking in the window hinted at something magical. We walked in and, for the briefest of moments, enjoyed our first Christmas tree. My father promptly unplugged the pagan symbol and dumped it on the porch as my mother took the box of food into the kitchen.

My father did not unplug the TV. He was maybe trying to be nice, or he had just given up, believing that the ever-reaching tentacles of sin had finally grabbed the ankles of his family. We were slowly being dragged into an unrighteous world while a fuzzy, gray Annie sang "Tomorrow" in the background.

Then my mom showed up wearing jeans and makeup. This alone may have shocked him into surrender. I can never be sure.

Finally, one day, my mom returned home from work and told my father once and for all that she was leaving him. This time, he did not clutch his chest.

In that moment, everything in the room vanished except my mother, sitting in a single chair, and my father standing over her. My father yelled at us "Get out!" and suddenly me and my brothers and sister were all outside, running in different directions.

I ran straight into the woods, alone, and lost sight of my brothers and sister. My feet were bare. As I fled, I had forgotten the woods were a place to go slow, a place of rattlesnakes, poisonous vines, and blackberry canes that reach and whip at you with a bitter sweetness. I cataloged the dangers beneath my feet and against my skin with their afflictions, mysteries for me to unravel later. My sweat dripped into my eyes and stung like his words: "Get out!"

Yet, scarier than the terrors in the woods, was my father's face staring at my mother. It's the one memory I have of him where he looked strong, and now it seems more like a possession, as if Satan himself had seized upon the briefest doorway and entered through the crack in my father's heart.

I ran faster and faster into the woods as a horrifying shadow of fear grew larger and larger behind me. Tears were mixing with the sweat now. I had always promised I would go with her. Instead, I ran scared and left her behind to face the Devil. Worried and guilty, I bit into my lips, but I kept running; the taste of blood, the penance for my betrayal.

Eventually, I came out of the woods and continued running down the road to my uncle's house. My siblings weren't faster runners than me, but I always had a notoriously terrible sense of direction. They had already arrived and told the story multiple times before I even made it into the driveway.

I felt like shit, but no one made a fuss over me. I assumed they were immune to feeling sympathy for a child with a hundred snakebites, multiple skin lacerations, and a bloodied lip. Or, maybe it was possible I had survived my woody ordeal in better shape than I imagined.

Our uncle loaded us into his pickup truck and returned us to the home where our mother no longer lived.

The following day, my mother returned and asked if any of us wanted to go with her. My siblings stayed behind. I, on the other hand, had been waiting for her to come for me; I had a promise to keep. Within minutes, I was packed and exited the house. My dad stood frozen, as if shocked and paralyzed by my betrayal, while my siblings waved goodbye. My mom and I turned out of the driveway and onto the dirt road in her little red car, never to call the green house home again. We were also no longer Pentecostal.

2

THE DEVIL'S MUSIC

After my mom left my dad, she and I moved from the woods of Maplesville into the town of Maplesville. There was a constantly blinking red light, a post office, a sheriff's department, a barber shop, a few random small shops, and a Dollar Bills. It wasn't very exciting, but everything was changing so fast that I didn't notice. My mom had cut her hair and now wore makeup and jeans all the time. She had even recently gotten her ears pierced and had become the most scandalous person in the town. Even though there were only 700 people, it remained quite a distinction.

Before, we could only listen to old Christian music. Now, we would drive around town in her new, gray Ford, listening to Bruce Springsteen and Elton John. I had only heard about Bruce Springsteen from a religious tract that I had found at the old green house. On the front of the pious pamphlet was a black and white drawing of a possessed man. The inside informed me that "I'm on Fire" was a song about a pedophile that could no longer control his urges and that Bruce Springsteen must be stopped before he raped every young girl that was home alone and unsupervised. The Devil lived in music. We must remain constantly vigilant to not let the hooky horns of rock & roll earworm us toward a life of pedophilia and tortured darkness.

My mom either didn't read the tract, or maybe she did and just considered it an invitation. Either way, being in her car and listening to "Born in the USA" and "Sad Songs (Say So Much)" made me feel like the arms of the world had just opened up and were giving us a great big hug.

We rented a small white house with a fenced-in yard. It smelled completely different from our old house, like chemicals instead of old wood. It wasn't an unpleasant odor, just foreign. Even after cleaning the entire house, the smell still lingered. My mom has always been the cleanest person I know, so I'm sure we would've cleaned it even if it smelled like gardenias.

For the first time in my ten years on earth, I had my own bed and my own room. My excitement faded to terror as I realized that I had never slept by myself before. My two older brothers had always shared my bed with me, with my sister a few feet away. They would torment me sometimes by making me sleep next to the window and telling me if a monster or madman broke in, he would get me. My death wouldn't be in vain because my screaming would wake them. They would wake my parents and escape to safety as my mangled corpse became sweet candy for a demon, or worse, just chopped into pieces and not savored by a Michael Myers type.

Now, without my siblings around, my muffled screams wouldn't save anybody. I would just be dead meat without a purpose. I ended up staying up as late as possible, hoping that as soon as my head hit the pillow, I would be out. Otherwise, I would lie in bed staring at the darkness, wondering what would come for me and from which direction.

Once, I even endured sitting through two hours of Geraldo Rivera as he explored "The Mystery of Al Capone's Vaults." If you missed it because you had a life or hadn't been born yet, you missed absolutely nothing. Turns out that the mystery was that there was no mystery, and Geraldo Rivera solved it all by himself. Fortunately for me, watching nothing happen for two hours is a great way to fall asleep. Also, fortunately for me, my mom's boss had been coming over a lot, and he would carry me to bed when I fell asleep in front of the TV. I'm sure my father would have found my mom a different house to clean if he'd known that her new boss, Lee, was single and attractive. But my father was not really known for doing his due diligence.

Lee had just retired from his job as an electrician in Anchorage, Alaska. He moved to Deatsville (near Maplesville), to be closer to his mother and siblings. His red-brick house sat on a hundred acres of land with a pool and a large, black walnut tree in the backyard. He wasn't rich, but he had so much more than we did that I assumed he was a millionaire. Besides being an electrician, he seemed to know how to do everything else too. He was building onto his house almost completely by himself, and always seemed to carry a hammer or a screw gun. My dad lacked tool-related skills, so it amazed me to see a person doing handy things so easily.

Lee also had twin sons, just like my mother, but his sons were older and not nearly as nice. Being from the north explained some of their lack of manners, but as they became increasingly less friendly with each visit, I realized it had more to do with us and less to do with which part of the country they were raised in. Mostly, they avoided me, so it was easy enough for me to avoid them back.

My mom and I still frequently went by our old house to see my siblings. One day, after school, we stopped by to drop off some fresh strawberries. Before we had even parked the car, my sister threw open the front door and came running down the creaky steps of the old green house. The brown and yellow dress my mom had sewn for her flew behind her as she moved. She made it to my mom's car window and said, "I want to go with you, Mama." With that, she collected her things while we talked to my brothers. By the time my dad arrived home from work, my sister was already miles away, listening to the Devil's music.

Then there were three of us living in the little house in town. My sister adjusted quickly to having a color TV and learning the heathen ways of the world. She could wear blue jeans and the slightest hint of makeup. In no time, she was singing the words of our songs from the front seat, while I sat in the back trying to drown out her and Bruce Springsteen.

Occasionally, we would bump into someone who took it upon themselves to remind us of our destiny. We ran into the preacher from our old church one day at my aunt's gas station. He politely stopped my mom as she was leaving, her body halfway out of the building, and said, "You know you're going to burn in hell forever, right?"

"Yes, I know," she said with a weak smile as we continued out the door. She had probably gotten used to it by now because a lot of relatives had suddenly become very interested in the future safety and wellbeing of my mother's soul. She was backsliding at warp speed and taking her children with her. I didn't mind because the soundtrack was good.

It had also become apparent that my mother's boss, Lee, was going to be taking the ride with us. My mom would work for him a few days a week and then fill in at the gas station on some of the other days. She was soon financially stable enough to go get my brothers. So, one day after school, she went back to the green house. She loaded up my brothers and all of their things and brought them to live with us in town.

A NORMAL PERSON DOING NORMAL THINGS

When my dad came home to an empty house, the Devil felt the event important enough to leave Bruce Springsteen and once again enter my father.

Before he had even finished parking his truck in our driveway, my dad was yelling like a crazy person. He burst through the door, poking his finger at my mother and pushing her back out of the kitchen and deeper and deeper into the hall. All we could do was follow and watch. My dad's hands became fire and his words brimstone as he pulled hell up from the floor of the shrinking hallway.

Finally he trapped my mother in the corner of the hall, but she had anticipated trouble. She reached behind the door of her bedroom and pulled out a rifle that she had borrowed from Lee. Satan then lost all interest in my father and abandoned him, and my mother now became the crazy person, pointing the gun at my father's chest and pushing *him* backwards, back down the hall.

"You better get out of here and leave us alone," she demanded.

"I'm a going! I'm a going!" he said as my mom bruised his sternum with the rifle.

Moments before, my brothers and sister and I had all been deathly afraid for my mother, but now we were deathly afraid for my father. We were trying to push the gun up toward the ceiling and away from my dad, but she kept finding the same spot on his chest. His face was the color of his hair as he retreated, walking backwards with his arms up. And then he was out the door, jumping over the hood of his car and driving away before my mom had even lowered the gun.

A nervous, curious neighbor waved from behind her chain-link fence. My mom waved back with her free arm.

"How ya'll doing over there?"

"We're fine, thank you," my mom said, passing the gun off to my oldest brother. "Ya'll doing alright?"

"Can't complain. Just doing a little yard work while there's a breeze," our neighbor responded, wiping her clean hands on her pants. "You turn your back for one minute and the weeds take over. They're like the Devil; you constantly have to keep guard."

"Yeah, I understand that." My mom tucked a stray piece of hair behind her ears. "Keep up the good fight."

The neighbor gave a clean-handed thumbs up and tried to fake doing yard work for a moment as we slipped back into the house.

Once again, we were all living together in a two-bedroom house. Now it was just a different house, one with air conditioning and without a father. Even without him, it felt smaller. My brothers were months into their teenage years, and my sister was just months away from hers, so they all wanted to stretch their growing legs out a bit. Our new living arrangement, when coupled with blossoming teen hormones, felt like a flower garden over a minefield. We were all still well behaved, but the clock was definitely ticking. Something would have to give... and soon.

Fortunately, something did give. Lee decided to go back to Alaska for the summer with his sons, and he asked my mom to stay at his house and take care of the property. She was still working for him, but she probably wasn't getting paid for all the time she was spending there.

So, my mom packed us up and moved us from Maplesville to Deatsville. We didn't know where we would go after the summer, but I had dreams of spending the days swimming and riding ATVs around Lee's property, so I didn't worry about it. My mom, however, didn't consider this a vacation; it was a summer work program with free housing.

Lee's house sat a mile from the main road, surrounded by a sprawling lawn and then fields and beyond that, trees. At the end of the driveway, near the house, a barbed wire fence lined one side and an area of thin trees and brush ran along the other. Unfortunately for us, my mom became fixated on clearing both areas and then keeping them clear. We spent hours pulling weeds along the fence row, and clearing brush, limbs, and leaves from the other side of the road.

Most people don't know that weeds are perhaps the most organized and spiteful life forms on the planet. I'm not fluent in the science of it, but either through chemical signals, telepathy, or purely spiteful will, they can respond quickly to any assumed attack against them and immediately summon reinforcements. By the time you finish, five weeds with a grudge against you have replaced every weed you pulled. If there is stillness in your soul, you can put your ear to the ground and hear them laughing at you. There was never a stillness in my soul because I hated pulling weeds on the fencerow and only wanted to be practicing my backflips into the pool. Instead, I was wilting in the heat and humidity while vengeful weeds slashed at my hands like miniature Leatherfaces. They are probably the main reason I never became an Olympic diver or married Greg Louganis.

I found an arrowhead one day while pulling weeds from the fencerow. The weeds had probably teamed up to bring it to the surface and were trying to figure out how to throw it at my head. In another day or two, they probably would've figured it out and slung it right into the center of my forehead. I may be giving them too much credit, but as a believer in evolution, I'm inclined to think weeds are probably the fourth most probable cause of our eventual demise. Obviously, global warming, nuclear weapons, and penis envy take the top three spots, with AI sitting in fifth. Fortunately, neither weeds nor any of the others got me that summer.

Lee came back from Alaska and didn't seem to notice the great battle that had been waged at the fencerow. He came home to a house full of another man's kids, while his own sons had stayed behind in Anchorage. My siblings and I were all very respectful, but it was surely a change for him. It obviously didn't faze him too much, as he and my mom married almost immediately after his return. Our temporary living situation had become permanent.

That meant my temporary bedroom was now my permanent bedroom, so my mom took me to buy curtains and a matching bedspread. Somehow, I ended up with a print of ducks walking through cattails. It is one of the greatest regrets of my childhood. I was so excited to have my own bedding and curtains that I said yes to the first design my mom liked. I had nothing against ducks, but I wasn't a hunter or an ornithology enthusiast, so it left me feeling unfulfilled.

Lying in bed that night, I hoped God would send my mom a vision of me in a room with leopard print bedding and window furnishings, and my mom would change her mind and take the ducks back to Sears the next day. I hoped for a miracle, but it never came.

As school time got closer, my second brother, Daniel, went back to live with my dad. I think he felt bad that everyone had abandoned him. My father had moved away from the green house and was now living in Clanton, in a small house that he rented from a man who lived in a large house nearby.

Once, my mom brought me over to my dad's to stay the weekend, and the man who owned the larger house met us in the driveway. He said to my mom, "That boy is funny."

My mom has a great sense of humor, and she always said that maybe I inherited it. But I think the man's statement probably concerned my obvious lack of masculinity rather than my comedic skills, because I had never even talked to the man, nevermind told him a joke.

"Thank you...?" She said, her response sounding more like a question.

After the divorce, my dad silently slid from the Pentecostal side of the church to the heathen Baptist side (they were all going to hell too). My dad was originally Baptist, and even preached occasionally at Baptist churches. Eventually, though, he got kicked out for preaching that divorce was an unforgivable sin.

When my parents met, I think my dad represented freedom and a bit of rebellion to my mom, who was raised strict Pentecostal. However, as soon as they got married, my dad became Pentecostal, so my mom's dreams of exploring the world of sin suffocated in her wedding vows.

Now that my dad was one of the divorced sinners, I think he thought it was best to make peace with the Baptists and rejoin their slightly more forgiving belief system. He had even started listening to 50s rock again. Whenever I visited, we would eat fried bologna sandwiches and drink sweet tea as the Devil's music slowly drowned out the memories of who we had been at the old green house in Maplesville.

3

MR. GAY MARBURY

I attended Marbury High School from fifth to ninth grade. At the time, it had around three hundred students from kindergarten through twelfth grade, and out of everyone, I was the gayest. I didn't want the title, but I didn't have a choice. They crowned and sashed me, and I didn't even know what it all meant.

There were three extremely butch sisters that went to Marbury too, so in retrospect, one of them should've won, but maybe they split the vote, and I only won by default. I really can't be sure they were lesbians because nobody ever asked them. Stupid people surrounded me all the time, but no one was stupid enough to ask them something like that. Plus, I carried a clarinet and they carried softball bats, so I was a far less formidable target.

In fifth grade, I didn't even know I was gay, but I did like to twirl things and turn cartwheels. Living in the woods with limited entertainment choices, I assumed it just meant I was artistic and resourceful. I would twirl every kind of stick I could find and even make my own flags out of PVC pipe and old cloth. Hanging out in the yard, I would listen to music, turn cartwheels, and twirl stuff. My family was probably grateful that we lived in the woods and nobody could see me exploring my talents. It's probably the reason they bought me a clarinet and put me in music class my first year at Marbury, just to give me something else to practice.

I would get called faggot a lot, but I wasn't exactly sure what that meant. Plus, during the 80s, faggot was the most popular putdown. You almost couldn't watch a movie without hearing the word multiple times. I didn't start putting it all together until I came home from school one day and told my mom and Lee that someone called me a faggot. I didn't see the need to say many someones did it practically every day. They handed me a big red dictionary and told me to look it up. I sat at the kitchen table and opened it to the F section.

faggot - a bundle of wood

- (slang) a homosexual

What was so bad about a bundle of wood? So weird. Well, I guess wood could be dumb, especially if it just sat there tied up to other wood. Stupid wood. I'm not stupid enough to be wood.

I knew nothing about the homosexuals, except the Pentecostals didn't like them and there was a billboard in town that featured one clutching his head while burning in a lake of flames. Once, on the bus, an older boy asked me if I was a homosexual like Elton John. My mom and I both loved Elton John, so I giggled, noticing that the word had "sex" in it. I hardly knew anything about sex except that it was cool and that I should be having it. My young and innocent mind then interpreted homosexual as someone who has sex at home (like Elton John). I was normally a bright kid, but that was not a shining moment for me. He repeated the question, and I giggled again. I wasn't sure how to answer; I didn't want to lie, but I didn't want him to know I wasn't having sex, especially not at home.

So, a faggot is slang for a homosexual male? Well, that doesn't sound that bad. I looked it up anyway, just to be sure.

Oh. My heart sank into my stomach and was digested immediately. Fumbling between embarrassment and devastation, I realized I was being called *the abomination*. I was the detested one spoken of so frequently in movies and school classrooms and hallways. Even though I still didn't even know that I was gay, it didn't matter. I closed the dictionary and left it on the table. Then I tried to creep to my room before my cracked spirit shattered to the floor in a million pieces.

From that moment on, I tried to watch how I moved and talked. I even tried not to smile because I wasn't really sure what I did that was getting me so much negative attention. It didn't make a difference. For almost five years, I felt like I was under attack.

In sixth grade, I could've taken up football to toughen my image, but I took the opposite route and joined the marching band. I was a decent clarinet player for a beginner, but the director insisted I play the bass drum on the field my first year. The tiny band only had eighteen members. Half were twirling things, and the other half were better or louder than me, so I became the obvious and only choice to fill the vacant position.

The drum was bigger than me, so I had to stick my pelvis out and my shoulders and chest back just to hold it up. Being a relatively new musician, I didn't exactly know how to keep the rhythm. The drum major would swing her arms at me a lot, but I could barely see her. When I could see her, I didn't know what she was doing. I would just hit the drum when my gut told me to. It turns out that intuition isn't the best substitute for talent and practice.

I never got better, but it didn't matter. Every Friday night during football season, I put on my 100% polyester band uniform and hit the field at halftime, heaving my bass drum. I would march back and forth across the field, trying not to pass out from the heat and the stress. My entire body would be sweaty, but especially my hands. I was so afraid of dropping my mallet that I would clench my fist until it was white. If the mallet fell out of my hand, I couldn't bend over to pick it up because the drum was too big and heavy. I would have to do a backbend just to attempt a rescue, and even then, there was only a very slim chance that I could pull myself back up. Mr. Gay Marbury would be stuck in a backbend in the middle of the football field long after the other members had marched off. I would be frozen in place with my bass drum pointed to the heavens. They would probably just continue the second half with me still there. After we lost the game (which you didn't need intuition to know was going to happen), all that would remain of me would be my sixth-grade hand triumphantly clutching a mallet.

Fortunately, my clenched fist never failed me, and I always made it back to the stands safely, where I could play my clarinet. Then, one of the twirling people would play the bass drum, since they had nothing else to do and were better at it, and I would happily hang out with my friends in the woodwind section.

Almost all of my friends were in the marching band, except Dani and Amy. They were into hardcore rock music and wouldn't have been caught dead holding a clarinet.

Before the internet and cell phones, Metal Edge magazine connected the world. At least, it connected my world. Every week when my mom left to get groceries, I jumped in the car with her. *"Going to town..."*

beat sitting at home in the woods, but more importantly, I needed fresh reading material. While my mom shopped, I'd go straight to the magazine rack and look through all the hard-rock publications. It now seems illogical that so many of these magazines existed, but music fans demanded a constant examination of every detail of their favorite band's life. Being hardcore, I was no exception.

I liked a lot of different bands, but if I saw Def Leppard on a magazine cover, my heart would jump. Music had become my life support, but the *Hysteria* album hit me in an entirely different way; it wouldn't let me go. I addictively flipped the cassette from Side A to Side B and then repeated the process. From beginning to end, it rocked. Every. Single. Song.

The title track, however, spoke to every part of me: the sad part that wanted to be loved; the hopeful part that imagined love; the loving part that didn't know it already had a home. Many songs moved me, but "Hysteria" wrapped my heart in bubble wrap first. It took me to a place where sadness and joy merged like warm and cool currents, a place where the temperature of water could not be measured in singularity. I made a one-song mixtape in order to not disrupt this state with constant rewinds.

My mom didn't know or care that music, especially Def Leppard, was the third most important thing on the planet (after air and water). She had once described her marriage to my father as a "fifteen-year survival course" and had struggled to keep food on the table throughout my early childhood, so a magazine with long-haired men on the cover would never qualify as a necessity. Our history had been about *actual* needs. I couldn't say to her, "*I need this mag, Hazel.*" Thus, every magazine I acquired came only through negotiation or an act of trickery.

I would offer to mow the lawn or do other seasonal chores or clean out the fridge, sweep the garage, or whatever she needed me to do. I had no actual power because she could just tell me to do those things anyway and I would have no other choice. We both knew it. My best bet was to wear down her "no" with my youthful enthusiasm. If that didn't work, I walked around the store with the magazine until checkout time, and then would read the situation for my next move. Sometimes, the only option was to sneak it into the cart under a loaf of bread or something, and then offer to unload everything myself. This rarely succeeded, because she usually paid close attention.

However, if she picked up an Enquirer or other tabloid, my fortune might change. Covers with Oprah's weight loss, preventing bug bites, or a Debbie Reynolds exposé doomed me automatically. However, salacious ones about sex scandals, Madonna's mental health, or aliens doing anything, were almost a guarantee that I would be able to make my purchase. I'd watch my mom's eyes for clues about her level of interest, but she rarely gave anything away. She'd thumb through the first few pages, and then it either went back on the rack or onto the conveyor belt. The rack screwed me completely and left me at zero. But if she dropped The Enquirer onto the conveyor belt, I'd say to her sweetly, "Can I have mine now?" Denying me now would be very selfish, and my mom was rarely that.

"Alright, but I don't know why you like those."

Seeing no need to draw out the conversation, I shrugged and dropped my Metal Edge over her Enquirer, where the cover story about a female celebrity that couldn't keep a man didn't seem destined for a Pulitzer either.

The next school day, I would drop my loot into my backpack and take it with me. My only non-band friends were the rock girls, Dani and Amy, and they appreciated a music magazine as much as I did. Conveniently, we all had different favorites.

As quickly as I placed my Metal Edge in front of them, it succumbed to their lusts. They pulled out page after page, like cavewomen plucking a chicken. Soon, all that remained of the carcass were random pictures of Tesla, Winger, White Lion, or other great bands that just weren't wall-worthy. Some not great bands also remained, but they were pretty much torn to pieces.

Dani loved Mötley Crüe, especially their bassist, Nikki Sixx. Normally, liking a bass player disqualified cool, but he had recently survived a heroin overdose, which made it ok. Possibly cooler even. Dani stood taller than most students in our class, and with her pitch-black hair and large breasts she couldn't be ignored, even though she wanted to be.

Amy stood out too. She had some sort of hip or leg disorder. I never asked her about it, and she never brought it up, so I can't be sure what it was. It caused her feet to point in and her gait to be jerky, rigid, and slow. Amy loved Poison, but like a normal person, she wanted to marry the lead singer, Bret Michaels.

Whereas I knew little about Dani's home life, I knew more about Amy. She lived with her dad and three younger siblings in a small house and they always made noise in the background when she and I talked on the phone. Amy broached the subject of her mom rarely, and in limited ways, such as, "When she comes back," or, "My mom was like that too." I felt connected with her beyond the music.

I didn't have a hard-rock honey. Lita Ford melted icebergs everywhere she went, and even though the ladies of Vixen wore a lot less makeup than Poison, they were still sexy as hell. Yet, I focused on them as artists and not sex symbols. I had no desire to marry any of them. For me, it was all about the music.

Until it became about the music and the tight pants. Specifically, the bulges.

People think 80s rock was about the music and the hair, but those in the know will tell you it was about the music and the bulges; the hair was just to distract your mom. Of course, it only worked if you didn't make the bulges the focal point. I hung a Def Leppard poster too high once, making Steve Clark's crotch eye-level. After my mom asked if he had a potato in his pants, I lowered it and never made that mistake again.

In no time at all, I was looking everywhere for bulges. At first it was rock bulges from Metal Edge, but I soon added JC Penney and Sears catalogs, and then quickly moved up to International Male. My addiction peaked as I began stealing my mom's Adam and Eve catalogs out of the mailbox. My body was reacting to my new favorite pastime, and I had learned a new trick.

It's weird that no one has to teach a boy how to masturbate. It's probably even instinct. Like suddenly, your body starts creating semen and tells you, "Hey, I'm making white stuff in your balls now. Let me show you a pleasurable way to get rid of it. Give me your hand." Then you just practice every day (or multiple times a day if you're super dedicated). Unfortunately, instinct doesn't give you very much information. I thought that each set of balls came preloaded with a set number of ejaculations, so I was afraid I would run out. I tried to practice in moderation, but I still worried every time. Afterwards, with great relief, I would say a brief prayer, telling God that I wouldn't do it anymore. Then at bedtime, I would say the prayer again.

Even though I worried about my balls, I shuddered to think about my soul. Obviously, if I liked bulges, I liked boys. *Oh fuck, I'm gay.* We were no longer Pentecostal, but years and years of sitting in church had imprinted upon my psyche the idea that being gay was the worst offense to God. If ever there had been even a sliver of a chance for me to get into heaven, it had evaporated.

It was official now; bulges were my one-way ticket to hell. I prayed again and again to not be gay, but God wouldn't cooperate. For months, I would go to bed terrified of spending an eternity in a lake of fire. I was just a kid, but I believed that my sin-shackled soul would never be more than a hell-bound pervert. It's hard to find joy or purpose in your life when you feel you were born an abomination, that you'lll die an abomination, and then will burn for eternity because of it.

Eventually, I gave up praying and accepted that I would just be going to hell. It was not a peaceful surrender. It was the utter letting go of a young boy who had not yet developed or inherited the tools to fight a battle of that magnitude. I accepted the inescapable reality that my soul was going to burn in hell forever. The only upside was that I would finally meet a lot of other gay guys, and they were all guaranteed to be hot.

I tried harder to pretend to be normal, but I knew I wasn't normal, and I hated myself for it. All the negative messages from movies, peers, and religion had absorbed into my being and were slowly poisoning me against myself. A part of me detached and looked the other way while my remaining joy and light realized that its life was actually a snuff film. On some level, I knew that after their untimely death, depression would take their place.

In ninth grade, when I was feeling extremely out of place in both my life and small-town Alabama, I gained a brand-new bully. He differed from the others because he wanted a committed relationship. Instead of "Hi baby" and stolen kisses, it was "Sup fag?" and shoves. He was on me like paparazzi, and I couldn't get away from him. We even shared a few classes.

In English class, he would sit right behind me and call me names the entire time. Once, I became frustrated and raised my hand.

"Yes, Jason?" Mrs. Cole said.

"Nic is calling me names," I replied, begging for rescue.

"Just ignore him." An audible sigh escaped her as she looked back down at the papers on her desk.

My unheeded SOS severely angered my non-romantic beau. He was also in the next class with me, PE. My band friends and I weren't athletic and had no desire to engage in any physical activities at all, so we were hanging out on the bleachers in the gym. Nic came over, grabbed my hand and pulled me to the gym floor. It kind of felt like he wanted to dance with me or rip my arm off. He picked me up by the neck and said, "If you ever tell on me again, I will kill you." He then threw me across the gym floor while my band friends all became interested in studying their fingernails.

I didn't like it rough, but Nic had a simmering kind of masculinity that sometimes boiled over. He was a thick Italian and looked like a bull wrestler. While not overwhelmingly attractive, he definitely would've been my type had he not wanted to murder me. But, since he wanted me dead, I tried to cool things down by staying away from him as much as possible. I would take a detour around the entire school if I needed to, just to avoid him. For months, I only felt safe if I saw him from far away. I feared him up close, but I was more scared of him when I didn't know where he was. His attendance was horrible, which you would think would be great for me, but it wasn't. When he was absent, I just assumed he was skipping class so he could catch me unaware and chop my head off with a machete. I had nightmares about Nic and no wet dreams. It was doubly unfair.

For months, any time I was outside alone, I looked over my shoulder. It terrified me that he could materialize out of the blue and chop me into pieces, or even use his muscular arms to pull my head and limbs from my torso. I imagined him throwing my bloody body aside like it was nothing and walking away. He might not even realize it was a bad thing. In his head, he might have thought: *Gays are bad. I killed bad. I am good.*

I didn't know what kind of value a soft boy such as myself had, but I felt equal to something in the neighborhood of a flat basketball or seventeen pounds of wilted kale. Killing something of that value would probably result in a citation equal to jaywalking. Hell, for all I knew, they might even have a special ceremony for him and give him a medal. They would display a picture of him holding my disembodied head in the trophy case next to his MHS Hall Monitor of the Century award.

Despite the potential for decapitation that lurked around every corner, my worst fears were never realized, because one day, he just stopped coming to school. And I had nothing to do with it.

Other than the occasional headbutt and fight in the halls, most people never showed as much dedication as Nic. There was always someone calling me names, but no one else threatened to kill me. Most were just happy to bully me recreationally. Even my band friends dabbled in it a bit.

My friend Stormy was a twirler. She had black hair that was short at the back with long bangs in the front, and she styled into a rapturous wave. It crested magnificently a foot above her head. When she started calling me Gayson (instead of Jason), it shocked me. Besides being mean, it wasn't very original and sounded kind of stupid, so she stopped soon after she started. I tried to not get upset. Maybe she had caught whatever hateful virus infected the halls of Marbury High School. At least her affliction passed quickly.

My best friends at the time were Josh and Jon. Josh wore glasses but never shorts. Freckles mapped his face with a thousand possible constellations. At the top of his thin frame, his slightly chaotic hair resembled a

29

freshly lit match that lacked the confidence to burn fully. He played the saxophone, but it didn't make him look cool.

Jon played the snare drum, so he was cooler than both of us. He had black hair that went casually to the side without screaming for attention. Even his smile moved lazily across his handsome face, seemingly in an effort to not be disruptive. Nothing about him asked to be noticed. This could have been because of his large number of siblings or an inherent coolness that I obviously lacked.

We were hanging out on a trampoline at Jon's house one summer night, staring at the sky, looking for UFOs, and talking about horror movies. Out of the blue, Josh asked me, "Why are you so gay, Jason?"

My spirit crashed silently, like an imploding skyscraper on mute. All my pieces were still there; they just weren't being held together anymore.

I was never good at magic, but I tried to disappear anyway. It didn't work. Luckily for me, Jon said to Josh, "That wasn't very nice." I realized I hadn't been breathing, so I took a deep breath. We went back to talking about UFOs, but Josh had hurt my feelings and I felt betrayed.

I didn't figure out the answer to his question, but I realized three things that night:

1. UFOs have committed to no longer interfering with the needs of humanity.

2. I cannot, and probably will not, ever figure out how to disappear.

3. Jon was definitely cuter than Josh.

I revisited Josh's question on multiple occasions. *Why am I so gay?* I could never figure it out. And then, as I grew older, the question became:

If I am so gay, how can I be so bad at it? And I never even came close to figuring that one out.

I wrote Josh a coming-out letter soon after moving to Alaska, but he never wrote me back. Years and years later, after I moved back to Alabama, I Googled him. The only place he showed up was on a church newsletter's prayer request page. *Josh Jones (son of Mary and Greg Jones) – unspoken request.* An unspoken request usually means that someone is struggling with something that they don't want to make public, like drugs or something. I sent him a prayer, but never learned what happened to him.

4

LOSER VIRGINS, AKA NOT FOR SENSITIVE READERS

I rarely responded to being called a faggot. I'd just absorb it and move on, hoping that whoever said it would get bored. This tactic worked most of the time, but not always.

Once, I was eating lunch with my friend Amy at my favorite spot—a bench under two gnarly trees on a hill near the football field—and a guy who was two years ahead of me caught me. He wanted a response to his aggression and had no intentions of leaving without it.

"Fucking faggot! Why don't you say something?" I stared at him, wanting it to be over, but still having no words for him. He shoved my shoulders, and I dug the tips of my shoes into the red dirt and tried to maintain my balance. I thought he might push me hard enough to knock me backwards and kill me. While it seemed like a decent option at the time, surviving seemed slightly better. "You too big of a faggot to stick up for yourself?"

I didn't have a brilliant answer for that. He obviously hated me, which was understandable because I probably hated me too, but his anger confused me. Was my mere existence enough to cause such rage?

"Are you a fuckin' pussy or just stupid?" He wore a silver necklace that swayed every time he came at me, and I watched it instead of his eyes. "Fuckin' do something!"

I did do something, once in the hall after a guy called me a name. Everything that normally stayed bottled up exploded out, and I jumped on him. The element of surprise benefited me briefly, but it ended in a draw when my favorite teacher came by and broke it up.

My mom brought me to school the next morning because she wanted to talk to the principal about me being bullied. The school didn't have air conditioning, but most classrooms at least had a single ceiling fan. His office didn't. The hot, stagnant air practically dripped from the ceiling. I spent the entire visit wiping beads of sweat from my forehead while trying not to get splinters in my lungs from the old wood smell.

"Who is calling you names?"

I preferred suffocation to this conversation, but he and my mom stared at me, awaiting my answer. She knew who it was, yet she still wanted me to participate.

"You said his name was Nestor, right?" my mom said helpfully.

"Yes, ma'am." Short and sweet.

"Nestor Williams?" I'm not sure why the principal wanted the last name verified. MHS didn't have a large student body, and there certainly weren't multiple Nestors.

I squirmed a bit in the wooden chair as I answered, "Yes, sir."

"What is he calling you?" He straightened his solid yellow tie casually.

My face drained at the thought of saying the word, and my mom noticed.

"A faggot." My mom stated it matter-of-factly. "He's calling him a faggot."

Looking at me in horror, my principal said, "What a terrible thing to call somebody." He then scribbled something on a piece of paper that I assumed was Nestor's name, but it might as well have been a bounty on my head. I knew it would probably make things worse. I also knew that the principal's horror wasn't about the fact that someone called me a faggot. It was more about the *"terrible"* accusation of being called gay. He promised action and my mom left.

Walking the empty hallways of Marbury High School, I hoped the credits would roll before I made it to my English class. I arrived and stood at the door, waiting, but I didn't fade out. Instead, I entered the room.

After the bell rang, my favorite teacher kept me behind to say how disappointed she was in me for fighting. My shame afforded me no explanation.

"Fuckin' do something!" my tormentor yelled in my face, but I couldn't figure out the "something" to do. Nothing made sense anyway, so I just kept watching his silver necklace as he moved closer, took my head in both his hands, and headbutted me in the forehead.

Thunder and a brilliant flash of lightning introduced a black sky. Matte silver confetti floated through it like lost sequins trying to find each other, as if they knew they were incapable of being beautiful alone. Swooning, I opened my eyes, pulling myself from the blackness and back to my returning world.

His thin face appeared mildly shocked, as if pain wasn't a rational consequence of his actions. Uttering one final, half-hearted slur, he turned and walked away. I tried pinning sequins to the ass of his acid-washed jeans as he moved.

"Are you alright?" a girl's voice asked.

I had completely forgotten about Amy, who had been there the whole time.

"What are you gonna do when you graduate?" my father asked as he drove me to his house for a rare weekend visit.

I didn't have an answer for that. In kindergarten, I wanted to be a fireman, but that had long passed. Recently, I had briefly considered being a horror writer, but changed my mind after producing only two handwritten pages in two days. Only one answer remained. To me, it made all the sense in the world.

"Move to California."

He didn't seem to believe me, but he still warned me against it. "That's not a good idea. California's gonna slide into the ocean soon."

I didn't know if I believed me either, but all the gay people lived in California. Obviously, I would need to be with my people in order to survive. And if I slid into the Pacific Ocean, at least I wouldn't die feeling alone. Until then, I would suffer through straight people. They weren't *all* trying to kill me.

In late October of that year, the school had a haunted house. Five or six very straight guys were hanging out together after it ended, just chatting and not chatting (*me*) about girls. One of the older guys suggested that we have a dick-measuring contest. Obviously, if he suggested the contest, he would probably win it. I didn't feel good about my chances, but I was definitely interested in judging. I hoped like crazy that someone would nominate me as an impartial judge, but no one else showed any interest in the contest or in picking me. It was a severely disappointing evening, especially when coupled with the fact that the haunted house wasn't scary at all. Apparently it was coordinated by weak-hearted members of the local senior citizen center.

I finally got to see another guy's dick when I officially lost my virginity a year later at 13. A friend brought him over to my house one day, and he returned alone a few nights later. We ended up standing side by side in the barn as he smoked a Marlboro Red. He offered to share. Although I didn't smoke, I wasn't going to miss my chance to share a cigarette with a fifteen-year-old boy. I said, "Yes." He took a drag and pulled my mouth to his mouth. I inhaled the smoke, feeling his lips on my lips and smelling his black leather jacket. The masculine scents of the cigarette and the leather became tied to that moment. For months after, the smell of either would give me an erection.

Beneath the smoke and leather, a slight scent of cologne still lingered loosely on his neck and shirt. I pulled away to exhale, and he pulled me back to his lips. His tongue slipped into my mouth, and I clumsily tried to follow his lead while trying to discreetly adjust my now-throbbing dick. I had never kissed a boy before, and it felt like a primal secret was being revealed to me. His left hand dove slowly into the hair on the back of my head and pulled my mouth closer to his lips, while his right had dropped the cigarette and was sliding down my back and pushing beneath my shirt. Then his hand was against the skin of my back and on my side, sliding up my chest to my neck. His touch was a nomadic storm moving over every inch of my body. Drifting and electrifying, it left me disoriented. I offered myself to this force of nature, asking that it overtake me.

He grabbed my hand and led it to the front of his jeans, where his cock was heaving against the fabric. My heartbeat was now louder than all the night bugs. It drowned out everything except his breathing. Soon, the sound of his zipper stopped my heart all together. My hand was sliding beneath the waistband of his white underwear, feeling his thickness wet against my palm as he unbuttoned my pants. His hand was on me then, pushing lightning through my entire body.

"Put it in your mouth."

I was on my knees in the dirt almost before he finished the sentence. He had an easy confidence when he spoke, and I would have done anything that he asked me to, even if I didn't want to. Of course, at that moment, I wanted to do everything.

"Come here," he said, pulling me up.

I got off my knees, and he brought me to his lips again. It was something like heaven, but grounded and real. I felt it in his lips, in his cock, and in the air stirring around us. He then found my spot in the dirt and put my cock in his mouth. I wasn't sure if I should ask him if he liked it. I definitely did. He knew what he was doing, and I wasn't ready for it. Fortunately, he stopped and came back to my lips, where I tasted myself for the first time.

Suddenly, someone inside the house turned the outside light on. We pulled ourselves together, slapped the dust off our knees, and started walking toward the house. He lit a cigarette, and we talked nonchalantly, as if my lips weren't silently screaming for every inch of him. When we walked back into the house, he started making small talk with my mom while I stood there awkwardly looking like a freshly sexed teenage boy. She wasn't familiar with that look, so she told him he could stay the night. However, she insisted we sleep on the foldout couch in the living room next to her room. As we prepared to go to bed, she left her door open, an obvious sign that she was suspicious of one of us.

This did not deter him. Within five minutes of her lights going off, his hand was pulling my underwear down from behind. He pulled closer to me, and I felt his hard cock against my lower back. I watched my mom's bedroom door as he entered me. I gasped into the pillow, hoping that the whirring of her ceiling fan was loud enough to cover the sounds coming from the couch. He was breathing heavily in my ear and his pushing into me was coaxing the creaky choir of the mattress to sing out joyously. I worried that the song would betray us, but I couldn't stop myself from pushing closer and closer to him to feel him deeper and deeper inside of me. His breath was growing heavier and faster on the back of my neck, until, suddenly, he stopped and turned me on my back. Before I knew what was happening, he was coming on my belly. I realized then that I like a guy to come on me, but I don't like it to stay there. It goes from sexy to gross in a matter of seconds. I went to the bathroom to clean up, and when I returned, he was sleeping.

This incident left me in a horrible bind. On Monday, I went to school no longer a virgin, and there was no one I could tell. All I wanted to do was yell, "I'M NOT A VIRGIN!" but it probably would've gotten me killed. I sat with my band friends in PE class, feeling like I was going to explode. Plus, they were all still virgins and would've been so jealous. I'd never had a chance to make anyone jealous, and my first chance locked itself in the closet with me.

"Hey, guys, I got fucked this weekend. Cool, huh?" or "Hey, have any of you guys ever tried anal? I did this weekend, and I really liked it." Instead, I just said, "I had an awesome weekend." Loser virgins just wouldn't understand anyway.

I really wanted to see him again. Partly for making out and sex, but partly just to be around someone else like me. When our paths finally crossed again, he didn't see me at all. He was kissing a girl, so I went the other way.

He called a few months later and asked, "Is your dick still growing?"

"Uhhh, I'm not sure," I said, feeling kind of confused. I'm sure he said some other stuff, but "How are you?" isn't nearly as memorable as "Is puberty done with your penis yet?"

He disappeared after that, and I returned to being the only gay person in my life. It saddened me. And, it also left me in a new predicament: before sex, I was abstaining; after sex, I just wasn't getting any.

ALASKA

5

MOOSE SUCK MORE THAN MOSQUITOES

When I was in ninth grade, Lee and my mom decided we would move to Alaska. In no time at all, they sold the house and moved us out of the woods of Deatsville to the sleepy city of Prattville, where we waited out the school year.

My brother David drove us the extended distance to school. He had purchased an old sedan the color of recently dried blood and dedicated a large part of his life attempting to eradicate the perpetual corpse smell that traveled from the trunk to the cabin. It made me question if the car had a secret death compartment, and also if it was possible for a corpse to have BO (the smell that assaulted us was an odd mixture of old body odor and decaying flesh). David sprayed, sprinkled, and spritzed every chemical imaginable, but the overwhelmingly dominant note remained the same. Only now, it wasn't alone. *Eau de Corpse* became *Corpse with Spring Jasmine, Corpse il Drakkar Noir,* or worst of all, *Pine-Sol Corpse.*

Every trip to school had me in the backseat, slightly nauseous, even with the windows down. On cold or rainy days, when the windows were up, I practiced holding my breath. Coming home in the afternoon usually started with a prayer. The hotter the day, the longer the prayer. I thought it was possible that this car had made a deal with the Devil to capture our souls, so even though God and I weren't really on speaking terms, maybe Divine intervention was our only hope. I assumed God wasn't petty enough to take his relationship issues with me out on my brother and sister's souls, but maybe I assumed incorrectly.

That last year I spent in Alabama as a kid was memorialized by the squeaking of the car door announcing the smell of melting death rising to meet me. And even though I knew it was coming, preparing for it was impossible. It just punched you in the nose and then sat beside you the entire ride home, trying to pick a fight. You would think that the smell would fade or lessen over the year, but it didn't. It gave 100% every day.

While I didn't process it at the time, as I impatiently counted down school trips in David's haunted car, an invisible wedge was forming between me and Alabama. In June, when we left that red state, what had been Pangea, became a much smaller piece of itself: an island with jagged coasts still bleeding from the separation. I floated away—knowing it was with the same dirt and breathing of the mainland, but free to evolve and become something new.

We left Prattville, Alabama, and started our almost 4,500-mile drive north to Alaska a few days after school ended. I would miss my brothers, who had just graduated and decided to stay with their feet on familiar ground, but I was more than excited to be escaping the backwoods of Alabama. My sister's enthusiasm for our new adventure was dampened, however, since she was leaving to finish her senior year without her friends. In the end, Alaska probably seemed like a warmer option to her than moving back in with my dad. Her relationship with our father had become frostier after the last time she had stayed behind with him, and then changed her mind.

I rode in the moving van with Lee while my mom and sister followed in the car, and watched from the window as the world I knew faded behind me. Thick Southern accents became thinner at each stop, melting slowly and retreating like a honey glacier, until they were no more.

Lee and I spent the majority of our trip in silence. Ours was less of a relationship and more an act of acceptance. I don't think either of us knew what to do with the other. Plus, my mom had been the source of my affection for my whole life; I had learned to expect nothing from men. I appreciated that Lee was there, but I didn't know how to be there with him.

I had made a lot of mixed tapes for the trip, which made it less awkward for both of us. Listening to my Walkman almost the entire time, I pretty much only broke my silence to ask for new AA batteries. Usually, requests for new batteries or cassettes were swiftly denied, but Lee bought them for me each time, at the next gas or bathroom stop. He even bought me the *Bloodletting* album by Concrete Blonde.

By the time we got to Montana, I couldn't listen to my favorite songs anymore. My ears needed a break. "Hysteria" and "Joey" were replaced with the silence of a trillion stars shining down on me from an expansive sky. As we drove in the darkness, I looked out the window and got lost in them. For a few hours, my eyes remembered every magic that my soul had forgotten.

The next day, we arrived in Canada. I only met a few Canadians, but they all seemed very nice. Possibly too nice. Like they were warming you up for something. I always expected them to end our conversation with, "By the way, do you have a couple of bucks I can borrow so I can buy a Bryan Adams tape and some licorice?" All of my interactions were with Canadians working at gas stations, restaurants, and hotels, so maybe they just had great customer service. But I couldn't be sure.

A strawberry blond attendant at a gas station in Alberta made me extra suspicious by being ten times sweeter than the average Canadian. To be that nice, I assumed she must have needed me to do something big, like kill someone. I believe no one deserves to be murdered, but any person who could be mean to this woman would have probably been the person to change my mind. I figured I'd be out of the country soon anyway, and no one would think to suspect someone as innocent-looking as myself. Luckily, she never asked me to murder any of her current or previous boyfriends, so I left her and potential prison time behind in Calgary. I really had no time for murder anyway.

At the US border, I realized border agents were also suspicious—of Canadians or people that had recently associated with them. They looked at us once and asked us to come inside. While agents searched our vehicles and distracted our parents, a different agent asked me questions.

"Are these your parents?"

"Yes."

"Are you carrying any drugs or firearms?"

"No."

"Did you murder anyone in Calgary?"

"Um... no."

Whew, dodged a bullet there. They might have worded that last question differently and left out the word murder, but paranoia is a bad processor of information, so I don't know what they actually said. Fortunately, I answered the question correctly, they released us back to our parents, and we continued our journey to the Last Frontier.

One of the first things you learn when arriving in Alaska is that Alaskans are very proud of their mosquitoes. Every gas station, gift store, grocery outlet, and possibly even church (I never went to church in Alaska, so I can't rule it out) had an endless array of mosquito-themed items for you to purchase. I didn't buy any because I was constantly under attack when not in a structure or vehicle, and I didn't need a t-shirt or magnet to remind me of a bad thing that was still happening to me. It's very odd. Alaskan mosquitoes are like the fanged chihuahuas of the mosquito world; they are small, bitchy, and have a chip on their shoulder. They also love me.

Probably the second thing you notice is that Alaska is amazingly beautiful. Though, it's not a sudden thing, like, you leave ugly-ass Canada and suddenly everything is better. Canada is also lovely. Alaska just gradually takes it to the next level.

You've most likely seen Alaska in the background of one of those weird reality shows on television or possibly in a documentary about mosquitoes or grizzly bear maulings. But nothing does it justice except being there and experiencing it for yourself. The mountains embrace everything in sight and reflect in an endless number of crystal lakes and rivers. Bald eagles stare at you from treetops, mountain goats ignore you from their ledges, and thousands of other species of animals drop gratuitously in and out of the frame.

There are also tons of moose. I don't include them in my list of Alaskan marvels because they are extremely doofy. Don't call them that to their face because they will stomp you to death. They may look like idiots, but they are actually the serial killers of the Last Frontier, the same way that their more attractive cousins, deer, are for the lower forty-eight states. That's not just an opinion; I'm adequately sure it's a proven fact. *(**Googled: do deer kill people? Deers kill an average of 120 people per year vs bears only killing 1 per year.)*

I also believe moose have JBS (Jan Brady Syndrome). Bears kill fewer people, but they get all the attention. While a mauling is front page news, a moose-related death doesn't even get mentioned in the obituaries. You might hear the moose wining about it... *"Ursa, Ursa, Ursa! It's just not fair."*

The good news is, it's pretty easy to see moose in the summer. At the end of June, the sun only goes down for a few hours, but it comes back up again so quickly that it never really gets dark. That doesn't mean moose won't kill you. It just means that you will see them sooner and have a lot more time to process your certain death. It's the same difference as being hit by a bus versus falling from the sky for five minutes after the plane's engines stop working.

At first, all the light in Alaska was extremely cool to me. Dusk and dawn had formed an alliance to squeeze out the darkness. After we arrived in Anchorage and unpacked all our things, I would stay up for hours exploring the neighborhood with no night to turn me away.

I had never lived so close to so many people before, and there were houses everywhere. There was even a 7-Eleven around the corner from our house. I had my first Slurpee sitting on a curb in my new town, trying to absorb the wonder of it all. Suddenly, I was a city boy, and the world was easily within reach of my sweet, sticky fingers. I just needed to find some gay people. Surely, all the Alaskan gays hadn't made it to California yet.

6

DRAMA!

I signed up to be on the swim team at my new school before my tenth-grade year started. Schools in Alabama didn't even have money for air conditioning, so a pool was definitely not in the budget. I was eager to take advantage of my new school district's wealth and start fresh, make lots of friends, and win some stuff.

I showed up on my first day of swim practice in a Skid Row t-shirt and ordered my speedo from the swim coach, but before I even made it in the water, I noticed that everyone else was faster than me. I tried discreetly watching the divers to gauge if I might be a better fit with them, but they were all a century ahead of me in skill. The boards were also a lot higher than I thought they would be, so I stuck with swimming for the day.

A girl with curly red hair and a friendly smile complimented me on my shirt as I was taking it off. Her name was Ann, and she was in my grade. We talked for a few minutes before the coach told me to get in the water. I got in and followed the rest of his instructions while constantly looking for a way out. Swimming isn't nearly as fun when someone tells you how to do it. It's even less fun when everyone else seems to love being told how to do it and does it a lot better than you. I had my own lane, but I felt like there was a line of swimmers behind me waiting for me to pull over. I kept looking over my shoulder just in case I needed to stop and wave someone past me, saying, "Go around." In Deatsville, I was awesome, but in Anchorage, I was just a guy that didn't drown.

As I was leaving, Ann asked if she would see me tomorrow. I gave her the biggest smile and lied through my teeth, "Of course, you'll see me tomorrow. I wouldn't miss it for anything."

I never picked up my speedo, and I didn't see Ann the next day. She became a state champion and even though I was a swim team drop-out, she and I became great friends.

Due to my early retirement from all competitive water sports, I sought a new way to express my talents. Almost immediately, I met Garrett. He was tall and had a mullet and was in my second period English class. Garrett was super easy to talk to because he just kept asking me questions about myself. At first, I thought maybe he wanted me to talk so he could laugh at my accent, but after a few minutes, I realized he was just friendly. Then he showed up in my sixth-period acting class and asked me even more questions, including why I was taking an acting class. I wanted to tell him that all gay boys should have to take at least one acting class, if not for fun or educational purposes, then at least for survival. Instead, I told him we didn't have acting classes at my old school and I wanted to try it.

It turned out he was also a member of the East High Thespian troupe.

"You should join. It's a lot of fun."

"Can you win stuff?" I asked with a laugh, hoping to make him think I was joking.

"Yes. I mean, we have an award ceremony every year," he said without indicating how he had perceived my question.

"Plus, we'll get to hang out, right?"

"Yes. It's actually a lot of work and a big-time commitment, so we'd be hanging out a lot. You'll meet a lot of cool people."

He almost lost me at work and commitment, but the silent call of the red carpet quickly drowned out the bad stuff. "As long as it's fun, I'm in."

If you don't know any actors or theater types, you might make assumptions that aren't true. Most of them are not eccentric, and only a tiny percentage are crazy. Those who are both, are extremely rare but also extremely easy to recognize. For these folks, if they are crying, they make sure that everyone *knows* they are crying. If everyone within shouting distance does not witness their complete and utter dissolution into hysteria, then it doesn't even count. For them, it's comparable to doing a play on Broadway versus performing a reading of The Night Before Christmas for your grandma's corn-shucking club.

If you happen to find an eccentric-crazy type, be warned: a tilt of the head and a gentle quiver of the lips indicates the fuse has been lit. It is no longer safe. Hyperventilation announces that all exits have been locked and sealed from the outside. You are now on lockdown for twenty minutes to two hours, witnessing the greatest tragedy to ever befall humanity in a painstakingly, slow-motion explosion. Afterwards, you stumble away, completely disoriented, trying futilely to wipe whatever just happened off of your traumatized psyche. By the third or fourth time it happens, you seek it out like an addict. You begin to recognize the most likely candidates for a full-on, engorged, dripping-from-the-tip nuclear meltdown, and you try to be near them.

The Thespian troupe president was just such a person. She was amazingly exuberant and always primed to go off. Her name was Julie, and she did not gently ease me into my thespian-ism. She spit on it, stuck it in, and said, "Now act surprised."

I spent my entire sophomore year shell-shocked, as I watched her pin-ball from one crisis to the next. When the new drama teacher didn't give her the starring role in the first play of the year, her response was like the eruption of Mount Vesuvius and we were the helpless Pompeians. Three hours later, everyone was exhausted, extremely confused and secretly wanting to hide in a closet with a pillow over their head.

Julie was a senior trying to get into a prestigious arts school; playing the ingenue's grandmother would not score her any points with the application review board. Plus, the character only had a handful of lines and no costume changes. It was like Meryl Streep doing a local pizza house commercial, getting to say "Pizza good" at the end. It was disgraceful and a complete waste of her expansive talents.

For my stage debut, I played dead guy #3. I knew with only one line, I had to possess it fully, milking it like a man who stumbled on a busty cow after wandering in the desert for forty days. Plus, a dead guy would naturally talk slowly, so I could draw out my eight words for almost a minute. The audience could read through the entire program as I owned the stage with, "Aye, Mrs. Winston. I knew her quite well."

Julie was too good for milking, so she refused the role. She decided that if she couldn't bring down the house, she would instead focus on bringing down the drama teacher. I loved Mrs. Harrison, our drama teacher, but Julie never asked me my opinion. Like most of my fellow thespians, she just asked me to say stuff.

"Say guitar."

"Gittar," I would respond. I had learned that even negative attention is attention, and attention is like oxygen. My accent was affording me a brief spotlight, so I soaked it up like a vine busting through the rainforest canopy.

"Say ruined."

"Rurnt," I agreed while I relished every ray of this new brightest of suns.

"Oil, do oil," they said, as if giving me their blood.

"Ull, ull, ull," I said, simultaneously filled and released.

Garrett still talked to me about other stuff, excluding girls and sports. From day one I was mildly suspicious, but after multiple conversations about George Michael, I was almost sure that he was gay like me. He wasn't in any rush to come out first and neither was I, so we both just kept circling it from a very safe distance. Then one night, on a phone call, we both apparently showed up intending to wait the other out.

"You gonna have kids one day?" he asked.

"Probably not. You?"

"Probably not," he said, closing the topic.

"You gonna get married one day?" I asked, undeterred.

"Probably not. You?"

"Not likely," I answered honestly.

After five hours of subtle interrogation, drama gossip, and George Michael conversation, something happened. One of us summoned up the courage to come out, and the other immediately followed.

"I'm gay," one of us said.

"I'm gay too!" the other followed.

Circling all night had exhausted us, so after receiving the information we needed, we said goodnight, hung up the phone, and went to bed. I was too excited to sleep though, because for the first time in my life, I had a gay best friend. I just lay all night feeling a hundred pounds lighter and wanting to be somewhere screaming, "I'M GAY!"

The next day at school, Julie came over to Garrett and me as we were talking during class. Looking at us both suspiciously, she asked, "Did you guys have sex?"

"No," I answered dramatically before pointing at Garrett. "But he's gay, though."

"He's gay-er," he added, pointing back at me.

"So, you're both gay, but you're not having sex? That's almost impossible, you know that, right?"

From that moment, she became the shepherd of our burgeoning sexuality. Both Julie's best friend and her brother were gay, so she considered herself an expert on the subject. "Do you guys know how to take it up the ass? It's not as simple as just shoving a cock up there. It really is a process." She followed that up with, "I can show you how to suck a cock if you want. It's important to remember to play with his balls. Guys love it when you play with their balls." And then, "You into armpits? Some guys are into it. You just gotta find your thing, though, you know?" She even gave us porn bags on the last day of school before the holidays while singing "I'm dreaming of a white Christmas." I was slightly embarrassed, but I thanked her and gave her a hug. After the hug, she looked at my hand holding the bag and said, "I'm going to know where your hands have been, so please don't hug me when I see you in January."

She invited Garrett and me to go with her to a party mixed with high school and college drama kids. I think we were meant to be her gay-boy entourage, but Garrett couldn't go, so I went without him.

Within minutes of arriving, Julie disappeared with a boy and I had a very strong drink in my hand. I stood in the kitchen feeling extremely out of place as people came in and out, refilling their drinks and staring at me. This made me feel anxious, which made me drink faster. Julie had led me to that spot, so I remained there like a faithful puppy, waiting for its master to return.

On my third or fifth strong vodka drink, a random stranger saw my distress and invited me to join a group of people in the hot tub.

"I don't have anything to wear," I said.

"That's alright. You don't have to wear anything," he responded with a smile.

"Ah, ok." I suddenly had a feeling that I had gotten myself into a naked situation.

My body and I hadn't always had relationship issues, but I had learned not to trust it. Beyond being a sinful thing, mine was also a shameless gossip. Limp wrists and girlish giggles told all my secrets before even I knew them. I'm sure my parents watched in horror as it delivered my first steps triumphantly with a swish.

Then, after I knew what it was doing, I couldn't stop all the ways it wanted to yell, "Gay boy!!!!" My body had mouths everywhere. And after a few different guys told me I had breasts like a girl, me and my body broke up. We kept living together; I just made it keep its shirt on unless it was drinking.

Fortunately, gym class in Alabama was a very casual affair that never resulted in anyone taking a shower, so I only had to take my shirt off once a year while the PE teacher checked me for scoliosis. That was uncomfortable for me. I would sometimes even wear a t-shirt while swimming around strangers. I knew I would get painfully chapped nipples from breaking the suction between the shirt and my skin, but that would be less uncomfortable than exposing my body.

I didn't want to be naked, but I also didn't want to be standing alone in the kitchen looking crazy. The vodka made the hot tub seem like a potentially better option. They were drinking anyway, and it was relatively dark outside, so I thought I had a good chance of sneaking in discreetly.

He led me through the house to a dimly lit room in the back.

"It's just through there," he said, pointing through a set of double doors. "I'll get you a towel after I use the bathroom."

"Thank you," I said to his back as he disappeared.

Men are usually fast in the bathroom. If he only peed and didn't wash his hands, he would be out in under a minute. I took off my clothes slowly, folding each piece neatly and placing it on a chair. If I took long enough, he would return, and we would walk outside together.

After a few minutes, it became clear that his bathroom trip would be an extended one. I couldn't just stand there naked because it would be obvious that I was waiting for him. I reluctantly walked outside.

The cold winter air hit me immediately, and I headed toward the hot tub. The six or seven people occupying it didn't seem to notice me as they engaged in conversation, so I felt like my chances of sneaking in unnoticed were pretty good. However, as I was trying to get in with one hand on the ledge and the other holding my privates, someone said, "Come on in." At that point, I panicked and just fell in, splashing everyone in the process. I noticed almost immediately that the girls were wearing swimsuits. This led me to believe that everyone except me was wearing a swimsuit. I sat there terrified, hoping some mass migration event would occur so I could jump out and run for my clothes. It didn't, so I retreated to the farthest corner, waiting instead for Bathroom Guy to rescue me again. That didn't happen either.

Hot tubs are very popular in Alaska, but no one warned me about how dangerous they can be. Apparently, hot-tub water is just a soup of body fluids (and solids), parasites, and germs. I later realized that I caught something really irritating that night. His name was Chad.

Chad was outgoing and swarmy as hell. He resembled a dark-haired Disney character with questionable intentions. I was shy and naked, so he easily caught me off guard with quick compliments. As soon as he had my attention, he changed the subject to discuss his favorite topic – himself. At first, I thought he was talking the entire time to make me more comfortable, which was extremely generous of him. Then I realized he wasn't going to change the subject. I went along with it because he said I was cute and nudity trapped me in the hot tub.

Finally, we were the last two people left in the hot tub. Seizing the opportunity, I jumped out as quickly as humanly possible.

"Let's hang out again soon," Chad said.

"Sure," I replied, grabbing my crotch and running for the door. I heard him getting out of the hot tub and hoped he wasn't staring at my pale ass as I disappeared inside. He caught up with me moments later and asked for my phone number.

A few weeks later, Garrett invited our theater friend Monica and me to hang out at his place for the night because his mom was out of town. Someone had managed to get multiple bottles of Boone's Farm Strawberry Hill and Wild Island, so we were going to drink, smoke cigarettes, and get a little crazy. I invited Chad to come over, with Garrett's permission, and he showed up with his friend Nelly and more Boone's Farm. The party was really just a Strawberry Hill sleepover, but the music was loud, and the boys were restless. The girls were out of luck, but they were still in good spirits. It didn't take long for us to be boozed up and dancing in our boxer shorts.

Chad and I went outside together a few times to smoke. The temperature had tripped over zero and seemed satisfied to lie face down with its nose stuck in the snow near the 3°F point. I didn't care about the seemingly lifeless body of weather before me because Chad and I were on a countdown to kissing. The moment hadn't revealed itself yet, but the mixture of hormones and booze awaited the slightest spark of bravery to ignite it.

"May I kiss you?"

It sounded effortless coming from him, but it threw me off. I knew proper English, but in Alabama, my English teacher had been the only person who had ever used it. "I don't know if you *can* go to the bathroom or not, but you certainly *may* go to the bathroom." The memory of Mrs. Pringle vanished before our lips met.

At the end of the evening, Chad asked me, "Do you want to be my boyfriend?" Of course, I wanted to be his boyfriend. There were red flags, but he was a cute guy asking me to be his boyfriend, and I wanted a boyfriend. Plus, red flags probably didn't mean the same thing on Wild Island and Strawberry Hill. They just waved gently in a tropical breeze singing "The party's over here." At that moment, it sounded like an invitation to fun. Plus, I figured having a boyfriend meant having a constant supply of cock and sex.

"Sure," I responded. Nothing that grew on Boone's Farm could beat this buzz.

"Okay," he said "but I have to warn you, I have a really big dick." Suddenly, I was over Strawberry Hill, and unsure if I should have taken more time with the question.

"Um, ok."

I am not against big dicks, or any dicks of any size for that matter, but the statement turned me off. I thought maybe he was underestimating my sexual abilities. "You don't know what I can take," I thought to myself.

"I'll just have to go slow," he added, as if not killing me with his cock made him a gentleman of the highest caliber.

"Thank you," I said.

He looked me deeply in the eyes and said, "I always want you to be okay." Then he kissed me, and the flags were invitations again. He big-spooned me as we were all crashing on Garrett's floor, and I went to sleep feeling excited to have a boyfriend, nervous that he may be a bit off, and slightly worried that he would get a night erection that would sever my spinal cord.

Thankfully, I survived the night, but within a month our relationship was growing cold on the embalming table. A malignant darkness flowed through Chad and it didn't take me long to realize that it didn't feel good to be around him. His arrogance and vanity were also huge turn offs; he should've warned me about the size of his ego instead. Plus, we had oral sex a few times, but my dream of having a steady supply of sex withered away unfulfilled.

I stopped answering Chad's calls without ever breaking up with him. Being extremely sensitive to other people's emotions made avoiding him forever a better option for me than hurting his feelings or pissing him off. I looked like an asshole, but I just wanted to disappear and pretend the messy bits would dissolve in my absence. At the same time, he might have only been calling me to get his Spin Doctors CD back.

7

OH BROTHER TYPEWRITER

My mom met Garrett for the first time one afternoon when he came over after school.

"Is he gay?" she whispered at the first opportunity.

"No, ma'am; he's just Alaskan." The answer made little sense, but I hoped it would at least change the subject. A conversation involving the word "gay" wouldn't lead anywhere good. Plus, outing someone would be rude and would only lead to questions about me. I had no plans to come out to my family, ever.

My mother didn't get the memo.

My original intention had been to avoid the subject of girls, dating, and marriage, and run like hell as soon as I graduated from high school. I imagined that, upon my escape, I would instantly meet the love of my life (possibly even on the plane to Paris), and we would live off love for the rest of our lives in a handsome villa somewhere in the French countryside. I would write poetry and raise pygmy goats while he would make cheese and soap from their milk. With one shaky semester of

French under my belt and an ever-wavering relationship with reality, I felt like the hands of destiny had no other option than to lovingly edge me ever closer to his waiting arms.

My mother was obviously far less romantic because she destroyed the idea of my dashing French husband before I could even buy a ticket. She was also far better at finding things than I was at hiding them.

When I was sixteen, I came home from school one day and was going into my room to throw my backpack down, when I found my mom there, in my room. She was sitting on my bed, holding the single piece of evidence that convicted me before I could even sit down. It was an anthology of gay fiction. In retrospect, I shouldn't have bought a book with the word "gay" on the cover.

My Jansport backpack and my stomach were suddenly in a race to my feet, and I looked down, realizing my shoes had become concrete. I couldn't move. I could only sway gently in the waves of silent disappointment and anger that emanated off my mother like a silent, deafening scream.

Oh fuck. *I was reading the book to study up on gay...* ummm... Don't say gay... *I found it outside by the fence and hid it under the mattress to keep it dry...* That's stupid... *I have become ravenously addicted to literature lately. It started innocently enough with the Hardy Boys, then recently moved onto Chaim Potok and Stephen King books, and now I just need a bit of something harder.* I thought I could throw in a twitch or two and really try to sell it, but all I could really do was stare at my stomach and shoes and say to myself, *Oh fuck.*

My plan to run away forever had left me ill-prepared to respond to this moment. I knew I was in trouble. Every bit of shame and self-hatred that I had been fighting off for years suddenly overwhelmed me, It was like a horrible dinner party of unwanted guests—speaking loudly over each other, and then turning to devour their host. I swayed as a thousand teeth gnashed at my soul. I swallowed hard, hoping that my throat was still there, my heart galloping faster and faster toward a certain cliff.

"Where did you get this? Did Garrett give it to you?"

"No, ma'am," I answered in words that felt like gravel in my mouth.

"Where did you get it?"

"Um... I bought it." I knew no words could save me. There was only me, the truth, and a reckoning.

"Why did you buy it?"

"I don't know." I decided that one truthful statement was enough for the day, and maybe the tears welling up in my eyes would soften her.

"Tear it up," she said. So much for the softening.

"No," I murmured. To this day, I don't know why I said no. It was probably the only time I said no to her in my entire life. We were both equally stunned. However, I knew I was now in deeper shit.

"Tear it up or I'll whip you!"

"No." I was committed to my futile rebellion.

My mother laid the book on my bed and left the room. She returned moments later with a belt. "Tear it up," she said, offering me one last chance.

I shook my head, knowing that I was signing my own death certificate. *Cause of death: Stubborn Gay.*

My mom, who I loved and respected, grabbed my arms and pushed me onto the bed. I didn't resist. She whipped me with the belt repeatedly, her arms heavy with sadness. It was not abusive or hateful; it was just the way her parents had raised her, and how their parents had been raised. The Bible clearly states that "sparing the rod spoils the child" and no one wants a bad apple. I had long since decided that my husband and I would spare the rod by making our children clean pygmy goat shit instead.

After she completed my punishment, she reminded me of her initial request.

"Tear it up."

Without hesitation, I tore it apart at the seams, gnashing at the throats of my brethren and silencing them with my betrayal. She left my room and closed the door behind her, leaving me alone to bury my dead.

I kept a very low profile for the rest of the night and the next morning. For once in my life, I rushed off to school like it was the happiest place on the planet. Then, after the fastest school day of my life, I returned home and tried to slip into my room unnoticed. Within moments, my mom was in my room.

"What can I get you to not be gay?" she asked.

I had never once considered the value of my sexuality. There isn't a Kelley Blue Book (or pink one either) for this sort of thing, so I was a bit stumped. Plus, we weren't Alabama poor, but we were still in the lower, lower middle class. I couldn't be sure of our exact financial situation, but it was much closer to the basement than the penthouse. Even if my gay was worth $1,000, I don't think she could have afforded it, and I didn't want the family to not be able to eat because they had bought my gay for the MSRP.

Then, I realized only one thing would avenge the gay writers that had suffered at my hands.

"A typewriter," I said.

"Okay," she replied, as if the answer was so obvious. "Of course, a typewriter. I'll get you one." With that, she left my room.

I didn't think that she would actually get me a typewriter in exchange for my sexuality, but the next day, when I returned home from school, there was a Brother typewriter and ream of paper on my bed. *Fuck, now I'm straight*, I thought.

Gay or straight, I couldn't type at all. I would sit on my bed and peck out a few words, but then get so frustrated that I'd stop. The next semester, I signed up for a typing class, and when I showed up the first day, I felt alive and connected to my greater purpose. By the third day, I realized that I just sucked at typing, so maybe I wouldn't become a writer after all. Plus, it already dawned on me that my mom hadn't paid nearly enough for my sexuality.

I dropped out of my typing class and broke my contract with my mom. Since our recent episode left me questioning my acting abilities, I replaced typing with another semester of drama.

8

BOYS VS BUDDHA

When my drama teacher, Mrs. Harrison, found out Garrett and I were gay, she started sponsoring a gay support group once a month during her free period. I would go to my history class, get marked present, and then walk back to her classroom to meet with other gay, lesbian, and questioning students. We hadn't figured out marketing yet, so there were only four gay guys, two lesbians, and a bisexual girl—with the occasional questioning girl who sometimes showed up.

In Alabama, my school had been a hostile place. I never even imagined the possibility of being out to a teacher, having a group of queer peers, or a safe space to be together and talk. East Anchorage High School gave me all of those amazing things. While I was there, only one guy called me a "faggot" and that was only because I bumped into him; we didn't even know each other.

I also went from having around thirty classmates in Alabama, to over 500 in Anchorage, and that made me just another face in the crowd. Of course, my theatrical prowess had made me a minor celebrity, but my fans were shy and very discreet. (Had I been able to find them, I would have encouraged my fans to be more aggressive with their enthusiasm.)

Once I arrived, I felt I had always belonged in Alaska. It occurred to me that maybe a miscommunication between my soul and God had resulted in me being born in Alabama. Maybe my soul had gotten distracted by one of God's angel assistants during my Life Planning meeting, and the first state instead of the second one was accidentally selected on my destination file. Instead of an epic origin story that involved volcanoes, earthquakes, and bald eagles, I came forth from dirt, and by the time God noticed I didn't have talon marks on my back or ash in my hair, it was too late. Then it took fifteen years of rearranging millions of lives and moments to correct the error.

I appreciated all the effort, but the fact remained that God and I had a strained relationship. At some point later, after certain life events transpired, I thought maybe Alaska was really just part of a plan to kill me off or something. Whatever the plan was, moving to Alaska definitely wasn't going to make me a Christian again, because I found myself surrounded by heathens. And it felt like coming home.

My new heathen community was mostly Garrett's fault. He made friends easily. I made straight A's in social studies, but I still hadn't learned how to *be* social, so I just followed him around. In his shadow, I met people. They used words I knew, like *reincarnation, karma, energy, aura, and spirituality.* It felt like people were speaking my language. They also used words that were foreign to me, like *chakra.* Whenever someone used it, I thought they had suddenly segued into a conversation about something car related. If I had a car, I probably would've realized that chakras don't get realigned at the mechanics.

For the first time in my life, I felt like my feet were standing in the right place. At the same time, a familiar feeling of disconnection grew stronger in me, and with it, the uncomfortable sensation that something was not right.

I wrote the words *Belief Creates* on a note card and put it above my bedroom door. I don't know exactly why I thought of it, and I don't remember spending too much time contemplating it, but I think that was when I began to recognize that my view of reality was questionable, because my entire life had been programmed by the beliefs of others. It only made sense that I would feel disconnected and uneasy.

Plus, the slow stirring of my soul had begun whispering that I was connected to *everything,* which was in direct contrast to the way I was feeling. I understood that being free of this dissonance was going to require spiritual exploration, so I put enlightenment on my to-do list.

Unfortunately, I put enlightenment lower on my list than finding a boyfriend.

After Chad, I found another one briefly. Having checked "boyfriend" off my list, I was about to take up meditating, but then we realized we were both bottoms. I thought I would automatically get to be the bottom because I had much better hair. He didn't know that rule (or I had possibly made it up), so he and I couldn't make it work.

The issue never came up with the next guy.

We met at a mellow heathen gathering at someone's apartment. There was no music, but instead was soundtracked by multiple conversations spread throughout the room. He sat across the room from me, talking calmly to a very animated red-haired girl. I could hear her, but not him, so I imagined that maybe his lips were just moving without sound, because she wasn't listening anyway. Moments later, she burst into a show tune.

It petrified me briefly because I would never have the balls to do such a thing and I would wilt under the responsibility of owning so much spontaneous attention. Most of the room instantly joined her in singing, and he slipped away. But then he walked directly toward my corner of the room.

"Hi. I'm Neil."

"Jason."

"Why are you standing in the corner by yourself?" His voice was calm and soft.

"It's a small corner, so there's really no room for a lot of people, but…" I slowed down and moved closer to him until my lips were close to his, and then, almost whispering, I said "Now that you're here, I see it's perfect for two."

If it happened like this, I would've pulled him to me and kissed him forcefully. However, I think liquor and my love of romantic French Films possibly bastardized my memory of the moment. In all actuality, I probably shrugged my shoulders and said, "My friend is here somewhere."

Neil had a blush on his cheeks that made him look like he had just come in from skiing. It also made him look younger than me, even though I found out he was actually a few years older. At the end of the night, we traded numbers.

After our first date, he bought me flowers and had them delivered to my school. They called me out of class and I returned with a dozen red roses. I tried to hide my red face behind them, but the teacher stopped me.

"You can leave them on my desk, if you want."

My relief was obvious, but putting them down also revealed to everyone the truth; I had just returned from gay skiing.

On our third date, we were hanging out in his bedroom. The flame of a single candle danced timidly with the reluctant darkness, maintaining a safe distance as if being chaperoned. Enigma played in the background as we lay on his bed, making out in the flickering shadows. He paused.

"Are you alright?" I asked.

"Yeah, sorry. I'm alright. I just have a lot on my mind."

We continued making out, but something was obviously bothering him. I asked him again, "Are you sure you're okay?"

The smile of reassurance that was beginning to blossom on his face backed out as if retreating. An army of untrained tears moved silently down his cheeks; each one a muted syllable of truth that his lips dared not betray. Finally he said, "I took an HIV test two weeks ago. They wouldn't tell me the results over the phone, so I went in this afternoon. It wasn't good."

It was obviously extremely difficult for him to share that with me, so I reassured him it was okay. After I left that night, I never talked to him again.

I knew I was an asshole. I didn't mean to be one, but I didn't know how to process it or figure out what it all meant. We had kissed so many times and that worried me, but I also assumed he would be dead in a few years and that scared me more. Plus, I was a teenage boy trying to get through high school. I hadn't even figured myself out yet. The easiest thing to do was disappear.

Finding a boyfriend might take longer than I thought.

9

THE CALL OF THE MILD

Hgh school had given me structure and halls to navigate, but after graduation, I had no direction at all. I felt like a pinball that had fallen out of the game. There was no one plunging me into action, no bumpers pushing me along, and no flippers to save me from danger. I just landed in the world and waited for some outside force to propel me forward while the emptiness inside me yelled, "Give me love!" to any guy that didn't have a swastika tattoo on his forehead.

A boy named Tony answered my call and disrupted my inertia. His motivation and sense of direction were slightly better than mine, but his inner emptiness was also louder. We played house with the idea that two dry wells could somehow quench the thirst of the other and then spent two years together dehydrated and digging deeper and deeper into dry darkness.

In order to do my part to support our dysfunction, I found a job at a video store. Temporarily.

The owner never said why they fired me, but I assumed that the video camera that I hadn't noticed before probably had something to do with it. That, and the riveting VHS rental, "Pro Bono" that I had actively watched the previous night, after closing the store alone. I only made it through the first 10 minutes of the movie, but I don't think the skinny, uncut lawyer actually helped anyone but me. He probably didn't have the legal skills required to get me my job back, so I just tried my best to forget the embarrassing situation.

I didn't mention to Tony that porn contributed to my unemployment. Instead, I got another job at a coffee shop... and then a very brief stint with a collection agency... and then, finally, a less temporary position at the cinnamon roll shop in the mall... and then, Tony moved to Arizona, and I found myself alone again.

That's when I decided to make the move to California for the first time. A large contingent of my heathen Alaskan friends, including Garrett, had moved to San Francisco, and I still had my childhood dream of living there. So I followed them.

In my youth, I had assumed that all gay people would just naturally want to be my friend. If not for my sparkling personality, then at least for our shared trauma. San Francisco taught me that wasn't the case.

When I first got to SF and went to the Castro, I was so excited to be around so many gay people. I was wearing an Old Navy t-shirt that I had just bought from a thrift store for $2. Old Navy was a relatively new brand at the time, so I thought it was a college football team and wearing it would butch me up a bit. It didn't take long for a couple of gays on Castro to remind me I sucked.

When they passed me on the sidewalk one guy said, "Wow, Old Navy, psshh!" and then they sucker-punched me with their rolling eyes. Reluctantly, I had to accept the fact that gays might not like college football and were possibly not a big fan of me either. Having survived straight people, I hadn't realized that I'd have to survive gay people too.

Being in San Francisco was like advancing to the final boss after only barely beating level one. It was super stressful if you're not great at being gay in the first place. I have absolutely no experience at being a great gay, so I can't even be 100% sure what that means, which makes winning the game a near impossibility.

According to legend, a perfect gay is a horse-hung top that only wears $500 t-shirts because it's sacrilegious to hide his visible abs under an article of clothing that costs any less than $499. He's under thirty-five, earns six figures, and swallows (but only because it's low in carbs). I didn't have visible abs, and I sometimes stressed about buying a shirt that costs over $10, which left me meeting only one requirement.

If I had a perfect body with visible abs, I would probably never wear a shirt again anyway. And there's no telling what I'd do if I were a horse-hung anything. Fortunately, the gods have decreed I live a humble gay life. This may have kept me from going completely crazy and fucking every man that could pronounce my name correctly. It actually sounds exhausting, so I probably wouldn't have done that anyway. We'll never know. However, I am sure that I would have probably made at least a few more gay friends in California if the gods had been more generous.

I did meet my next boyfriend there, though. Steve approached me while I was sitting on the couch at the Alaskan's apartment. It was my second day in town and by some twist of fate, I had gone from Alaskan, to Californian, to freak of nature.

The plane ride the day before had made me sick. I had rubbed my nose raw from wiping it so often, and that night, I had gone to the bathroom to find something to put on it. I didn't really live there, and I didn't want to be disruptive, so I just opened the medicine cabinet in the dark and selected a tube of something. I opened it and rubbed it on my nose. It felt better for a moment.

The next day, however, my nose had gone from discreetly dry and irritated, to obviously angry and looking for a fight. I did my best to hide it by keeping my head down. When Steve introduced himself, I tried to make eye contact. I couldn't do it without betraying the red monstrosity above my lips, so I stared down the entire time.

"Do you not want me to talk to you?" he asked.

I did want him to talk to me, but I didn't know how to answer the question correctly. "Yes, I do" or "No, I do" so I went with the obvious answer, "Jason."

Fortunately, he didn't notice my nose and just thought I was shy or a simpleton. When I finally lifted my head a week later, he probably just assumed I was coming out of my shell.

Steve and I were together for around six months after that. It was the most mature relationship I'd ever had up to that point. We had a lot of great experiences and even a bit of magic. However, I had no clarity about anything in my life, so eventually Steve broke up with me. I quit my job at Hot N' Hunky (a burger joint) and moved to Alabama to live with my brother for a bit, before making my way back to Alaska. The experience hadn't spoiled me on California, though. I still loved the Bay Area. I had met a lot of great people there, including my future spiritual coach, Vera.

After I returned to Alaska, I went to work at a gift shop in downtown Anchorage for one or two years. I honestly can't remember. It feels like Father Time took the years from 21-32 from my timeline, put them in a vodka snow globe and smashed me over the head with it. We didn't sell alcohol assault souvenirs, so I'm not sure where he got his. But we did sell normal stuff like t-shirts, postcards, stone carvings, magnets, and some weirder stuff like reindeer jerky, dried moose poop, and oosiks (walrus penis bones).

I can kind of understand buying reindeer jerky, especially if you hate Christmas, but moose poop, not so much. It also can't be good for moose morale to have their most popular tourist item be their shit. They probably don't even know how lucky they are not to be reindeer. Or a male walrus. Even the most well-endowed walrus probably wouldn't want its penis bone displayed on a shelf in a tourist shop. Plus, after being removed from the walrus, one would assume they would be completely useless. I can guess that people would buy them only as a conversation piece.

"Wow, what's this bone-looking thing on your shelf?" say your amazed friends.

"That's my oosik," you reply proudly.

"What's an oosik?" they say, obviously very interested in the item.

"It's a walrus penis bone. Do you want to touch it?"

You quickly realize you spent $500 to make your friends uncomfortable when you could've just said, "I want to be inside you," and achieved the same thing for free. At least you'll remember your trip to Alaska while dusting around the remains of your social life.

I don't have an oosik, but when people find out that I lived in Alaska for twenty years, they do ask me about all my hunting and fishing adventures. "I didn't go hunting or fishing while I lived there," I tell them. They quickly find out that I was a boring Alaskan. I try to rebound by mentioning that the Northern Lights are amazing, but by then I've lost all credibility.

I did do a few Alaskan things over the years. One time, Steve (my ex from California) came to Anchorage to run a marathon and wanted to go to Mount McKinley National Park. I had gained some weight at the time, and I was hoping he either wouldn't notice, or would still love me, regardless. After he told me I "wasn't aesthetically pleasing," I realized he had noticed. I didn't know why he was judging me about my weight while wanting to go see a mountain named after a fat white guy.

White politicians thought it was a good idea to name the huge mountain outside Anchorage after President William McKinley (a fat, white guy) instead of using its original name, Denali— an Athabaskan word meaning "the great one." Fortunately, in 2015, they changed Mount McKinley National Park back to its original name, Denali National Park, but that was after Steve and I went there.

Steve wanted to see the mountain, but he also wanted to see a bear, his favorite animal. We hopped on a bus and rode around the park looking for bears, which were also fat during summer. I wondered if I was the only fat thing in Alaska that he didn't want to see. The clouds obscured our view of the mountain, but we did see a few fat-ass bears.

After getting off the bus, we explored a few safe areas of the park. Steve reminded me that he was there to run a marathon, which meant effortlessly going up and down slopes. I had not trained for any kind of activity and smoked almost two packs of cigarettes a day. Getting on and off the bus had almost killed me. Now I had to climb some fucking hills. He may have been trying to get back at me for gaining weight and ruining the marriage proposal he had planned. Anyway, I would have said no if he had asked. Not in the moment, but years later, after really thinking about it.

Besides Denali, I also went on multiple "short-term" camping trips. Camping isn't much fun in Alaska. I think I went four or five times and it rained six of them. It also doesn't get dark in the summertime, so you're just sitting in a tent in ankle-deep water, staring into the miserable eyes of your friends, hoping that the chicken you've been trying to cook for five hours will give you a fast-acting strain of salmonella so you can die or at least go home.

Eventually, someone can't pretend to be having a good time any longer and brings up the possibility of going home. Everyone instantly agrees, so you put all of your wet stuff in your car with your wet friends and drive back home wondering whose stupid idea it was to go camping in the first place.

As unpleasant as those trips were, misery made all of my camping experiences memorable. I love every person I was ever in a tent with in Alaska—even if we never lasted the night.

Since camping and other outdoor activities rarely worked out, I spent most of my off-the-clock time drinking with friends in their homes, drinking with friends at karaoke and gay bars, or once, accidentally drinking with a couple of Belarusian guys that definitely weren't my friends. Well, one of them was friendly enough to tell me that the other one was probably going to kill me, so I should run before he got back from the bathroom. To be fair, they should have told me they were extremely homophobic. Had I known that, I probably wouldn't have gone back to their place after the bar closed, and I definitely wouldn't have mentioned that I wasn't into girls. I ran out the door and promised myself to most likely never go home with Belarusian guys again.

Drinking, while popular everywhere, is especially popular in Alaska. It's one of the favorite pastimes for Alaskans that don't like to kill things, and the second most popular for those with blood on their hands. It's probably connected to people living through six months of winter, only to feel stalked by it for the other six months. Imagine Julia Roberts in *Sleeping with the Enemy,* but cut out the middle of the film where she's happy. Then add an eighteen-month supply of vodka and you have a year in Alaska.

If you don't drink, that's okay. Alaska's unofficial state motto is "Alaska: Not Just for Drunks Anymore." It may be a relatively new unofficial motto, so you might not find it on a t-shirt just yet, but always ask for it at the gift shops. As soon as someone sobers up on the state marketing team, I'm sure they'll get around to getting it out there.

Drunk or sober, if you want to see the Northern Lights, you're going to have to go to Alaska in the winter. It's a beautiful time to see Alaska, but not to drive. All roads lose a lane after the first snowfall, and people just kind of start driving wherever. If you're on a two-lane road, it's safer to just drive on the sidewalk. There aren't very many pedestrians, and moose only use sidewalks to poop and stalk their victims. If you're not comfortable improvising pathways, you should leave the driving to an experienced Alaskan. It's better for you, Alaskans, and the pooping moose.

Fortunately, it doesn't get very dark during the winter. The snow reflects and magnifies even the smallest glimmer of light and seems to glow.

There is a certain peace that only blooms on a winter's night in Alaska. You can't access it while driving. But when you're miles away from everything, with nowhere to go and nothing to do, there is an opportunity to be with what is around you. This union is the one of the most gentle ecstasies available to a human being. It's a subtle calling beneath the wind, woven into the hidden rhythm of the snow and in the dervish-like dancing of the Aurora Borealis against the ceiling of the world. Everything is poetry. The deepest parts of ourselves echo it, asking us to be free and to come sing the song of our innocence that has waited patiently in our throats for an eternity. It beckons us to birth the song that will awaken our magic and pull us into the cosmic dance.

And, if you're not ready for the cosmic dance yet, or just not into that sort of thing, there's always vodka.

10

A NOSFERATU TRIPTYCH:

THE LOST BOYS, NEAR DARK, BAD BLOOD

I spent the first half of my life being almost completely lost. If you've ever had that anxiety dream where you're on stage and you don't know who you are or what lines you're supposed to be saying, then you can understand. I just kind of woke up on stage every day, said some stuff, exited stage left ungracefully, then woke up on a new stage the next morning and did the same thing again. Repeatedly. Sometimes, it was a musical, though, and I got to sing a bit. There was rarely dancing and never good dancing. That's where Felipe found me – not dancing at a club.

It was a weeknight in the middle of winter, so there weren't many people out. He looked slightly out of place and a little suspicious, but he was also handsome, so I walked past him. Then I walked past him again, but slower, pretending that I was looking for someone. It wasn't a well thought-out plan, considering there were only ten people in the bar and it would be hard to miss anyone, but I was counting on a strong acting performance to distract him from that obvious fact.

"Did you lose something?" he asked.

"Um, maybe," I answered, wondering if my acting was really that bad or if he was drunk. "I lose stuff all the time, so if you found something, it's probably mine. And if you found money, then it's definitely mine."

"I didn't find anything, including money," he said.

"Well, I would have bought you a drink," I added. "What's your name? I'm Jason."

"Felipe," he answered as he reached his hand out. "Nice to meet you. Would you like a drink?"

"Yeah, sure. Vodka seven with a splash of cranberry."

We sat at the bar and chatted over drinks. He was a little shy, so I talked more than him. At the end of the night, he offered to take me home. I wanted more time with him, so I accepted, even though my car was outside in the parking lot.

There was a magical tension in his truck as he pulled up outside my house and parked. Everything was slow but moving too quickly. His hand was on my leg, and my heart was soft but screaming, "You're alive! You're alive! You're alive!" and I wanted to share it with him, to pass it from my lips to his. I wanted him to take part of this message from me because it overwhelmed me.

Then he kissed me. Suddenly, I was in the eye of all storms, anchored by his lips to something new and more powerful than anything of a lesser nature. An unfamiliar god was pulling this deepening magic, extracting it, and with alchemy, creating the universal ingredient for infinite possibilities. It was there in our kiss. A taste of blue, electric honey exciting all my neurons and making my body a place that I could no longer safely inhabit. Yet my anchor, his lips, wouldn't let me slip away. I could only swim against it, with his body a new river swelling against my own. Felipe did not come inside my home, but he kept me awake all night.

I was a lost boy in a man's body. Felipe, on the other hand, didn't seem lost at all. He knew exactly what he wanted and worked hard every day to move himself closer to his goals— saving money, sending money to his family, and building a home in Mexico. He also didn't talk about emotional things very often. I mistakenly considered it a sign of strength.

The only thing that seemed complicated about him was the fact that he was deep in the closet. He was from a very conservative Mexican family that would rather have a dead son than a gay son, so for him, coming out was not and would never be an option. Most of his family didn't live close by, but he lived with another family that knew his family, so I could rarely visit him at his place.

I spent the night once though. He brought me over to make chili relleno for me when the family he lived with was out of town. We were listening to music and laughing in the kitchen. I was helping him cook, but mostly being in the way, when he kissed me. There was never anything else when we kissed. It was the kind of freedom that said, "No matter what happens, everything is okay." In his arms, I was safe from everything. Even when he turned me around and made love to me on the counter, his hands on my body grounded me. There was nothing to want or need with him near me.

That night, I lay beside him in his bed in a room full of his things. I wanted to feel like I belonged there too, but I knew I didn't. I was simply getting an unauthorized glimpse into a world in which I would never belong. I closed my eyes and tried not to think about it because, at that moment, he was holding me in his bed in a room full of his things, and maybe, just maybe, I could be one of them.

II

Felipe worked a lot. During the winter, he would work multiple jobs in town, while he spent most of the summer working out of town. We talked on the phone regularly, and I would usually see him every other weekend. As soon as he got into town, he would pick up his truck and come to my place.

I lived in a small house owned by my step-dad and I was giving him almost half my salary every month for rent, and he would turn around and give it to my unemployed step-brothers. It was not a perfect arrangement, but I accepted it because I had my own place and room for my dogs, Tico and Antonio. It was especially worth it when Felipe came by. He always wore a baseball cap and a belt, and I would take them both off as soon as he walked into the house. It wasn't always sexual, though. Sometimes, it was just nice to lie naked in each other's arms.

I was still completely lost as a person and had no direction at all. I would work all week, and then on the weekends I would party with my friends. Drugs were never my thing, but I was very into vodka, so my goal on weekends was to get as fucked up as possible. Maybe it was possible to get so lost that I would disappear. It never happened. I would usually end every Friday and Saturday night drunk off my ass with my friends, slow-dancing in my back room to the same three or four songs. Garrett was almost always there with me and a few other people, chatting and dancing while we listened to John Mayer's *Slow Dancing in a Burning Room* fifteen times in a row. They never once asked me to stop playing a song, which was a miracle in my mind.

Felipe would sometimes meet me when I went out, or he would pick me up at the bar. I would be a drunk mess, but he usually tolerated me.

At some point, I think he started seeing me less as a boyfriend... and then just seeing me less and less. I knew we were in trouble when he came over one night and told me he had seen my friend Gerald on a bareback website. Felipe pulled the website up on my computer and showed me. I didn't care what Gerald was doing. He was an adult living his own life. But, I knew that in order to see someone somewhere, *you* have to be there as well.

"Why were you on a bareback website?" I asked, with a mixture of concern and confusion. This was before PrEP (the HIV prevention pill), so alarm bells were going off.

"It just popped up on my screen and I clicked on it," he answered. "Then I closed it right back. It's no big deal... Do you want to go to Taco King for dinner?"

I now had an ever-tightening vice grip on my chest, so, even though it was our favorite Mexican restaurant, I answered with the enthusiasm of someone giving a thumbs-up while being stomped to death by a moose. *"Sounds great. Just dying over here."*

Dinner wasn't good. My torta tasted like two slices of puffy cardboard stuffed with chopped Styrofoam and cilantro. Felipe had even somehow made my soda flat. I wondered if his suspected betrayal was turning the world against me, but I didn't want to jump to conclusions too quickly.

It was possible he wasn't having unprotected sex with other men. Maybe my food had lost its flavor because I'd developed some new nervous system disease. For a moment, the thought comforted me. It was born, took a breath, and then slid to the floor, flipping its tail and gasping for air like an unfortunate fish in a Faith No More music video.

Yeah, Alzheimer's or Parkinson's disease wouldn't be an epic win in this situation, so I would just need to do some investigating to close the matter once and for all.

The next night, I went back to the website. It asked for an email to login. I knew his email address, so I entered it. It then asked for a password. I didn't know what that could be, and it was probably in Spanish anyway, so I was going to give up. Instead, I clicked on "forgot password." It then gave me the option to reset my password or answer a security question. Resetting was not an option, so I chose to answer a question. It relieved me to see that the question was multiple choice:

What size cock do you prefer?

6 inches

7 inches

8 inches

9 inches

10 inches

11 inches

12 inches

It disappointed me to see I barely qualified as a choice on the list, but I was even more disappointed when I selected 12 inches and was correct. Maybe that was why he was almost definitely cheating on me. I had a sinking feeling.

One look at his messages confirmed it. He was meeting with someone in the next few hours, even though he told me he had to work. I also saw that his message history went back further than only a few days. From the looks of it, it could have gone as far back as the Pleistocene Epoch. I'm sure there were tons of horny men back then who wouldn't have ever even thought about wearing a condom.

I didn't contact him right away. If he didn't want me, bringing it up wouldn't change that fact: it would only make it true. I wasn't ready for that, so I just doubled-up on my ice cream and tried to watch a movie. I made it through the ice cream, but I couldn't focus on anything else except crying. It felt like amateur macrame students were using my stomach to make a plant hanger out of it, while simultaneously playing tug-o-war with my intestines. In between tears and tugs, I left Felipe a message. I was pathetic, and I knew it. I was sitting at home crying and feeling sorry for myself while my boyfriend was fucking or getting fucked behind my back. All I could say was "Hey Baby. I love you. Call me when you're not busy." He was busy the rest of the night.

III

We didn't break up after that. We talked about everything, but I didn't want to fight, so I dropped it. It was a lose-lose situation for me, so I took the "lose" that let me keep him as a consolation prize. I assumed that our conversation had solved the issue, but in actuality, my consolation prize was still being shared with the community. I didn't have any love for myself, so I settled for whatever love he had leftover to give.

At the time, I had no, even vague, awareness of our relationship dynamics, nor was I aware of my silently raging lack of self-love. I only knew that something was missing and maybe he had it. I was Frankenstein's monster; dead pieces on a table waiting for lightning to bring me to life. He was my greatest storm and my greatest chance for this charging current.

Our relationship didn't end; it just kind of faded out until I eventually asked, "Hey, what happened to the music?"

It started with a phone call. I had never seen or heard him cry, so it alarmed me when I answered and he was crying. He said he was coming over to my house. When he arrived, he walked straight into my arms and told me he had tested positive for HIV.

I held him as we lay fully clothed on my bed. He couldn't stop crying.

I said, "It's okay. Everything will be alright," but I had no confidence in my words. "I'm sorry" was the only thing that I could say with any certainty.

"What am I going to do?" he sobbed.

I had no answer to that question, so I just told him that everything would be alright. He was not in a space to be concerned about me. He didn't tell me he loved me, nor say that he hoped I would be okay. There was only "What am I going to do?" There was no "we."

Eventually, he stopped crying and told me he was going out of town for a while to be with his family. He couldn't tell them he was positive, but he just needed to be around them.

As soon as he walked out, a sinkhole formed in the pit of my soul and began pulling my now unanchored pieces out of orbit. These untethered bits were quickly reduced to space debris as they swirled into a black hole as if being flushed. A herd of Pamplonian bulls stampeded into these now-empty spaces and gored into me like sperm racing to enter an egg. They soon also disappeared into the black hole, and then there was nothing left. He had completely hollowed me out, and all that remained was a stabbing pain.

Felipe never moved back to town. He would come in occasionally to see his doctor or to fly out of the airport, but his visits were brief and increasingly rare. He was still working constantly and sending money to his family. When I saw him, he would always ask if I needed any money. I didn't, but it made me feel like I mattered to him.

Even though he hurt me by lying and cheating on me, I never got angry at him. I thought he was basically a good person. He loved and supported his family, even though he knew that they could never be allowed to know him fully as a person. I think he was just his own kind of lost, and we were meant to find each other on the path.

"There is nothing that way," I said, pointing behind me.

"There's nothing behind me either," he responded.

We had stood in that spot for three years, staring at each other and waiting for something to happen. Then, one day, HIV struck a match and set everything around us on fire. Felipe ran while I stood frozen in place, waiting for a new path to emerge from the ashes. After the smoke cleared, I stood alone in the destruction of it all. He had made the better choice.

I considered going to get tested, but I decided against it. Instead, I made a truce with HIV. I would ignore it, if it would ignore me.

I kept my part of the deal for the next four years.

I'm not sure which part of me didn't want to know my status: the part that wanted to live or the part that wanted to die. Or maybe neither part wanted the other to know. I can't be sure. The fact remained that knowing didn't feel like a weight my foundation could support.

Years earlier, when Steve and I first started dating, we went for an HIV test together in San Francisco. Even though I had hardly had sex and hadn't engaged in any unsafe activities, I was nervous. For two weeks, my mind became an echo chamber with the *ki, ki, ki, ma, ma, ma* sound from the Friday the 13th soundtrack being replaced with *AIDS, AIDS, AIDS, Die, Die, Die*. It only made sense to worry because I wasn't a virgin.

AIDS was my destiny. I had heard it many times from multiple sources, and though I didn't think about it every day, it had collected like litter in the middle of my neural pathways. Faggot = AIDS. I didn't have to like the math or acknowledge it, but I definitely couldn't recalculate. Everyone knew that God punished gay men with AIDS.

After my mom found out I was gay, she lived in worry mode for me. It was bad enough that I was going to hell for being gay, but AIDS would pick me up at my front door and drop me off there, probably long before I had even packed. "You're gonna get AIDS. You're gonna get AIDS." Her worry spoke the words, but they blended in with the other math and became part of the equation.

One issue of Metal Edge had a picture of one of my favorite lead singers wearing a t-shirt that read: *AIDS Kills Fags Dead.* Reading it dropped an angry hive of lidocaine bees directly into my solar plexus. I thought he was the coolest, sexiest rocker ever, and the second-best lead singer (only behind Joe Elliott of Def Leppard), but his shirt stung and numbed me at the same time. Maybe AIDS was God's bug spray and I was just a disgusting insect that ran when the lights came on.

And, even though I didn't like Guns N' Roses, my band friends did. They sang along to *"One in a Million"* as Axl Rose lamented about faggots spreading disease. I sang with them, casting off pieces of myself in the process. I was a faggot singing about a faggot, and while it felt terrible, it didn't feel wrong.

If I knew my status I would be stepping into my shameful destiny, and I wasn't ready to do that yet. I crouched down and pretended to tie my shoes, hoping that destiny would get bored and leave.

Neither hope nor destiny cooperated.

Destiny is the slasher that follows you with a machete through the woods. No matter how fast you run, it doesn't fall behind. While you're zigzagging through the woods and breathlessly running for your life, an internal GPS is secretly navigating you to your kill spot. Somehow, destiny always makes a straight line to the rendezvous. Then, when directed by the script, it leaps out from behind a tree and gives you a machete to the face or uppercuts your head off.

Of course, destiny could also be someone with a million-dollar check, enlightenment, or a little dog on the side of the road. It could be anything. But at that moment, destiny was just a bitch with a big blade.

CALIFORNIA

11

ON THE ROCKS

If you've ever tried to fill a bucket with water only to find out the bucket had a hole in it, then you can understand my relationship with vodka. However, you probably stopped when you noticed the hole. I didn't; I tried to drink faster.

Vodka had never been a great friend, but it helped me forget how much I hated myself sometimes, however briefly. Then it would trick me into believing that change was as easy as buzzing all my hair off or shaving my head. It got me with that one more than a few times. I would wake up the next morning, not only hung over but also with no hair (and once also without eyebrows).

Vodka was my attempt to escape my feelings of self-hate and disconnectedness. I also studied Buddhism, so I knew that these dark parts could not be escaped, only healed, but at that time, I wasn't ready to make a commitment to healing. Plus, drinking always started off fun, like 10 PM vodka saying, "I'm on top of the world..," and then 3AM vodka finishing the sentence with, "...now how do I jump off?"

On one such vodka morning, a deeper sober part of myself took advantage of my drunken susceptibility and I sent an SOS message to my friend Vera on MySpace. She was a spiritual coach that I had met years ago in San Francisco, and she was actively working with my friends there.

When I woke up, I ran to my computer and immediately deleted my MySpace page. I assumed that deleting my account would also delete my messages. I didn't want to look like the crazy person who had drunk messaged a spiritual coach at 3AM. Plus, I knew it would be a vulnerable message and vulnerability made me extremely uncomfortable. Sober-me definitely had no interest in reading what vodka-me had written.

Fortunately, I did something wrong when I deleted my account, because I got an email from Vera later that day. Garrett and I were going to San Francisco in a month for a visit, so Vera and I made plans to meet while I was there.

I arrived at her front door with a recent vodka haircut, thinking that she already knew I was a crazy person from my message, and that this should go smoothly. Even though I imagined we would probably end up having a very Zen herbal tea while she talked to me about how I wasn't actually crazy at all, I was still nervous.

As soon as she opened the door, I knew that conversation wouldn't be happening. She offered me a seat and before I even hit the chair, I had an inner meltdown. She remained calm and unchanged, while every crazy piece of me started an internal screaming match. I felt like a teenage driver with drugs, sex toys, and a machine gun stacked precariously on top of a headless corpse in my passenger seat, as a cop pulled up behind me. Every darkness I owned seemed on display and just dying to be noticed. My body couldn't be still as they all jumped up and down inside, dripping with anticipation, and screaming out my guilt repeatedly, "I'm a murderer! I'm a murder! I'm a murderer."

I had murdered no one in this lifetime, but the part of me capable of murder was still there, and I wanted it to be quiet.

The hour passed quickly, and at the end, I knew she was the perfect coach for me. She didn't even mention me being peculiar or acting oddly, so I also held on to a bit of hope that maybe I wasn't that crazy after all.

Two nights later, I went to a group meeting with slightly renewed confidence that I was indeed not a crazy person. And if I had a bit of quirkiness to me, I knew I would not expose it so brazenly as I had before. Plus, out of a group of spiritual types, I figured I would definitely register as the mellow, normal one.

Then, as the meeting commenced, I had a physical reaction to Vera and couldn't stop moving my body. Obviously, I had the most uncomfortable chair in the room, because I explored every way to arrange myself around it, and could not settle for even the briefest moment. She noticed and had me come sit next to her. For the rest of the evening, she held my hand, and I settled down.

I returned to Anchorage, ready to make a much deeper commitment to my spiritual path and knowing that vodka and I were on the rocks.

Months later, I got utterly, embarrassingly, fall-on-the-floor drunk at my favorite karaoke bar. All I really remember of the experience was falling and almost getting into a fight with some guy. I had been preparing to quit drinking for a few months by pissing off all of my friends and drinking buddies, and that guy had probably smiled at me or something. Unwilling to risk making a new friend, I fortuitously fell into him and eliminated the possibility of us ever hanging out together. As I stumbled out the door, the last drink of my life dripped off his jacket. I also quit smoking ten days later.

I knew I had taken a big step toward spiritual clarity, but life without friends, drinking, or cigarettes was pretty boring. I decided that now was the time for me to focus on my dream of being a musician. I had taken up the guitar recently, but I wasn't very good. I was already in my early thirties and sensed that something bad was coming, so I started visualizing a new friend that played guitar and didn't want to drink with me.

The Universe delivered almost immediately. I met on a guy on Facebook who had just moved back to Anchorage from Texas. He sent me a message and we chatted and connected over our love of music. I invited him over to hang out. This was before all the Grindr murders and maybe even before Grindr, so I wasn't worried. He came over one afternoon after I got off work, and we hung out and he played guitar. We actually had a bit in common. He was gay and recently formerly Christian. He had even been in a Christian boy band—though I don't think they danced.

His name was Jared. By the time he left that night, we decided to work on music together. I would write lyrics and sing, while he would play guitar and sing backup. We would meet up at my house and practice two or three times a week. And just like that, I became part of a musical duo.

In no time at all, we had seven or eight songs. We were actually pretty okay. Our first performance was for my mom and Lee in their living room. We followed that up with a warehouse performance for family and people that were still talking to me. By the end of the summer, we had recorded a short CD and got a gig at the Alaska State Fair.

It was the most exciting thing to happen to me in a very long time. We were on a stage singing in front of my family, Garrett, and a few others. Occasionally, people who had come to look at large vegetables would stop and listen to us as well. I was excited that I was probably receiving as much attention as 2,000-pound pumpkins and 4-foot-long rutabagas. Afterwards, the organizer even invited us to perform at a different stage a little later.

Then, we were performing in front of a hundred people. A lot of them were drunk and noisy. Halfway through our set, Jared's guitar string broke and he didn't have a backup guitar, so he finished clanking through the song as best he could. We grabbed our stools and exited the stage, feeling grateful that the audience hadn't seemed to notice. The next act, however, noticed, and swarmed the stage to take our spots. They pushed past us, making it glaringly obvious there was no sympathy in the musician brotherhood. Suddenly, we were outside in the rain, listening to the heartless bastards bring down the house. At that point we felt like we had done Alaska, so we made an escape plan.

"Do you want to move to Northern California?" I asked Jared.

"Sure. When?"

"Before winter. Maybe right after my birthday."

"Okay," he said. It was that simple. That gave us two months to plan.

My friend, Nia, who I knew from high school, lived north of San Francisco. She had an extra room that we could use until we found our own place, so housing was taken care of right away. Plus, Vera was there, so I had connections.

We decided to drive and we needed to find a vehicle to make the trip. Jared's truck was too old and the back was uncovered, which meant we couldn't pack it, and my car was too small. So, Jared sold his truck and bought a slightly younger SUV, and I sold my car and saved the money for the trip.

Coincidentally, I had been working with Jared's father, but we didn't know it until a month or two after Jared and I met. When we announced we were moving, Jared invited me over to have dinner with his family. Jared was still in the closet, and his parents were religious, so I was a little nervous at first. However, his mom made a great dinner, and the conversation never veered into Jared "finding a wife" or "making us grandparents" territory. I was relieved and left feeling like I had been worried about nothing.

We planned to leave Anchorage on October 6th, two days after my birthday. I was in the midst of having a not-great birthday at my mom's house when Jared called me. I could hear the tears in his eyes. Apparently, his mom had found a message on his phone that related to him being gay and all hell had broken loose. They had kicked him out. As he was leaving, his mom told him she regretted inviting me over and wanted her food back. Obviously, that was impossible, and if it was possible, it would be an extremely unpleasant retribution for her to exact.

My favorite college football team was getting beat by a nobody when Jared showed up, still crying. I wasn't in a great mood because of the game, but my mood instantly worsened when my birthday was hijacked by his accidental coming-out day. I knew I was being a bad person, so I tried to be supportive. However, once my team lost, it became an increasingly arduous task. He stayed with me for the next two days until we left, so I tried to make it up to him by being extra nice. I don't think he even noticed my attitude because of his emotional distress.

We woke up early the morning of our departure and left for our new beginning. Three hours later, after passing Glennallen, the truck broke down. We opened the hood, and I stared at stuff while he started touching and wiggling stuff. He seemed to know what he was doing, so I volunteered to let him be in charge of this situation and I would take the next one. Fortunately, we were only a mile or so outside of town, so we walked back to a gas station where he bought some repair supplies. Two hours later, we were back on the road. It relieved me that he had solved the problem, but it didn't give me faith that the vehicle was going to get us to our final destination.

Once it got dark, it became apparent that the headlights were not working. Jared turned on the fog lights, but that was as effective as throwing Dasani at a vampire (there is nothing holy about that water). I sat clenching my ass cheeks together and barely breathing until we finally pulled over at a hotel. We decided not to drive so late the next night.

However, the next night, we got stuck driving in the dark again, except this time it was snowing and we were on top of a mountain with nothing but the slightest sliver of road in front of us. I don't like heights of any kind, but it usually offers me some comfort to see the ground below and know that I'm not falling towards it. I gripped the oh-shit! handle and gasped every time I caught sight of the mysterious darkness falling miles below my window, just beyond the confines of the barely visible mountain road. I wasn't ready to die yet, especially without a Grammy or visible abs.

Thankfully, we arrived at Nia's apartment, tired but extremely relieved. The mountains of British Columbia had taken years off my life. We quickly unpacked the truck and settled in within the hour.

I didn't know that I would be deathly ill at the same time the following year.

I met Nia through Garrett and Julie when I was sixteen. It might have even been the night I smoked pot for the first time. All I really remember is hugging the speaker and listening to Sade's "No Ordinary Love" on repeat. I was terrified, and Sade's voice seemed to be the only hope I had of not having a panic attack. Now and then I would drift away from the speaker, then realize I might be floating. I would once again embrace the speaker and hang on for dear life. The next morning when I woke up, I knew I preferred a Boone's Farm hangover to a traumatic marijuana experience.

When we first met, Nia and I spent a lot of our time partying or having coffee and smoking cigarettes at Denny's. Sometimes, we were drunk and listening to Tori Amos or Counting Crows. Other times, we talked about spirituality while over-caffeinating in a smoky haze. She loved Renaissance Festivals, but my inability to smoke marijuana greatly diminished my ability to find them enjoyable.

By the time I moved to California and was living with Nia, she and I had evolved and were no longer drinking and smoking together. We now chatted over ice cream and tea. One night, outside of a Baskin Robbins in Mill Valley, I told her about a weird feeling I was having in my lungs.

"It kinda feels like I pulled a muscle in there, but I think that's impossible. Other times, it feels like my lungs are just slowly being taken over by fuzzy caterpillars," I said.

"You better get that checked out."

"Yeah, I know, right," I said before taking a bite of my waffle cone. Then I changed the subject back to ice cream. "How's yours?"

I went about my days normally at first because the situation was developing as slowly as a twenty-six episode special on the letter origins of the alphabet.

Jared got a job at an upscale Chinese restaurant and wasn't around so often, but we would practice and run errands on his off days. His truck continued its steady march into decrepitude and began smoking heavily from somewhere under the hood.

Northern California is not a friendly place for smoking vehicles or for those that drive them. Anytime we had to go anywhere, we would put on baseball caps to hide our identity. The smoke was even coming into the car, so we would have to keep the windows rolled down. We took the car to an auto shop, and they said it would take $2,100 to fix it. We probably had about $1,000 between us. We were saving to get our own place, so getting the truck repaired wasn't really a viable option.

One day, we made a quick dash to Trader Joe's for hummus. As we were leaving, looking like the Beverly Hillbillies in witness protection, a teenage girl rolled her window down and yelled, "Time for an upgrade!"

I wanted to roll up the windows and let the fumes take me, but Jared wouldn't allow it. Instead, I slunk down as far as possible, pulled my hat down to my chin, and asked the Universe to teleport us back home.

We planned our next outing during school hours to avoid getting read by teenage girls. On the road, we were sending smoke signals to every other car on the highway: "*We are rednecks. We come in peace. Sorry about the smoke. Do you know anyone in the music business?*"

People responded to our message with shaking heads and looks of disgust and judgment.

Once, when I took a trip to Japan, a lady told me I looked like a famous person. I had buzzed my hair off and was a little overweight at the time, but I was still ready for a compliment, so I asked her, "Really? Who do I look like?"

"You look like fat Bruce Willis," she said, puffing her cheeks out and imitating a fat kid straining to show his guns.

I remembered that, and thought hopefully every Prius that passed us was thinking, "Wow, Bruce Willis really let himself go and he's obviously bankrupt. Even his driver looks miserable. He probably knows he's not going to get paid." The prospect of sullying Bruce Willis's reputation wasn't desirable, but it almost had me sitting upright again.

Finally, after getting pulled over by a cop for being a hazard to the world, we took the car to a new mechanic who said that he could fix the car for under $200 if we could just leave it with him for a day or two. We found that to be a very agreeable proposal, so we left the truck and walked home on foot, discussing how grateful we were that Officer Charles had pulled us over.

A month later, we had moved into our new studio apartment, and I had started working at a non-profit doing direct care. Jared still worked at the Chinese restaurant and would always bring food home for me. He even joked that he was jealous I could eat so much and still appear to be losing weight. I wasn't exactly sure what was happening to me with the weight loss and the now-rapidly multiplying caterpillars in my lungs that had recently taken to biting. I was also exhausted and developing red spots down the back of my neck. The most logical explanation was that I had developed an extreme poultry allergy due to eating so much Kung Pao chicken. It seemed plausible, if not highly likely.

I had left my two dogs with my friend Teri in Alaska with the promise to send a ticket for them as soon as we had our own place. Tragically, Antonio developed a heart problem and passed away before he ever made it back to me. I cried like a baby, and also felt horrible that my gentle and lovely friend had to deal with Antonio's last days. As soon as we had our apartment key, I sent for my remaining dog, Tico.

When Tico arrived, he wouldn't make eye contact with me. He gave me attitude for an entire day before turning to me and licking my face. The thing with Tico was that he loved women and other dogs. Our living situation didn't satisfy his needs. Not having the space or desire to have a woman in the house, we looked for another dog. Jared had always wanted to have a dog, but I insisted the dog wouldn't belong to us; it would be Tico's dog.

Soon, Jared found a dog for Tico. His name was Oscar. He looked like Tico on stilts but with a longer snout. They quickly became friends, and on his very first night, Oscar came to my futon to sleep with Tico and me. Jared had wanted Oscar to sleep with him, so he didn't appreciate the sleeping arrangements. I, however, didn't mind at all. In fact, soon after that, I started spending more time on the futon with Oscar and Tico. Then I started calling in sick for work because I could hardly move off the futon. I realized that it was time to stop eating Kung Pao chicken and go to the doctor; the caterpillars had completely taken over.

12

FELIPE FOREVER!

In October of 2009, death came for me. I think he may have stopped by the store for cigarettes and sunscreen, so by the time he got to my apartment, I was already driving to the doctor. I hadn't wanted to go, but my lungs hurt and I could barely breathe. The walk to my car had been difficult and painful. It took every ounce of strength I had just to pick my leg up and put it back down a few inches in front of where it had been. My heart rate would go up and I would have to stop for a moment. I would try to breathe, but every breath felt like someone tattooing my lungs. I imagined the name of my infectious ex constantly being needled into my chest. It was not cool at all. In retrospect, he wasn't that cool, either.

When I arrived at the clinic, the doctor hooked me up to a machine and asked me to walk down the hall. I obliged, though with little grace. He didn't attempt to hide his concern about the state of my health as he first watched me and then glanced at the results on the machine. I returned to the exam table where he removed my socks and checked my feet. As his frown burrowed ever deeper into the skin of his face, I realized he would not be delivering good news.

"I'm sending you to the ER."

Yeah, that wasn't good news; I didn't have health insurance. His concerned face showed me I had no other choice. He already had a nurse calling ahead to reserve a room.

I trudged to my car and then drove less than a quarter mile to the hospital parking lot. It crossed my mind that I should've packed a bag or something. All I had with me were car keys, an empty wallet, and my phone. I paused for a moment at the doors of the ER, feeling woefully unprepared for any possibility that lay beyond them. The ER nurses were waiting for me when I entered.

As the doors closed behind me, I started to cry.

After settling in at the hospital, they asked if they could do an HIV test. I politely declined because a part of me didn't want to be a guy with HIV. That would be the horrible ending to my story that everyone would've seen coming since the Felipe chapters. I wouldn't even be the writer of my life, and instead just a sad character drifting aimlessly through a plotless book. The reader would probably skip to the last chapter just to make sure I died and then return the thing for a complete refund.

I still held out hope that it was something else. I figured, these were talented people, I'm sure they could find another cause of death, if not for me, at least for the reader. My roommate could've been poisoning my chicken the entire time. Or maybe I was allergic to California. That made little sense, but at least it was original. And my father did warn me about California years back, so that would be something close to foreshadowing.

However, the doctors didn't want to make a creative effort and were firm in their commitment to kill me off with AIDS. I declined their request to take an HIV test a second time.

Since my illness technically still qualified as a mystery, they treated it as such; I had an unknown infectious disease which required me to be quarantined. Healthcare professionals could enter my room practically dressed in hazmat suits, and the few visitors I was allowed could only wave at me from the other side of a window. The mask I wore at least partially concealed my wretchedness, as I waved back weakly. A part of me was relieved that they probably couldn't see my pained expression.

I was supposedly being given pain meds, but I believe I was in the placebo group. The only time I wasn't in pain was when I was lying in bed, not breathing. I could spend all day in bed, but not breathing wasn't an option. So I kept breathing, taking the smallest breaths possible.

At night, when I had finally shallow-breathed my way into sleep, my body would revolt and demand more oxygen. It would naturally take a deep breath. Then a thousand needles were stabbing into my chest, again screaming "FELIPE!!" I would jolt awake in intense pain with my heart jumping out of my body. I developed a fear of falling asleep because I knew that my body's desire to take deep breaths waited for me like Freddy Krueger.

Misery never let me out of its sight. Rolling over to get a B12 shot in the ass was horrible; getting up to deliver a stool sample to the nurse was even worse. But the ultimate painful experience was attempting to masturbate:

jerk, jerk, jerk
stop and try to take small breaths

jerk, jerk, jerk
"FELIPE!!"

fuck.

jerk, jerk, jerk
be very still, small breath, small breath
jerk, jerk, jerk
"FELIPE FOREVER!!"

double fuck, ugh.

After I repeated that for what seemed like hours, I finally achieved the most painfully unsatisfying orgasm I've ever had in my life. I then had to lie completely still for twenty minutes to catch my breath, and then get out of bed and dispose of the soiled paper towel. It took an eternity to make it to the toilet, hoping like hell that no one walked in on me, as I slothed my way to the bathroom to flush the humiliating incident away forever. It wasn't even close to being worth it. Masturbation, my once-trusted friend, had betrayed me. I would not let it hurt me again.

Even though I lost one friend, I had plenty of opportunities to make new ones. You can't help but meet tons of people while in the hospital. It's something that I'm naturally horrible at, like rapping and dancing, so I reluctantly accepted the opportunity to improve my social skills.

I met an amazingly compassionate, gay nurse. He was older than me and would always take a bit more time with me than necessary and then hang by the door for a moment before leaving. Once, he looked back at me with tears in his eyes. I imagined I reminded him of a person or time before that was painful, beautiful, or both. His tearful exit, a soft kiss on my forehead. Gentle and loving. I could almost feel his soft breath move over my face, his full, normal lungs connecting us for a moment. But these moments could only be imagined. The unknown distance between us filled by two souls blindly following sounds that may have only been echoes of themselves.

I met another male nurse that I enjoyed seeing but hated experiencing. When he gave me my B12 shot, the needle was ten times larger than the needles used by the other nurses. I could think of four possible reasons for this:

1. He may have been homophobic. He probably stared at me through the cracked room door, saying to himself, "You like big things in your ass? I'll show you." He would follow that with a soft, maniacal, evil nurse laugh while flicking the top of a needle the size of a railroad spike.

2. Since he was relatively hot, maybe he was a simple person who wasn't good with numbers or measuring stuff.

3. Maybe he was really new and hadn't learned shots yet. Being a generous student, he volunteered to cover for the other nurses so they could go smoke or make out in the drug closet.

4. The only other reason he could have for making my ass a stabbing victim was that he was in love with me. He probably just wanted to make an impression. In that scenario, we would call him Carlos...

Carlos was a young soul. He preferred bungee jumping to talking face-to-face with the love of his life. He was awkward and had a hard time expressing himself in painless ways. To him, a 10-inch needle screamed, "I LOVE YOU MORE THAN MY OWN LIFE!" Carlos felt things deeply. There was a place inside his eyes where, if I could go there, I could feel only love and no pain. Unfortunately, he was always behind me when he gave me the shot, so I could never find that place. But he loved me, so I endured the pain.

I'm not 100% sure how I feel about Carlos anymore.

There were also two doctors that were complete opposites. The first was gentle and put lavender-scented pillows around all her words. I remember only a few things she said, but I know her words were always kind. I know nothing else about her, but I will also mention the possible, yet unproven, facts that she loved grape gummy bears and wrote haiku in her free time.

Her counterpart displayed a horrifying lack of pillows of any kind (except possibly the ones used as murder weapons). He would say things like "If you make it out of here..." or, "If you do get better, you'll probably be in a home after this," and "Who do you have to take care of you, for the rest of your life?"

There is no way for me to 'Carlos' him. He was the type of person who volunteers to write obituaries, maybe even for living people. He was just mean. It wasn't the slap-you-in-the-face kind of mean, but more the DL variety. It's like he tried to take a tiny piece of my soul every time he came into the room, slowly trying to lull me into death. Each syllable he spoke was a tiny cut, and with every droplet emitted from those syllables, a tiny poison built up in my system. He enjoyed playing the long game and had probably already written my obituary. The fact remained: I had cowritten it.

Occasionally, when Dr. Obituary was out of the room sharpening his words, I would be visited by the hospital chaplain. Hers is the only name I remember from the entire thirteen days I was in the hospital: Charlene.

Her soft beauty and sweetness hung closely around her like a euphoric stalker that remained unseen to her but was visible to everyone else.

In a different life, we probably danced together in a meadow, with a Scandinavian breeze painting soft pink roses on our cheeks.

She would sit with me, and I would imagine that place for a few minutes. The sore over my lips that scarred, and now hides behind my facial hair, disappeared when she was with me. Something in the room breathed for me, moving the curtains ever so slightly.

After she left the room, she lingered. A piece of her called for me to come with her. When I think of her now, my heart jumps, and I am reminded that the world is a beautiful place.

Dr. Obituary would always try to follow up with me after her visits.

"How are you feeling?" he would ask.

"I'm feeling a bit better," I'd reply while managing a slight smile.

"Oh good. Well, you may never walk again. We should probably do another test on you."

Then he would send me downstairs to have one of his associates stick a tube down my throat. They just needed a small sample from my lungs. I wanted to ask why they needed an enormous tube for a small sample, but I couldn't because of the enormous tube in my throat.

"Ah yeah, you like that big tube, don't you? Tell me you like it."

No, I didn't like it. I really didn't like it. Back upstairs, I'd feel like I'd just been face-fucked by a 30-inch lead pipe.

The doctor would return yet again, this time to tell me I had Pneumocystis pneumonia, and that I was most likely still in pain. I think it's the only time I ever saw him smile. He was probably feeling pretty accomplished, his mind whirring... *"In lieu of flowers, please send..."*

The kind, haiku doctor talked me into getting an HIV test after informing me that my immune system was dead and AIDS was the only rational explanation. They would basically need to nuclear bomb it to start it again, and my body would be vulnerable to everything until it got stronger. Without a positive test result, they couldn't prescribe me all the medicines that would allow the healing process to begin.

I agreed to the test, partially for her, and partially because I had no fight left. I became an AIDS patient by the end of the day. And that sucked. The fact that my poultry allergy was now most likely just a sensitivity, did nothing at all to cheer me.

As if on cue, my mom showed up. Someone from the hospital had called and told her my health situation was now an AIDS situation. I cringe when I think about how she must have felt at that moment. I knew that everything they told her caused her pain, and all that pain had my name on it.

She flew into town with my sister and the prayers of a hundred Alabama women. An amazing thing about Southern women is that they pray fervently without asking questions. My mom probably said, "My son Jason is in great need of prayers," and then suddenly everyone was praying.

I'm not sure how long after praying that the questions start, but the great thing is that gossip isn't as strong as prayer. The other great thing is that they were all 2,000 miles away, so I didn't have to answer questions. Well, not their questions anyway. My mom was a different story.

Our relationship wasn't complicated, but it did complicate my relationship with myself.

I was a sissy. I didn't know that at first, but I'm sure it was probably the third word I learned after mama and Jesus. Fortunately for me, everyone was more than eager to help me understand who I was. Over time, I absorbed the fact that I was sensitive and soft.

My father sensed this and took a hands-off approach, which meant my mom went the exact opposite direction. Possibly, she interpreted my softness as weakness and raised me that way. She was never cruel. In fact, she loved me more than all my siblings combined. She's very diplomatic though, so even if you asked her that today, she wouldn't admit it.

Since my parents were poor and kids were expensive, after the birth of my sister, they took measures to ensure she would be the last. However, I triumphed over their efforts and arrived anyway. My mom said I was a miracle baby because I defeated the IUD and survived a knot in my umbilical cord. I'm not so sure though. Maybe the knot was God's attempt to stop me after my parents had failed. Obviously, it's more comforting to think I was a miracle than to think that God was trying to kill me. I may never know. The only thing I'm sure of is that my mom has probably blamed my homosexuality on that knot more times than she blamed it on my friend Garrett. Garrett or the knot? The knot or Garrett? She probably still debates it some nights when she can't sleep and, of course, my current situation ensured that she would have plenty of sleepless nights.

It's an emotionally taxing event for a Southern boy to hurt his mama. Whether intentionally or unintentionally, it's traumatic. One day, after watching me struggle to walk to the bathroom and back, my mom told me, "I would give you my lungs if I could." It was emotionally and physically painful. Sobbing when it hurts to breathe is double murder.

My mom stayed with me until Dr. Obituary informed her she should return home. Even though my body was responding well to the treatment, he told her she would need to rest up for when I got out of the hospital and needed her constant care. Reluctantly, she went back home and took my sister and her good lungs with her.

It was probably for the best because I'm sure I was starting to smell. I had a nasal cannula in (to help my oxygen levels), so I couldn't tell, but I was feeling a little less pain and a lot more gross. Hospitals aren't a great place to be if you like daily showers. I would sponge myself off, but it was as useful as spitting on a forest fire. My hair stuck to my head in a sweaty, unflattering style, and my entire body felt like it had a thick layer of grime clinging to it. I shuddered to think of the places that the light didn't hit.

That thought alone willed me out of bed. I stopped listening to Mindy Smith's "Couldn't Stand the Rain" on repeat, took off my oxygen, grabbed a walker, and worked my way out of my room and down the hall to the shower. It was my first solo trip out of my room, and even though it was painful and took forever, it was also liberating.

I took off my hospital gown and sat on the bench in the shower. After the water warmed, I turned the showerhead towards my body. It was like a baptism of hope. I felt the water on my hair and my face and then my skin. Even though I still couldn't bath myself as thoroughly as I wanted, for a few minutes, I felt alive again. I also knew that if I could walk and shower, I might be able to leave the hospital soon.

I didn't get to take many more showers, but I started taking more brief trips up and down the hall. Soon, I didn't need oxygen or a walker. I wasn't moving very fast, but I was moving on my own. Dr. Obituary gradually had to accept the fact that I was getting better. Then, soon after, he said the nicest thing he ever said to me, "I think you will be ready to go home tomorrow." He may have been crying when he said it, I can't be sure.

I was extra excited because I was getting out on October the 30th. I would be home in time to celebrate Halloween! It wouldn't be festive, but I could watch horror movies while eating Chinese food and ice cream. Plus, the only people living in our apartment building were those who had given up on life or hadn't yet figured out how to give up drinking. Either way, none of them had kids who would knock on our door. I wouldn't have opened the door anyway, because I would've probably scared them.

They wouldn't let me walk out of the hospital. Instead, they put me in a wheelchair and rolled me to the front door. I assume it was to charge me an extra $7,000 for transportation expenses, but it might have been for liability purposes. There was also the slim possibility that I was still shaky on my feet. Maybe they didn't want to see me fall and break my neck, just as they were tearfully waving their goodbyes.

My roommate Jared met me at the door and drove me back to our studio apartment. The climb to the second floor required more help than I had hoped. I hadn't encountered a single stair at the hospital, so I was woefully unprepared for the experience. I tried to hide soft tears as he helped me take each step.

Tico and Oscar heard me at the door and welcomed me home with viciously wagging tails and tongues gently licking the tears from my cheeks. I lay on my futon and decided to just stay there with my dogs for as long as possible. I was horrible company, but they didn't mind at all.

13

SWEEPING JESUS

A fter leaving the hospital, I was left to deal with the parts of myself that had led me to the hospital in the first place. My overwhelming feeling of relief quickly faded, and a once-subtle emptiness returned with aggressive heaviness.

I had always felt like I was missing a spark that everyone else possessed, but now its absence ping-ponged pointedly against the infirm borders of my soul. It was as if the Divine had lit a fire in everyone's chest and somehow forgotten about me. Maybe I was in the bathroom at the time, or I had bent down to pick up a lucky penny. Regardless of the reason, a cold vacancy remained. Suddenly, it was as if someone had taken the blinders off, and I could finally see clearly that I didn't care about being alive. I realized AIDS didn't come to kill me; it basically came to say, "Die or get off the deathbed."

I wasn't actively suicidal, but I had been passively suicidal for years. This liminal state was now evicting me, and I needed to walk into the light or flush myself headfirst into the land of the living. I had to decide to live or die. The problem was that I still just didn't care. I really only wanted to sit in a dark room and gradually make a wingless snow angel on top of my futon mattress.

I talked to my spiritual coach about it. She said, "If you don't want to be alive, pray to *want* to be alive."

As a gay guy raised in a conservative Christian household, the mention of prayer sent a chill through me. I didn't want to pray, and I definitely didn't want God to get involved. He wanted me dead anyway, according to my raising. If I called him for help, he might show up in a really bad mood. "Now why the fuck did you call me?" the incredibly muscular man would say, as his glorious gray mane and beard rustled furiously in the winds of his wrath. He would then shoot a lightning bolt from his hand into my skull and call out a shirtless Jesus to sweep my headless corpse off to hell. Afterwards, over dinner, God would ask Jesus, "Didn't we send AIDS for that guy already?"

"AIDS isn't as reliable as it used to be," Jesus would answer. "I'll follow up on it though."

"Alright, you know the lightning bolt thing stings my hand a bit, and I really don't like to do it if a lot of people aren't watching."

"Yes, sir," Jesus would respond, thinking to himself, *You think you know hand pain? Whatever, dude.*

So yeah, I wasn't much in the mood to call heaven's 911 service.

I told Vera, "I don't think I even want to want to be alive."

"Well," she said, "if you don't want to want to be alive, pray to want to want to be alive."

Okay. I saw the only option for me at this point in my life was prayer. I only hoped the person answering was more like Tammy Faye than Hannibal Lecter.

This uncertainty meant I had to reconcile the God of my youth with the god of my deeper experience. It didn't really make sense to me that an old, white, straight man in the clouds created me, expected me to be perfect, and then made an eternally burning place to send me if I wasn't perfect, or if I enjoyed sucking cock. God, most likely, wasn't a flying Republican.

Plus, I figured the Divine was probably too vast to be comprehended by human brains that are still debating the existence of dinosaurs. I envisioned someone staring at a star in the sky and then proclaiming that they knew the entire universe. To me, religions had arrogantly done that to God. With little imagination and no knowledge, they shrunk God down, put him in a box, and claimed him as their own. I didn't want to claim God as my own. I just wanted a god that was on my side. I just wanted a chance to start over and figure out our relationship together, without all the gossip that had influenced it before. God and I could hang out, get to know each other, and maybe he would love me so much that he would even give me abs like Jesus (I'm a big fan of Jesus, but not because of his abs).

I found the popular quote, "*We are not human beings having a spiritual experience; we are spiritual beings having a human experience*" and it offered me an entirely new perspective on the situation. I thought, what if we are all just little pieces of God that were sent out to explore the world like little vessels from a huge mothership. Maybe there is no such thing as sin and the Divine wants us to show up on this planet, investigate everything with innocent curiosity, and have a fantastically messy human experience. Maybe we learn and grow, not by being perfect and judging others, but by making horrible mistakes, fucking up everything, and realizing that everyone else is doing exactly the same thing. This idea makes everybody's experience equally valuable.

This also means that when we judge someone else, we are taking ourselves out of our own experience because we have lost the sense of our own value. Murder, rape, hate, other negative actions... they only take us farther out of our experience, which is farther away from our connection with the Divine.

Obviously, our experience doesn't *require* us to totally fuck it up, but it would be completely acceptable and expected if we did. I went big with AIDS, and that was definitely not required or even remotely suggested. And, while I have met a few babies that seemed to have evil tendencies. I think most people are born into a pure experience; it's just quickly tainted.

Nia gave me a three-drawer accent table once. It was a cool light-green color, but it matched nothing I owned, so I painted it brown. Then I decided I didn't like brown either, so I painted it black. It now matched my other furniture, but it became boring and almost invisible. The drawers also became nearly impossible to open because of the layers of paint.

Maybe we are like that accent table. We are born with our spirits ablaze with brilliant colors, and the song of our soul is moving in these colors and waiting to be sung out loud. But colors are dangerous in a black and white world. We are painted over, with layers of black and white in order to fit into someone else's vision of the world. Before we even know our own song, it's buried beneath gray layers of beliefs, expectations, and judgements.

These layers led me to hating myself, and hating myself got me to where I was: fresh out of the hospital with an AIDS diagnosis, sitting numbly in a dark room. So, I prayed, not to the God of my childhood, but to a new one that hopefully belonged to everybody.

"Dear Divine. Sometimes I feel like I'm just missing something that everyone else has, and it makes me not want to be here. I don't even think I

want to want to be here. At the same time, I know there's got to be more to my life than this. Please, please help me."

God didn't reach down and bitch slap me. It also didn't rush out a response. Feeling ignored, but safe, I started saying some version of the prayer multiple times a day. Nothing happened, and I assumed nothing would happen. Then one day, I woke up wanting to want to live. Honestly, I can't be sure if it was an answered prayer or my spiteful response to the Divine's indifference to my prayers. Either way, I didn't want to sit in a dark room anymore.

I was considering opening the curtains of our home when a knock on my door distracted me. Maybe the Divine had decided on the bitch slap after all.

I opened the door reluctantly. Two women and a man stared back at me.

"Hi. Are you Thomas?" the woman in front asked.

Nobody calls me Thomas unless I owe them money. It then dawned on me I probably had a significantly destructive hospital bill sitting in the unopened mailbox. Great. The bill collectors found me on the same day I finally decided to want to live. I nodded anyway.

"I'm Jan. I'm a social worker with the county and my colleagues and I just wanted to stop in and check on how you're doing." They all smiled sincerely. "Do you mind if we come in?"

I looked into the stale darkness behind me. The apartment suddenly felt like the tomb of Dracula. I really wished I had made it to the curtains before the door. "Sure," I answered unconvincingly.

I moved to the side as they entered. The other female paused as she stepped inside and brushed her hand repeatedly against the wall. It confused me, but then I realized she was probably trying to find a light switch. I moved to the window and opened the curtains.

As the light came in, a part of me detached and I was watching four strangers instead of three. Who was this zombie doppelgänger, and when had he hijacked my life and crashed into this scenario? He shouldn't be answering their questions as if he knows me. And they shouldn't be here asking questions. None of it made sense. At that moment, I realized I didn't want to be a zombie anymore. I also realized that wanting to want to be alive wasn't enough.

The social workers left after thirty minutes with a promise to be in touch. While they were all very nice, I didn't want them to be in touch. I wanted them to go back to their office, stamp *Case Closed* on my file, and then forget about me. It wouldn't hurt my feelings at all if they never thought about me again.

However, by the end of the week, someone from the county called asking if I needed more information about filing for disability. I'm pretty sure Jan put them up to it. Since I spent our time together out of my body, she probably thought I was experiencing debilitating mental anguish. The thought of being a thirty-four-year-old man on disability shook me; it felt like a dead end. "I'm good. Thank you though," I informed the caller.

The possibility exists that Jan had nothing to do with it. Maybe the Divine answered my prayers by showing me what the path of not wanting to be alive looked like. It felt mostly easy, like lying on a conveyor belt and falling asleep to the siren lullaby of a guillotine. The peaceful, steady rhythm of the belt joining the whistle of the falling blade in a misleading duet. At the end of the belt, I would realize that it was the worst song ever, and the blade racing toward my throat would not be hitting a triumphant high note. After an anti-climatic metal whack, my head and headless body would fall into a timeless void. My brain would work just long enough to process the thought that their horrible song was on an uninterrupted loop.

This path didn't appeal to me at all. Even though I lacked enthusiasm, I chose the other one.

14

DISCOMFORT

A IDS didn't make me skinny. It's true, but apparently, it's not very funny. I've tested it out on a few different doctors and nurses, but not a single one has ever laughed. Even if I served it with a big grin, the most I ever got back was a half-hearted pity smile. I felt like it explained more about me in five words than a chart or complete medical history could ever do, and I just wanted them to get the joke. But no one ever did.

I briefly thought I was skinny when I left the hospital. I went to see a new doctor, feeling like I had barely missed the off-ramp to death, but it might have been worth it since I had lost weight. The first thing she did was put me on the scale and tell me I was overweight. I felt helpless because the only way I could lose more weight was to have something amputated. It felt almost as bad as being in the hospital, but not quite.

After my release, I assumed I would soon be living a life without pain. However, in no time at all, I started finding fresh new ways to experience "discomfort."

Within weeks of my release, I developed an angry sore on the roof of my mouth. Nothing has ever stopped me from eating. I'm the kind of person who gains weight with the flu, so I persisted. I would just eat and cry. One of my worst moments was sitting on my futon bed in my studio apartment, trying to eat a shrimp egg roll. I love Chinese food, so it was a heaven and hell experience. On my tongue it was amazing, but when it hit the roof of my mouth, it felt like sandpaper on a third-degree burn. I just kept crying and eating.

I attended a potluck dinner at Vera's while experiencing this affliction. I brought brown rice. Intuitively aware of my pathetic state, she praised my brown rice as if it were the most difficult dish imaginable. I really needed a win, so I absorbed all the praise I could get.

When it was time to eat, I fixed a small plate of salad because it seemed like the safest option. It was actually just a few pieces of shredded lettuce, but I was really trying to fit in. I failed miserably, as I sat chewing lettuce with tears rolling down my cheeks. I realized at that moment I was not ready to be out in public. It was too late, Vera had noticed and the rest of the evening became all about me. I cried the entire time while trying to talk about my recent experiences without using the words HIV or AIDS. I'm not sure if my glorious brown rice was enough to compensate for hijacking the evening, but everyone was gracious and supported me.

Vera once told me that some people experience more emotional pain on their spiritual path, while others experience more physical pain. At that point, I realized I was straddling both categories. I hoped the two wouldn't keep trying to one-up each other. Eventually I'd find myself in a fit of hysteria while simultaneously falling onto a bed of nails and getting struck by lightning. If it took that to get enlightened, it would be worth it, but I'd prefer a bee sting and low-grade depression. Both seemed like better options than my current experience.

That potluck at Vera's convinced me not to leave the house again until I had healed.

Hoping to speed the healing process, I talked to my doctor, who then told me to take ibuprofen. I feel mostly immune to pain meds anyway, but ibuprofen was as effective as swallowing toothpaste for a nosebleed. It's really not worth the effort of taking the cap off.

I realized this years ago in Alaska when I received a prescription for Ibuprofen after breaking my ribs.

I'll mention first that I was drinking and possibly very drunk when it happened. My inability to remember probably disqualifies the notion of 'possibly' and means that I was extremely drunk. I was sitting on a barstool at my favorite karaoke bar in Anchorage. A bar gremlin had tied my legs in a knot. As I was trying to stand up, my legs stayed behind and my upper body crashed to the floor. Felipe had taken the night off from cheating on me (or had possibly finished early) and had stopped by to have a drink with me. The drink he bought me might have been the one that put me over my limit. Actually, maybe this was his first attempt to kill me, though he didn't come nearly as close as he did the second time.

I woke up (or came to) the next morning feeling like a semi had run over my chest while the driver had tried repeatedly to shoot my eyes out with a nail gun. I got out of bed and staggered to the shower. It was immediately clear that something horrible had happened. I stood in the shower for a few minutes, scared to move. Eventually, the water was turning colder and colder, so I got out, dried off as best as I could, and went straight to the ER.

At that moment, I had no recollection of the gremlin incident. When I finally saw the doctor, he asked, "What happened?"

"I don't know," I said honestly. "I just woke up with my chest hurting."

He looked at me suspiciously. I think he was trying to figure out if I was a victim of domestic violence, but settled on the possibility that I was a complete idiot. He showed me the pain assessment chart and asked me to rate my pain. There were six colored faces, from smiley green to teary, frowning red.

"The orange one," I indicated.

"Which orange one?"

"The very severe orange one." I had selected only one shade under the worst pain possible. Then I worried that I might have been overly dramatic because one step below the crying Red Face may not be exactly right. You would pass out at Red Face, and I wasn't even close to passing out, so I changed my mind. "Or maybe just the Severe one." I think he was giving up on me because I didn't know what happened or how bad it felt.

"Let's send you down for an x-ray," he said. He left the room and was almost immediately replaced by someone entering to push me to radiology. Once there, they stood me up against the wall and asked me to take a deep breath and hold it. One reason I was in the hospital was because I couldn't take a deep breath, so I just held my breath and hoped they didn't notice.

"Can you take a deep breath for me?" the tech requested after the first failed attempt.

"Okay," I responded, knowing that I had agreed to do the impossible.

"Ready?" she asked. I nodded. "Okay, take a deep breath."

I took a small breath and was rewarded with a thousand burning spears in my chest cavity. I held my breath while clinching my teeth and praying like hell that I was doing it right this time.

"I'm really going to need you to take a deep breath for me," she said, oblivious or indifferent to the tears in my voice.

"Oh yeah, okay." I pretended I had just misheard her the first two times. But I didn't even try again. I just closed my eyes and made a constipated face.

"Sir, I can't get a good x-ray if you don't take a deep breath," she said, completely emptied of her backup patience reserves.

"I don't think I can," I replied. "It hurts too bad."

"Alright," she said. My confession had laid claim to the failure. She released me back upstairs, content with the fact that I had fully absolved her.

Once I was back upstairs, the doctor reentered the room. "The x-rays were inconclusive because we couldn't get a clear view of your ribs," he said. Rather than running more tests, he opted to send me home with a prescription for hardcore ibuprofen. It then dawned on me that maybe he didn't think I was a victim of domestic abuse, but a drug addict. I reluctantly took my prescription and went back home.

Later, I was mentioning to Felipe that I had somehow gotten hurt. He reminded me I had done a belly flop from my barstool the night before. Then it all came rushing back to me. Oh yeah. I was hurting too badly to be embarrassed because solving the mystery didn't solve the real problem. Felipe was also showing minimal empathy for me because it was all my fault.

I spent the next month taking small breaths and trying like hell not to cough. It was mostly impossible, but I did it because I had no other option. Sneezing was a completely new level of hell that I had never experienced before. I'm also not the one-and-done kind of sneezer. I'm more the six-and-please-no-more kind. Every sneeze felt like someone was ripping me open and sucking the meat off my ribs. I was almost sure each one sent me straight back to start where I would have to heal all over again.

The entire situation also put both my drinking and karaoke dreams on hold. I sat at home miserably sober while, unbeknownst to me, Felipe was out fucking or getting fucked by boys without broken bones. To relieve the stress, I tried to smoke, but I could only take small, unfulfilling drags. I would sit there holding my cigarette and feeling like the biggest loser in the world. I had never been cool, but this was an all-new low. However, now having achieved AIDS, I realized that there were previously unknown depths to be explored.

So, no, ibuprofen didn't really work for me.

Within a few months of being able to eat without crying, I was back into the ER with a mysterious pain. It felt like I had pulled a muscle somewhere between my front and left side or I had been impregnated with one of those alien babies that like to chew their way out. The doctor looked over my body and sent me for an ultrasound that showed nothing. I wasn't pregnant with an alien baby, but that was all I learned. The doctor had no other answers. He told me to "rest up" and sent me home.

I was midway through my painfully ineffective resting-up treatment when the entire front and back of my lower torso starting erupting into fiery red blisters. I returned to the ER, where a different doctor told me I had shingles. He was also polite enough to inform me that if I had come in earlier, they could have given me a shot that would have made the outbreak a lot less severe.

"Um, thank you," I responded. I wanted to add, "Can you let the other doctor know?" But I wasn't in the mood to be a smart ass because half of my body was melting off. He gave me a prescription for Percocet and I went back home.

Shingles suck hardcore. It feels like every nerve in that area of your body becomes an electric eel and starts fighting with all the other electric eels to break the surface first. I couldn't sleep on my back, stomach, or left side, not only because of the pain, but because I felt like all the blisters were bursting and gluing me to my sheets.

Shingles is very painful, but also unattractive. I stared at my body in horrified awe, but it was so gross I couldn't stop looking at it. It was like red islands had turned up on the map of my body and little volcanoes were constantly going off and making the islands larger and larger. My body had seemingly committed itself to a kamikaze study of human volcanology.

It also didn't take long for me to remember that I am mostly immune to Percocet, but not to the side effects. I would take three pills at night, not for pain, but hoping the drowsiness would hit me before the nausea. On a great night, I would get a few hours of sleep and not wake up sticking to a sheet.

This affliction passed, but my body quickly replaced it with gallstones.

A gallstone attack feels like Freddy Krueger trying to open a Christmas present, with the present being a small, balloon-like organ in your digestive system that deflates when you're not eating. After the first attack, I realized that there is nothing you can do except curl into the fetal position and try to pass out. I honestly considered hitting myself over the head with a frying pan just to knock myself unconscious for a while. Seriously. I would be on the floor, writhing in pain, slipping in and out of a fetal position for hours with no relief. In that situation, cookware to the head sounded like a tender mercy.

The first time it happened was in Anchorage. I thought I had a three-hour spell of horrible gas or killer indigestion, so I didn't really think about it much afterwards. I just said to myself, "Wow, that really sucked. Hopefully, that never happens again." I went about my business, and I completely forgot about it.

However, after recovering from shingles and feeling confident that the worst was over, it made a vicious return.

One night, after a huge cinnamon roll with double cream cheese frosting, I was under attack again. I was back on the floor in the fetal position, trying to figure out if someone was voodoo dolling me. I couldn't think of anyone who would want to hurt me, but I wished they would just chop off my head instead of continually pricking me. I would even open the door for them if they wanted to hit me over the head, but the knock never came.

The third time it happened, I went straight to the ER. This doctor was one of the friendliest doctors I have had in my entire life. His voice had a lilt to it, and every sentence he uttered felt like it was spoken to his best friend.

"Sorry you're not feeling well, bro. I'm going to give you a shot that'll take the edge off. Then we'll send you for an ultrasound and hopefully have you back outside enjoying this beautiful day in no time at all." He must have been working a very long shift because it had been raining most of the day, but I agreed because we were bros, and I didn't want to be the one to break it to him that the weather was uncharacteristically shitty. Plus, maybe this time they would find an alien baby and I would have to have an abortion.

The shot took the edge off, and I gradually blossomed out of the fetal position. It still hurt, but it didn't feel like I was being murdered anymore. After my ultrasound, he broke it to me that I had gallstones and that I would probably need to have my gallbladder removed.

"Don't worry. It's a fairly simple procedure," he assured me. "They usually have you in and out in just a few hours." He smiled at his joke, and I felt like we should hug, but he rolled toward the door before I could embarrass myself. "I'll get you the referral to the surgeon," he promised before disappearing behind the closed curtain.

A few days later, I sat in front of the surgeon, listening to her describe how easy it is to remove a gallbladder. It almost felt like an elevator pitch, because in under a minute, I had agreed to let her have it. She was very enthusiastic about it, so I'm sure she was probably high-fiving everybody in the office after I left.

"I got another one, you guys," she would have beamed.

"Wow, Sheila! Great job!"

Sheila would leave the room for her next appointment, and they would remain huddled together, wondering aloud, "How does she do it?"

By cutting three holes in my abdomen. But no one asked me.

After Sheila took my gallbladder, I returned home to convalesce and wonder if I had given it up to her too easily. I was probably just another notch on her out-patient bedpost, and all I got out of it was another prescription for ibuprofen.

While Sheila could've done a better job explaining the digestive side effects, it turned out that she was pretty good at taking out gallbladders. I was a little nauseous and sore for a few days, but experienced only minimal pain. "Wow, Sheila! Great job, even if I meant nothing to you."

I'm not sure if I meant anything to my next doctor either, and she penetrated me. My HIV doctor had done an anal swab, and the results showed I had abnormal cells in my anal canal. This required me to be sent to a different doctor to be investigated further. She put me in stirrups, put a speculum in my ass, and dug around curiously. She had explained electrocautery, but I really should have researched it more thoroughly, because before I knew it, my ass was on fire, and the entire place smelled like a witch burning. Apparently, electrocautery involves using heat to destroy and remove cells. It was an incredibly intimate experience, and I wondered what life decisions had led her to a career in burning gay men's anal cavities. I see her waving the smoke from her face and explaining to me that "It's a labor of love." I would've bought that too, because she was very into it, even if I was so not into it.

I had an appointment to go back again for another round of burning, but I ditched her. I had spent weeks walking like a robot and trying not to poop. Going to the bathroom felt like giving birth to a backward porcupine and always resulted in hours of bleeding afterwards. I would stuff my underwear with toilet paper (not the front), just so blood wouldn't seep through. My underwear didn't look like a crime scene or anything, but there was enough blood to make me uneasy.

I felt pretty bad for not making my appointment. I'm almost sure that she didn't pull a Miss Havisham after I stood her up, but part of me wonders. Maybe she still wears the remnants of her doctor's gown while sitting in her office with all clocks stopped and curtains drawn, What was once a labor of love was now a poisoned promise, lying broken in a putrid place of no expectations.

Realistically, I doubt she even noticed that I didn't show up, but on some level I wanted her to hurt like she hurt me. And she hurt me deeply.

15

HAMMERED

The most unfortunate aspect of being alive is that it requires a lot of money. Having recently decided to reinvest in life meant I needed a job or a rich husband. Unfortunately, acquiring either seemed daunting, considering my interest in the endeavor stemmed more from need than desire. I had found multiple jobs in the past and zero husbands; therefore, gainful employment seemed the obvious choice.

I visited my spiritual coach in order to discuss the issue. "I need a job."

"Well, get a job." She had a way of always making the difficult things seem like the easiest things in the world.

"It's not that easy."

"Yes, it is. Just walk right down to the natural food market and tell them you want a job," she said, as if it was already a done deal.

I didn't want to go to the market. And if I did go, I certainly didn't want to talk to anyone. Talking to people made me uncomfortable, and asking people for something was even worse. In an emergency, I could probably ask for the number of the ice cream aisle. Even then, it would only be after considerable consternation.

Since most of my issues stemmed from religion, I blamed it on church and the fact God required me to be seen and not heard. Not being heard also meant not asking for anything (except possibly forgiveness). Growing up, when I wasn't outside playing with my siblings or other kids, I needed to be quiet and cause no disturbances. I didn't take to it naturally, but I had an aversion to getting whipped, so I strived to be extremely well-behaved and nondisruptive around adults. Around God, I barely dared to breathe.

Then, one Sunday morning, an oddly traumatizing event occurred that caused me to make an unnatural commitment to being not heard.

During the beginning of the preacher's sermon, the sound of a man urinating came loudly through the thin wall separating the men's bathroom from the nave of the church. I gasped and turned my head toward the bathroom in shocked awe. Occasional "amens" and "hallelujahs" belonged in the moment, but the splashing sound of a man relieving himself did not. A man touching his sinful bits and announcing it so proudly in the church seemed an affront to all things holy. Frozen in place, I unflinchingly watched the wall, hoping the sound would stop before God brought the roof of the church down upon us. The man, however, seemed to be channeling the Alabama River and showed extreme indifference towards my safety and that of those still blissfully unaware of the danger.

The blasphemous act finally trickled into nothingness, the spell over me dissolved, and I turned back to the front quickly. I then realized no one else seemed to have noticed the offending incident. The only witness to the greatest crime to ever befall Vermont Holiness Church sat quietly with a mortified face that loudly proclaimed, "I know what you did!" I didn't want to see him and I certainly didn't want him to see me, so I grabbed a hymnal from the back of the pew in front of me and brought it to my face. It practically touched my nose. *Ah, safety.* I wouldn't see him and he wouldn't see me.

My mom tapped my leg. I peeked around the side of the book. Her eyes whispered forcefully, "*Stop being weird,*" as her hand pointed to the back of the pew. My face could only stare back blankly. She took the book from my hands, closed it, and returned it to its slot. I maintained my stare. Sensing a distress in me, she leaned in and whispered, "Do you need to go to the bathroom?" I shook my head confidently. First, I did not want to come face to face with the loud man. Second, I never wanted to use that bathroom again. If I did, I would sit down and say a prayer first. Good boys make no ripples in the toilet and no waves in the world. I wanted to be the best of the good boys. Right then, I decided that being seen and not heard was the safest course of action.

Obviously, I couldn't tell my spiritual coach that my childhood had been so marred by a man pissing loudly in church that I was left with a crippling inability to talk to people. Not only did it not make total sense, but she might suggest that bringing up the incident more likely represented an unexplored desire to engage in watersports (or something like that). Knowing her psychology skills trumped mine, I reluctantly agreed to stop by the market. Plus, I had to pass it on my way home anyway, so it would require minimal physical effort to stop.

A young guy with dark hair and untrusting eyes greeted me at the customer service desk of the small market. He looked almost young enough to be my son.

"Can I help you?"

When I opened my mouth to speak, my words slipped out as if lubed in an accent of panic.

"Are you guys hiring?"

He paused and possibly considered if he could stand working with me. Then he responded hesitantly, "I think so. Let me get the department manager." He picked up the phone, dialed a number, and briefly talked to the person on the other line. As he talked, I stared at his name tag: *Will – Supervisor.* "He'll be up in a minute."

I wanted to run out the door because my potential new supervisor was probably going to be graduating from high school that year. He had a shifty eye on me, though, so I just looked around nervously. This only increased his suspicious gaze. The manager appeared and offered no relief. I could instantly tell he was the serious type. His name tag said *Brad – Team Leader.* He handed me an application and said, "Fill this out. You can do it here or bring it back later."

"Okay, I'll do it here," I said as I took it from him. I sat in the dining area and attempted to fill out the form. My memory, however, chose not to cooperate. I couldn't remember details about any of my previous jobs. I wanted to add a disclaimer stating that all dates, phone numbers, and addresses were potentially incorrect because of a system error, but I didn't think he would find that funny. Instead, I just hoped he didn't call to verify anything.

As soon as I finished my inspired-by-true-events application, I took it back to Will. He had either warmed up to me in my absence, or had forgotten that I had bothered him earlier. This time, he smiled. "Let me get him back up here." He called, and Brad returned shortly to take me right back to the dining area.

We sat quietly as Brad read my application thoughtfully. "Alaska, huh?" he said finally. "What brought you here?"

"I just got tired of the winters," I responded. I don't think he would've appreciated the fact that I really moved to win a Grammy.

He didn't follow up with a fishing or hunting question, so I assumed he didn't care much for killing things or he wasn't straight. Instead, he asked questions about being a team player, how I handled conflict, and my availability. Not wanting to draw out the process, I kept my answers as short as possible. He showed no interest in hanging out either, so within five minutes, the interview had ended. He gave me a sincere smile, stood up, and told me to bring my ID and Social Security card to orientation on Monday.

I wasn't super excited to be starting a new career as a bag boy at thirty-four years old, but I was moderately excited to be alive enough to be doing something. So on Monday, I returned to the store with my documents. My moderate excitement, however, had spent the weekend going from mogwai to gremlin, and dread now seeped from every pore of my being, including my hands. I hoped that no one would introduce themselves with a handshake; it would not be pleasant for both of us.

Brad greeted me at the customer service desk with a slight smile and an outreached hand. "You're a little early."

Instead of my hand, I offered him my driver's license and soggy Social Security card. He accepted them reluctantly. I immediately hoped the *ugh* echoing through my head hadn't made its way out of my mouth. Instinctively avoiding a damp handshake probably made me look rude, or worse, like I had just arrived from the wilds and hadn't yet learned the ways of civilized men. My awkward offering of an overcompensatory smile satisfied any doubts he had about me. At least a smiling idiot wouldn't piss anyone off. And if I could learn to put eggs at the top of the bag, even better.

"I like to be early," I replied, while hoping he wouldn't follow up on that statement. I hadn't even meant to say it.

"You're probably the only one." He smiled. "Come on." I followed him through the supplements and natural beauty aisles, through the swinging doors labeled - *Team Members Only* and into the back of the store.

I passed through those doors thousands of times after that, sometimes as a bagger, a cashier, a supervisor, and sometimes as an associate team leader. Brad had been gone for over a year when, one day, I walked through them and met a new guy in our department.

I don't know what made Matt special. Like everyone else, he seemed to have no knowledge of it at all. In fact, it might've been a secret only I knew. It wasn't obvious the first time I talked to him; it revealed itself gradually over a few months.

We didn't seem to have a lot in common. In fact, at first glance, we probably seemed like complete opposites. He liked girls, beer, and baseball, and I liked boys, milk, and college football. Plus, I was more than a few years older. We became fast friends anyway.

"Peter Coyote tried to get a voucher for a *raw* milk bottle earlier." (Glass milk bottles required a deposit that would be refunded when the empty bottles were returned. We didn't sell raw milk, so we couldn't refund a deposit for it.)

"The gall of Peter Coyote." Matt faked a look of shock. "Does Peter Coyote need $2 that bad?"

"Not fucking likely." I knew very little about Peter Coyote and couldn't be sure that Matt knew anything about him. "He probably hasn't even spent all of his *E.T.* money yet."

"Did you tell him you couldn't take it?" he paused and looked at me seductively, "But you could refill it for him?" A shit-eating grin blossomed on his face.

"You're stupid and that's so fuckin' gross." I grinningly appreciated his warped sense of humor. "It would probably hurt like hell too. I'd probably be too dehydrated to cry before I even filled half of it."

"That's not even that gross. There's this video online about two girls and a..."

"Don't even bring up that fuckin' thing again. That is so fuckin' gross."

"Yeah, but art is subjective. It's gross to us, but some people might think it's a nice film about friendship and sharing. I mean, if I saw you suffering with a half-full raw milk bottle, I'd help you out."

"Ah, for real?" I answered with the enthusiasm of a nine-year-old being told to take the car to the store for ice cream. It also hadn't passed me that he would consider the bottle half-full and not half-empty.

"Yeah, sure buddy." He grabbed my shoulder. "That's what friends do; we have each other's back."

"Man, that's so awesome. Hopefully, he comes back in."

"Hopefully, not. I mean... that's just twisted. Plus, I gotta go for a run later and running with sore balls is murder."

"Where are we running?" I hadn't meant to try to move our friendship out of the store and into the real world. It just kind of came out. Plus, I had started running, but stopped months ago. I could probably fake it for at least a few minutes. He probably wanted to run more than a quarter mile though. I couldn't really solve that problem at the moment because I worried he would decline my self-invitation.

"Wherever you want."

Later, he picked me up in his little black car and we took our first trip to Tennessee Valley together. I rolled my window down as we listened to "The High Road" by Broken Bells and "Little Secrets" by Passion Pit. A remembrance of innocence flooded me and I felt like I was being given a moment of freedom that had been intended for a much younger version of myself. As if a sliver of joy had gotten trapped somewhere in my body twenty years earlier, and now, Matt, the wind, and the music magically worked together to release it. The pain and swelling disappeared as my heart welcomed the long-lost visitor.

On the trail, we started jogging slowly. I felt him next to me talking, reminding me to breathe naturally. He mentioned something about the wind. I listened, but a deeper part of me was still having a reaction to him. Life didn't have questions anymore; the moment contained every answer. I didn't need to discover it, touch it, or force it in any way. I just needed to be in it. My focus returned to his words and the sound of our feet hitting the path in unison. For the first time in years, I felt connected and alive.

The trail ended at a beach. When we reached it, the edge of the ocean had just swallowed the sun and the sky burned with the panic of reds and yellows fleeing the loss of their god. We watched briefly before walking quickly back in the direction of the car.

We made the trip regularly after that. Sometimes, we ran straight to the beach and back. Other times, we stopped to rest. On one especially sunny day, after we completed our run to the beach, Matt climbed up on a large rock and took his shirt off.

"Take your shirt off and get your ass up here," he said.

"I don't like to take my shirt off," I responded while climbing up on the rock.

"What are you talking about? We're the only ones here." He slipped his hand out to pull me up. As soon as I was on the rock, he pinched my nipple and again told me to take my shirt off. "Don't be a pussy," he added.

"You're a bitch," I said as I removed my shirt. I tried to lie on the rock as quickly as possible so my belly would look flatter. He didn't care about his belly. While I was in conflict with my body, he seemed to be completely at ease with his. And even though nothing about him was perfect, everything seemed to fit perfectly. I wasn't jealous. I just wanted to lie on that rock for as long as possible.

Being around him had become an excruciating joy. He was an unwritten Rumi poem, incessantly unraveling before me. I begged to be brought into this poetry, to smell the gardens beyond the gate, to feel the slightest mist of his rains brush against my face. But I stood weakly in a place I had yet to interpret, my heart an interloper, and my knees unsteadily hoping to learn his words. He sensed my predicament, but didn't seem to care. He even flirted with me, which helped but didn't.

At work, some people started asking if we were a couple. He went along with it coolly and said, "I don't care if they think we're dating. I mean, we're a cute couple, right?"

"We're probably the cutest couple in town really, and there are some pretty fuckers around here." I didn't really believe that, but I wasn't against working with him to disprove it. At the same time, everything was right and as it should be. I didn't want or need to possess him, I just wanted to be near him. As inappropriate as we were together, being around him felt like being plugged into something good and pure. It even crossed my mind that the Divine had sent him to deliver a message that I was only now ready to receive.

Sometimes, he would stay the night. We would go for walks, watch movies, or play video games together. I sucked at video games, so I always got us killed by a zombie. He never got upset with me, even though he really wanted to win. I, in turn, didn't get upset when he hated the ending of *Martyrs*, my favorite horror movie at the time. We would be up talking long after we had turned the television off and the living room had become dark.

"What's the scariest dream you ever had?" he asked as we lay on the living room floor.

I had to think about it for a second. "One time I dreamed I was standing by a lake or something and there was a body in the weeds. I could hear people coming, so I ran because somehow I knew I had killed her. When I woke up, that feeling stayed with me. It was creepy. For three or four days, I was paranoid."

"That wasn't scary," he scoffed.

"Yeah, I'm not sure it was a dream, either. Anyway, the police never came by, asking questions, so..."

"Whatever."

I turned to look at him and said, "Well, you tell me a scary dream, then."

He looked back at me. "All of my dreams are scary," he whispered.

"Good, then pick one." I turned back to the dark ceiling and waited.

"I have a dream sometimes where my grandma is shaking me and crying and trying to tell me something, but the dream doesn't have sound. I just see her in a panic yelling something at me and she's crying harder and getting more and more frustrated because I can't hear her. It always wakes me up."

"Damn, that would be intense? Is she still alive?"

"Nah, she died years ago."

"Do you think she's trying to tell you something?"

"Maybe, but I try not to think about it."

Eventually, he would go to sleep on the couch or the floor. I would bring him a blanket and go to my bed.

Even though HIV was usually just a thing in the back of mind, like a balloon that had slipped away and bumped occasionally against a corner of the ceiling, I wanted to tell him. We had been friends for over a year and he knew everything else about me anyway, so I brought it up to him on one of our night walks.

"Can I tell you something?"

"What's up?" he said. "Everything okay?"

"Yeah, of course. It's not really a big deal." I was lying and doing a horrible job of it. I was much better at stalling, though.

"If it's not a big deal, then just tell me. You get a girl pregnant?" he joked.

"Yeah, I was so drunk, I thought she was a power bottom. Now I got an ugly-ass baby on the way." There were so many things wrong with that response.

I think he was preparing himself for me to tell him I was in love with him.

"I'm HIV positive," I said.

"Thanks for letting me know," he said.

"Are we still cool?"

"Yeah, of course we're cool, dummy."

We talked about it more while we walked, but I started feeling like I should've told him I was head over heels in love with him instead. It's possible I was slightly regretting being so honest. The more we walked, the more I believed we were both regretting it.

Maybe he didn't care about my status, or maybe he did. I tried to be ultra-Zen about it and accept that everything was as it should be.

He got a job in San Francisco soon after that, so I hardly saw him anymore.

One winter morning, I bumped into him on a street corner in Oakland. I struggled to make eye contact with him because I had gained thirty pounds and he had gained a girlfriend. Instead, I stared at the white t-shirt he wore under his black zip-up hoodie. We talked briefly and made a promise to get together soon. As he walked away, I remembered my heart had a nail in it.

I never saw him again.

ALABAMA

16

NOT SO GREATNESS

I haven't won a lot of awards or trophies in my lifetime. I think I won Best Supporting Actor in an East High School production of something, and the Best-Behaved Boy one week during vacation Bible School, but the shine has long worn off those accomplishments. It's been one long and dry awards season for me ever since.

For a brief and magical moment, I had thoughts of being an Olympic runner. One spring morning as I ran through the park, everything seemed perfect. The sun on my skin, my rhythm as I breathed deeply, and the wind on my face as I ran faster and more effortlessly than ever. I had already decided I wouldn't be disappointed with a silver or bronze medal, when I noticed a slightly overweight 15-year-old girl lapping me for the second time. My quest for Olympic gold was immediately put on hold while I reevaluated my abilities.

I tried to run in Alaska, but it was hard and I didn't know what I was doing. You would think that running is easy: just put one foot in front of the other as quickly as possible until you get somewhere different from where you started. But I would start with feet of fire and, one minute later, be hunched over and breathless, only yards away, realizing that running is one of the most idiotic activities of all time. You show up, get out of your car, run in circles, and then get back in your car and leave. It makes no damn sense. You can't even smoke while you run.

I took up running again in California after getting out of the hospital. Running made a little more sense then, since I didn't have a car. I showed up at the high school track one day with Vera. She told me to "Just go slow and take your time." So, we started running together.

I quickly realized that she was taking the slow and steady approach. My feet didn't like that, so I took off and then circled back. And then I did it again. Her movements suddenly looked less slow and more zen-like. In that moment, it occurred to me that if I'm only going in a circle anywhere anyway, then why the rush? By then, she had warmed up and I had tired myself out. Her approach had been better than mine. She stopped and walked around the track with me.

After that day, I worked myself up to running a mile. I didn't have to go fast; I just had to keep moving. I learned to focus on my breathing, and then just settle into a comfortable pace. Running is mostly a mental and breathing exercise. When my mind told me I couldn't, I just kept breathing and did it anyway. Sometimes, I had to slow down, but eventually, I found my rhythm. In no time, I was up to a mile. Some days were a lot faster than others, but that didn't matter. For months, I would show up a few times a week and run a mile, and that was enough.

Soon after, I noticed a flyer at work for a 5K that was coming up in a few weeks. I didn't think I was ready for it, but I decided to think about it anyway. On the day of the event, I woke up early and went.

I paid my registration and got my bib number – 1401. I walked around while I waited for the race to start and tried not to look like a fraud while half expecting someone to sniff the air, point at me, and yell "Imposter!!" Then a ton of runners would descend on me like a ravenous horde of zombies, and since I was an imposter, there was no way I could outrun any of them. My only revenge would be causing them to lose the race. Everyone knows you can't run after a heavy meal.

No one noticed me at all. And my only goal became to stay unnoticed. That would mean no passing out, no pooping or peeing myself, no crashing into anyone, and definitely no dying. I honestly wasn't confident that I could achieve any of those things, but I got in line with the other runners anyway. The faster runners were up front, so I stayed closer to the back. There were hundreds of us, and I was surrounded. They fired the starting gun, and we were off.

It was a beautiful spring morning that was suddenly alive with the sound of a thousand footsteps hitting the pavement. I wasn't sure where we were going, but there were plenty of people in front of me I could follow, so I just fell into the flow of it all and focused on my breathing. When I passed the 1km marker, I relaxed and realized that I probably wouldn't ruin my underwear. Everything and everyone was just effortlessly moving forward, and I was in the middle of it all. At the 2km, I had almost fully settled in and wondered why I had been so worried.

Then, halfway through the race, I remembered being at the hospital. I thought about how painful it had been for me to walk and breathe. Now, I was running in a 5K and I was nothing special, just one of hundreds of people running in a circle. My vision became blurry with joyful tears for a moment, but I wiped my eyes and kept running.

I didn't know anybody in the race, but toward the end, there was a guy cheering everybody on. He was yelling at everybody: "Great job!", "You got this!" and other supportive statements like "Alright!" and "Wooo!" while clapping his hands furiously. I know he wasn't there for me, but I felt like he was my witness. I did have it and I did do a great job. Of course, I was just one of the 99.99% of runners that lost the race, but I was the proudest loser of the day. Not just because I didn't poop my pants, but because I showed up and did something that I wasn't sure I could do.

Over the next few years, I would go in and out of running—running regularly and losing weight, and then stopping, gaining weight, and getting depressed. Then, I'd have to start back over from the beginning. I repeated this cycle many, many times.

During one especially brutal cycle, I went from extremely happy and fit, to fat and completely depressed. A fog settled over me and I couldn't find myself anymore. My hip also started hurting me so badly that I had a hard time standing. I decided to quit my job at the natural grocery store and move back to Alabama and stay with my mom who had recently returned there.

I loaded my clothes, stereo, and extra stuff into my trunk, strapped my concrete garden statue of a meditating Buddha in the back seat with a seat belt, and put my dogs in the passenger seat, and left Northern California. I didn't know exactly why I was leaving, and I felt like I was giving up and running away. All I knew for sure was that I couldn't be that person in that situation anymore; I needed to break up with my life.

In an attempted rebound, I detoured to Austin for a day to audition for *The Voice*. I got a hotel room for the night, and the next day, I walked to the audition because I didn't know the area or the parking situation. It was not a wise decision. I showed up sweaty and looking like complete shit. Everyone else was cute or cowboy-hatted, while I looked like a 252-pound red crayon that had melted into a t-shirt and cargo shorts. I felt miserable and out of place.

They eventually gave me my group, and we finally made it into the audition room. I still had not stopped sweating, so it relieved me that the room was relatively dark. Everyone in my group could sing, but no one was that special. The producer said, "Thank you, but we won't be moving forward with any of you." I think they really wanted me, but maybe they didn't think Jon Bon Jovi would give me the rights to perform "Blood Money" on television. It was either Jon Bon Jovi or the lights. Obviously, they weren't looking for overweight, sweaty, gay guys with a sensitive rocker's edge, so my dreams of an instant life makeover were derailed.

I continued towards my mom's house in Chilton County, Alabama, muttering to myself the rest of the trip – "*The Voice*, my ass."

I had put the name of my mom's town in the GPS instead of her address and forgot about it until I pulled up to a church and my GPS helpfully stated: "*Arrived.*" I suddenly felt like my escape from California had been an elaborate plot by Southern Christians to reclaim my soul for the Lord. I quickly noticed my mistake, called my mom for her address, and continued the last few miles to her house.

My mom always greets me one of two ways when she hasn't seen me for a while. It's either "You're getting skinny" or "You're getting fat." She doesn't ever actually say that I'm getting fat, because she's way too sweet for that (and I'm her favorite, in case you'd forgotten), but anything other than "You're getting skinny" really means "Wow, you've gained a little weight since the last time I saw you." When I arrived at her house, she met me in the driveway. As I got out of the car, she looked at me and asked, "Did you have room in your car for everything?"

Ugh! I had really gotten fat if she was asking how I fit anything else in the car.

"Yes, ma'am. I got rid of all the other stuff I didn't need." I mean, other than the extra 42 pounds I was lugging around. If you went by my BMI, I was supposed to weigh 128 to 162, so maybe I was lugging around 90 to 124 extra pounds. Obviously, I won't use the BMI in this situation because it totally sucks, and it would be a bummer if it were accurate. Instead, I settled on my hospital weight as my low weight. I figured, if I was 187 at my worst, then 199 pounds would be perfect, and 210 would be acceptable. Being that I'm a reasonable person, I would never expect to be perfect. Plus, the world doesn't need more perfect people; it just needs more people doing their best. I wasn't very close to that either, but I was looking to turn it around.

Ever since we moved to Alaska in 1991, my mom had been threatening to move back to Alabama. Lee was always doing or saying something to upset her, so it had almost become her catchphrase. Finally, after twenty-two years, she did it. She told my stepdad that he could stay in Alaska, but she was moving back home. She then enlisted my cousin in Alabama to help find her a house. In no time at all, she was in Alabama, signing paperwork and picking out paint samples. By the time I arrived, the house was already completed to her satisfaction.

After seeing that my mom was serious and wouldn't be coming back, Lee rethought his decision to remain in Alaska. Days after I arrived, my mom flew back to Anchorage to help him pack up their things.

Suddenly, I was alone in the house. There was a bit of joy underneath it all, but the not-so-gentle truth was that I was an overweight, thirty-eight-year-old gay man living in his mom's house. Every morning this Truth bitch-slapped me across the face and yelled, "What the fuck are you doing?" It then cold-stared at me with a tilted head and a WTF look. "Wake the fuck up!"

The truth didn't seem to care at all that I was depressed or that my hips hurt. I even tried feeling sorry for myself, but it didn't work. It was just vicious. "You gonna wait for Mommy to come home and make it better, huh?" I would then reach my hand out, ready to be lifted up, ready to change, but instead of helping me up, the truth would kick me in the chest and knock me on my back. "Oh, hell no, bitch! That's not my motherfucking job." The truth is an asshole.

I felt like I was at rock bottom, but I tried not to entertain the thought because I didn't want to tempt fate. You know when you're having the worst day ever, and you think, *How could this day get any worse?* and then the answer repeatedly reveals itself to you throughout the rest of the day. I was already having a horrible time with Truth, so I definitely didn't want to invite Fate to the party. They would tag-team me and make me their sore-ass bitch. I was nowhere near prepared to take on both of those studs, so whenever I started feeling like I was at my lowest, I would try to distract myself. I would say, *"Good things are happening"* and look the other way, hoping not to make eye contact with Fate. Sometimes, I would even whistle just to sell the nonchalance. Nothing to see here. Nope. Nothing. Uh uh. *Whistling sound.*

Truth sees right through whistling, though. Once it's on top of you, you just have to relax, accept it, and then try to change what you can. With my current issue being that I was a thirty-eight-year-old, over-weight, gay man living at my mom's house, it really only left me two truths within my control: lose weight and move out. I had no problem with the thirty-eight-year-old gay man part.

My mom had an elliptical machine in the garage, so I lugged it upstairs to my man den. Every day, I put on some music, jumped on the elliptical, and pulled and pedaled my ass to nowhere. At first, it was boring as hell. Then, after a few days, it became even more boring. If my heart rate hadn't been so high, I probably would've fallen asleep. The only thing keeping me from a threesome with Ben & Jerry was the knowledge that I would need to follow it up with seven hours of foreplay with the elliptical just to break even. No, thank you.

One day, after I caught myself seriously debating which one of us I was going to throw out the window, I broke up with the elliptical. It was a mutual decision because I hadn't realized how hard our partnership had been on it. We kept living together, though, because it was bulky and hard to move down the stairs.

I had lost a little weight and was feeling a little better anyway, so I took up running again. I would prefer to run outside in 100 degrees with 99% humidity than exercise indoors at any temperature. Plus, I like sweat to be dripping off me like grease off a rotisserie chicken. I started wearing lighter-colored running clothes just so my sweat would be a lot more obvious. It sucks when you wear black, sweat like crazy, and then have to strain to see the sweat stains. After a run, I want to look like I just came back from conquering something from the deepest, darkest depths of the ocean. If I'm wet from my head to my toes, I really feel like I crushed it. I read somewhere that sweating more doesn't mean you're losing more weight; it just means your body is hotter. I stopped reading because I didn't want to get bogged down with the science of it all, but I got the gist of it – sweat more and look hotter.

I wanted to look hot, but my short-term goal was just to look warm enough to be alive, so I put on my running shoes and started running around outside my mom's house. I would start from the garage, go to the storage shed, back past the garage to the mailbox, around the circular drive, briefly hit the road, and then back past the mailbox to the garage. This would be one mile, so then I would keep going on the same route for two or three miles until I got tired. I was scared of being on the road because Alabama law allows you to be on your phone while driving, and they were always going 90 miles an hour, so I would always speed up on the road leg of my run.

Country drivers are nice, though. They will usually wave, honk, or lift two fingers from the steering wheel as they speed past you. If they kill you, at least you were hit by a friendly person who might have possibly known you (or was at least briefly cordial).

Eventually, I couldn't force myself to do another driveway circle, so I got on the road. I was like one of those people from *Friday the 13th* (just heavier and having a lot less sex) that was running for their life, but kept looking back to see if Jason Voorhees was catching up. If I saw a car coming from either direction, I would go a good yard off the road on the opposite side, just to be safe. They would usually honk or wave while I stumbled through three feet of dense kudzu, trying to wave back and look completely normal.

The other thing about Alabama country people is that they have a lot of dogs and not a lot of fences. I had completely forgotten this helpful information, but it returned to me in no time. As I started running in a four-mile loop, it seemed that a dog waited for me at every turn, and even though I love dogs, and had initially assumed that all dogs felt the same way about me, it didn't end up being true.

Country dogs don't see a lot of runners, so I think most of them were just confused by me and were coming to check me out. Unfortunately, there were other dogs that were less curious about what a runner is doing and more curious about what a runner tastes like. The good and bad thing about these dogs is that they were easier to identify because they ran at me much faster than the other dogs. A dog would start running at me, and I would slow down, saying "Good boy," hoping it was a good boy (or girl). I learned quickly that fast dogs are not 'good boys' and fat boys are not as fast as bad dogs. I would scream like a girl and run in the other direction, praying like hell that a squirrel would run across the road, or a texting driver would speed by.

Most dogs lose interest in a minute or so, but if you're ever chased by a pack of dogs, they are competing to take you out. The game doesn't end until a dog tastes blood. I didn't know the rules at first, but I learned them after a bulldog mix clamped onto my outer left thigh and five other dogs just stopped, put their asses on the ground, and started panting. I couldn't quite make out everything they weren't saying because I was screaming and swatting at the dog on my leg, but I was almost sure I heard one of them say, "Who's the bitch now?"

I really love dogs a lot, so once my bulldog attacker, Cookie (most likely not her real name) let go of my leg, I didn't hold it against her or the others. While she licked her lips, turned around and trotted back to her loser friends, I just kept running.

After I made it to safety, I looked at my leg. Cookie had left a bite that resembled a smiley-faced monkey head. It was weird that the monkey was happy because it was bleeding from its eyes and mouth, but simian mood analysis didn't interest me much at the moment. I was caught between worrying about a potentially fresh case of rabies and finishing my run. Being less than a mile in at that point, going back would've been the best option, but that would mean another encounter with Cookie and that would just be asking for it. She had already bitten a hole through my boxer briefs and tasted my blood, so she probably thought she owned me at that point. I decided to tough out the next three miles to avoid her.

I started running the opposite direction after that, so if Cookie attacked again, I would be at least 75% done with my run. Oddly enough, I never saw her again. After it was clear that I didn't have rabies, I even worried about her. I knew she had recently had puppies because I had gotten a really good look at the size of her nipples while she was hanging off me like a Christmas ornament. She might have stopped running with the boys to focus on being a mother. The other dogs slowly lost interest in me now that she wasn't around. Maybe they had figured out they weren't her puppies' daddy or maybe because I screamed like a banshee every time one of them even blinked at me as I passed. There is also the slimmest possibility that Cookie slandered me and said something like "His blood tasted off."

Her gossip circle was small because other dogs on my route still showed interest in me. But it just wasn't the same. She had my blood in her mouth, and I had her saliva in my leg. Once you've had this kind of intimate experience with another creature, it bonds you. This theory of mingled body liquids = bonded for life obviously doesn't apply to two members of the same species.

If I was bonded for life with everyone I had ever kissed or shared body liquids with, I would be severely tempted to jump off something tall. I wouldn't actually do it because I would probably be followed over the edge by somewhere between one to five hundred gay men (and possibly a female or two that caught me off guard) who couldn't imagine a life without me. Considering they would be bonded for life with so many others, I could potentially wipe out the entire gay population. That would be a mega bummer. I would also need a lot of lives to burn off all of that bad karma, and that would push my enlightenment back centuries. In case you didn't know, it takes longer to burn off bad karma than belly fat. I still have a belly, and I've been working on it for twenty years.

Running away from dogs did help, though. I lost thirty pounds in three months and was feeling a lot better physically. Resurfacing in the back of my mind was the once-lost thought of being an abbed gay. I tasted a hint of greatness in the idea of running shirtless, while drops of sweat surfed their way down my glorious abs. Men and women would tilt their sunglasses down to discreetly watch me gracefully bound by like the offspring of a gazelle and a Greek god. I wouldn't want them to be jealous or turned on; their appreciation of my perfection would be enough for me. Seeing me would remind them that the world is a beautiful place and lead them to search for even more beauty. They would stoop down to sniff every flower and climb higher into the trees, desperate to taste the juice of the fruits closest to the sun. From these heights, they would rise up to protect the earth and start a movement that would unite all nations in the fight against climate change. My abs could save humanity and the planet.

I wasn't inside yet, but I stood at the Doorway to Greatness, waiting to be let in. When the door didn't magically open, I tried to find the key in the pockets of my sweaty, gray running shorts. With a 5-inch inseam, you would assume that finding a key would be easy. However, every time I stuck my hand into a pocket, I felt astral breezes brushing through the downy softness of my arm hair. I searched through a thousand other dimensions and worlds looking for my key, but I couldn't find it. I don't actually remember ever having it, but I'm sure I must have. It's incomprehensible to me that I could've been born without it.

Gradually, I concluded that the key to the Doorway to Greatness is like your virginity – once you lose it, it's gone forever. Mine was probably in some bar somewhere, or maybe a drive-thru, or worse yet, I might have lost it at that one guy's house that gave me a pack of powdered donuts after I used my feet to jack him off through his underwear. It wasn't my idea, and I didn't ask for the donuts, but I assumed if there was one moment that I had probably lost the Key to Greatness, that moment was the most likely candidate. Hell, I probably didn't lose it at all. It had probably just abandoned me after watching me awkwardly trying to maneuver some guy's erection with my feet. "Yeah, I can't do this anymore," it probably said, as it decided that its entire life purpose would never be realized at the hands (or feet) of this moron. "I'm embarrassed for both of us," it said, as it jumped into the unknown.

Fuck. I looked for a doorbell, but there wasn't one, so I started knocking like a crazy person and begging to be let in. "I just want to be beautiful and save the world. Please, let me in. Don't you want me to save the world?" Absolute silence. "Please. I'll settle for a four pack. The world needs us." Still nothing. It then dawned on me that greatness is a cunt. I was much too friendly to be hanging out with a bitch like that and maybe there was a friendlier door close by. I was sure that I could get into the Good Enough door. A flat belly would turn enough heads to at least create a slight movement. That would almost certainly be enough to save snow leopards and lessen the intensity of hurricanes. No one really wants to save mosquitoes, moose or tsetse flies anyway. I'd probably be doing the world a favor by letting those assholes perish. As for polar bears and tornadoes, I could work on them later. For now, I would just focus on having a flat belly and figuring out if chronic masturbation was a symptom of rabies.

17

LOST SATELLITES

Soon after moving back to Alabama and losing a bit of weight, I got a job as an assistant manager at a supplement store in Birmingham. I was still living at my mom's house, and the first part of my plan was to get a job and move out ASAP. Only then could I focus on finding a husband.

I knew a little about supplements from working at the natural grocery store, but most of my knowledge came from informal conversations with helpful friends and acquaintances. It's impossible to live in Northern California without everyone sharing their vast knowledge of natural healing and asking you if you've tried this supplement or that herb for every affliction known to man. That excludes HIV because no one ever offered me a cure for mine (or else they just didn't know I was positive). However, for everything else, try turmeric or colloidal silver. Turmeric is more fun because it can also be used in rituals and to dye fabrics, while colloidal silver just turns your skin blue. Neither will give you abs.

If someone somewhere had somehow gotten belly fat reclassified as an affliction, I'm sure I would be skinny by now. I would just post a message on social media and all my Northern California friends would come to my rescue.

Hi guys.

Sorry I've been out of touch. I've got a severe case of belly fat, and it's really got me feeling down. I've only left my house once this week, and that was just to stock up on ice cream and cheeseburgers. I'm asking my Southern friends for prayers, but maybe you guys can advise me on which supplements to take. Thank you so much in advance. I'm hoping to be in a Speedo soon.

Much love,

Jay.

I saved the message as a draft, just in case. Plus, I passed the interview and was now going to be receiving supplement discounts.

It quickly became very obvious that many people were looking for miracle supplements to lose weight. There were generally three kinds of customers: fit people trying to get bigger, fat people trying to get smaller, and older people just trying to feel normal again.

Sadly, there was also a thin, female customer that was trying to lose weight for her wedding. She had a personal trainer and worked out for hours a day. I didn't think she could get thinner, but she would come back smaller and smaller every week. I wasn't sure what size dress she was trying to get into, but she must've ordered an XXS from Wish. Realizing that a Wish XXS had less fabric than a night-stand doily, she committed to fitting into it rather than sending it back or just letting the $8 go. I told her a few times that she already looked great, but she told me that her trainer thought she could still lose a little more weight. I wanted to cut her off, but we weren't allowed to judge customers, so my only recourse was to hope like hell that her damn wedding day would just get here already. Eventually, she stopped coming in, so I assumed she was off the market or serving time for killing her trainer. Either way, I hoped she was healthy and safe.

One of the diet products we were selling at the time was on the news one night because it was causing liver failure and killing people. It instantly became the most popular item in the store. Everyone wanted it or wanted more of it, but then it got banned by the FDA and disappeared off the shelves. A lot of customers were very unhappy about the development.

"Man, they finally make something that works, and then the government bans it," or, "Just because some people died in Hawaii doesn't mean they should ruin it for everyone."

It seemed ridiculous to me that someone would hold a grudge against dead people for interfering with their weight-loss goals, but after hearing the same thing multiple times, I realized that this wasn't an isolated way of thinking. I've always known that people were crazy as hell, but sometimes I forget it. This served as another reminder that people were indeed still fucking crazy. I would much rather live overweight than go into liver failure, have a heart attack, and then die slightly less overweight. No, thank you.

Then my coworker with 12% body fat offered me the rest of his bottle of death pills and I changed my mind. My liver was probably strong enough to take a few punches anyway. I thanked him for the pills and quickly swallowed the fact that I was a crazy person. No need to dwell on the negative stuff. Maybe I could find the bride's trainer; I'd heard that he really knew how to get results.

I survived the banned supplement and even lost some more weight. Damn government and Hawaiians. I briefly achieved enough confidence to almost attempt flirting again. When I first started there, I had tried to flirt with guys, but I had forgotten that Southern guys were usually raised to be polite and address their elders as "sir."

"Hi, how are you doing today?" I would ask with a big smile and a twinkle in my eye.

"I'm doing well, sir," they would respond.

I was not at all into being called "sir." Plus, I was only in my mid-thirties. I couldn't possibly be older than every cute guy that came into the store. I would instantly feel like a pedophile and back away, letting them know to find me if they needed help. They can put you to death in Alabama for putting salt on train tracks, so I'm pretty sure it's illegal to have sex with someone that calls you "sir." Prison would be an even worse place to practice flirting and I would be the one calling everyone "sir."

I wasn't earning enough money to move out of my mom's house, and my thoughts sometimes felt the need to convince me I was a failure.

"You're fat and living at your mom's house. Now you're going to put on the same tight black shirt you wore yesterday and go earn eleven bucks an hour at a job you don't like. You're such a loser. Loser! LOSER! And you'll probably be single forever because no one wants a boyfriend with HIV."

A large part of my life after puberty was spent in low-grade depression and sometimes even three-ton-leg depression. Occasionally, I could glimpse the city lights of normal up ahead, but I could never get close enough to bask in their warmth. Sometimes, I couldn't move at all. I would stop in place and suddenly feel like I couldn't take another step or even sit in my car for hours after work because I couldn't bring myself to walk back into my life.

Unconsciously, I constantly looked for something greater than myself to belong to, as if I was something of little significance. A lost satellite on the coldest edges of the universe, battered by meteorites and the cries of lost worlds, searching for even a Pluto to orbit. Not daring to ask for the sun, only to be a set distance from it, only to drift from it no more. Depression and a lack of self-love made my search seem impossible.

One morning, as I sat on the top of the stairs at my mom's house, I froze. I had to be at work at the supplement shop, but I couldn't move. An untied black shoe dangled in my hand as I felt suffocated and helpless.

My depression had teamed up with all the unhealed parts of myself to paralyze me. It told me what to believe about myself with each word weighing a thousand pounds. The force of them on my shoulders and against my lungs made them indisputable. That I couldn't breathe was real; that my shoulders drooped was undeniable.

"Your shoes are cheap. You're a fat guy in a tight shirt and cheap shoes sitting at the top of the stairs at your mom's house. This is as good as it will get for you. Such a loser."

The attack had started the minute I woke up and had been relentless ever since. That I had made it as far as the stairs seemed like an amazing feat.

From somewhere else, a small but determined voice asked, "Is there another voice?"

Suddenly, complete silence exploded in my mind, leaving nothing behind. I became just a man holding a shoe at the top of the stairs. For the first time I could remember, I was at complete peace. I put on my shoes and went to work, knowing that my thoughts were probably out to get me. At the same time, I resolved to no longer be an easy target.

Finally, almost a year later, I quit the supplement shop to become the people manager at a fast fashion apparel store. As soon as I got my first check, I applied for my apartment in the big city. In no time at all, I was out of my mom's house in Verbena and living in Birmingham.

I spent the first night in my new place listening to "Budapest" by George Ezra on repeat and dancing around my empty living room by candlelight. For the first time in a long time, I felt young and alive.

The feeling didn't last too long, though. If you've never worked retail or as a server, you must have had money or parents that didn't care enough about you to make you get a real job. Congratulations, I'm sorry. Fortunately, I was born poor, so I've worked plenty of retail and customer service jobs. Just in case you feel you missed out or need a reason to hate people or your life, get down to the mall and find a job at an apparel store, where it can take one person fifteen seconds to undo five hours of your work.

The particular brand I started working for made its money selling a lot of clothes at lower prices, so every t-shirt design was stacked fifty shirts high with twenty XSs at the top and possibly an XL or two at the bottom. First of all, we only sold two XSs a year, so it was a horrible idea to put them out in the first place and an even worse idea to put them on top of anything. Team members would spend their entire shifts just circling tables, rebuilding t-shirt towers. It was a special hell to turn and see five hours of work collapsed on a table behind you. People wanted to see the design on the largest shirt possible, so they would pull the shirt from the bottom, destroy your tower, and then toss it back on top of the carnage after deciding that they didn't like that design after all. I tried to be Zen about it and whisper, "Thank you," to the customers for reminding me of the timeless lesson of impermanence, but more often than that, I just rejected the urge to whisper, "Fuck you." I would circle back with the smile of a person about to crack and then start all over, hoping the customer would see me and realize the error of their ways. It never worked. All the employees would just show up every day, clawing at the floor while the retail demon pulled us back further and further into the darkness.

In January, we breathed. There was still tons of work to do, but at least the people stayed home. We pulled out bins and bins of go-backs that had been accumulating since Black Friday, and gradually started rebuilding our shattered lives. We would start every morning with soft tears and a solemn group chant of "We're going to be okay." It was as if the holidays had almost killed our spirit and we were now able to grieve for what we had almost lost. We would stand silently engaged in our tower rituals, listening to tears falling onto miles and miles of freshly folded XS t-shirts. Then a stray Christmas song would reemerge on the store playlist, and PTSD would overcome everyone. Anguished cries of hysteria would arise from the children's department, men's activewear, and women's separates as people dove for shelter under the newly made tower tables.

The fitting room had once been a place to seek silence and reflection during these situations, but a customer had taken a shit in stall number three and permanently defiled the place. The store bathroom was pretty close by, so I'm not sure what event led to the defilement. I can only assume that it was an act of revenge or excitement. Hopefully, it was because someone had too much holiday joy for their system to process and it pushed out all the vile darkness remaining in their earthly vessel. Maybe they even transcended something. In that case, it might have been worth it. I'm sure the person who cleaned it up didn't think so, nor did the other customers in the area. Some say they still smell the ghost of it today. I got a chill throughout my entire body every time I came within twenty feet of the place. The hair on the back of my neck still stands up whenever I think about it.

I'm not sure if it was the shit or the holidays, but our store manager just stopped coming to work. He made one last call to tell us if his boyfriend called, tell him he was out of town at a district meeting. He must not have known that his boyfriend was the rude type that didn't call before showing up at your front door. Suddenly, he was in the store, marching toward the back and repeating contradictory things like "I know he's here" and "Where is he?" Then he was knocking on the locked backroom door like the spurned southern lover in an old black and white movie. His anger quickly dissolved to desperation. "Oh, won't you let me in, Johnny? Won't you let me in?" he cried, gradually collapsing against the unwavering metal door. Johnny wasn't there, and I didn't know his current location. He finally gave up and left. We never saw Johnny or the door belle again.

This drama didn't deter me from my quest for love. Since starting there and getting my apartment, I had decided to be open to people and just go on dates with anyone that didn't seem dangerous. It had become obvious that an enlightened top wasn't going to come into the store, buy a $5 t-shirt, and then fall in love with me after I asked him if he wanted to apply for a branded credit card. In fact, no one was coming in and even accidentally blinking in front of me to give me hope. *Did he just wink at me?* Not even close.

18

ROOKIE SEASON

Taking into consideration the fact that men weren't making an effort to date me, I decided to be proactive and posted my profile on a few dating websites. Plus, I could just disclose my HIV status immediately in my profile without worrying about being rejected for it later.

My first date seemed pretty normal, other than mentioning more than once (in a short period) that he could only meet after dark. We agreed to meet at a California Pizza Kitchen an hour after sunset because he lived further away and needed extra time to drive. I worried he might be a vampire, but he had posted a picture, so I assumed he had a sun allergy instead.

The guy in the picture looked darker and more handsome than the pale, okay guy that showed up. Usually, guys post multiple pictures, with each getting progressively less attractive, but he had posted only the one. I figured the guy I got would've matched the eighth photo. The hostess seated us, and he placed all his weight on my nerves before the server had even brought us our water. I quickly found out that, to him, conversations weren't to be had; they were to be won.

"Did you ever see any famous people in California?" he asked.

"I pissed off Bonnie Raitt when I worked at a natural food store because I wouldn't turn the air conditioner off."

Years ago, she had beaten Queensrÿche out for a rock award at the Grammys and had, in that moment, set a stinging in my soul that screamed for retribution. "I Can't Make You Love Me" had numbed the pain significantly, but seeing her face again brought the pain back to the surface.

She had come to the service desk to complain about it being too cold in the store. The day must not have been going in her favor because I tasted her sour mood as she spoke. She seemed to want to take her revenge out on me. She demanded that I turn off the air conditioner. I said, "No, I'm sorry. I can't do that." I really couldn't because I had no power over the store temperature, but she interpreted my honesty as a refusal to comply with her demands. She promised never to shop there again and shuffled toward the door of the building. I hummed "Silent Lucidity" to myself as her red hair blazed off into the horizon of the temperature-appropriate produce department. Organic cucumbers must remain cool.

I have since healed that part of myself pained by her Grammy win and am completely open to doing the duet we would've talked about had the store temperature not put her in a bad mood.

My date didn't know or care about Bonnie Raitt because he was already talking about the time he shared a mimosa with Cyndi Lauper. They met and instantly became best friends, and now she called him whenever she came to town. You would think she had a winter home in Birmingham or something, based on his enthusiasm.

I mentioned I didn't drink.

He responded, "Well, me neither, but a drink with Cyndi doesn't really count. You know, True Colors and all." He giggled, and I tried to figure out how that sentence worked in his head, because I couldn't do the math of it in mine. I took a big drink of water because I also didn't know what facial expression to make.

He then mentioned seeing Bill Clinton buying hot dogs once at Piggly Wiggly.

"Before or after he became president?" I asked.

"I'm horrible with dates, but it was obviously before he went vegan," he responded with a laugh.

I had actually shaken hands with Bill Clinton twice as a teenager in Anchorage, but I'm not a one-upper, so I didn't mention it. I don't know what he was doing in Alaska. The only obvious explanation is that they were buying oosiks or refueling on their way to a state with more electoral votes. Whatever the reason, it wasn't very important because they were in downtown Anchorage greeting people lining the streets. I shook his hand and then ran another block to get ahead of him and shake his hand again. It was before everyone found out where his hands had been, so it was still cool to me. Honestly, I was really there to see Hillary. I caught glimpses of her waving from the limo as it drove slowly on the street behind her husband. If I could go back in time, I would try harder to get her attention and say, "Hey girl, can we talk?" She would pull me into the limo, and I would tell her all the things to look out for in the next thirty years. The entire world would thank me, except Russia and the red states. I would spend the rest of my life running every time I saw an umbrella or an NRA sticker, but I would at least be on speaking terms with Michigan, Wisconsin, and Pennsylvania.

"I liked the Clintons," I responded graciously. "Especially Hillary."

"I don't think she put out very often. If you asked me, Bill had no other choice. Poor thing, I'm sure his heart was in the right place, even if his dick wasn't."

I really wanted him to switch places with the server because she was great. She was a slightly overweight twenty-something that perceived my distress. She would bound over every few minutes like a blond superhero that had no actual powers except interruption.

"How are you guys doing over here? Ya'll okay?" she would ask while standing next to him. All of her sentences became one long sentence, so there were no gaps in between. Just a steady chain of normal words, whose only punctuation was the subtle hints of concern dotted throughout. She would stare at me and then point at him with her eyes while nodding. I couldn't decode the message, but I worked on it while my date started pulling her into his theory about Hillary.

"I think I need more water," I said finally, realizing that I couldn't break the code, and she would probably slap him before I even came close. She disappeared and reappeared within forty-five seconds, but this time she stood next to me, pressing her apron against my shoulder. She placed my water in front of me on the table and waited, presumably, for me to slip a folded note into her pocket. I appreciated the effort, but being relatively new to dating, I hadn't anticipated the need for a written SOS.

"Thank you," I said sincerely.

"Okay, I'll be back to check on you in a few minutes," she said, staring deeply into my eyes and walking off.

My date had somehow moved from Hillary to talking about his dog and hadn't noticed that she had said "you" instead of "ya'll." At least he was talking about something that really interested me. Everyone knows I love animals, especially dogs. I had recently watched *Best in Show* and asked him if he had seen it.

"I'm not sure. Who's in it?" he asked.

I named a few of the cast members, and he interrupted me.

"Oh yeah, of course. That *Best in Show*. Catherine O'Hara is my cousin. Well, older cousin. Ha ha!"

I decided to stab him with a butter knife if he said one disparaging thing about Lady O'Hara. I'm sure I would get off on parole for defending her honor. Fortunately, my savior server heard my eyes rolling and immediately appeared at my side.

"Ya'll want to hear about our desserts?" she asked.

"No. Thank you. I've had more than enough."

"Sure," my date responded. "I would love something."

"Well, you can definitely get it to go," the server said triumphantly, as she could finally help move this evening to its rightful euthanasia.

"Yeah, you can just take it with you to your house," I said.

He listened intently to the dessert options and asked her to repeat them.

"Does the red velvet cake come with ice cream?"

"You can add it."

"How cold is it?" he asked, determined to pull every minuscule bit of air from the lungs of the evening.

"It's room temperature," she said, her voice slowly losing faith.

"Not the cake, the ice cream."

"It'll melt before he gets to his house," I interjected. "So he'll just have the cake to go and we'll also get our check, please."

Mercifully, she was back before he could finish asking me about what we were going to do next.

"Do you just want to split the bill?" I asked.

"Are you kidding me?" he said. "This is my treat."

First of all, this wasn't a treat for anyone, including the server. If he enjoyed it, he was completely oblivious or just a psychopath. But by that point, he had patted his pockets and started looking at me like a lost puppy.

"Gosh, I think I left my wallet at home."

"I'll get it," I said. This put me over my limited budget for the evening, so I had to use my emergency credit card. At least this allowed me to control the tip situation because I didn't even trust him to remember that we had a server.

I signed the check, and we got up to leave. The server and I looked back at each other as if we had just gone through something horrible together. We gave each other a single nod and parted ways forever.

In the parking lot, he wanted to keep chatting, but I told him I really needed to get home to walk my dogs. He offered to help me.

"No, thank you," I said with a hint of panic in my voice. "They don't like strangers in the house."

"Do you have a lot of strange men in your house?" he asked flirtatiously as he moved in for a kiss. I diverted his kiss into a side hug and then stumbled backwards towards my car.

"Have a goodnight," I said, edging backwards, keeping my eyes on him the entire time.

"Oh, shit!" he exclaimed, closing the distance between us. "I just remembered that I've got no gas in my car. I don't have my wallet. Remember? I can get my mom to bring it to me at your place in the morning. Dogs love me."

"I'm sorry, I gotta go." A sudden rush of wings started beating furiously toward me as I stood at the car door, fumbling with my keys. I was in the car and pulling away as the sound of fangs cracked against the glass of my driver's side window. I breathed a sigh of relief, knowing that I was one less crazy away from meeting my future husband.

Maybe it had nothing to do with him and more to do with me watching "The Lost Boys" again the night before. Either way, my next date definitely wasn't a vampire.

I remember little about it except the end. I left my neighborhood to drive thirty minutes to his neighborhood. Once I picked him up, he didn't want to tell me where we were going, so he directed me back to my neighborhood to a chain steak restaurant less than a mile from my apartment. Our server didn't try to conceal his disappointment when we ordered a shrimp appetizer, a cheeseburger, and two sodas. We struggled through bits of unmemorable conversation as we quickly finished our food.

Before long, we were in the car driving back towards his place. He initiated handholding, seemingly because we were obligated to hold hands, but it didn't feel romantic at all. In fact, in no time, it started feeling angry. Then it was like a game of chicken. Neither of us was going to let go for anything. It was surreal. It felt like we had committed to jumping off a cliff together, but we were angry with our choice of suicide partners. We wouldn't let go because we didn't trust the other one to jump or not to push the other one over.

The conversation was uninspired and seemed only to serve as the boring soundtrack to the drama not unfolding in the space between my car seats. Yet each syllable came out tensely and covered in sweat. Our hands were wet and pale, as if they were clutching a bitter, invisible jewel. I finished the drive one-handed and somehow arrived safely back at his house. At that point, he let go of my hand, kissed me goodnight, and got out of the car.

"I'll text you later," he said as he disappeared up the steps and into his house.

I wasn't sure what had just happened, but I didn't want to figure it out while parked in his front yard. I pulled out of the driveway slowly and punched the gas as soon as I hit the main road.

I rolled the windows down and tried to process the evening, as the wind circulated through the tainted car air and escaped back out. There were only two scenarios that would explain the handholding situation:

1. He housed a demon that could only be evicted by being transferred to another through hand-holding. He probably didn't know it had to be the hand of his true love, so he clutched at my hand the entire time while asking himself, "Why isn't this working?" Fortunately for me, I didn't love him.

2. He was a rookie witch who could make things happen but couldn't dictate *how* they happened. For example, he cast a spell to convince me that I must keep holding his hand, but he had no control over how my mind rationalized the demand. And my mind processed his spell as a game, which is not as strong as desire, or love.

I don't know what would've happened if I had gone on another date with him. He could have potentially cast a spell that turned me into something unimaginably uncomfortable, like a top.

I received a text from him soon after returning home.

Had a great time. Wanna see you again soon.

I responded because we had held hands and I felt obligated, but I kept my response brief.

Me too.

We didn't communicate for a few days, but then he texted me again.

Are you seeing someone else?

I wanted to respond that I wasn't seeing anyone at all, but I ignored him instead.

Are you breaking up with me?

I blocked him after that.

I'm not known for my strong people-judging skills. In fact, I have historically trusted everybody. My mom even told Garrett once (with me in the room), "Yeah, Jason is so gullible. If he had a man in front of him with a big sore on his penis, he could tell Jason that it was a birthmark and Jason would just put it in his mouth." I was glad that my mom could finally make a joke involving my sexuality, but I didn't really think I would've sucked that guy off. At least not with the light on. Plus, that didn't necessarily mean that he was a bad guy.

On my next date, however, I knew within seconds that this was not someone I wanted to be around. When we stood in front of each other for the first time, I felt a buzz through my entire body and saw static electricity repelling us from each other. It felt like urinating on an electric fence, but not in a good way. Again, I'm not known for my intuitive gifts, but at that moment, the message was undeniable: STAY AWAY FROM THIS GUY. I'm almost sure he wasn't a serial killer, but I sensed he would bring something negative into my life that I definitely didn't want or need. But, I didn't want to be rude and back out of the date at that point, because it would seem like I was ditching him only after seeing him in person. Not wanting to be an asshole, I stuck to our original plan of going to Atlanta for a coffee and tea expo.

An almost three-hour car drive is not the best time to find out that your date has an encyclopedic knowledge of conspiracy theories. I think watching people get killed in a horror movie is awesome; hearing how the government is killing people isn't awesome at all. I didn't want to disagree with him too strongly because I wasn't sure of his mental state. Even though he was short and half my weight, my intense focus on driving and pretending he wasn't there made me vulnerable.

He closed out the ride with a stirring oration on the perks of global climate change. With great relief, we finally pulled into the venue parking lot and exited the car.

Once inside, I tried to fake interest in how many ways there were to make a cup of coffee. After a while, I couldn't do it any longer. It was like when you're having sex and you keep moaning, but all you really want is for him to come already, roll off you, and fall asleep. And I love coffee.

We walked together for a while, but after sampling some abomination at the quinoa milk booth, I excused myself to go to the restroom. I made no effort to find him when I returned. Instead, I walked around, smelling and sampling tea until we finally bumped into each other.

"I was looking all over for you." I tried so hard to sell it.

His indifference made me feel foolish for all my efforts at deception. "They had kopi luwak at a booth! Can you believe that?"

"Uh, yes?" I asked, not having a clue about kopi luwak.

Fortunately, I think he only went on a date with me for a free ride to Atlanta and to sample some free beverages. Later, he asked me to drop him at a hotel so he could attend day two of the weekend-long expo. It didn't surprise me that he already had a reservation, and I didn't attempt to hide my delight. I enjoyed the quiet ride home and never heard from him again.

A few days later, I received a message on a dating website. The profile had no photo and belonged to someone in Turkey. The message had four words.

Hi. How are you?

I had committed to being open to everyone that messaged me (that didn't show they were crazy right away). *Hi. How are you?* is as normal as it gets. Plus, a Turkish person probably wouldn't stalk or kill me because it would be expensive and probably not worth all the paperwork required to enter the country. There were plenty of people in Turkey that were much more convenient and inexpensive targets anyway, so I responded to him.

His next message read *Hi. How is your health? Are you looking for local one?*

My health was good, but obviously required a conversation. Hopefully, *undetectable* could be easily translated into Turkish. I hadn't really thought about that last question too much though. Was I looking for local one?

At that point, I assumed my next date would have to be normal and fabulous because I was way past due for some normal and fabulous. He was probably already in some invisible queue somewhere, holding a bouquet and double-checking his back pocket for his wallet. To be fair, there could have been another guy in that same line, killing everyone off to get to me sooner. Maybe a bloody bouquet wouldn't be so bad coming from a guy that was really going to buy me dinner. He would have to be very hot and somewhat rich, or very rich and somewhat hot for it to be worth it. The chances of that were pretty slim, so I ended up letting that guy go.

I had only met six gay men in Birmingham up to that point, but five of them were at least a little crazy. The sixth one was my co-worker and new friend, Ricky. I hadn't figured out for sure if he was crazy or not, but I had collected enough data to officially decide that, no, I was not looking for local one.

19

... FOR YOU TO SHOW ME ONLY HILLS

Once I started dating, I made it a point to meet anybody I chatted with as soon as possible. Sometimes crazy takes a while to really show up while chatting. When you're face-to-face, it usually reveals itself within an hour or two (sometimes minutes). This had been relatively simple to accomplish until I met Arman, the Turkish guy, online. Complicating it even further was the fact that he actually wasn't from Turkey. He had been afraid to put the truth in his profile because he worried that someone from his country would recognize him.

He was giving his countrymen way too much credit. They would have to have been severely intelligent (and bored) to discover his true identity based on a profile with no picture, a fake homeland, and a screen name stolen from a British luxury and cigarette brand. Of course, the government would've probably had a much easier time.

He admitted in his third message that he was actually from Kazakhstan. I knew nothing about Kazakhstan except that it was in central Asia and that plane tickets would probably cost more than I earned in three weeks of folding t-shirts. However, after two weeks of chatting and video calls without any red flags, we planned a visit. He had a US visa from a previous work trip, so that made the process a lot easier. Still, the earliest he could come was the end of April. It would have to do.

Since he lived on the complete opposite side of the world, he would be getting ready for work while I was getting ready for bed. I video called him at night and then the next morning while he was getting home and I was getting out of bed; he did the same. I really enjoyed talking to him and getting to know him better, but it also worried me. Usually, little bits of crazy starting creeping in the longer you know someone, and I had over two months to get through before we actually met.

I counted down the days while growing increasingly nervous. I just knew that one morning I wouldn't answer the phone fast enough and then he would come on the line yelling because I kept him waiting three seconds too long. Or I would video call him and he would answer wearing nothing but cocaine on his nose and a bloody "SOMEONE I KNOW WENT TO THE RNC AND ALL I GOT WAS THIS LOUSY T-SHIRT" shirt. But crazy never happened. Instead, I learned that he and I had a lot in common and shared a lot of the same dreams.

Then I asked him, "Do you want to get married?" and realized that I probably sounded like the crazy one. I wasn't proposing, but I did want to know if he was looking for a serious relationship. I didn't want to fall in love with him and then find out later that his biggest dream in life was to visit Birmingham, Alabama, and I was just a guy he was staying with.

Two months later, the day arrived for me to drive to Atlanta to pick him up. I had very little vacation time, so I went to work that morning. My coworkers thought I was crazy to have a foreigner (that I had never met in person) come all the way from the other side of the world and stay with me for ten days.

"Ya'll better hope ya'll get along or that's gonna be a long ten days," everyone said in their own way while laughing or shaking their head. I was slightly worried about that, but I was up for taking a long-shot at love. Plus, living for ten days with a Kazakh that hated me probably wouldn't be as bad as folding t-shirts for that amount of time.

Wanting to make a good impression, I spent my lunch break walking through the mall looking for a pair of dress socks that matched my outfit. It should've occurred to me before then that I needed matching socks, but that morning, I woke up in a sweat with the realization that my outfit was horribly incomplete. Arman would exit the terminal, notice my unimpressive socks, and turn back toward the ticketing counter while shaking his head and muttering the Kazakh word for redneck. Avoiding that scenario would require the perfect pair of socks. I would even pay extra if they were magical and guaranteed that the first person to notice them would fall instantly and madly in love with me. I would settle for non-magical socks as long as they were a great match for my white and creamsicle, vertical-striped shirt.

I ended up running out of time and buying a $15 pair of socks that weren't really a great match at all. They did have a hint of autumnal orange in them. Maybe he wouldn't notice the shade difference since my pants would put some distance between the two oranges. Plus, I'd never asked if he was colorblind. If he was colorblind, that would solve everything. Maybe for $15, my orange-striped socks couldn't make him fall in love with me, but maybe they would be magical enough to affect his vision.

I finished my shift and ran home to walk and feed my dogs. They became a little suspicious when, after my shower, I didn't put on my pajamas. They watched with tilted heads as I buttoned and tucked in my shirt, belted my pants, and put on my hopefully magical socks. I was extremely proud of myself for having brown shoes to match my brown belt, but it dissatisfied me to discover that my socks had all but vanished inside of them. Tico and Oscar couldn't comprehend my dilemma, but they still watched me silently as I straightened myself out.

"It's okay, guys," I said reassuringly.

I doubled up on my lucky cologne just in case. Once I was in the car, the artificial, musky masculinity of it overwhelmed me. I drove the 130 miles to Hartsfield-Jackson Atlanta International Airport with all the windows down, trying to soften the scent. By the time I arrived, it wasn't as overwhelming, but it was still strong. I figured it would just make him a little dizzy instead of completely knocking him out. If it knocked him out, at least there wouldn't be any uncomfortable silences or talk of conspiracy theories on the drive home.

I made it to the terminal and started waiting around with a lot of other people for our passengers to show up. Steady streams would exit the terminal, join our group, and trickle out to the exits and baggage claims. After watching hundreds of joyous reunions, I finally saw my passenger.

Two things happened simultaneously:

I noticed he was shorter and smaller-framed than I thought, dressed casually and wearing no socks at all. I had not expected that. I could accept the fact that we probably wouldn't be dressing up like twin lumberjacks for Halloween, but this was practically our first date, and he hadn't stressed out about socks at all.

At the same time, a huge electric "Yes" went through my entire body and I knew instantly that this person and I would be together.

I greeted him and took his carry-on bag as we walked to the baggage claim. I asked him about his flight. He answered with the shortest sentence possible while staring at his sockless feet the entire time. His trip had started almost twenty-four hours ago, so I hoped he was tired and hungry and not woozy from my cologne fumes. After retrieving his bags, we made our way to the car and headed back to Birmingham.

"Are you hungry?" I asked.

"Yes, Mister Jason," Arman responded while still staring at his feet.

I wasn't sure that I had heard his answer correctly. I had my window down slightly for purification purposes, so I assumed that his accent or my window had distorted it. Being almost sure that I misheard him, I asked a follow-up question just to be sure.

"Are you hungry for anything in particular?"

"It's okay," he said.

That wasn't very helpful, but at least he hadn't called me "Mister."

"Do you like chicken?" I asked, thinking it was a safe choice to offer almost anyone from any culture.

"Yes, Mister Jason," he responded.

Oh fuck! "Mister" is obviously the Kazakh equivalent of the Alabama "sir." I was days shy of being ten years older than him, but I didn't think that qualified me to be his elder. It seemed slightly possible that his "mister" might be more closely related to the California "sir." If that was the case, he was misusing it. Its usage is generally reserved for more specific situations, like when you walk into a room, take off your shoes, get on your knees, and only speak when you're told to speak. "Yes, sir" is the answer to every question until you put your shoes back on.

Between the culture and language difference, I couldn't really be sure of his intention.

We stopped at a fast-food restaurant and ordered two spicy chicken sandwich meals. I hoped he didn't taste the homophobia gently fried into the deliciousness. If he did, he said nothing. I think he was just happy to have food and something besides his shoes to look at for a few minutes. While his head was up, I showed him that French fries are best eaten with a mixture of ranch and ketchup. He appreciated the important cultural lesson and graciously offered me a "Thank you, Mister Jason." We would definitely have to work on that.

After we arrived home, he opened his bags and gave me the twenty-five pounds of chocolate that accounted for half the weight of his bags. I gratefully accepted the gift and eagerly shared with him something I believed wholeheartedly: chocolate is best eaten with crunchy peanut butter. He had never eaten peanut butter before and didn't take to it. When I had discovered he didn't like horror movies, I had been skeptical, but adding the peanut butter issue made me wonder if this had been a big mistake. Ten. Whole. Days.

At bedtime, he and my dogs were equally shocked that they would now share a bed. Apparently, dogs aren't popular in Kazakhstan, and we had somehow missed that in our chats. I had talked about them, and he had seen them during our video chats, but we hadn't discussed their sleeping arrangements. My queen-size bed instantly felt like a mini-twin as the four of us tried to get positioned for the night. He was tired and almost instantly asleep, while I stared at the ceiling. Tico found his spot between my legs, while Oscar had rolled himself up into a ball between us and stared with one eye at the softly breathing stranger. I thanked the Divine for delivering a non-snorer to my bed, and as everything fell into peace, I followed.

A NORMAL PERSON DOING NORMAL THINGS

The next day, I set out to impress him with my fabulous life. Our first stop was Walmart to buy groceries. It was by far the largest grocery story he had ever seen. He had me take numerous pictures of him pushing the increasingly full shopping cart throughout the store. Standing on the back of it with one sockless foot sticking out, he smiled warmly at his friends at home. He found it odd that they had ten thousand different kinds of yogurt, but not even one kind of horse milk. After he explained that it makes you drunk, I said, "I don't drink anymore, so I'm not sure, but maybe they'll have it at the liquor store." I had never even heard of it, much less seen it. To be fair, I'd never wandered past the vodka section, so I couldn't really be 100% sure. I was at 99.99% though.

We dropped off the groceries at home before running to the mall to meet my coworkers. On the way, we stopped by Starbucks for coffee. In Kazakhstan, he bought his coffee from Starbeans (Starbucks' completely unrelated non-cousin), so he tried to translate the menu into something close to what he usually purchased. It didn't work out at all. While I enjoyed my vanilla iced coffee, he took one sip of his warm interpretation and promptly decided that Starbeans was better. I admitted Starbeans had a magical sound to it, but I would reserve judgment until I tried it for myself.

At the mall, he met my coworkers. He spoke great English, but he had never encountered Southern accents before, so he just nodded a lot and answered "yes" to everything that sounded like a question.

"How was your flight?" Ricky asked.

"Yes," he answered, nodding enthusiastically.

"Oh, that's good. Make sure Jason takes you out to do something fun. He doesn't do anything but run and work. He's pretty boring," Ricky said.

"Yes," Arman responded with a smile.

"I may be boring, but I'm never bored," I said, pointing at my head. "It's like an amusement park in here." I left out the adjective *abandoned*.

After he had answered everyone's questions in the affirmative, we exited the building and he asked, "Were they speaking English at all?"

"Mostly," I answered.

I hadn't really considered the possibility that my life was boring, but after Ricky had planted the seed in my mind, it suddenly overtook me. It wasn't at all boring to me, but it would obviously be a major snooze-fest for anyone outside of my experience. I would really have to up my game tomorrow if I didn't want Arman to be sleeping for the remaining nine days.

Being a relative newcomer to Birmingham and not one to go off exploring on my own, I didn't know where to take him or what to do to impress him. I remembered going to Moundville Archeological Park as a young child, and it had made an impression on me. Obviously, this place would impress the hell out of him. He would probably even fall deeply in love with me there. I had forgotten that it scared me and made me cry.

The next morning, we drove an hour to Moundville. Upon arriving at the park, we stopped at the first building we came to, paid the admission fee, and then got back into the car to drive around the park. I had picked up what I thought was an information pamphlet, but it was just a vague map with the hours of the park printed beneath it. I figured we probably wouldn't need a lot of info anyway, because the museum would have tons of it. We would just follow the map and let everything be a surprise.

As we drove deeper into the park, the mounds appeared. Without knowing the full story of the mounds, they weren't too impressive. They just looked like hills with the tops cut off. Arman looked curiously out the window in all directions, trying to figure out what made the place so special. We soon arrived at a parking lot. Obviously, we were supposed to stop and discover something, so we got out. There was a mound to the left and a trail to the right. Being in Moundville, we went to the mound route first. We climbed up the mound, walked around it for a few minutes, and then walked back down the mound. Uh oh. I was beginning to worry that I had made a mistake. Hopefully, the trail would offer redemption.

We wandered onto the trail, and I was immediately hit with the realization that this would not be the moment that he fell deeply in love with me. It also became more apparent that it probably wouldn't be anytime that day either. He wiped at the beads of sweat dotting his face as the heat and humidity bore down upon us. I was grateful that most of the mosquitoes were attacking me, because I don't think he could've handled any additional misery. We both tried to finish this leg of our journey as quickly as possible so we could get back to the air-conditioned, bug-free car.

We then drove around more topless hills until we arrived at a new parking lot near the Black Warrior River. We got out and walked around for a moment and discovered a village exhibit nearby. It was a tableau of a family burying someone in the floor of their hut. They had broken through the concrete, dug a hole one foot deep, and placed the dressed body inside. The head of the body looked like a rectangular football with a nose on it. The designers of the display had probably decided not to put any effort into her because she was dead and going in the ground anyway, or maybe they were over-budget and had no money left by the time they got to her. She didn't even have hair. The younger lady looking over her had tons of hair. Dad and Grandpa were adequately thatched. Even the toddler standing nearby had enough hair for at least a few more toddlers. Grandma had normal gray hair, but the yellowed choir robe she was wearing overshadowed it. It seemed out of place, as if someone had thrown it over her at the last minute.

"Something's missing. I just can't put my finger on it," said the designer.

"It's the dead lady's hair," responded his astute apprentice.

The designer either wasn't listening or didn't want to look stupid. With a point of his snapping fingers, he responded, "Of course. Get my church bag out of my trunk." Five minutes later, Grandma was standing in the background with her arms up, looking like someone had frozen her right as she was hitting the high notes in her first solo performance.

This was nothing like the exhibits from my childhood. I remembered seeing tons of cool artifacts, learning (and forgetting) tons of interesting information, and most significantly, recoiling in horror at a pit of skeletons displayed in a real burial site. At that point, I would rather he be traumatized by death than hoping for his own. I can read a map, but I'm not fluent in that either, so I couldn't figure out where the skeletons were. I meant for them to be the highlight of our trip. We drove around and saw more mounds, but we didn't see the museum. At that point, we really just wanted to find a bathroom and go home.

We hadn't seen a single person or car since paying our admission fee. If a guy hadn't taken our money, I would have thought that the park was actually closed and we were trespassing. Maybe he didn't work there at all. I was suddenly paranoid that we were now those people that were "in the wrong place at the wrong time." If I wasn't trying to woo him, I would've told him to just find a tree, so we could get the hell out of there. However, I didn't want to alarm him, so we drove around some more until we found a building.

Once inside, an elderly woman approached us. I asked for the restroom and she pointed up a set of stairs. I didn't engage her further because I wasn't sure that she really worked there. Plus, she could have been trying to trap us upstairs until the guy from the entrance finished counting our money and arrived to hang us on a meat hook. Thankfully, Arman wasn't a bathroom diva, and we were quickly back outside, getting into the car, and driving hopefully toward the park exit.

I was sure at that point that once we arrived home, he would pack his bags and ask me to take him back to the airport. He would turn to me and say something like, "I came from a land of mountains for you to show me only hills." He would then have more fun sitting in the Atlanta airport for eight days than doing anything with me. It also occurred to me on the silent ride home that viewing desecrated burial sites of Native Americans shouldn't be an activity for anyone. I imagined my husky skeleton on display at my unearthed burial site. Not cool at all.

After we got back home and he didn't ask me to drop him off at the airport, I decided we should just hang out and get to know each other rather than trying to stay busy. For the next few days, we did just that. We cooked together, listened to music, and began working on his relationship with my dogs. We would go to the park together in the morning and he would walk Tico and Oscar around the lake while I finished my run. He had told me that Kazakhs love tennis, so we also bought some racquets and played tennis together at night. After showering and before going to bed, we would lie together on the couch. I would hold him in my arms as we watched television or talked.

It was beginning to feel like a life that I wanted to slip into.

The day that I had planned to take him to meet my family finally arrived. They never really know what to expect me to do next, but inviting a strange Kazakh to live with me for ten days probably seemed as likely as me getting someone pregnant. Of course, I'm sure they would have strongly preferred me to bring a baby over. Nevertheless, my mom met us outside with hugs and a smile. Arman gave her a handful of chocolates. She thanked him and introduced him to her dog, Minnie, before asking us to come inside.

We sat at her kitchen counter while she walked to the refrigerator. "Do ya'll want something to drink?" she asked.

"Yes ma'am," I replied.

"Water or tea?" she asked as she filled two cups with ice.

Arman had recently tasted Southern sweet tea and had thought it was just golden sugar water, so he answered, "Water for me, please," with a trailing emphasis on the word "please."

My mom poured water into both glasses and set one in front of me. As she gave him his glass, she looked him in the face and asked him softly, but with sincere concern, "You aren't a terrorist, are you?" There was a smile beneath it, so he wasn't sure how to answer the question. I knew she was sweet like crazy, but she also watched Fox News, so I was going to answer it for him.

"No. Not at all," he answered before I got the chance. She had already asked me the question a few times since I announced his visit, and I thought my repeated answer of "Of course not" has assuaged all of her concerns. Obviously, she needed further convincing.

"I don't think you can be a terrorist and give blowjobs," I added.

My mom had returned to church since moving back to Alabama. I knew that the best way to put a nail in the coffin of any conversation with a Christian mom was to mention a gay sex act. She instantly changed the subject.

"What time are ya'll going to Rachel's house?"

We hung out for a bit with my mom and Lee before heading over to my sisters to meet her family and my two brothers.

After leaving my sister's house, everyone in my family had met Arman and hopefully realized that he wasn't a terrorist. At that point, even though it wasn't currently legal in Alabama, I asked him to marry me. This might seem like a rushed decision, but our situation was not a normal one. First of all, the moment I met him at the airport, everything inside of me just said "Yes." And everything about our visit and our time together confirmed those feelings.

I was also very aware of the possibility that our being together wouldn't even be allowed. The Supreme Court had yet to rule on Obergefell v. Hodges, which meant that they could decide if I would need to move to a different state before I could even start the complicated immigration process. And then we might have to wait years to find out if our application had been approved. I wanted to begin the process of making it happen as soon as possible.

I asked Arman to marry me because I wanted to be with him—and I also understood that no matter how much we wanted to be together, it ultimately wasn't up to us. If we applied for a marriage visa and it was denied, being together would be almost impossible.

"Do you want to get married?" I asked, and I instantly felt like I needed another shot at it. I had briefly thought of making a grand gesture, but I didn't have enough friends to do a big dance number or enough money to rent a plane. Plus, I had already brought up the possibility of us getting married before, just to gauge his interest. I didn't really have a good plan, so I just brought it up while we were driving home. I sounded way too casual, like I had just asked my best friend "Are you gonna eat that?" while staring at the uneaten remains of their juicy cheeseburger. Fortunately, he already knew me well enough to know that I was sometimes only slightly awkward, but usually a complete mess. He held my hand and said, "Yes, I would like that."

We continued home in a completely new kind of silence.

And that was that. Until it almost wasn't.

The next day, I made a ton of guacamole and we went back to my sister's house to play cards with my siblings. We ate tacos and sat around chatting as we played Phase 10. Later, I noticed my new fiancé had gotten quiet. I assumed he was just focused on winning the game. After he won the game, I just assumed his victory had taken everything out of him. He remained quiet for the rest of the evening.

The next day, I knew there was a real problem. We were sitting at a restaurant about to share plates of pad thai and orange chicken. It thrilled me to be having two of my favorite dishes, while his face looked like we had just driven back through the entrance gates of Moundville. I scanned my mind to find out what I had done to offend him. I have a tendency to say stupid shit all the time, but I usually know it's stupid right away. Maybe my filter had gone from having a delay to not working at all. It would be my luck that it broke a day or two after I proposed. I tried scanning again, just to be sure. All results came back negative.

Whew! Not my fault.

I was relieved to find that I was still a good person, but upset to realize that I hadn't been able to pinpoint the source of his angst. Determined to get to the root of it, I asked him, "Are you okay?"

"I'm okay," he said, as if nothing in the world was okay and would never be okay again.

I could've just accepted his answer and started eating the food while it was still warm, but I offered a follow-up: "Are you sure you're okay? You seem upset."

"You didn't bring me guacamole," he admitted after a prolonged moment of silence.

Guacamole? Guacamole? Guacamole? Hmm. It didn't ring a bell. My perplexed expression led him to repeat it. "Last night. You didn't bring me guacamole."

Ah shit. I had gone back for guacamole during the game and hadn't offered him any. Now I was going to be single forever because of an avocado dip. "I'm sorry," I said, fully aware that it was woefully inadequate and unlikely to exonerate me or lessen his feeling of disappointment. I felt like an asshole.

"It's okay," he said as he mindlessly stabbed at the orange chicken.

"Don't take it out on the chicken," I joked. "It's already dead." He gave a weak smile and dropped the fork. "I will never not bring you guacamole again. I can order some now if you want," I said, hoping that he didn't take me up on the offer. It was an Asian restaurant, and they had no guacamole. If he wanted some, I might be able to order all the ingredients separately and make it at the table.

"No, it's okay. I'm not sure if I like it anyway. Just don't forget about me next time."

"I will never do it again," I promised. With that, the subject changed, and we started eating our twice-killed orange chicken and now-gelatinous ball of pad thai. The guacamole conversation had turned our food into something cold and miserable. Afterwards, we bonded over how bad the food had been, even though it had been guacamole's fault.

I didn't want him to go back to Kazakhstan with any lingering doubts about his soon-to-be husband, so that night, I made him guacamole. It didn't take him long to realize that he was most likely allergic to avocados. I had probably been trying to protect him at my sister's house all along by intuitively not serving it. This made me feel a little better, but did him no favors at all. He was a hot mess. He spent his last night in town huddled in the fetal position on the couch and regretting that he had ever broached the subject. I threw away everything green in the house and promised to never bring him guacamole again. It also reassured me that he didn't assume I had poisoned him.

His unfortunate condition probably contributed to him agreeing to watch one of my favorite movies with me. At least, I think he agreed.

"Do you want to watch *Martyrs* with me? It's scary, but really, really good," I asked, making it obvious that there was really only one appropriate answer. "It's in French." Surely, that would convince him.

"Bahhuhh," he responded. His lips were swollen a bit, so it didn't really sound like a word I had heard before. I assumed it was a Kazakh "yes" rather than ask him again and have him endure another painful round of answering questions.

He didn't enjoy the movie at all, but to be fair, I don't think he could've enjoyed anything at that point. He even uncurled himself out of the fetal position to go throw up. On the way to the bathroom, he begged me not to pause the movie for him.

"Are you sure?" I asked.

"Yes, please don't do it."

"I'm sorry you're sick," I said as he disappeared into the bathroom. "It's just the avocado, right?"

He probably didn't hear me because he didn't respond, but minutes later he reemerged, looking worse than he had before. I hugged him and continued playing the movie. He only vomited once more before bedtime.

The next morning, he was feeling much better. He was also starving, so I made us cheesy grits, fried eggs, and turkey sausage for breakfast. After explaining what I thought grits were, we began discussing what we would have to do to get married. We didn't know the entire process, but we knew it would take time and money and also require us to send a lot of paperwork to the government. I had always paid my taxes on time, so I felt like I should've been on good terms with "the Man." However, a large part of me was very concerned that I might catch him on a bad day.

20

A SAFE PLACE FOR CHRISTMAS

After compiling a Britannica-sized collection of documents (nearly five sets of the Harry Potter series if you're younger than the internet) and paying an application fee, we applied for Arman's visa. From there, it was a waiting game while the government looked at us from every angle. They checked our criminal backgrounds, our communication history, and they were also checking my finances. Fortunately, I had never been arrested, but I had to prove that I made enough money to support both of us. Soon after applying, however, I found out I was losing my job at the apparel store because of restructuring.

The district manager came in to meet with all the managers. She called us into the office one by one, and as she moved down the short line, we realized she was shuffling our responsibilities. We didn't have a store manager at the time, so it made sense. When my turn arrived, I was feeling okay about it. However, being last also felt dangerous.

"Tell me what you know about visuals," she said. The feeling arose that our meeting was about to take a turn for the worse.

I answered the question and felt that I had passed the oral exam with at least a strong C. She and I were obviously on different pages.

"We're going to have to let you go," she said and pulled my separation paperwork out of her briefcase. I realized there had never been a possibility of me answering the question correctly. My apparel career was over.

I had gradually been developing and strengthening the belief that everything always works out in my best interest, so I wasn't extremely worried about the job. However, it concerned me that even a brief period of unemployment would cause our application to be denied. She gave me my pink slip and the rest of the day off to process my job loss. Ricky was still crying when I walked out of the building.

The very next day, I received a call from a man that I had only met once. He had just quit his job managing a store of the same brand at a different mall and was starting a new management position with a major beauty store chain. He was a shameless flirt, so at first, I wasn't sure why he was calling me.

"Are you looking for a new job?" he asked.

"Yes, and as quickly as possible." I had also just started the process of buying a house, so I didn't want to mess that up either.

He was looking for an assistant manager and wanted me for it. I would just need to apply with the district manager. I knew less about hair and makeup than most straight guys, but I needed a job in the worst way. The very next day, I interviewed with the DM.

Fortunately, she asked very little about my makeup skills and hair products and more about my management skill set. I made it through and had a verbal offer a few hours later. I started training there by the end of the week while I was still finishing out my final two weeks at my other job. My bad news had resulted in a severance check, a slightly higher paying job, and earning extra money from briefly working both positions. I would also probably be running into a lot more gay people at a beauty store. It crossed my mind that all my customers would probably know more than me.

I had made an agreement with Arman; I would have our house ready for him if he could be there in time for Christmas. He agreed to the proposal, but we were both aware that it completely depended on his K1 visa application being approved. We checked the website for updates multiple times a day, just to read that our case was still processing. I seemed to have plenty of time to find and purchase a house.

My realtor tried to remain patient as I asked him to show me affordable house after affordable house. They had only pre-approved me for a few dollars over six figures, so his commission wasn't going to be great. He was going to be driving all the way to the "less-expensive" neighborhoods and spending money on gas. I apologized after every stop as his smile eroded as quickly as a treeless hill in the rain. On the last day, we were going to look at three houses, but I worried he would hate me by the time we got to the third, so I told him we could just look at the first two. When we arrived at the second house, I instantly knew that it wouldn't do. I think we heard three gunshots before we even got out of our cars.

"Let's just go to the third one instead," the realtor said. "I don't think you'll like this one."

I was in my car and texting him, *I'll follow you*, before he finished speaking.

The third one sat on a quiet street between two less desirable neighborhoods. The backyard was just one big hill, but beyond it stretched nothing but miles and miles of trees. It had a basement, a fireplace, a garage, two bathrooms, and three bedrooms. There were also two enormous oak trees right outside the front door. It was almost perfect if you didn't pay attention to the millions of leaves and acorns carpeting everything outside. It didn't bother me much because I would have a husband soon, and I could teach him to rake.

As I was looking out over the back deck, thinking that I might've found our house, a giant hawk landed on the fence, looked at me, and flew away. Never one to ignore a message from the gods, I told the realtor that I wanted the house. He exhaled, and we were friends again. Before I left the house, I went into our future bedroom and lay on the floor. I made Arman a video of the ceiling with the ceiling fan whirring and told him, "Soon you and I will lie in this spot together every night." I didn't lessen the magic by mentioning that Oscar and Tico would be right there with us.

I put all of my money with money that Lee and my mom gave me and started the home-buying process. Within days, Arman's visa was approved, and we were each racing to fulfill our end of the agreement. He would need to take an eighteen-hour train ride back to his hometown to see his family and tell them he was moving to the United States. They didn't need to know that he would marry a man. After that, he would have to go through all of his things and bring only what would fit into two bags and a carry-on. As he was wrapping up his life in Kazakhstan, I was signing paperwork and moving into our new house.

I didn't love my new job, but I hated it after being denied two days off in a row to move. I didn't own a lot of stuff, but I needed more than one day to get moved and situated. Fortunately, my entire family showed up at my apartment to help load my stuff and move it to my new place. When we arrived, Lee went to work repairing the light over the garage, while my brothers and sister helped move things inside. My mom immediately went to the store for shelf liners. She returned in no time and began lining every drawer and shelf in the kitchen, as well as the hall closets. To this day, I cannot sleep peacefully in a house that has unlined shelves or drawers. It feels unnatural, like a portal to hell has been left open, and at any time, demons will spring from beneath the plastic silverware holder and come for me. My mom probably sensed early in my life that demons had an unnatural affinity for me and had since devoted her life to securing every portal that could possibly exist. Since my soul is also probably susceptible to household demons, she has always ensured that shelves and drawers in my surrounding area have lining. She also still calls me and asks, "Have you changed your oil lately?" I think there's a portal in cars as well.

"Yes ma'am," I always respond, because I don't want her to worry.

Buying a house left me with a Christmas budget of $maybe.nextyear. I knew it wasn't too important to Arman, but it was going to be his first Christmas, and I wanted it to be great. I had ordered him a lot of clothes for his new life in America and was so excited when they started arriving. Mistakenly, I had taken the buy-a-lot-of-inexpensive-stuff route instead of the buy-one-or-two-really-nice-things route. When I started opening the bags and boxes and realized that I could read my palm through every item I had ordered, I panicked. My soon-to-be husband was going to be wearing transparent clothing that was most likely two sizes too small. My current offerings would not fulfill my desire to give him a great first Christmas unless he planned on becoming a prostitute.

I warned him we would not have money for a year or two, but I didn't want him to walk in the door and immediately realize that we were poor. We would take the luggage containing his entire life up the stairs and into an almost completely empty house in a not-so-great neighborhood. He would look at me with the tears in his eyes screaming the words his mouth could not find, "What have I done? I have moved from the other side of the world to be poor." It wouldn't be in English, but I could understand it. This would be before he even saw his gifts. Oscar would probably growl and bark at him for having loud eyes, and the chaos and drama would cause the house to fall down upon us, closing the sad chapter forever. We would, however, survive for a few days on the chocolate he had brought with him.

My family had gotten used to me being the broke one after receiving bath salts, cabin socks, or Skin Bracer for the last few years. I wanted to at least ease him into it. My mom gave me a three-foot-tall table Christmas tree, which I set up while also hanging two stockings over the chimney. I hoped it would look so festive that he wouldn't notice that we didn't have a lot. I bagged and wrapped his gifts and placed them on the floor under the tree. For his stocking, I bought small denomination gift cards for fast-food restaurants and donut establishments that he needed to experience as a soon-to-be American. I also added some cologne samples.

He arrived the day before Christmas Eve. I showed him around our house and then we put away his things. Afterwards, we lay on a blanket on the living room floor under the soft glow of the Christmas tree lights. Oscar and Tico recognized him but still didn't seem sure about him yet, so they lay by me. Even if they weren't sure, I was still at 100%. We were a family now, and we were starting a new life together in a new house with all shelves and cabinets lined for our safety.

21

STRANGER COTTON

The last time I saw my dad alive was in 1997. It was when I moved from California to stay with my brother, Daniel, in Alabama. With no plan or direction, I slept on his coach, chain smoking and occasionally going out with some new friends. I worked a few hours a week at Food Land to earn cigarette money, but otherwise, my brother took care of me. In retrospect, I'm not proud of this period of my life, and my brother was a saint to tolerate me for as long as he did. I borrowed his truck frequently to go drinking. I would pick up hitchhikers, then he would hear about it (coincidentally, I had picked up his coworker one night) and have to tell me that picking up hitchhikers isn't safe. I also cussed at one of his acquaintances who had stopped by to invite us to a KKK meeting. "Are you fucking kidding? Why the fuck would we want to go to a clan meeting? That is the stupidest shit I've ever heard." My brother warned me after he left that I shouldn't have said that to him because he was crazy. So, I'm sure my brother worried about me getting murdered by almost anyone I came into contact with or possibly just killing myself by drinking and driving into a tree. Again, not proud.

One day, Daniel and I drove an hour away to the house where my father now lived with his new wife. I hadn't seen him in over seven years, but my brothers were both regulars, so everyone knew them.

Soon after arriving and meeting his wife, my father asked if I wanted to go fishing with him. Obviously, he must have forgotten the little he knew about me, because fishing isn't my thing, and fishing in the blistering sun is only okay if I drown in the first two minutes. However, deep down, I thought maybe he wanted to reconnect with me and start building a relationship. So, I said, "Sure." We walked for a bit to a pond and then got into his boat.

I probably wasn't very good company because I kept praying the whole time.

Dear God, Universe, Divine, All that is. Please don't let us catch anything. It's not the fish's fault that my dad chose the pond as the place to bond with me. Thank you in advance.

I try very hard not to kill things, and I was definitely not looking forward to my father hugging me while we were both covered in fish guts.

But my father only offered more small talk. First about snakes. "Yeah, I don't like snakes," I replied. Then about the weather. "Yeah, it is really hot." And it *was* really hot. Alabama summers are hot, humid, and sticky. Being in a boat under the sun for an hour, trying to make conversation with someone that only really wants to talk about how miserably hot it is (and the occasional snake anecdote), while trying to pray all the fish away, is not a rewarding or relaxing experience. It is stressful. Finally, he decided we would go back to the house. *Hallelujah!*

When it was time to go back to my brother's house, my father did not hug me. He casually mentioned maybe coming to see him again. And that was it. For a moment, a fish guts hug didn't seem so bad.

I returned to Daniel's house, moved back to Alaska, then moved back to California and then back to Alabama before I ever heard his voice again. He didn't call, send a card, text, or email me for almost twenty years.

I think about it and wonder, how could a man never think about his child? Was there one moment when he just decided that I wasn't worth it? Was it me or something I had done? Was it my softness when the other boys were tough? I tried to investigate all the parts of myself to find the one that had ruined everything; the one part that made me unworthy of his love. It is an impossible case to solve. I saved a place for his love inside me, but it remained empty. This emptiness dug into me like a trapped miner clawing the earth, desperately waiting for the light to hit his face. But emptiness is heavier than love and never reaches the light: the light must be brought to it. I, however, had not been trained in bringing the light.

In 2016, while Arman and I were making our new life together, Daniel called me. He was at my dad's, visiting, and my dad had asked to speak to me. I knew my father had been fighting cancer for a while, but I had heard no updates, so I had assumed the best. When my dad got on the phone, his voice sounded normal, so I thought nothing about it. I was just happy to hear it after such a long time. We talked for a few minutes, and I promised I would come with my brother to see him soon. After we said goodbye, my brother got back on the line, and we made plans to meet in a few days to drive to my dad's house.

I arrived at Daniel's house, and he met me in the driveway.

"He's gone, Jay. They just called a few minutes ago."

I didn't have a response. We just stood in the driveway for a moment, him with tears in his eyes and me not knowing how to feel. "I'm going up there now. Do you still want to go?" I nodded. We got in his truck and drove away in silence.

I returned to my father's house for the first time in almost twenty years, to see his dead body, lying on a hospital bed in the living room. I couldn't help but think that he looked like Abe Simpson because his skin had turned yellow and his face had become old and shrunken. It wasn't a funny thought, but one of devastation. How did the person I went fishing with so long ago become this thing before me that I no longer recognized? I was also stuck with the reality that I would never know why he didn't love me.

A few days later, my mom and I drove to Selma to attend his funeral. After debating it quietly for a moment, we sat on the friend's side of the church. The air was thick and unmoving.

Some man stood up, walked to the front, and started talking.

"Thomas 'Cotton' Colburn was a good man." He talked for twenty minutes about a man that I knew almost nothing about. Apparently, my dad loved riding horses, woodworking, and spending time with people other than me.

After the service, more than one unfamiliar face thanked me for coming. I assumed these were the people he was hanging out with while avoiding me for the last twenty years. My brothers were pallbearers, while I felt completely out of place. I didn't even know if I had earned the right to grieve. My sister opted not to attend the service.

I cannot speak of my brothers' or sister's experience of my father. I only know that my sister and I's experience differed completely from our brothers.

Imagining my dad as a boy, I put him in all kinds of scenarios: throwing a ball, climbing a tree, killing something (because that's what boys do), or maybe riding a bike in the sun. His white hair would be short, probably in a buzz cut. I paint a smile on his face because I want him to be happy, but I really know almost nothing at all about his experience. I put him in a thousand places, but he never gives up his secrets.

On the night of his funeral, I was at home preparing to meditate. I put an extra cushion in front of me and invited my dad to take a seat. I sat in my meditation, holding a space for him, and trying only to focus on my breathing. Afterwards, I stacked our cushions together in the corner and went to bed.

That night, I dreamed of meditating with his cushion still in front of me. But this time, he showed up. He appeared in the room and sat on the cushion. He looked at me with eyes the color of robin eggs and smiled at me. At that moment, I felt release. I knew we were okay. It didn't fix me or heal my wounds, but we were okay. With that, he got up from the cushion and disappeared behind me.

22

HOUSE TRAP

When I was a kid, I quickly learned what was expected of me. It was a generationally demonstrated map of how my life should look. I was to be born, go to church, be born again, work hard, get married, buy a house, have kids, have grandkids, maybe have great grandkids, then die, and go to heaven. If I lived a safe and discreet life, played by the rules, then I could live an abundantly joyful afterlife.

While I was not capable of living up to the entire assignment, I held onto some parts, hoping for a passing grade. I should still work hard, buy a house, get married, and live a safe and discreet existence. That was the destination point for the majority of my life. Even as I explored the idea of being a spiritual being having a physical experience, my programming was defaulting me to my factory setting. Yet there had always been a persistent gnawing in my soul for freedom.

Days after Arman arrived, and before we got married, I had an important conversation with him. I told him that I wanted to be free in all areas of my life and I didn't know what that would look like exactly. Maybe I'd go vegan again, tell people my HIV status, shave my head, or move into a cave. I didn't know what I might want or need to do in the future, but

I knew I needed to be free to do it. So, I asked him to accept that I may change.

I added that I wanted to be happy, and that it was 100% my responsibility to make myself happy. I told him that when I'm happy, I could share it with him. And that while I couldn't *make him* happy, I would always be by his side, supporting him as he worked to make himself happy.

I also told him that I wanted us to be partners in every sense of the word. I wanted us both to know that, no matter what happened in our lives, there would always be one person by our side, supporting us and helping us work on achieving our dreams.

I think with my mouth, so it wasn't very eloquent, but it needed to be said.

Even as I spoke those words, I was still actively working on completing my life assignment. I had bought a house. I was working hard, and I was about to get married. My childless dad bod probably even counted as some kind of extra credit. I was doing exactly what I was supposed to be doing.

Arman and I were married by my friend Ricky in our living room. We had no reason to have a wedding— I had one friend (who officiated), Arman's family didn't know he was gay or getting married, and I didn't want to make my family uncomfortable by giving them an invitation that they would have almost definitely declined. Even though they liked Arman, they didn't like gay marriage. I didn't bring it up to them. Instead, I told my mom afterwards, and let the news trickle down to my siblings.

A few days later, we had a few people over from the apparel store. They came with gifts and a de facto wedding cake. We didn't think to buy liquor because I didn't drink and I'd never hosted this sort of thing before. I made some Thai sandwiches that ended up being dry and horrible. Ricky made some punch that was great unless you were drinking it to chase down the sandwiches. It was an unfortunate collision of tropical flavors and cilantro fish sauce. Thankfully, we had chopped fruit, Kazakh chocolate, and cake to dull the memory of my Asian-inspired hand-food disaster.

After that night, it felt like I had achieved my default goals. Now all I needed to do was keep working hard and die. I tried to distract myself from the "die" part and just kept working hard. Arman couldn't work until they approved his employment authorization, so I didn't have any other options anyway.

I would come home from working another understaffed shift at the beauty store, and Arman would be bored to death or upset because he'd gotten into an argument with Oscar. He would ask me to take him anywhere, just to get out of the house. I didn't want to tell him I was exhausted from running away from customers that needed a color match or smokey eye demonstration. We would go to Target to walk around for a bit, and then, at the end of our outing, we would buy a few things. We were living off my credit cards at that point, because everything I earned was going towards bills. Thankfully, Arman was mostly low maintenance.

One rainy afternoon, after returning from one of these trips, we passed a spot where people dumped trash, mattresses, and other things they didn't want or need any longer. A small white dog ran out onto the road right in front of me. I pulled over and called to her. She ran towards me, wagging her tail and possibly smiling. I scooped her up in my arms and we continued our drive home. Arman had become a little more friendly with Tico, but Oscar still barely even tolerated him, so the sight of another dog brought an ashen look to his face. I asked him to hold her, even though his silent face screamed, "Please don't ask me to touch that." She was soaking wet and smelled like someone had brined her in urine, but he took her anyway.

Once we got her home, we saw she was super skinny and covered in fleas. Her mostly white fur was yellow from what I guessed was her own urine. I could only assume that she had been confined in a tiny space and had never been housebroken or let out to do her business. Someone probably never loved her and just dumped her off like trash. I loved her from the second she crossed my path, so I couldn't understand who could do that to her.

We washed her three or four times to get rid of the fleas and urine smell. The smell faded but didn't go away entirely. Tico was very interested in all the activity around the new arrival, while Oscar and Arman were showing a decidedly less optimistic reaction. After the baths, we put her in a crate in the garage for the night to give everyone a little time to get adjusted.

Arman was beginning to plan a rebellion, as the reality dawned that there was about to be a new and permanent addition to the family. He would reluctantly hang out with her while I was at work because they were stuck at home together, but when I got back, he would explain to me she was bitchy and a smartass. I wasn't sure what he meant, unless Kazakh was the one language that dogs could speak. I didn't think that was it, but I had no appetite for drama. She was super sweet to me, but he and the other dogs weren't sure if it was going to work out. I asked if he would talk to them about giving her a little more time.

Gradually, the urine smell disappeared and Arman started thawing to her. He even named her Gulya after his friend back home. Before anyone knew what happened, she had become queen of the house. He had begun to love her more, but he was also growing tired of being stuck at home with her under the new hierarchy.

Arman was still months away from being able to go to work, but, in order to prepare him for future employment opportunities and get him out of the house more, he needed to learn to drive. Birmingham may have had public transportation; I was never really sure. There was definitely nothing near our house, but about every month I would glimpse a bus passing by like a ghost ship. It hardly seemed fair to put him on a bus that probably wouldn't drop him off again for weeks.

At night, after I got off work, I would come home and take him out for driving lessons. He had driven nothing in his life, so it was a completely new experience for him. It was a completely new experience for me also – a terrifying new experience. I naturally lack trust for other drivers, but this one had rarely even been in the front seat of a car before. I would have whiplash fifteen times before he even got the headlights turned on.

He had always dreamed of getting his driver's license, so as scared as I was with him in the driver's seat, I was happy to be supporting him in achieving something that he wanted. I also realized how joyful it was for him because he was always studying the driver's manual with a huge smile on his face.

He passed the written test with no problem and we celebrated with Thai food and a $3 bottle of wine for him.

A few weeks later, I took him for his road test. I was sitting on a bench with another guy, watching as Arman handed his paperwork to a DMV employee and got behind the wheel of my car. I was very proud until the guy turned to me and said, "Is that your son?"

I always considered myself young for my age, so I couldn't comprehend how he came up with the question. I guess I was old enough to be a dad, maybe even a great granddad by Alabama standards, but I had never considered that I could look like one. Even though Arman is ten years younger than me, we look absolutely nothing alike. He is also Asian.

"No," I responded, like a person who had just been slapped by his pimp. "He's my friend." I felt disappointed that I had mislabeled our relationship, but his question had disoriented me. I tried to take it easy on myself. Plus, the guy was older and didn't seem like the type that wanted to get into a discussion about what "that's my partner" means. I looked back at the car as Arman was driving out of the parking lot without stopping at the stop sign. Yeah, I was definitely not his dad.

We didn't celebrate that night because Arman failed the test. He attributed it to the guy being racist or homophobic, but I assured him it was probably due solely to the test administrator being scared for his life. We agreed to disagree and instead decided to focus on him being a better driver, just in case I was right.

The next week, after reviewing stop signs and three-point turns, we went back for his retest. I watched proudly as he stopped at the stop sign before leaving the parking lot. I had shaved my face to look younger, just in case someone asked if we were related. Maybe, at least, they would think we were step brothers this time. No one asked, so I regretted shaving.

This time, he passed. We could then go to the next item on the list: getting a job. As soon as he received his employment authorization card in the mail, he applied to be a cashier at the same natural food company that I had worked for in California. We were both grateful and excited when he got the job because we had maxed out all of my credit cards except one. It was my JC Penny card, and we were using it to buy restaurant gift cards when we didn't have money for food.

His new job also put us into a car-sharing situation. He would drop me off at work sometimes, and other times, I would drop him off at work.

Most of the time, our schedules didn't match up, so it was difficult to make it work. It was quickly clear that he would need his own transportation.

As soon as he received his second paycheck, we went to look for a car. I tried not to act completely shocked when they approved us for the one he wanted. It wasn't fancy at all, but it thrilled him as he drove out of the parking lot with me behind him.

Arman eventually got an IT job, and then another, and then another, until he was making more than me. I thankfully left the beauty store and got a job at a handbag store.

It was around this time that my dad died of cancer, and I found myself watching as our lives were gradually passing by. I continued watching as an aunt died, followed by a cousin, then another aunt, an uncle, Oscar, another uncle, my step-dad, and then Tico. Watching others close out their life cycles left me to realize that I was just on a conveyer belt to the afterlife. Death was never a stranger to me, but life had always been. I had been checking off the boxes, but they hadn't even been my boxes. The thirst for freedom went from a sensual whisper to a *Metal Edge* scream, and it was no longer to be ignored. I wanted a life of rich experience and hardcore freedom.

At some point, life had just become a one-way maze with ever-shrinking walls. I would go to bed every night and speak to the Divine about how grateful I was that I didn't need a single thing in the world. Even though we weren't rich, I had everything I needed. I wasn't worried about food, past-due bills, or not having my medication. It was an amazing feeling. Yet, beyond that, everything else seemed like a trap: our house, my job, and even, to some extent, our marriage. I also had an experience around that time that left me wondering if my identity was a trap as well.

One morning, I brushed my teeth and got dressed for running. Arman had left for work already, and the dogs were napping quietly in the living room. I stopped to make the bed before leaving the house, and as I finished, something strange happened. A blackhole opened in my head. I sensed it, but my mind also processed it visually. In the shortest moment possible, I felt my entire identity being pulled into it. Panic and fear rose quickly to meet it, and it disappeared.

Freedom has been my deepest wish for a large part of my life. The realization that my identity was not a solid thing, and possibly not a requirement for my existence, made me begin to question it. Was my identity a trap also? I didn't sit with it every minute of every day, but it led me to ask myself, in quiet moments or during meditations, "Who am I? How much of my identity, if any, is who I am?" And some nights, while in bed fighting court battles in my head about why I was right about things or why someone else was wrong, I asked, "Who am I defending?"

I didn't really have an answer. At that point, I don't think the answer would've accepted an invitation anyway. The VIP, the only required guest, was the question, and freedom lay somewhere beyond it.

I didn't know how to move closer to freedom, but I knew that my current life had its nose against the wall, and something would have to change. I believed deeply in the Zen proverb that stated, "Move and the way will open." Even though I'm sure it wasn't meant to be taken literally, moving seemed like the obvious thing to do. We decided to sell our house.

We had no actual plan other than that; Just sell the house. So after almost four years of living in our house, we sold it and moved into an apartment. I signed the paperwork, and as I handed the keys over, I realized their extreme weight.

23

SHIRTS AND SKINS

After moving out of our house and into an apartment, we were suddenly close to a great park. In our old neighborhood, there were no good parks for running. I would get up three or four times a week and drive six miles to an okay park. Once, I saw the police searching a pond for a body, so I liked it even less. I wasn't sure if someone had fallen through one of the many broken boards on the bridge or if they had only gotten murdered. One corner of the pond always had the bodies of fish floating upside down in it, and it smelled like death. If someone had fallen through a broken board into the water, they probably didn't even have a chance to drown because the toxic water would have gotten them first. I always tried not to breathe or open my eyes in that corner.

My new park was extensive, with many places to run. It was also only a mile from my house. An added bonus was that it had firefighters exercising in it, instead of police solving murders. They were always running one-mile laps around the sprawling, body-less pond.

I was still overweight, but I had kept the idea of being an abbed gay in the back of my mind. It hibernated safely behind the thought of having a flat belly and saving snow leopards. I assumed at some magical point in the future that all the pieces would come together, and I would then become a shirtless runner.

Off one of the larger trails, branched a smaller trail that was seldom used by anyone. I liked to take it because there was a stream running along most of it. Sometimes, I would even stop and meditate or do a walking meditation there before continuing my run. While running there one morning, it crossed my mind again that maybe one day I would be thin enough to run shirtless. I would just need to run more often and more miles. Suddenly, that thought made no sense at all. I stopped running, as I realized I didn't need to lose weight to run shirtless; I could just run shirtless. For a long time, I had focused on the wrong thing. It wasn't the shirt or the weight. It was my own shame and self-judgment. Being overweight was just a small part of my experience that I had magnified into something greater and more powerful than it actually was. I didn't know if I would be overweight forever, but I knew I could take off my shirt instantly. I looked around me in every direction, like a man about to piss on a tree. There was no one around, so I took my shirt off. I continued walking and thinking about how crazy I had been.

It felt amazing to be shirtless. I looked down at my belly and felt love for it. Every dripping piece of sweat and every fine peach fuzz bit of hair was magical. I felt completely free. When I came back to the main trail, the spell was broken, and the old voice came back.

"You're fat. Everyone will judge you and laugh at you. Stay safe. Keep your shirt on and your head down. You can always try again in twenty more pounds. You may be worthy then."

That made perfect sense to me, so I put my shirt back on and continued my run onto the main trail. I felt disappointed that I wasn't stronger, but I had put up at least a small fight. I would try again in the future.

The next day, I ran back to the same spot, vowing to fight harder. I took off my shirt and hung it on a limb of a tree. This trail was a half-mile loop, so I would leave my shirt behind and walk the loop bare-chested. If I saw anyone approaching me, I wouldn't be able to cover myself.

The sense of freedom returned to me instantly. The trees, the water, and the breeze all felt connected to me and me to them. I asked the Divine to help me free myself of all my craziness and bullshit. I didn't like how attached I was to the idea of not being good enough, and I wanted my life to be led by freedom, not fear. I walked the entire loop while thinking about it all.

When I returned, I put my shirt back on. Today would not be the day. I got back on the main trail and started running again. It crossed my mind that, if I am 100% in my own experience and not judging myself, then it is impossible for me to judge others. Letting go of my self-judgment in that moment would instantly make the world a less judgmental place. I wanted the world to be a better place, so I took my shirt off and continued running.

Soon after, I passed an older couple on the trail. I looked straight ahead, but I kept thinking that I'm making the world a better place. *You're welcome.* I felt like they were staring at me and redressing me with their eyes, but I kept running. Every time I passed someone, I would stare past them and repeat to myself, "I am making the world a better place."

I was running faster than normal just to get back to my truck sooner. When I arrived, I put my shirt back on and walked around for a few minutes to cool off. Then I went home with my win.

The very next day, I felt like I had to start all over again. I sat in my truck trying to talk myself into taking my shirt off and going for my run. I repeated, "I am making the world a less judgmental place," for twenty minutes before finally summoning up the courage to do it.

Running shirtless wasn't that hard. It was the simple act of taking off my shirt and stepping out that was difficult. For some overweight people, this might not have been a big deal, while some thin guys might have the same struggle. However, everyone has battles on their path, and this was a big one for me. I had to repeat the same twenty-minute routine every day for over a month before it even came close to feeling natural.

No one ever stopped me to tell me to put my shirt back on, but occasionally, a bigger runner would give me a thumbs-up as we passed each other. I realized gradually that maybe only a slightly overweight person could deliver my message at that moment. I didn't see overweight guys giving skinny or fit guys a thumbs-up, so maybe me having abs wasn't the answer to all the world's problems. Maybe just showing up every day, as I did, was the best solution I could offer. Maybe you don't arrive at greatness; you show up to it. I would still work on losing weight, but from then on, my weight would not stop me from being shirtless. I committed fully to just showing up.

Becoming a shirtless runner made me want to be free in other parts of my life. Around that time, I sat Arman down and told him I had something important to talk about with him. His mind instantly went to divorce, but that wasn't it. I wanted our marriage to be open.

I had brought it up before, but he wasn't really open to talking about it at that point. This time, he listened as I laid out my position. I wanted to have an open marriage because I wanted to be free in all areas of my life. It wasn't about sex; it was about being able to do whatever I wanted. I wanted him to go out, make friends, and do whatever he wanted in his life as well. Our happiness is our own responsibility, and I wanted us both to have our own and share it with each other.

I had seen so many miserable couples sharing their unhappiness with each other and never even questioning why. Relationships are one of our greatest teachers, so I wasn't trying to judge anyone else. However, I didn't want our marriage to feel like a plastic bag tied over our heads. I loved him and was still committed to our partnership, but I needed to be 100% free in all areas of my life.

"So, you want a divorce?" he asked.

"No. This could be the best thing for both of us."

Arman and I are almost completely different people, so the casual observer might try to figure out why we're together in the first place. He doesn't like horror movies and doesn't relate to anything spiritual, so it's not obvious. When I try to talk to him about my spiritual experience, he gets a blank look and waits for it to be over. I get the same look when he talks about computer stuff, so I don't get upset.

No one can be everything to everyone, but I want us both to have everything we need. I'm almost certain our souls made an agreement before we were born to share a part of our time together on earth and to support each other. I don't know what his soul was doing for the ten years between our births, but his past is his business. Either way, I want him to be as happy and fulfilled as possible while he is on this planet. Plus, he shouldn't have to wait for me to die to feel free.

He had never had a fabulous gay life, and I really wanted him to be free to have that experience. I wanted him to go out and dance with boys and be free to kiss them if he wanted. I didn't care what he did, but I wanted him to have experiences he hadn't had before. Frankly, I didn't expect him to go to orgies or dance on a pride float, but he could do it if he wanted. He was always free to do anything he wanted while in our relationship, except dangerous things like driving drunk and hard drugs. He wouldn't do those things anyway, but I thought I should mention it to him.

We had gotten into an argument once when we were on a road trip to New Orleans with a few friends. It was my birthday, and they were going out, but I didn't want to go. He felt like he couldn't go without me because we were married. I tried to explain that he could do whatever he wanted and it was fine with me. I just wanted to stay in the room and watch a horror movie. In the end, we both did our own thing, but he showed an extreme lack of enthusiasm about it.

In California, Matt and I had spent a lot of time together just hanging out and running. If I had been in a relationship at that time, I don't know that I would have been able to have that friendship. I never wanted to be in a position where a relationship kept me from exploring friendships, hanging out with other people, or doing things alone. I didn't want to make myself small in order to fit into someone else's limited version of what my life should look like. Plus, I'd probably done enough of that already.

That was my closing argument for my open-marriage proposal. He was still reluctant, but after I insisted that our partnership was as solid as ever and I was still committed, he agreed. We would have rules, and he didn't want to know what I was doing, but from then on, we could do whatever we wanted whenever we wanted to do it. Yet, nothing changed. We were the same people in the same relationship, except now we were free to explore the world in any way that we wanted.

The thing I realized quickly after opening our relationship was that it's easy to pack up your insecurities, roll them up in your marriage vows, and pretend they never existed. When we became open, I remembered right away that I was very insecure about my body. And not in a way that running shirtless could cure.

I wasn't sure exactly of the cause or the cure; however, my exploration of Grindr only compounded the problem. I wasn't even ready to hook up with anyone, but suddenly I felt like my ass wasn't bubbly enough, my penis wasn't big enough, and I was too old, too fat, or too unattractive to even fuck in the dark. On top of that, a lot of uneducated people still equate *undetectable* to being dirty.

Of course, beneath it all was the silent truth that my body is exactly as it needs to be for me to have the experiences my soul wants me to have. My heart always knows this and tries to remind me to be gentle with myself. However, my ego gets triggered by my heart. It gets an angry hard-on and fucks me dry while whispering in my ear that I need to renew my subscription to *Men's Health*.

24

RIDING TO NIRVANA

Arman loves Miami. We took our first trip there right after Hurricane Irma, and since then, we had gone a few more times on shorter trips. Our last trip was during the "incident" at the US Capitol building in January 2021. Ricky and Arman's friend from Kazakhstan joined us and while they went to work on their tan, I stayed behind.

Our place was a mile from the beach but two blocks from a psychic's shop. I love psychics about as much as I love the beach, so I stopped in for an impromptu reading. The décor instantly overwhelmed me. Every deity, stone, and tarot deck in the world was displayed together. It was like a schizophrenic collage made by an unhinged person who had recently been asked to "Show me how you feel." I was disoriented, but still curious about what guidance she could offer me.

I sat in front of her as she took my palm. After sitting silently for a moment, she began speaking. She said that I would receive a promotion or a new job in five or six months. I would be worried that I wasn't qualified for it, but I would be successful in it. I would also go to New

York as part of my new position. She continued talking for a bit, but then, towards the end of our session, she offered me very helpful information. She explained to me that in my near future, I would meet a lover. During our time together, my third eye would be opened while we were making love.

"You mean, I'm going to get fucked into enlightenment?" I asked in complete awe and delighted surprise.

"Yes. You will get enlightened, and after that, he will leave you forever."

If she was a great psychic, which I wanted her to be, I would be the luckiest gay man in history. I wouldn't be hurt at all if he left me, especially after fucking me that well. I could then become a great spiritual teacher, and my gay brothers and sisters would come to me and ask to be shown the way.

"There are many ways on the path, but the quickest way is the way of the bottom," I would declare to the bang-bang sounds of minds being blown.

I really wanted it to be true, so I asked a follow-up question. "Do you know where I'll find him, by any chance?"

"I didn't get that information," she responded.

Well, shit. Now I was going to have to get fucked by every man I met, just so I didn't miss him.

"Just remember, he will be your lover for a short while," she added.

Ah, that made things a lot easier. There are probably a few gay men out there that would fuck me, but very few that would also hang out with me afterwards and listen to Sade by candlelight. I just needed to look for that guy.

Afterwards, I paid her and went back to our apartment. As I walked back, I started thinking about all the things she said were waiting for me in the future. I really wasn't attached to anything she mentioned.

Of course, the lover part would be amazing, but I probably wouldn't get fucked into enlightenment. I could accept her being wrong about everything. What had become unacceptable, however, was the fact that I no longer wanted to live a life where most of what she said couldn't even be slightly possible. Selling the house had been a start, but it was nowhere near enough.

For the first time in my life, I wanted to let go of the attachment I had to always being and feeling safe. I felt like I wanted to burn that safe place down. I wanted to step outside, rip open my shirt and yell to life, "Come and get me!" I wanted it to throw all the shit and magic it had at me, and I was ready to take it. Beneath this desire was the steady belief that everything always works out to my benefit. I was ready to be completely open and give life all the space it needed to move me closer to freedom.

Arman had never lived anywhere in the US other than Alabama. Although Birmingham is a great city, both of us wanted him to experience living in other places. Plus, he always wanted to live by the ocean, and while Birmingham was a lot closer to the ocean than anywhere in Kazakhstan, it was still four and a half hours away. He loved Miami because of the ocean, but also because it was more diverse and gay friendly. I liked Miami, but I also liked silence, so I wasn't really dying to live in a bigger city. However, after my visit with the psychic, I decided we should move.

The next day, I submitted a verbal proposal to Arman. We would move to Miami by June 1st if I could take a year off to find myself. After that year ended, we could think about our next steps.

This proposal excited Arman and he agreed immediately. As soon as we returned home from our vacation, we made our timeline. Everything on our list was given a deadline and transferred onto our wall calendar.

In order to make moving something we were doing and not something we were going to be doing, I started going through every room of the house and getting rid of things we didn't need or love. I also told my coworkers that I would quit my job in four months to do my own thing for a year. Initially, they didn't really believe me, but the more and more I talked about it, the more real it became for them and for me. Our former boss and friend Mimi had quit two years earlier to start her own business, so I used her as a role model. I wasn't entirely sure what my own thing was, but I knew I wanted to write a book. I would start with that and go from there. The simple act of doing it would hopefully create new doors with new possibilities lying beyond them and Miami. Maybe I could even check getting killed in a horror movie off of my bucket list or, better yet, write a horror movie and get killed in it. Hopefully, there would also eventually be doors to enlightenment and a cabin by a lake somewhere. If nothing else, I could at least work on my tan.

25

PROSE AND KOANS

A s I walked through the parking lot of the mall on my last day at the handbag store, I felt a pebble digging into my foot. I stopped for a second and shook my foot around trying to dislodge it, but it wouldn't budge. The June heat had quickly brought a glisten to my forehead and the t-shirt under my black dress shirt already hinted at moist danger. Not wanting to make it worse by stopping and untying my shoe in the parking lot, I continued on quickly, but gingerly.

A blast of cool air welcomed me into the store, followed immediately by my coworker. "Hey Jason." Her black clothes were almost identical to mine. She put her hand on her hip and asked, "Why are you walking crazy? Did you hurt your foot?"

"Hey girl. No, I just have a rock in my shoe." I took off my shoe and emptied it into my palm. Instead of a pebble, something else fell out. "Never mind," I lifted the offending item and beamed, "It's just a stale piece of curly fry."

I couldn't remember the last time I had curly fries. This could explain the extreme staleness of it, but not how it showed up in my shoe months later. I'm pretty sure it wasn't mine anyway because it definitely didn't look familiar; somebody probably sharpened it and put it there. Or maybe the Divine was sending me a message. Like, maybe life isn't like a box of chocolates; it's like a stale curly fry in your shoe. Maybe we just need to stop now and then and try to figure out what's slowing us down or making us walk funny.

Fortunately, I had a full year. I was almost sure I would have time to write a book *and* to contemplate curly fries.

MIAMI

26

THREADS

D ulat, Armand's friend from New York, visited us in Miami and his first question to me summed up my entire year off:

"Why are you so pale?"

I stammered for a moment and put three incoherent excuses into one statement. Neither of us understood it, so we chalked it up to the language barrier and changed the subject.

He was right, though. I should've had a much better tan, especially since it was the easiest thing to achieve on my Miami to-do list. But, I had kinda fallen into a spiritual hole and there wasn't a lot of sun in there. It was kinda like the 2005 horror movie "The Descent."

If you haven't seen it, it's basically about a woman with issues who goes spelunking with a group of female friends who also have issues and then they get acquainted with some grotesque and hungry creatures called crawlers. Whether the crawlers have issues is secondary to the fact that they have sharp teeth.

Being on a spiritual path is like being the main character in that movie. You go into a deep dark hole, realize you're fucked, realize that everyone else is fucked, and then your headlamp dies. Then scary white creatures jump out at you. Eventually, you start to think the darkness itself is trying to kill you. You finally almost escape, but there's actually a sequel called "The Descent 2." Even though you don't remember a damn thing that happened, and you're practically still wearing the blood from part one, you have to go back to the cave and get chased in the dark again by some janky fanged assholes. Not only is it scary and painful, but it's almost impossible to look cute.

Obviously, it would be much easier for someone to tell you about the cave than to explore it yourself. Or you could pretend it doesn't exist and instead focus on tree climbing like your parents raised you to do (trees are indeed very real). There are hundreds of ways and reasons to not choose the cave. Isn't spelunking out anyway? Even the word sucks.

The reality, whether unfortunate or not, is that you're in the goddamn cave anyway and it has never even been a choice. The choice has only been whether or not to realize it. Choosing the cave gradually makes you aware that the illusion of not being in the cave was the trap and that the cave is actually the path to freedom. Once you know it, you can start working through all the shit and trying to find a splinter of light somewhere that will eventually lead to a way out of the darkness. Albert Pike probably said it better when he wrote, "We must pass through the darkness, to reach the light."

Miami helped me realize my cave has unlimited shades of darkness. It also made me question whether I was the gutsy girl with issues or just a pale-ass crawler, which is probably the whole point of the cave anyway: to find out who we are. I'm still working on that.

The truth is, I am a product of collective delusions. They have programmed me to be a sterile thing, wingless and unwild, and not a threat to the comfort of others' conditioning. Through a generational amalgamation of beliefs, mythologies, superstitions, judgments, and every experience of pain imaginable, an unconscious course emerged to train me to believe that life is not to be lived, but disarmed.

This led me to live my life under the influence of many delusions, and one of the most powerful ones is shame. Shame is a lie that sucks the joy out of living. Shame just sucks.

I have been ashamed for being gay, for having HIV, for not having a perfect body, for masturbating, for being depressed, for masturbating while being depressed, and for thousands of other reasons. There's not even a good explanation for it. It's like someone gave me a shame coat at an early age and I accepted it because I'm a polite person.

"Thank you. I didn't even know I needed this," I said.

"Oh yeah, you're gonna need this for sure. And since you're a Christian, I got you the one with the really big inner pockets."

"Why?"

"Hey! Shhhh. Only heathens ask questions." He probably noticed my confused, yet gay smile and said, "Ahh. Just trust me on this one," before patting my head and disappearing in a cloud of red smoke.

Well, now I would never know why the coat smelled like sulfur. And, even though it was ugly and smelled funny, I put it on.

From that day forward, I never took it off. It became like a second skin. Even as it became heavier and heavier, I didn't think about it anymore. I just walked through life collecting things to hide inside my pockets. The heat of it made me sick and the weight of it pulled me down, but I had forgotten that it was a separate thing, so I kept wearing it.

Until, one day, I felt the roughness of the fabric brush harshly against my bare skin and I remembered it.

When I sat down to write for the very first time, I did not know what I was doing. My only plan was to show up with a pencil and some paper and see what happened. I tried not to think about it because my brain doesn't work when I think. And then, before I could fuck it up with thinking, my hand had written "AIDS didn't make me skinny." This made me suspect that my hand was out to get me. We had had some good times, but it had obviously turned. It must have forgotten that I am a person who says, "please" and "thank you." I give a big smile so people know I am not a threat, so they feel safe with me and know I can be trusted. There is nothing else to me. I am just a normal person doing normal things. I do not make waves. I do not seek to cause others discomfort. I am a nice guy. Basic math, uncomplicated. I want neither trouble nor attention. I am definitely *not* a guy that says, "AIDS didn't make me skinny."

For a second, I wondered if my hand was channeling some other cool guy living with HIV and weight issues, but it seemed like a long shot. Even though I was sure there were plenty out there, they were probably having game night with their friends, eating ice cream, or, if they were lucky, giving a friendly handy jay to a stranger.

I was almost sure my hand wasn't channeling a dead guy because even gay guys don't stress about abs in the afterlife. But if I was wrong, gay hell would be worse than I thought. Having to spend an eternity never being good enough or happy with yourself would be horrible. Not to mention that your ice cream would melt before it got delivered and even though you weren't eating anything and living in a fire pit, you still couldn't lose weight. To be fair, heaven probably doesn't come with abs either. Honestly, I don't think heaven and hell exist and I'm still on the fence about abs. Regardless, my hand was taking it upon itself to expose my messy bits.

It would've been a great time for an epiphany about shame being a lie, and my path to freedom moving downhill only in the direction of my own truth, but that didn't happen. I'm not saying the Divine was being stingy with epiphanies, but with all the shit going on the world, I imagine it could've at least been a bit more generous. *"Hey, the world is literally on fire and... DeSantis... so if not enlightenment, can I at least get an epiphany? Hello? I'm not sure we have much time left."* But, no. Instead, the Divine quietly dropped a realization seed into the inner pocket of my shame coat. Maybe my soul was no longer loamy enough for epiphanies, but it was slightly better suited for slow realizations and perfect for building patience. Actually, the Divine had probably even given me a different seed years earlier.

Months before leaving Alaska, I wrote a song called "Past Lives." Less than two hundred people have ever heard it and only one or two of them probably remember it. However, in my dreams, an unknown German DJ named Gunther did an underground, deep house mix of it and, incidentally, spiritually liberated everyone on the dance floor. It's not likely, but if anyone could do it, it would be Gunther.

The lyrics to the song were simple:

"Every breath, every mistake.

Every choice, good or bad,

that I made,

got me to now, this perfect now,

'cause I'm here with you."

I didn't actually feel like the guy in the song, but I wanted to be him. I wanted to arrive at every moment being okay with all parts of my experience and knowing that somehow even the fucked up pieces were a part of something perfect. Achieving that, at the time, seemed impossible. Instead, I kinda always just stepped over the moment—keeping one foot in the past, one in the future—and then trying to maintain my balance while shifting the weight of all the shit I was carrying.

I hadn't listened to the song in years and had actually forgotten about it. Then, one morning, I opened up my computer and sat down again to write. I had long since abandoned paper and pencil for a standing date with the blinking cursor. Months ago I had made it to the final chapter, but my brain had seemingly committed to a writer's strike and my hands had gone quiet, as if they had run out of gossip. I typed and deleted words repeatedly, hoping my brain or hands would eventually feel sorry for me and come to my rescue. They didn't. They just sat quietly by, as if they were waiting for me to do something. I didn't know what to do, so I decided the best option was to break the uncomfortable silence.

"Hey Siri. Play a song just for me." It wasn't an unusual request.

"Sure. Here's 'Just' by Radiohead."

I really like Radiohead, but that song is no "Fake Plastic Trees," so I tried again. "Hey Siri. Play music just for me."

This time, it played "Past Lives."

After listening to the first verse, I realized that my brain and hands *were* waiting for me; they had been waiting for months for me to catch up. There was nowhere else to go and nothing else to do. I just needed to show up to this moment, this perfect moment, and be the kind of guy that says, "AIDS didn't make me skinny." That guy could only show up to this moment soft and vulnerable, and free from the weight of shame. He would show up, hoping you would meet him with equal softness. Because in this softness lies the remembrance that we are both divine threads in the fabric of all things, and every thread, every expression of the Divine, deserves to be loved and free.

ACKNOWLEDGMENTS

So many people encouraged me before, during, and after writing this book. After reading it, I'm sure a lot of them will regret it and one or two of them may even faint. I am grateful for all of them, regardless. However, I didn't write it to offend anyone or inspire them to judge me. I wrote it because I want to remove all barriers I have to loving others. The part of me that doesn't want to be judged creates a wall. In fact, all of my unhealed places cast a shadow over my heart. *A Normal Person Doing Normal Things* is about ripping my chest open and bringing light to those places. However, it is also an invitation. It doesn't matter how you show up. Just show up. All of your messiness doesn't matter. Come as you are without judgment and with the intention to love. You don't need to be perfect because there is nothing more beautiful than openness and love. Plus, perfection is a goal of the darkness, but it's a natural state of the light.

I would like to express my gratitude to:

Arman for telling me to write a book and then supporting me while I did it. Hopefully, he doesn't regret it.

John F. for always showing up with me (to the cave and karaoke).

Nia for being there from the beginning and helping me get to the end. Plus, years and years of other stuff.

Sivan for always shining a light when I couldn't find my own.

All my Coach friends, especially Jon Tomas, Kenny, Kristy (Kritty), Mel, and Mimi for being like a family and keeping my inspiration battery charged. And Mimi again for a thousand other reasons.

Garrett for feedback, support, and years and years of friendship.

Andy F. for listening to me talk about this all the damn time and still being supportive.

My editor, Tracy, for bringing it all together and helping it make sense.

My family for everything. Especially my mom. Please skip chapter four. And Aleah, Alyssa, and Jason for games and Eurovision support.

Ricky. Thank you. I've finally figured you out.

Antonio, Tico, and Oscar for sharing so much of their lives with me.

And Gulya for being with me for every word.

ABOUT THE AUTHOR

Jay Colburn is the by-product of an inconceivable three-way between Maplesville, Alabama; Anchorage, Alaska; and San Francisco, California. When he's not searching for enlightenment or a good horror movie, he likes to drink iced coffee and reaffirm his belief that love can save the world. This is his first book.

jaycolburn.com

To Evelyn –
my most supportive and patient Fleet Street
'widow'

Arthur Butler is former political correspondent for the *News Chronicle, Reynolds News, Daily Express* and *Daily Sketch,* three of which newspapers died under him in Fleet Street's cut throat circulation battles from the 1950s to the 1970s. Such was his reputation as a news gatherer that, despite such catastrophes and fierce competition for jobs, he was never out of work. When the *Daily Sketch* merged with the *Daily Mail* he became overnight a pace-setting lobbyist, making news instead of reporting it.

Arthur Butler's previous publications include:

No Feet to Drag (with Alf Morris MP)
The Parliamentary & Scientific Committee (with Christopher Powell)
People, Politics and Pressure Groups – Memoirs of a Lobbyist (published in 2010)

Reviews of *Memoirs of a Lobbyist:*

Iain Dale's Diary Blog: "This book really is a good read… I highly recommend it."

Quentin Letts, *Daily Mail*: "One of Westminster's first lobbyists he has been one of SW1's more discreet operators. He writes with lovely understatement…"

Tom Easton, *Lobster Magazine:* "It is well-written British political life intelligently observed and reflectively considered."

London School of Economic journal *Connect*: "In this hard-hitting memoir Butler seeks to establish that lobbying is an essential tool of the democratic process."

CONTENTS

offer but confessed I did not feel ready to join such an illustrious journal. I felt in need of some basic training in the business of reporting. In fact, I was confident I would be accepted for the only training scheme for would-be journalists then in existence – run by stuffy Lord Kemsley's nationwide newspaper group. It was partly designed for graduates, had existed for only a few years and was introduced to take the heat off Kemsley when he was quizzed by the Royal Commission on the press. The government was concerned by allegations that journalistic freedom was being stifled by the concentration of newspaper ownership into the hands of a few powerful groups. Kemsley and Beaverbrook were the two main targets. However, when Kemsley told the Royal Commission he had a plan for training young journalists as a means of raising standards they were delighted.

I told the London University Appointments Board of my interest in the training scheme, but they gave me a wrong date for applying. I was told by Kemsley head office that I was too late for that year – 1951. Waiting for another twelve months was not acceptable to me. I decided to make use of an important contact.

Knowing I hoped to become a journalist, Lina had introduced me to Desmond MacCarthy, distinguished literary critic of Kemsley's *Sunday Times*. With his wife, Mary, he lived in book-lined style by the Thames near to Hampton Court Palace, where Lina had a *grace and favour* apartment in the famous clock tower. While at the LSE I was often invited to visit the MacCarthys at their first floor flat in Garrick's Villa (once owned by the famous actor) and they took a kindly interest in my activities.

I decided to tell Desmond about the training scheme setback. He immediately phoned Denis Hamilton, Lord Kemsley's right hand man, and succeeded in getting me considered for the one remaining vacancy – on the Middlesbrough Evening Gazette. I was accepted. I was about to become absorbed in Lord Kemsley's sprawling newspaper empire covering a great chain of provincial morning and evening papers and five national Sunday papers – the *Sunday Times, Sunday Graphic, Sunday Dispatch, Sunday Chronicle* and the *Empire News*. All but the first were to die in his hands. 'Lord K', as he was known, also owned the *Daily Dispatch*, published in Manchester and catering for a northern readership; and the *Daily Graphic*, sometimes entitled the *Daily Sketch*, his only national daily paper.

I was so keen to start working for him I declined an invitation for a two-week holiday in Rome. Instead, I headed north for gritty, grimy industrial Teesside. My baggage included a portable typewriter –a 'good luck' gift from my ever-supportive parents – and the collected poems of W.B. Yeats, a parting gift from Martin Wight who asked me to stay in touch. Martin told me one of his favourite lines came from Yeats' poem 'He wishes for the cloths of Heaven':

'I have spread my dreams under your feet;
Tread softly because you tread on my dreams.'

CHAPTER ONE
Teesside Trainee

As I approached Middlesbrough by train and looked out at the polluted industrial landscape intersected by rows of small back-to-back terraced houses, I recalled Mary MacCarthy's words in her letter congratulating me on my appointment.

"I expect you will, alas, find a good deal of rough with the smooth, but I am sure it will be interesting. I am afraid black smoke, endless business and money-making – little art."

Mary, I remembered, had been very pleased when I was elected president of the LSE's Art Society. I was never to see her again, but we kept in touch by letter. It was typical of the kindness and generosity of Desmond, one of the nicer members of the Bloomsbury Group, that despite failing health he found time to take an interest in young people and to follow my career. However, as he was busy with his writing and work as a leading member of the English section of the international P.E.N. club, Mary took on the job of corresponding with me. Sadly, too, Desmond's asthma was worsening.

On arrival in Middlesbrough, I made my way to the modern, well designed office of the *Evening Gazette* and was ushered in to meet the editor *"Jimmy"* James. He turned out to be a kind, patient fair-minded man for whom I was to form a great respect. A former chief sub-editor of a Manchester evening paper, he had the habit of addressing members of his staff as *"chief"*. He quickly introduced me to the graduate trainee already working on the paper – a charming, amusing young man and fine writer named

Terence Feeley, who took me to dinner that night at the Corporation Hotel – the smartest spot in town. He arranged for me to lodge with him in a comfortable house on the Marton Road leading out of town, saying, "The best thing about Middlesbrough is that it doesn't take long to get out of it."

He was right. But the people were warm, friendly and hospitable, and the surrounding countryside was spectacular. The *"Borough"* had earned such titles as *"Boom Town"* and *"Mushroom Town"*. At the beginning of the 19th century it had comprised of a few farmhouses by the River Tees. Then, in 1828, the Stockton and Darlington railway had extended a line to the village, and Quaker business families had bought land to build a small port from which to ship coal from the North East pits. The discovery of ironstone in the Eston Hills above Teeside then gave a great boost to development. The "iron rush" began in 1850, with people arriving from all over Britain. One local village was even called California to draw a parallel with the great gold rush.

A town began to take shape to house the hundreds of miners moving into the area –a Victorian town built for speed and economy on the gridiron pattern. By the 1870s some forty thousand people were living there. By the end of the 1880s a third of Britain's pig iron production was made in and around the town. The iron pipes for London's new water system were made there. The engineering and shipbuilding industries moved in and there was an air of prosperity and confidence, underlined by the building of a costly town hall in 1887. In 1888, Middlesbrough was granted county borough status.

There were to be times of depression, too, and the area was hit by heavy unemployment and hardship in the 1930s. But by the time of my arrival in the summer of 1951 there was renewed belief, as Imperial Chemical Industries forged ahead with an ambitious new petro-chemical works described as *"the greatest single industrial project so far announced by British Industry."* It was estimated that it would eventually employ some ten thousand people. On the downside the plant exuded a smell akin to cat's pee and this polluting stink filled my nostrils as I alighted from the train.

At night the sky glowed red from the iron and steel industry furnaces, and those Teessiders not at work got on with trying to enjoy themselves. Owing to the large number of thirsty workers manning the heavy industry plants vital for Britain's limping post-war economy, the town received a special ration of extra-strong export ale. As a result, it had at that time the highest drunk rate and the highest birth rate in the country. It also produced a lot of news.

Before I was allowed to get to grips with 'Big News' I had to start by covering the humdrum. I reported for daily duty to Chief Reporter, Tom Stake, famed in the circulation area as *"Tom of Teesside"* for his weekly football dispatches. In Middlesbrough football was king, and when Tom reported a win for the "Borough" productivity soared for a few days in the local industries. Wilf Mannion was the much-worshipped star of the team. Born into a poor family in South Bank, Middlesbrough, in 1918, he had become one of the finest footballers of the 1940s and was Teesside's *"Golden Boy"*. Blessed with superb ball control, dazzling speed and devastating shooting skill, the blond inside forward played 26 times for England and scored eleven goals. Treated unhelpfully by the Middlesbrough management he tried to leave the club in 1948, but the directors held him to his contract that had been signed on his behalf by his parents when he was a minor. At first, he refused to play but being short of money he returned to the field and continued to reward the fans until 1954, when the club was relegated to the Second Division – an appalling blow to the morale of the town. By the time he was allowed to leave he had scored 110 goals for the club in 368 games.

Decades later, watching the appalling performance of England's pampered football team in the 2010 World Cup tournament, I recalled the mean treatment meted out to magnificent Mannion and compared it to the huge sums of money expended on some of the overpaid, oversexed, overconfident 'stars' of the English side.

Tom Stake decided that my first assignment should be to visit the Tees shipping office to collect the shipping returns – details of vessels arriving at the port. Compared with that chore, writing up the activities of the local Darby and Joan clubs from scrappy notes left at the front office by aged members was positively exciting. Gradually the tempo increased from chasing accidents and fires to attending country fairs and court work.

Within six months of my arrival, however, the horizon widened when it came time for Terence Feeley to complete his training and move to Kemsley House in London, to become a writer for the *Sunday Graphic*. Regretfully, I never saw him again, but I enjoyed watching some of his fine adaptations of Henry James' novels for television and he wrote at least one play for the West End. Terence had reported on performances by visiting concert orchestras and productions at the local theatres; he had filled in when Sidney Jackson, the Gazette's leader writer was absent; and generally, he had been the *"colour"* writer for the paper. Editor Jimmy James now looked to me to fill the gap. My career as a local drama critic was short-lived. Most of the entertainment served up by the main theatre was composed of traditional music hall turns from singers and comedians to jugglers. With the steady spread of television across the country, however, this was a form of amusement struggling to survive. Television had just arrived on Teeside and my coverage of the shows at the theatre was no help. Most of the acts appeared to me to be tatty and third rate. But not content with slamming these, I criticised the state of the theatre itself, which was run-down, dirty and laden with the dust of years of neglect. I was reminded of it some years later when I watched John Osborne's play *The Entertainer* about a seedy music hall comedian named Archie Rice. In particular, one of Archie's quips touched a chord, *"Don't clap too hard,"* he told the audience. *"We're in a very old building."*

After a month or two of my critical reviews, Jimmy James received an indignant letter from the theatre manager. He threatened that if the Gazette continued to send me to cover the shows he would withdraw his advertising. Jimmy was sympathetic to my view and remarked that now TV had arrived in Teeside, the theatre would soon discover that the good people of M'bro would prefer to watch top-rate shows at home with a few cans of beer, than risk being eaten by fleas while they watched rubbish on the stage. However, with an eye to revenue, he assured the theatre that my reviews would end – but added that in future the Gazette would send a reporter only on those occasions when a big star warranted their presence. Such a star was Frankie Vaughan. On his arrival in town I was sent to interview him in his room at the Corporation Hotel. Only a year older than me, he was already a major name in show business. He had a reputation for wowing the women with his good looks, romantic songs, immaculate evening dress, top hat and cane. His signature tune was *Give me the Moonlight* – the ladies swooned.

Unknown to most of his fans, he was already involved in a lot of charity work and was supporting the setting up of boys' clubs in places like Middlesbrough, to get youngsters off the streets and away from crime. He said that as a young boy growing up in a run-down area of Liverpool, he had to thank his membership of the Lancashire Lads' Club for the fact that he did not get into trouble himself. He was then Francis Abelson and explained that he changed his name after his grandmother said to him one day, *"If you vant to be a singer, make sure you are a good vorn."* So he became a good *Vaughan*. Soon after his appearance in Middlesbrough he made it into films and in 1960 starred opposite Marilyn Monroe in *Let's Make Love*.

My presence at the rather sad local art gallery was more welcome, as my reports of visiting exhibitions began to be published in the national journal *Art News and Review*. In a letter to Mary MacCarthy, I was able to report that there was art in the North-East and sent her some of my cuttings to prove it. A highlight of the cultural scene in Middlesbrough was the occasional visit of John Barbirolli's Hallé Orchestra – known to some as Hallé's band. Based in Manchester, they would come to Teeside during forays across the border into Yorkshire. Under Barbirolli's baton the orchestra reached high standards of performance. They travelled in two motor coaches and a former member has described how the one carrying the ladies and principals was known as the *"posh bus"* and the other, carrying the brass and others, the *"boozers' bus"*. In view of Middlesbrough's reputation for strong ale the town must have been a popular destination with the latter.

The town, in fact, had a long musical tradition. In 1907, when a Japanese prince paid a state visit to England, the Lord Chamberlain prohibited Middlesbrough Amateur Operatic Society from performing Gilbert and Sullivan's light opera *The Mikado* – *"owing to buffoonery in certain parts"* – that he feared would be offensive to Japan. In contrast to Middlesbrough's low-calibre music hall productions, one amateur performance stands out in my memory of those days. In the bleak industrial suburb of Grangetown, where ears were normally attuned to the roar of the steel furnaces, the local boys' club staged Mozart's opera *The Magic Flute*. It was indeed magical. As I caught the smelly bus back to my lodgings with the boys' singing still in my ears, I decided to become more active in trying to win a better deal for the people in places like Grangetown. It was enclosed on three sides by polluting industry – the iron and steel works and I.C.I.'s Wilton petro-chemical plant. The hard working people who lived here suffered from a variety of respiratory diseases, with premature deaths from asthma, bronchitis and lung cancer taking a heavy toll on the population. Damp terraced houses and a poor diet added to the health problems. Eventually, some forty years later, the people of Grangetown decided to take legal action against I.C.I. and British Steel over pollution, claiming they were severely afflicted by the diseases it caused. They suffered some of the highest asthma rates in Britain.

In line with my desire to help improve living conditions in places like Grangetown, I had joined the Teesside Fabian Society and after a year took over as secretary. I had actively supported the Labour Party since the age of sixteen, when I had designed anti-Conservative posters for display in the local left-wing newsagent's windows during the 1945 general election. That year, on a visit to Foyle's bookshop in the Charing Cross Road, I had bought John Strachey's book *Why You Should be a Socialist* that was to have an important influence on me. An earlier influence had been my mother's descriptions of her life as a child in Dover during the Great War, with her widowed Aunt Nell and her five children. Nell's husband, a sergeant in the Queen's Royal regiment, had been killed in the bitter battle for Hill Sixty on the Western Front. Reduced to poverty, Nell suffered the humiliation of struggling to raise her family under the watchful eye of hard-hearted Government Means Test inspectors who would insist on her selling off items of furniture before granting her money she desperately needed to buy food and pay the rent.

In 1952, I became involved in local parliamentary politics when a by-election was called for the nearby Cleveland constituency. The man chosen as Labour's candidate was a certain Arthur Palmer who, in the 1945 general election, had won the seemingly impregnable Wimbledon seat from the Tories, only to lose it later. A chartered engineer and fuel technologist, he had been a great help to the bumbling, useless Minister for Fuel and Power, Emmanuel Shinwell, in the preparation of the Bill for nationalising electricity. As an active Fabian, he quickly made himself known to the Teesside Fabian Society and recruited some of us to help with his election canvassing. He won, and when we met up again at the House of Commons five years later, he was very helpful to me. Although he was to become Opposition Spokesman on Fuel and Power from 1957 to 59, he never held office. But, one evening, after campaigning in Cleveland, he told me over a cup of tea that there had been one occasion during Attlee's premiership when he thought his moment had arrived.

The Prime Minister's Parliamentary Private Secretary sought him out and said that Mr Attlee wanted to see him at No. 10 as soon as possible. Arthur hurried across and with expectation high was ushered into the Prime Minister's room. Attlee looked up from his desk. "Ah, Palmer, glad you could come. This wretched radiator has stopped working and no one knows how to connect the wires. Someone said you might have an idea about these things? Can you help?"

Arthur sorted out the wiring and wandered back deflated to the Commons.

I had first joined the Fabian Society while at the LSE. The school had been founded by Fabians to help make Britain a successful socialist state. When I told Desmond MacCarthy during one of my visits to Garrick's Villa he was pleased and told me that some of his friends had been active in starting it, including George Bernard Shaw, who edited the first book of Fabian Essays, and Sidney Webb. Clifford Sharp, editor of the *New Statesman* when Desmond had first written for it, was also a Fabian – indeed, the weekly magazine had been another of the tools forged by leading members of the society to achieve their socialist ideal.

In founding the Labour Party together with the trades unions, the society produced the most important tool that was eventually to bring about the achievement of its goal. When Fabian, Clem Attlee, led that party to power at the 1945 general election, he could count 229 other Fabians on the Labour benches in the Commons. Forty-one were in his government. During its six momentous years in charge, that government had put into effect the programme for the Welfare State drawn up and spelt out by Fabians over the previous fifty years.

It was put to me that Labour's defeat in 1951 was caused partly by the failure of local Labour parties to educate constituency members in the need to reconstruct society in the interests of the general welfare. The poverty I witnessed in the mean backstreets of Middlesbrough reflected that need. So the defeat gave a boost to the Society and its role in developing new policies to bring about equality of opportunity and decent housing for all. There was also found to be a need to give more thought to foreign and colonial policy – subjects of special interest to me.

I had written twice to Martin Wight to report on my new life and on 20 December 1952 received a somewhat belated reply. He wrote, *"Your letter came just as I had succumbed to an attack of 'flu: I do hope you will have attributed the delay in answering to some such cause and not have accused me in your mind of wilful neglect...*

Your career reassures me that International Relations has some excuse as a university degree. Here the machine grinds round in the familiar way and (between ourselves) I would rather be doing other things, but I try to make the best of it..."

It made me sad to discover how disenchanted he had become and hoped his students would not notice. In another letter he had described the latest batch of students in the department as *"satyrs cavorting on the slopes of Parnassus."* What he had overlooked to tell me was that during the year he had married a young woman named Gabriele by whom he was to have two sons and four daughters. No wonder he had not found time to reply sooner. He went on to become Professor of History at Sussex University and in 1972 died suddenly at the age of 58. In 1979, a revised and expanded edition of his *Power Politics* was published by the Royal Institute of International Affairs and Penguin Books. A foreword described him as:

"one of the most distinguished scholars to have worked in the field of international relations and who brought to it unusual qualities of intellectual depth and erudition."

I was pleased to discover that, in 1951, he had prepared a new edition of Harold Laski's little book *An Introduction to Politics*, the purpose of which was, in the author's words, *"to set out the basic problems in a form which will make them intelligible to the average interested reader."* That was precisely what Martin had done so well in his teaching of international relations.

During my second year in Middlesbrough a clergyman friend, whom I had known since I was evacuated from London to the Forest of Dean in the war, offered me a holiday in Belgium – and the opportunity to undergo a moving experience. Stephen Fowler, who had served as an Army padre in the First World War, had been appointed padre at the British Mission Church at Ypres. This ancient little town in Flanders, reduced to rubble and ashes in that World War, had been rebuilt and revived and stood surrounded by vast immaculate cemeteries of Commonwealth soldiers under the care of the War Graves Commission.

But thousands of those who died in the mud and blood of Flanders' fields were never found – and never buried. They had no cross to bear their name, standing in one of those rigid ranks, mile after mile, in the silent cemeteries. Their names, instead, were engraved on the monumental war memorial at Ypres' Menin Gate. There, every evening, a trumpeter sounded the Last Post for them. And there, on my first evening in Ypres, I stood with Stephen, head bowed, deeply moved by the short, poignant ceremony.

I had been raised on horror stories of the slaughter on the Western front. My mother, who served as a teenage Wren in the battered 'front line' port of Dover, told me often of her harrowing experiences in meeting the wounded and dying men as they were disembarked – maimed, disfigured, shell-shocked. It took my visit to Ypres to bring fully to my consciousness the sheer appalling enormity of the conflict. Out of every nine British soldiers who fought in Flanders five were killed, wounded or reported missing. On the first day alone of the disastrous Battle of the Somme some 20,000 were killed. Thousands more were slaughtered in such killing fields as Passchendaele, Arras and Cambrai.

Stephen drove me around the cemeteries. As always a generous host, he did his best to alleviate the horror of these vast burial grounds. There were sightseeing visits to Brussels and Bruges. There were daily opportunities to

17

enjoy the rich Belgian food. At the end of the holiday Stephen asked me if my study of international relations had given me hope that the world would not become submerged again in such a blood bath. I replied that it had not made me optimistic.

In line with the growing interest in commonwealth and colonial affairs, I took the opportunity as secretary of the local Fabian Society to organise a daylong seminar on some current issues, with John Hatch of the Africa Bureau as main speaker. He had come to my notice through his articles as Commonwealth correspondent of the *New Statesman* and his book *The Dilemma of South Africa* which led the Labour Party to offer him the post of secretary of its Commonwealth Department. At the seminar I was impressed by his knowledge and ability to express his views. We were to remain in touch throughout his career, one of the high spots of which was the release from jail in South Africa of Nelson Mandela, for whose freedom he had tirelessly campaigned. Apart from issues of colonial freedom we had another subject of mutual interest – rugby football. John was a successful referee in the 1950s and in the Middlesex seven-a-side semi-final at Twickenham in 1960 served as touch judge when Denis Thatcher was referee. John ended up in the House of Lords but never felt comfortable there. He would have felt more at home in the Commons.

My involvement in local politics had not passed unnoticed in the *Evening Gazette* office. Lord Kemsley might have twitched if he had known that the Teeside Fabian Society secretary was occasionally writing the Gazette's leading articles and getting regular reports published of Fabian meetings. My colleagues, however, were relaxed about the situation, and when the local trades council needed a representative from the National Union of

Journalists, they asked me to take it on. On attending meetings, I quickly fell foul of the tough old communist railway worker, *"Brother"* Feeney, in the chair who did his utmost to ensure that the council followed the Kremlin line. In February 1954, I was to make headline news in the local press when I accused him of *"deliberately misleading delegates in the interests of a communist sponsored organisation."* The row had erupted over an invitation to a Mrs Betty Ambatielos, Welsh wife of an imprisoned Greek trade unionist, to address the council on *"Greece Today"*. The League of Democracy in Greece, which was sponsoring her visit, was a communist front organisation proscribed by the TUC. When I challenged the chairman on this, he replied that, so far as he knew, it was not a communist body. In view of this misleading response I then moved a motion of censure against him and the invitation to Mrs Ambatielos was withdrawn. Next morning, the *Northern Echo* ran an inside page lead account, headlined, *"Middlesbrough ban on communist. Trades Council chairman accused by member."* The Middlesbrough *Evening Gazette* followed up with a story headlined, *"Reds, so Trades Council says No."*

At the next Council meeting, when my censure motion was due to be debated, I withdrew it in favour of a stronger resolution moved by another member to remove Feeney from the chairmanship. However, this went too far for the majority and it was defeated.

In the course of the debate I stressed that I "had no intention to emulate the hysterical McCarthyite anti-communist campaign, but there was an important difference between allowing communists to play a full part in our trades council and allowing ourselves to be duped and fooled by them."

The *Evening Gazette* carried a report of the meeting over two columns. I was confident *"Brother"* Feeney would never try to mislead the Trades Council again.

One of our visiting speakers at the Fabian Society was a very impressive and articulate young man named John Rex of Sheffield University. He persuaded me to become a lecturer for the Workers' Education Association and I launched a course on the principles and problems of international relations. After a few meetings, however, I realised that my students were not very interested in learning about the balance of power, international morality and international law. They preferred discussing current issues with a far-Left bias. The class lasted less than six months, as members drifted away and numbers dropped below the sustainable level. Later, I smiled knowingly as I read in Oswald Harland's book on *Yorkshire North Riding* of his experiences in lecturing to the iron, steel and coal workers around Middlesbrough. *"These people are not, believe me, any easy crowd to handle,"* he wrote. *"A more politically minded lot it would be hard to find."*

My short-live lectureship for the WEA was a blow to my pride. My self-esteem was in need of a boost – and one was on the way. To supplement our low wage from Kemsley newspapers there were opportunities to earn extra from *"lineage"*. Reporters had arrangements with national newspapers and Kemsley papers on Tyneside to send reports in return for payment based on the number of lines used. A senior reporter in our office named Charlie, who had been the *Daily Express* man in Liverpool when Atlantic liners brought countless celebrities to the port, was the local *"stringer"* for *The Times*. The responsibility had become irksome and one day he asked me if I would like to take it over. I was delighted and was soon phoning the great paper's office in Printing House Square with reports of industrial developments and other news. At local press conferences I would sometimes introduce myself as *"Butler of the Evening Gazette and The Times of London"*.

I found time, also, to enter an English Speaking Union essay competition on an international affairs topic – and in due course was informed that I had won. One of the judges was a politician named Denis Healey, elected Labour MP for Leeds South East in 1952, having previously served as the highly respected secretary of the Labour Party's international department.

As for Middlesbrough's MPs, I got to know them well – barrister Jocelyn Simon who won the West constituency for the Tories in 1951 and after a successful period in Government became Lord Simon of Glaisdale; and Hilary Marquand, who had been Health Minister in the Attlee Government, and became Member for Middlesbrough East in 1950. Urbane, courteous and a distinguished academic, Hilary was an economist and expert on industrial relations. At my request he addressed the local Fabian Society on *"Labour's Social Policy"*.

When I had been in Middlesbrough for three years I thought it was time to remind those running the Kemsley group in London that I had completed my training. Jimmy James undertook to inform them and to let them know that I was interested in specialising in political or diplomatic reporting. The response from London was slow and in my impatience I applied for a post on *The Times*. I was interviewed in London by Donald Tyerman, an assistant editor and a fine writer who had a well-earned reputation for encouraging and helping young journalists. However, he could offer me as a start only a job on the *Times Literary Supplement*. It would give me a foot in the door and provide useful London experience he explained. I asked for time to consider his well-meant offer and on the train back to

Middlesbrough decided to decline. The T.L.S. looked like a backwater to someone who wanted to report on important current developments. I never met Tyerman again but watched his career with interest as, having been passed over for the editorship of *The Times*, he went on to become a distinguished editor of *The Economist*.

Meanwhile, I witnessed the death of the first newspaper to die while carrying my by-line. Soon after starting work in Middlesbrough, I was approached by a bright young sub-editor who asked me to contribute to the North-Eastern Weekly News, published from the Evening Gazette office. It carried background stories to the local news; profiles of Teesside bigwigs; and features with a bearing on regional interests and the countryside. Pleased to have the opportunity to spread my journalist's wings I wrote regularly – and for no fee – for the struggling little paper. Then one day I learned that its circulation and advertising revenue had fallen too far. The remaining readers were told it was being closed down. I was sad. Perhaps the arrival of television had contributed to its demise. Soon I was to become accustomed to such deaths in Lord K's tottering empire.

I had continued to correspond with Mary MacCarthy and had congratulated Desmond on his knighthood. Mary sent me good advice:

"Do all the time be keen on improving your writing – that is, your style," she wrote. *"Do your best to be fully interested in what you have to write and avoid hackneyed phrases. Plain writing is usually the most expressive. Count Tolstoy (though he is quite too severe on human nature and belongs of course to an altogether different age to ours), has in his novels a most wonderful power of simple expression 'which comes across'. Obscurity – which is not your failing*

– often conceals a very muddled mind and is, I think, a bad fashion of the day."

In April 1952, she had written to report that Desmond had been seriously ill. *"He has a strong heart, that helps him, but he is very depressed and suffering. He has had such a very long endurance of chest, bronchial and asthmatic trouble and he now worries very much about his writing and feels his powers are weakening."*

Desmond was more ill than Mary realised. He died early in June, in Cambridge, two days after the university had conferred on him the honorary degree of Doctor of Letters. He was seventy-five. *The Times* described him as *"a dramatic and literary critic of much grace and accomplishments... at his best and most individual in writing on the theatre. Indeed there have been few more discerning dramatic critics and his early work on the plays of Bernard Shaw are models of the genre."*

I had good personal reason to concur with the words of *The Sunday Times* obituary that *"nobody was less Blimpish or more indulgent to the aspirations of the young."*

Desmond's close friend G.M. Trevelyan lamented that his failure had been that he wrote few books. Some twenty years earlier a collection of his articles had been published in two volumes – *Portraits* and *Criticism* – but these had been selected for him by friends anxious to see his work appear between hard covers. Trevelyan expressed the hope that *"someone will now make a further selection from his more recent articles and publish them as a memorial to a fine scholar and critic."*

Mary did her best and wrote to tell me that she had been busy preparing a book of his essays. She died the following year and *The Times* obituary writer noted that *"though somewhat overshadowed by her husband's genius, she had a gift for literature which had she chosen to develop it might have given her a greater reputation than she in fact enjoyed."*

I took the training scheme seriously and, much to the annoyance of Chief Reporter Tom Stake, insisted on getting experience in the sub-editors' room. Terence Feeley had not bothered to learn sub-editing so why should I? I believed, however, that such experience would make me a better reporter. There was a cold war situation between the reporters' and subs' rooms. Stake, his ego boosted by his local celebrity status as the borough's football columnist, did not cooperate smoothly with the sharp-minded, business-like chief sub. My determination to get subbing training intensified their feud.

In the subs' room my interest in politics was well known and so I was often asked to handle parliamentary reports. The parliamentary correspondent for Kemsley's provincial evening papers was named James Margach and his convoluted reports arrived in our office mid-afternoon, as the last edition time approached. All too obviously written in a rush at the end of Commons Question Time, they were clumsy in style and often difficult to understand. Nobody in the subs' room wanted to handle them. My heart would sink as I watched the chief sub look along the cluttered table in my direction and say something to the effect: "Arthur, you're our political expert – see what sense you can make of this."

The often ungrammatical reports had to be rewritten at high speed, as the hand of the clock moved mercilessly toward edition time. *"Bloody Margach"* I intoned – but did not know how to pronounce his unusual name. Nobody else in the room seemed to know – or wanted to know. But, in due course, I was not a little surprised when it appeared above reports in *The Sunday Times.* How on earth had he

24

earned such promotion? Well, at least he would not have to write at such speed aboard the Kemsley flagship.

In the years ahead our paths would cross again, by which time we had all learned to pronounce his name.

In the early autumn of 1954, *"Jimmy"* James informed me that he had at last received news from the London office that the editorial director of the Kemsley provincial network had a vacancy for a diplomatic correspondent for the group's evening papers. Would I like the job? As I stammered out my excited acceptance James said with a friendly smile, *"I thought you'd be pleased. I'll let them know."*

A few weeks later I boarded a London-bound train, having said my farewells to all the warm and friendly folk of this grimy town who had helped me at the start of my career. I could not have foreseen that in less than twenty years I would return in a different role, to repay the debt by helping to set up the new County of Cleveland with Middlesbrough at its heart.

But no amount of local government reorganisation could solve the town's social and economic problems. Early in the twenty-first century it was rated in one survey as the worst town in Britain in which to live. Middlesbrough-born journalist Tracy Corrigan, writing in the *Daily Telegraph* in September 2010 lamented that the population of her hometown had dwindled by 20,000 in the last twenty years. She wrote: *"It's a common tale of urban decay: unemployment is high and often long-term; much of the workforce is employed in vulnerable sectors; educational achievement and life expectancy are low; and more than two-thirds of council wards are classed as deprived."*

According to research commissioned by the BBC, it was forecast that Middlesbrough was the most vulnerable place in England to the coming wave of public spending cuts to be announced by the coalition government in October 2010. North East England was warned that it would be the region least 'resilient' to the expenditure axe, as it had so many public sector jobs provided by Whitehall in the previous decade to mop up some of the local unemployment.

For some six decades since I left the tough Teesside town, it had been failed by government after government, by politicians of the main parties served by incompetent civil servants manning departments unfit for purpose. Most recently, it had been disgracefully failed by the Blair-Brown New Labour administrations, mesmerised by the 'get rich quick' success of City gamblers and noted for their lack of interest in stimulating and supporting heavy manufacturing industry of the type that once provided good jobs for the skilled workers of the North East.

Would the Tory-Lib Dem coalition be more committed to encouraging investment in this vital area of industrial activity?

CHAPTER TWO

In the Snake Pit

London looked good to me that autumn of 1954. I took over the flat in Leytonstone that my parents had just vacated, as my mother had become housekeeper to a wealthy Greek family in Paddington. Everything appeared to be working out well.

When I reported to Kemsley House on Gray's Inn Road I was not worried, therefore, when the editorial director told me that it had been decided that for a start – to get me used to London office routine – I would work as a reporter on the Northern Desk, which supplied news to Teesside, Tyneside and towns in the north-west. I was given to understand that this would last for only a few months. I was not told that the diplomatic correspondent's job I had been promised had since been given to another journalist – Peter Kirk, son of the Bishop of Oxford. Kirk had been foreign editor of the group's *Sunday Chronicle*, edited by one of Lord Kemsley's family. In 1954, however, the group had suffered a number of blows. A month-long national newspaper strike, started by electricians and engineers, had hit the whole industry causing the loss of six hundred million copies. It had done particular damage to Kemsley's inefficient and uneconomic operation. The high-living press lord, faced with mounting financial problems, told the staff that the *Sunday Chronicle* was to be merged with the *Empire News*.

To get Kirk out of the way of the disastrous merger he was sent on a world tour. Now he was on his way home and, although he had political ambitions, he was prepared to take, as a stopgap, the job that had been offered to me. To be fair to Kirk, I am sure he did not know of my involvement – and in due course I came to like and respect him. When I complained that I had been misled, I was told I had misunderstood the situation. Now it seemed, I had been offered the post only if a vacancy occurred. I phoned Jimmy James who said unfortunately there had been no offer in writing, but he was sure that he had been told that the post was available. I decided to leave Kemsley Newspapers as soon as possible. The man who had taken the decision in Kirk's favour was the high-flying C.D. Hamilton with whom Desmond MacCarthy had dealt in helping to get me on to the group's training scheme. It had been passed down the line to me by a bibulous Scot nicknamed *"The Red-Nosed Courtier"*. I had heard about Hamilton in Middlesbrough because he had started his journalistic career as a junior reporter on the *Evening Gazette*. He had made little impression, but people remembered him as a well turned out young man active in the Territorial Army. As an ex *"terrier"* he had received quick promotion on joining the Army at the outbreak of war. Trim and dapper, he rose to become the youngest acting brigadier and was awarded the DSO. Covered with wartime glory he was then faced, on demobilisation, with the prospect of returning to the reporters' room in Middlesbrough. Someone then decided that he should be moved instead to the more prestigious Tyneside paper, the *Newcastle Evening Chronicle*. There, the chief reporter did not know how to use him and so, for most of the time, he did very little. Before long, however, a member of the Kemsley family, who had served with him in the war, recommended that he should be appointed as personal assistant to Lady Kemsley, a prudish, limited woman who needed someone to look after her diary, travel arrangements and sundry other chores. A story about Lady Kemsley concerned a prize-winning bull pictured in all its glory in one of the group's newspapers. Offended by the prominence given to the animal's reproductive organ she insisted that this should be removed from the picture. The owner of the bull was furious at this editorial castration and sued for damages.

Hamilton headed for London and before long Lady Kemsley's female secretary was complaining to friends that he was *"a creep"*. But Lady Luck was smiling on him. In 1946, Lord Kemsley himself needed a PA and his wife suggested that Hamilton was the man for the job. Having won his lordship's confidence, he was told to get involved with the group's flagship, the *Sunday Times,* edited by the elderly, unadventurous William Hadley. In 1950, Hamilton ensured that H.V. Hodson, a donnish man and a Fellow of All Souls, took over from the 80-year-old Hadley. In the eleven years he was in charge the paper's circulation doubled to over a million.

Hamilton, I discovered, was viewed with near contempt by the foot-soldier journalists of the Kemsley provincial empire. They knew he had not made his mark as a reporter and that he could not write well. An experienced feature writer ghosted articles that appeared occasionally under his name. He made some bad appointments of editors and London editors of provincial papers and at times interfered with unhelpful effect in content. One such disaster was when he stopped the *Newcastle Journal* running a *Peter London* gossip column that, according to the editor, had helped to put on ten thousand readers. In Hamilton's opinion, however, that was not what Tynesiders wanted to read. The scrapping of the lively column about celebrities in London duly coincided with the loss of thousands of readers.

When it came to managing staff, he has been credited with success in promoting talented journalists – but he had a reputation also for sacking youngsters for no obvious reason. Some members of staff reported that when called to his office he had subjected them to unnerving periods of silence. He added to the problems of the provincial papers by being unable, through lack of experience, to judge the merits of those appointed as their London desk editors. There were some pompous, unproductive and unimaginative duds among them, some of whom were promoted to editor's chairs in provincial towns at a time when local papers were increasingly threatened by the spread of television and local radio stations.

The main problem, however, with the London-based back up service for the Kemsley, and later Thomson, provincial network of over fifty papers was simple – and ridiculous. London editors and reporters were told that their job was to compete with Press Association reports and not to waste time looking for local angles. As a result, provincial editors were deprived of hundreds of stories and features that would have created local interest and boosted circulation. The stupidity and waste of the system is highlighted by this story:

Norman Riley, a senior London editor told his deputy Victor Reeve that a ship which had been to the Antarctic had docked at Southampton and, if he would like a day out, he could go to write up the event. Victor, a great believer in the local angle, interviewed so many of the ship's crew that he disembarked with material enough for seventeen articles in his notebook – local interest features for towns and cities such as Aberdeen, Newcastle-upon-Tyne, Cardiff and Middlesbrough. Back in the office he found that Riley had left for home so he typed out his seventeen stories, each starting with a different regional bent. All were published and the provincial editors were delighted. Norman Riley, however, was not so pleased. When he saw the copies on his desk he turned on Reeve angrily and told him never to repeat his performance. He should have written one story, he railed, like an agency reporter, and that is what he must do in future.

I first met Victor when I joined the Northern Desk in the Kemsley newsroom. The Northern Editor was the decent but pernickety Fred Moore, bogged down in petty admin. Most of the productive work was done by the energetic, highly intelligent Victor whose father had been an editor in Newcastle. After serving as a bomber pilot in the war he had been a reporter on the Newcastle evening paper, sitting next to Hamilton during the ex-brigadier's short stint there. Victor had found him unimpressive.

The atmosphere in the big news room was redolent of a snake pit, with the under-employed London editors eyeing each other suspiciously, jealous of any small favour that floated down to a desk from the top management floor. One day the Red-Nosed Courtier told Victor he had been chosen to carry out an important task for Hamilton. He was to go to vet a property that Hamilton thought might be suitable for his son. A London editor senior to Victor, on learning of his errand, pulled rank and insisted on taking it over – presumably as a means of ingratiating himself with the boss. Soon after, the creepy fellow was made editor of an important provincial paper.

The moment of truth arrived for many in the newsroom one payday. A plump, jolly young woman came in carrying the usual brown envelopes containing our pay, followed by a thin, doleful female carrying white ones. Those handed the latter read to their dismay that their services would no longer be required after whatever period of notice was written into their contracts. Not only had Lord K decided to merge the *Sunday Chronicle* with the *Empire News*, but he had sold the *Daily Dispatch*, based in Manchester, to the *News Chronicle.* As part of the downsizing of his empire he also sold two loss-making papers in Glasgow. The ending of wartime restrictions on competition had made newspaper ownership more risky, especially for the less adventurous. In 1952, Kemsley had sold the *Daily Graphic* to Associated Newspapers, owned by Lord Rothermere.

Frustration and a greasy canteen diet had caused me to have a stomach pain that was suspected of being a grumbling appendix. After an operation I decided to take a holiday in the sun. I signed up to join a group on a guided tour of Yugoslavia that was just opening up for large-scale tourism. Travelling by train across Europe on hard wooden seats we arrived, at last, stiff, tired and hungry at the busy little port and resort of Opatija, on the northern end of the Adriatic. There we boarded a small ship for a cruise down the Croatian coast to Dubrovnik. We had an overnight stop at Split, part of the town housed within the massive ruined walls of what had once been the spectacular palace of the Roman emperor, Diocletian. The next day, as we cruised southwards arid cliffs rose up like great slag heaps until we reached Dubrovnik, *"Pearl of the Adriatic"*. Set in an azure sea and encircled by 13th century walls, the beautiful little city more than fulfilled my expectations. I could not wait to disembark and explore its quiet streets, for motor vehicles are not allowed in the city.

That evening, I strolled over the broad flagstones towards the Italian Baroque church of St Blaise, then enjoyed a fish supper washed down with local Riesling. Next morning, I walked around the walls, enchanted by the jigsaw of sunlit orange tiles topping the buildings, a melange of Gothic, Renaissance and Baroque. Swimming from the rocks that afternoon, I was alarmed to see that the wound from my recent appendix operation had started to open up. Advised to attend a medical centre outside the city walls I made my way there. In a corner of the waiting room a bloodstained bucket contained used bandages to the interest of a swarm of flies. The doctor who treated me picked up an instrument that looked none too pristine and probed the wound before announcing that it was nothing serious. He applied a dressing and refused my offer of payment. Feeling a little queasy, I thanked him and left, pondering the extent to which medical practice and hygiene had advanced here since the walls of Dubrovnik were first built. Excursions took us from Croatia into Montenegro to the stunning scenery of the Bay of Kotor and the medieval Venetian town of Cavtat, paved in marble and once favoured by Edward, Prince of Wales and Wallis Simpson. To conclude the holiday we drove north to Bled, a resort in the forest, mountain and lake setting of Slovenia. From there I visited the then regional capital of Ljubljana, where I climbed to the hilltop castle for a view of the Baroque buildings cascading down to the river far below.

I returned to London full of praise for Yugoslavia – but with this caveat: beneath the colourful surface of daily life was a dark and sinister sense of interracial hatred. I recounted to friends how local people – whether Croats or Serbs, Christians or Muslims – would extol a neighbouring beauty spot only to add that it was a shame about the inhabitants, who were a frightful bunch. To emphasise their dislike, they would run their hands across their throats in an unequivocally murderous gesture. It was clear that only the ruthless power of President Tito and his own form of Balkan communism was holding the country together. In due course we would witness the terrible bloodshed and racial atrocities that marked the break-up of the region following the removal of Tito's iron hand.

Refreshed and healed, I, meanwhile, returned to Kemsley House. Amidst the carnage in the London newsroom our corner remained intact. I was kept busy reporting events for

33

the Northern papers we serviced and began writing features for the Newcastle *Sunday Sun*. One day, I was sent to cover a Girl Guides' parade in the grounds of Windsor Castle, attended by Princess Margaret. At one point I was very close to her and was struck by her exceptional loveliness. Petite and curvaceous in her Chief Guide's uniform she had dazzling violet eyes. The Queen Mother's Steward, William Tallon, told me many years later that he once heard her tell a visitor, *"I have the most beautiful eyes in the world."*

Unbeknown to me that day in Windsor, she had been in love for some years with the handsome and much decorated wartime air ace, Group Captain Peter Townsend, who had been equerry to her late father King George VI. He had divorced in 1952 and now the affair was moving rapidly to an end – an end that was to provide me with my first big scoop. In June 1953, the Sunday *People* had revealed that newspapers abroad were reporting a romance between the flirtatious Princess and the handsome divorcé. In March 1955, the *Sunday Pictorial* reported that the Princess was trying to decide whether to renounce her right to succession to the throne and marry him. It emerged later that the Queen had told her that while she could become his wife she would have to give up her title and her income from the Civil List. Under the Royal Marriages Act, she could not marry before her twenty-fifth birthday without the Queen's permission. She was twenty-two when they began to consider getting married.

As news of their affair began to spread, Townsend was posted away from the Palace to Brussels. Following her twenty-fifth birthday he returned to Britain. The scene was set for the final act in a romance now being conducted in the full light of media publicity.

Arriving at the office one morning, I was told by Fred Moore that it had been decided that I should go to Uckfield in Sussex as quickly as possible, to report for the provincial group on what was to turn out to be the finale. Margaret was staying with friends in a country house on one side of the town and Townsend, based on an estate on the other, was visiting her daily by car. National newspapers were already carrying reports of the assignations. Moore told me that I would have a car and driver and had been booked into a *"B&B"*. I had never been on an out-of-town overnight assignment before. I gulped my thanks, packed my pith helmet and headed for deepest Sussex. That evening, having bought a toothbrush and a change of socks, I settled into my lodgings and wandered into the biggest and best inn in town and surveyed the competition. It propped up the bar in the form of half a dozen national newspaper reporters. I sidled up and, on seeing the doubles being ordered, decided I could not afford to get involved. I had never been on this type of expense account operation before and Moore had omitted to tell me how much I could spend. I watched my rivals roll into the dining room and command three-course meals, with wine. I ate a frugal supper and went to bed early.

The next morning, picked up by my driver, I joined the media motorcade as it followed Townsend's car along the country roads to the estate that hosted Princess Margaret. The reporters were prepared to hang around the gates together to await his departure. The most stylish of the pack was a young man sporting a cravat and driving an M.G. sports car, who worked for the *Daily Mirror*. His name was Desmond Wilcox and he eventually became a successful broadcaster and producer and married TV celebrity Esther Rantzen. I left them and walked up the road. Pushing through a hedge I saw Margaret and Townsend in the distance, strolling hand-in-hand and presumably trying to decide what to do. I wished I had a photographer with me.

In due course, our motorcade returned to Uckfield without a statement having been issued. I decided to adopt a different tactic the next morning. I asked my driver to arrive earlier and to wait in a pull-in on Margaret's side of town. There we sat until Townsend drove by. We shot out on his tail with the competition trailing well behind us. We were bumper to bumper so that, arriving at the estate, we drove through the gates with him before they could close on us. Townsend's car stopped immediately. I jumped out of mine and ran up to the door of his vehicle. Wearing a sports coat and slacks, he lowered his window looking somewhat bewildered. As the gatekeeper approached me I quickly asked Townsend if he could say anything about his future with the Princess. With a strained and sad expression he replied that he would not be seeing her again after that day. The gatekeeper was tapping me firmly on the shoulder and so I stepped back and the car drove on. As my own backed through the gate I walked out to be met by the hung-over horde. *"What did he say?!"* they called out.

"Nothing of any use," I replied, and headed for a phone box down the road.

Luckily, it had not been vandalised. Dame Ann Leslie, doyen of Britain's female columnists and one time *Daily Express* junior reporter, has recalled how in those cut-throat days in Fleet Street she was instructed in how to disable public phones, to prevent rivals from filing their stories.

On my return to the office the next day, nobody commented on my *"end of the affair"* exclusive. Perhaps the sleepy bunch had not realised it was a scoop. But as I had no intention of staying longer than it could take me to get another job, it was of no great consequence.

After Townsend told me he would not be seeing Margaret again, they returned to London separately on Monday, October 31 – but, in fact, he made a final visit to her at six o'clock that evening. One hour later, Margaret announced that she had decided not to marry him and stressed that she had made the decision alone. She had no doubt been helped to reach it by the intervention of Prime Minister Anthony Eden who had warned her that, if she married the divorced Townsend, it would be impossible for her to remain in line of succession to the throne and receive her share of money from the Civil List.

Meanwhile, in the previous March, Sir Richard Ackland, the austere, quixotic 15th baronet who had won Gravesend for Labour in 1947, resigned from the seat in a huff. Disenchanted and opposed to Labour's support for the hydrogen bomb, he decided to force a by-election and fight as an independent. Before the contest could be held, however, the Tory government called a general election. Peter Kirk, who was taking up *"my"* diplomatic correspondent's job, was chosen to fight Gravesend for the Conservatives. He won the seat on a split vote. The Kemsley group had lost him. He was to become a conscientious, much respected MP and a leading pro-European. He received a knighthood and died young.

As I had started to look for a job outside the crumbling Kemsley empire, I did not chase after the post. I saw an advertisement for someone to fill a vacancy for editor of *Forward,* the left-wing weekly journal that was being relaunched by friends of Labour leader, Hugh Gaitskell, to act as a counter to the Bevanite weekly *Tribune.* I had already become involved in Labour politics by joining the Leyton constituency party and was active in the Central London Fabian Society. I was interviewed by two of Gaitskell's close colleagues in the Commons, the accountant Jack Diamond – who had raised the money for the venture – and George Thomson, himself an experienced journalist. They displayed a courteous interest in my career but no doubt thought me rather green. When I expressed disapproval of the effect of the Trade Union block vote on policy forming at party conferences they were clearly unhappy. If they could have foreseen the imminent capture of key unions by anti-Gaitskellite left-wingers, they might have taken a more sympathetic view of my remarks. Indeed, when in 1956, the extreme left-winger, Frank Cousins, became General Secretary of the powerful Transport and General Workers' Union, the days when Gaitskell could rely on the trade union block vote had come to an end.

Shortly afterwards I received a letter informing me that I had not been appointed and I replied offering my spare time services as a reporter free of charge to help get the paper launched. I learned that the editor was to be Francis Williams, one time successful helmsman of the *Daily Herald*, who had become a well-known, affable pipe smoking TV pundit. Francis had been approached by the Gaitskell gang when they had been unable to find anyone suitable for the job. He had agreed to take it on, on a very part-time basis, his main contribution to be the considerable prestige of his name, advice and a weekly column. A young man named John Harris, with even less newspaper experience than me, was to be assistant editor at a very low salary. He would be responsible for the daily donkeywork. My offer of help was therefore gladly received and a few weeks later, I climbed the steep narrow stairs to a first floor office in High Holborn to introduce myself to Francis. George Thomson was also there and so began a life-long friendship with this decent, charming and astute Scottish politician who began his journalistic career writing the utterances of Desperate Dan, the cowboy of the *Dandy* comic, which had been launched in 1937. George had become MP for Dundee East in 1952 and had edited the old, more left-wing *Forward* from 1948-1953. Francis, in his most avuncular manner, made me welcome. George and I had a great respect for him and could scarcely believe we were working with such a legend of Fleet Street. Following his editorship of the Labour-supporting *Daily Herald*, he had done an admirable job as press adviser to Prime Minister Clem Attlee at 10 Downing Street. Attlee was not interested in the media. The Press Association tape machine installed at No. 10, to keep the occupants instantly abreast of the news, was called the *"cricket score machine"* by pipe smoking Clem. As for the word *"spin"*, this would have meant no more to him than the twist a bowler might put on a ball in a game. When Francis showed him a particularly important headline on a front page, Clem would nod and immediately turn to the sports page for the test-match score. In his personal dealings with the Press for No. 10, Francis always played a straight bat.

Having failed to get the editorship of *Forward*, I decided to try for a job on a left-ish national daily newspaper. My preference was for the *News Chronicle* which for over a hundred years had been a champion of social reform and humanity. Launched as the *Daily News* in 1846, its first Editor was the 34-year-old Charles Dickens and it had attracted brilliant journalists ever since. The latest in that great tradition was James Cameron and his commentaries on world affairs had helped lead me to decide to write asking for a job as a reporter. I was interviewed by the news editor, Tom Steele, a gaunt, intense man. Within a few days I received a letter offering me a post. I lost no time in giving my notice to the Kemsley management and headed for Fleet Street.

No doubt I was not missed by C.D. Hamilton who in a rather shifty manner had blocked my promised promotion to diplomatic correspondent. Following Roy Thomson's purchase of the Kemsley group in 1959, he was appointed editor of the *Sunday Times* two years later and, to his credit, added the successful colour magazine and Business News section. When Thomson went on to buy *The Times* in 1967 he was made Editor in Chief of both the daily and Sunday newspapers – and picked up a knighthood along the way.

Chapter Three
On Opportunity Street

Entering Fleet Street as a member of the journalistic fraternity for the first time, I felt a flush of excitement. As I turned down Bouverie Street to the corner office building of the *News Chronicle*, my heart beat faster. It was part of the Fleet Street village, noisy, bustling, packed with pubs and eateries, haunted by the ghosts of Samuel Johnson, Charles Dickens, G.K. Chesterton and other great writers and outsize characters. In the newspaper offices that lined the thoroughfare and the side streets that ran from it, the clatter of typewriters, the jangling of telephones and sub-editors' hoarse cries of 'copy!' joined with the roar of the presses to produce a vibrant, persistent din. Adding to this cacophony, strident newsboys along the pavements proclaimed their wares:

'STAR, NEWS, STANDARD – STAR, NEWS, STANDARD!' – London's three hotly competing evening papers.

In the often squalid rooms where reporters typed their stories, notices exhorted them with slogans such as 'Be fast, be accurate.' To some this was the street of adventure, to some the street of shame. To me, at the age of twenty-six, this was the street of opportunity.

The *News Chronicle* had been owned since the Boer War by the wealthy, liberal Cadbury family. They had been persuaded by the Liberal politician Lloyd George to put some of their chocolate money into what was then the struggling *Daily News*. In 1912, George Cadbury had merged it with the *Morning Leader* and in 1926, Edward Cadbury had laid the foundation stone of the office I was entering now. A few years later, the *Daily News,* having first taken over the *Westminster Gazette,* took the ailing *Daily Chronicle* under its wing to form the *News Chronicle.* I had witnessed the drama of its latest acquisition, when the Kemsley journalists had been told that it had bought Lord K's *Daily Dispatch* (circulation 463,000).

I was about to meet someone with a bizarre story to tell about that deal. He was Bill Pattinson, the Chronicle's ebullient deputy news editor – and a distinguished naval officer in World War II. The day before the well-kept secret of the take-over was to be announced, Bill was summoned to the editor's office and given a special mission. The most important outside contributor to the *Daily Dispatch* was a certain Gipsy Petulengro, whose horoscopes and forecasts were read avidly by many. Bill was told to leave at once on a covert operation to sign him up for the *News Chronicle* and in so doing, ensure that his readers stuck with the new, combined paper. Appropriately, Bill tracked Petulengro to a caravan and informed the man who made his living foretelling the future, *"Hello, I've got some news for you."*

"What's that then?" asked the puzzled seer.

"The News Chronicle has bought the Daily Dispatch," replied Bill. *"I'm here to offer you a job."*

Unabashed by his failure to have seen this coming, the gypsy signed a contract on the spot, helping the Chronicle to retain 300,000 readers of the old Dispatch from the start.

The *News Chronicle* has been described by others as *"a reporters' paper – the one other journalists read."* Apparently it had a long waiting list of journalists keen to be taken on and was known to be one of the most difficult papers to join. If I had known that when at Kemsley House I might have thought it was a waste of time to apply. Certainly one did not join the *Chronicle* for financial reward. In fact, compared to staff on most other Fleet Street papers, members of the Chronicle team were underpaid. But as I was soon to discover, they had a great sense of pride and enjoyed camaraderie unequalled elsewhere. Entering through the glass doors I passed a bust of Charles Dickens before being ushered upstairs to the newsroom, where news editor Tom Steele gave me a friendly welcome and introduced me to Bill. Other characters around the table included Denis Weaver, the one-time intrepid foreign correspondent who, while covering the Spanish Civil War, had been sentenced to death by Franco's men. He was saved by the intervention of the British Foreign Office. He had been one of a small band of *Chronicle* foreign correspondents, including J.C. Segrue and Vernon Bartlett, who almost alone among British reporters exposed the true aims of Hitler's Nazi Party.

In the next door reporters' room, I was given a seat and well-worn typewriter and was introduced to several of the staff including Betty Williams, daughter of my new friend Francis, editor of *Forward*. When I explained to Steele that I had been working in my spare time for them, he said he had no objection if I continued to do so. Clearly, he made a mental note that I had political contacts, so when political developments occurred outside the parliamentary arena, I was usually asked to report on them.

In my lunchtime and evening hours I got to know some of the Fleet Street pubs. The newspaper business, I soon discovered, floated, sometimes unsteadily, on a sea of alcohol. On my first day I had lunch with another *"new boy"*, Norman Crosland, at the famous Mooney's pub. In 1700, S.G. Mooney and Son, a Dublin-based brewery, had bought The Old Boar's Head, a tavern that dated back to 1605. It became the first Irish pub outside of Ireland. Norman and I tucked into steak and kidney pudding washed down with Guinness in a pokey, packed upstairs room. On the other side of Fleet Street stands its most famous pub, the 17th century Olde Cheshire Cheese. Although used in their time by such writers as Dickens, Yeats and Conan Doyle, it was not much used by any of the journalists I knew. It was regarded by my drinking colleagues as a place to take tourists. They chose instead the pub or pubs unofficially affiliated to their newspaper. The *Chronicle's* pub was The Feathers or the nearby White Swan, better known as The Mucky Duck. *Daily Express* boys used the Red Lion in Poppins Court, which became known as Poppins, or went to The Punch Tavern, Olde Bell or The Albion near Ludgate Circus. The *Daily Mirror* mob used The White Hart in Fetter Lane, otherwise known as *"the stab in the back"* because of the vicious nature of the office politics played out at the bar. Daily Telegraphers used The King and Keys on Fleet Street and journalists from all the papers drank in the Press Club, situated for some years in Salisbury Square with shabby furniture and cartoons festooning the walls.

When I was too short of cash to join friends for a *"wet lunch"* I would sometimes wander down to Christopher Wren's St Bride's Church, standing discreetly back from Fleet Street, its elegant spire rising in tiers like a wedding cake. It was the tallest spire he ever designed but was not built until the start of the 18th century. The Great Fire of London destroyed over eighty churches in 1666 and Wren rebuilt fifty. In December 1940, St Bride's was once again in flames after being hit by a German incendiary bomb. Restored at great expense, it was completed in 1957 and rededicated by the Queen in time for me to enjoy it in my more sober moments. I learned that more elevated scribblers such as Milton and Pepys had links with it.

One of my first assignments was to be sent to report Winston Churchill addressing a pro-Europe rally at Central Hall, Westminster. The Euro-enthusiasts regarded him as a founding father of the Common Market. He was, however, very sceptical about what benefits membership of that organisation would bring to Britain. In fact, he is on record in private correspondence of underlining the fact that Britain had another role which it could not abdicate – that of leader of the British Commonwealth. In his conception of a United Europe he wrote that he never contemplated the diminution of the Commonwealth. He saw Britain as *"a friend and sponsor"* of the United Europe movement rather than as a member. At Westminster Hall, however, he said nothing to upset the pro-European *Chronicle* that led the front page with my report.

In April 1955, Anthony Eden had at last taken over as Prime Minister from Churchill and had wisely called a general election the following month. This resulted in the Tories being returned with an increased majority – 345 seats compared to Labour's 277, the Liberals limping along behind with only six. Eden's popularity, however, did not last for long. His lack of interest and knowledge of domestic policy issues quickly became a problem and he began to get a bad press – a situation not helped by worrying economic problems. Meanwhile, Hugh Gaitskell's election as Labour leader following Attlee's retirement had given a momentary boost to the morale of Labour supporters and posed a sharp new challenge to Eden, especially on economic affairs. In an attempt to counter growing disenchantment with his administration, Eden had a reshuffle of ministers at the end of 1955, moving Harold Macmillan from the Foreign Office to the Treasury and replacing him by Selwyn Lloyd, a colourless, unhappy man soon to be lampooned as Mr Celluloid by my friend Bernard Levin in his weekly political column in *The Spectator*.

Through my contacts at *Forward,* I learned in the following summer of 1956 that Selwyn Lloyd had given an off-the-record briefing on the Middle East situation to members of Labour's National Executive Committee. During this he asserted that President Nasser of Egypt was a megalomaniac whose aim was to destroy Israel. Lloyd had not seemed comfortable in imparting this information and it was assumed he was a mouthpiece for Eden who was anxious to get Labour onside. In July the USA, followed by Britain, withdrew offers of aid for the planned Aswan High Dam, a project vital for Nasser's ambition to boost Egypt's shaky economy. He responded by nationalising the Suez Canal Company, declaring that he would finance the dam from the revenues provided by users of the canal – and without Western aid. As I read the headline in the *News Chronicle* I gave a whoop of excitement. I had great sympathy for the poverty-stricken Egyptian people. Moreover, as a Labour Party supporter and believer in nationalisation as a means of dealing with certain situations, I thought Nasser had every right to do this. His action, however, was immediately condemned as illegal by the West and Eden told the Commons that Britain was consulting with other governments concerned. To my surprise and disappointment, Gaitskell supported his statement and asked whether the problem would be referred to the U.N.'s Security Council.

Despite Nasser's assurance that Egypt's international commitment would not be affected, Eden was determined to retaliate, in the ill-based belief that Nasser could no more be trusted than Hitler, with whom he had tried to negotiate as Foreign Secretary in the 1930s. With Britain, America and France deciding to set up an international agency to protect freedom of passage through the canal, Eden decided to prepare for possible military action by giving the Government wide powers and calling up recruits – a move that could affect me personally. Ever since my call-up as a Z reservist in 1951, I had been a member of the front-line reserve that could be mobilised without a special proclamation. I was by now Captain Adjutant of an ordnance vehicle company – just the type of unit that was likely to be involved in an operation against Nasser. My problem was that, while prepared to be in the front line of defence against an aggressive move by Soviet Russia, I was deeply unhappy at the prospect of being involved in an invasion of a poor Third World country desperately striving to use its few natural resources to improve the lot of its people. I decided that if I were to be called up I would refuse to go on the grounds that I volunteered in the face of a communist threat and that no right-minded Briton could have expected to be called upon to take part in a war of aggression against a country such as Egypt.

At a meeting of the Central London Fabian Society I was applauded when I denounced Gaitskell for his *"Palmerstonian utterance".* Like Barbara Castle, I took the view that Gaitskell had let down the Labour Party by supporting Eden's initial statement in the Commons. For the first time, I began to doubt Gaitskell's judgement and the excuse given later that he privately did not believe the Government would be mad enough to launch a military attack on Nasser was to me not a satisfactory explanation for his conduct. It was Gaitskell's initial mistake in supporting Eden's cynical ultimatum to Egypt that led to the Suez War that first brought his wife Dora to my attention. A Jewish refugee and passionate Zionist, she had considerable influence over the Labour leader whom she once described as *"too soft".* In my opinion this stocky, tenacious little woman had got him off on the wrong foot and she was deeply upset when he changed his views and led the opposition to Eden's war.

Following Nasser's nationalisation move, the top legal adviser to the Foreign Office warned the Government that a resort to force by Britain would not be permitted under the U.N. Charter. Lord Chancellor Kilmuir played the political game and over-ruled him, providing Eden with the advice he wanted. Matters got worse in mid-October when the French persuaded Eden to collude with an attack by Israel on Egypt's Sinai frontier. Appalled by the direction of events, Anthony Nutting and Edward Boyle resigned from the Government. William Clark, the able and honourable journalist who was Press Adviser at 10 Downing Street also quit. Foreign Secretary Selwyn Lloyd denied in the Commons that there had been collusion, committing what should have been the unforgivable crime of deliberately lying to Parliament over the country's involvement in war. In fact, Foreign Secretary Selwyn Lloyd believed he could have got a peaceful settlement of the Suez dispute at the U.N. tripartite talks between Britain, France and Egypt. He thought the Egyptians were sincere in wanting a peaceful solution, but the French were in bellicose mood. He was recalled from New York to take part in the secret invasion talks with the French and Israelis. The cynical plan, worthy of Hitler, was for Israel to invade Egypt and for Britain and France to call on both sides to cease-fire. Then each would withdraw ten miles from the Suez Canal under threat of attack by British and French forces if they refused. Egypt, justifiably, refused to comply with this outrageous demand and so the Anglo-French fleet set sail. Edward Heath, the Tory Chief Whip, revealed later how he witnessed Cabinet Secretary Sir Norman Brook sadly leaving the Cabinet room having been ordered to destroy Eden's copy of the secret invasion plan that Eden then denied had existed. The Israeli copy eventually came to light in 1996. The only ministers who knew at the time of the illegal operation were Selwyn

Lloyd, Chancellor of the Exchequer Harold Macmillan and RAB Butler. Of that group, only Macmillan at first completely backed the plan. In due course he was the first to accept it had failed when faced with massive selling of Sterling and a severe threat to the economy. Heath did his best to persuade Eden to pull back from the brink, fearing that this ill-judged act of aggression would split the country and seriously damage the Tory Party. The Attorney General, Sir Reginald Manningham-Buller, warned Eden that he was unable to devise an argument to justify the proposed aggression. The Lord Chancellor Lord Kilmuir, however, exceeded his role and, bending legal principles, sought to produce a case for Eden. He had no authority to offer this dishonest advice but to Kilmuir loyalty to the PM came first.

As for my military situation, the War Office decided that they were not so desperately short of officers that they needed to call on me. Certainly my unit would have been a liability at Suez, under-trained, ill equipped and inexperienced as it was. But I heard of some fellow officers who were called up to take part in the great fiasco and two of them, involved in the motor trade as self-employed operators, returned to Britain to find their businesses ruined.

As a dedicated supporter of the Labour Party at that time, I could not have believed that in due course a Labour government would be guilty of its own "Suez style' adventure – the appalling illegal war of aggression against Iraq. Like Anthony Eden, the vainglorious Anthony Blair, a second rate lawyer who if he knew any international law decided to ignore it, mislead an ill-informed Commons as he took Britain to war over the threat of non-existent weapons of mass destruction.

In holding the view that Nasser had the right to nationalise the Suez Canal Company and that Eden's attack on Egypt was in breach of international law I was in tune with the opinion of the *News Chronicle's* editor Michael Curtis. Unfortunately, Laurence Cadbury, the paper's owner, did not support the Curtis line and when 25,000 readers cancelled their subscriptions as a result of the paper's anti-Suez stance, Curtis' position was seriously weakened. Certainly the struggling paper could ill-afford the loss of so many readers, a large proportion of whom had been *"bought"* with the purchase of the right-wing *Daily Dispatch* title.

Curtis, formerly chief leader writer on the paper, had become editor in 1954. Robin Cruickshank, his predecessor, had warned him that the *Chronicle* was in serious financial difficulties and that, as a last resort, Laurence Cadbury was prepared to sell it to the *Daily Mail,* owned by Lord Rothermere. It was true that chocolate millionaire Cadbury was out of sympathy with the paper's great liberal tradition and as a moderate conservative, preferred to read the Mail. When in conversation he had an irritating giggle and the sick joke in the office was that Cadbury *"giggled while the Chronicle burned"*.

In fact, before taking on the task of editor Curtis had proposed that the paper be turned into a quality tabloid – easy to read and intelligent – aimed at younger people. Cadbury, however, failed to grasp the concept and the idea came to nothing. Later, Curtis suggested that the paper should merge with the *Daily Herald,* the decent but often dull T.U.C.-linked newspaper, by then also struggling to survive. That, too, received the thumbs down. Cadbury had no taste for becoming involved with a Lib-Lab daily.

When the loss of readers caused by the *Chronicle's* anti-Suez stand created a new circulation crisis, Curtis tried again. Assisted by Mike Randall, his deputy, whom he had persuaded to leave the *Daily Mirror* in 1956, he produced a plan for a broadsheet – a liberal *Daily Telegraph* in style. Once again, the board said *"No"*.

Randall provided some much needed technical expertise to the operation and in later years we became close friends. I contributed to his book of memoirs of life in Fleet Street. He had a number of stories about the fabled meanness of Cadbury. The old skinflint travelled to the *Chronicle's* office by bus and had even chosen a flat to live in because it was near the stop. It was a service flat that could provide good meals from the block's restaurant, but it was Cadbury's custom to inform guests that the food was not good and that he would be cooking himself. He would then put on a waiter's jacket, select packets of frozen food from his refrigerator and serve up an unappetising plate of meat and potatoes.

The *Chronicle's* Foreign Editor, Tom Baistow, was walking along Bouverie Street with Cadbury one day in the fifties and said he was on his way to lunch. *"Where do you eat?"* asked the boss. Baistow replied that he was going to The Wellington, a restaurant used by James Cameron, Michael Foot and other friends. Cadbury asked how much lunch cost there and Baistow replied that the bill was usually between five shillings and seven and sixpence. Cadbury emitted one of his famous giggles. *"That's more than I pay!"* he snickered, going on to explain that as a director of the Bank of England he was going there to use the subsidised canteen, that served a good lunch for only one shilling and nine pence.

I suspect he was tucking into *"subsidised"* turtle soup and other delicacies on the night I was sent to report on the Lord Mayor's autumn banquet at Guildhall to be addressed by Prime Minister Eden. The Suez mess was at its height, the country deeply divided, but Eden got a loud ovation as he entered the hall. What was noticeable to me was the glum visage of his cabinet colleague RAB Butler who followed him in a manner that suggested he was distancing himself from the architect of the crisis. Labour leader Hugh Gaitskell had appealed, in a broadcast about the invasion, to rebel Tory MPs to bring Eden down and find a new PM who would halt the military activity and order a ceasefire. Many in Parliament assumed that the appeal was aimed at Butler who was rumoured to be distinctly wobbly on the issue. In the run-up to the resignation of Eden in January 1957, following the breakdown in his health aggravated by the collapse of his Suez policy, Fleet Street's political correspondents had been speculating on his successor. The *News Chronicle's* Ian Trethowan, like most of his competitors in the Commons Press Gallery, was tipping Butler as the man most likely to take over at No. 10. I was surprised. It seemed to me that the Tories would not forgive RAB for prevaricating over the Canal. The word had got around that he was unsteady and unsound. In any case, his legendary ambiguity and privacy had not endeared him over the years to the blunt-speaking clubbable members of the Tory squirearchy. They were not sure if they could trust him. In my opinion, most Tory MPs would prefer Harold Macmillan, despite the fact that, as Chancellor, he had been the man to cause the retreat from Suez by warning of the devastating effect of American economic pressure on Sterling and the reserves. Drinking in the Chronicle's pub *The Feathers* I aired my views to Tom Steele and Bill Pattinson. With good reason they had a great respect for Trethowan and were surprised to hear me challenge his judgement. When I was proved right they remembered our conversation.

My ambition on joining the *Chronicle* was to become a diplomatic correspondent. In *The Feathers* I would hang around on the fringes of the foreign desk staff, listening to their stories, hoping to become accepted. Foreign Editor Tom Baistow, an uncompromising fighter for truth, had helped recruit James Cameron to the paper. Together they fought their battles for humanity and the dignity of the individual everywhere in the world. They were experts at puncturing cant and hypocrisy. Cameron, one of the finest, most travelled foreign correspondents of the 20th century, would entertain with his dry humour as he drank and chain-smoked through the evening. Tom, who had worked for five national dailies, had been *"splash sub"* at the *Daily Sketch* in Manchester before joining the *Chronicle* as picture editor in the mid 1930s – a period when the paper was noted for its stand against fascism. He could be very argumentative. Richard Crossman, when editor of the *New Statesman,* was to describe him as *"a cocky little Scotsman who liked his whisky".* Tom himself was to sum up his life in journalism as *"one long ego trip in excellent company... and all expenses paid."*

Often they would be joined at the bar by the grizzled Willie Forrest, a highly experienced foreign correspondent who had covered the Spanish Civil War for the *Daily Express.* The quiet spoken Scot had been a member of the Communist Party and assisted the Republican cause with political activities. In Spain he got to know Ernest Hemingway whom he described with distaste as brash and mostly drunk and rowdy in the bars and hotels. During the Second World War he met up with the author again – in London. It was June 1944 at the height of the VI missile offensive against the city. Invited up to his suite in The Dorchester Hotel, he found to his amazement that Hemingway had plotted on a map where the missiles had fallen and had concluded that the Germans were trying to destroy him personally. The doodlebugs, as he imagined, were closing in on The Dorchester. *"He was as mad as a hatter,"* said Willie.

I had a word with him about joining the Foreign Room team and his advice was to go away and learn Russian… a diplomatic way, I suppose, of getting rid of me for a while!

Then there was Norman Clark, the self-effacing former war and foreign correspondent, who was heading up the Foreign Desk when I joined the paper. Unbeknown to most, he was conducting a desperate battle behind the scenes to save the paper. Suspecting that owner Laurence Cadbury was planning to sell it off, he tried to persuade other members of the Cadbury clan to oppose such a move.

Some members of the foreign room were involved in the growing campaign against nuclear weaponry. Cameron had witnessed the atom bomb tests at Bikini Atoll and Woomera, Australia. After these experiences he became a founder member of the Campaign for Nuclear Disarmament. Earlier in his career his vivid reports from the Vietnam battlefront had done much to build up opposition to that war which he described as *"both imbecile and brutal"*.

Ritchie Calder, the *Chronicle's* outstanding science correspondent, was also a leading member of CND and together with their friend the left-wing Labour politician Michael Foot they would be in the front line of marches against the bomb. Ritchie had the gift of being able to accurately interpret science to the man in the street in language he could understand. He had reported for the *Daily Herald* from 1930-41, covering the appalling unemployment and social suffering of the period. As a result, he had become an active member of the Labour Party, but although aligning himself with the pacifist left wing he had done important government work during the war. As a member of the Army's feeble front line reserve I did not approve of the call for unilateral nuclear disarmament. On the grounds of self-preservation alone, we needed the bomb to deter the Russians.

With no foreign room vacancy in sight I continued my general reporting. One night, I was told to accompany a junior member of the City office staff to track down and interview Sir Bernard and Lady Docker – a fabulous, high-living couple who were once again in the news. Sir Bernard, the wealthy managing director of BSA (Birmingham Small Arms Company) that, among other things, manufactured motorcycles and Daimler cars, had been sacked. Lady Norah Docker, who had progressed from pretty barmaid to a hostess at the Café de Paris, was said to be very upset. She had a taste for gold-plated Daimlers upholstered in mink or zebra skin. Her often outrageous conduct made her a favourite of the gossip columnists who nicknamed her *"Naughty Norah"*. Our news editor suspected that on such a disastrous day for Sir Bernard, Norah might well produce a headline in her own right by blowing her top in a West End night club. My city office partner was a bright young reporter named Patrick Sergeant. In due course he became city editor of the *Daily Mail*, creating the highly successful *Money Mail* section and later the magazine *Euromoney*. His achievements earned him a knighthood and a fortune. Patrick was well known to the Dockers and Norah appeared to like him. We tracked them down to an expensive Mayfair restaurant and sat at the bar while they ate a gloomy dinner. Norah was very upset and, grateful that we kept our distance in the restaurant, invited us back to their apartment for a drink. Sir Bernard left her with us, tearfully sinking champagne. She had some hard barmaid's words to say about the BSA board that had finally had enough of her husband's expensive style of living. Not wishing to take advantage of a lady, however, we decided there was nothing more to report that night. But their exploits, sometimes featuring their luxurious yacht, continued to keep them in the headlines. The media made the most of the occasion when they invited a group of working dockers to join them for a party on the vessel. Then, in 1958, while visiting Monaco for the baptism of Prince Rainier's son Albert, Norah, feeling slighted, threw a miniature Monégasque flag on the floor at a royal function. Rainier, deeply offended by this insult, banned her and Bernard from the principality and, worse, by agreement with France, from the entire Riviera coast. This was a severe blow to their riotous social life.

On a more cultured level I was assigned one day in October 1956 to shadow members of Russia's superb Bolshoi Theatre Ballet Company who had arrived in London for the first time since the war to perform at the Covent Garden Opera House. The newsroom had decided that there was a good chance that, having been allowed to pass though the Iron Curtain to the West, one or two of the fabulous dancers might be tempted to defect. I spent tedious hours watching a hotel near Leicester Square where they were being housed and eventually followed them to the Opera House for their final rehearsal before the performance next evening of *Romeo and Juliet* danced to the music of Prokofiev. No other newspaper had bothered to shadow them and I skulked for a time in the dark outside the theatre with no one to talk or drink with. Unable to enter the theatre by the front door, I eventually wandered down a side street and there found an unlocked entrance. I climbed up many fights of stone steps until I arrived at a door opening on to a balcony. The rehearsal was in full swing, the orchestra playing the haunting music that I had never heard before. Alone, I sat in the darkness. The Prima Ballerina Ulanova was billed to dance the role of Juliet and I could only assume that it was her I watched. The combination of her dancing and the music nearly moved me to tears. Then came the magnificent stately dance of the Knights. I had to restrain myself from jumping to my feet and shouting *"Bravo!"* Instead, fearful of being locked in by the doorman whose earlier carelessness had enabled me to trespass on the sublime performance, I scurried back down the steps to find a telephone. The night news editor, a stiff-collared, white-cuffed ex-Foreign Office man named Jim Barnes told me to phone in a colour piece – a curtain raiser for what was to be London's cultural event of the year. Then he made the mistake of phoning the *Chronicle's* ballet critic. Fearing that my enterprising 'advance' report would not make either the newspaper or her popular with the stuffy Opera House management she insisted successfully that it should be spiked.

On Britain's political stage the leading man, handsome Anthony Eden, had taken his last bow. Aggravated by stress incurred by the failure of the Suez campaign, his health had failed and he announced his retirement. RAB Butler, misled by the press, expected to replace him at No. 10. Every newspaper except one had been forecasting that he would get the job. It was for members of the Cabinet to decide. Lord Salisbury, as senior Cabinet Minister, assisted by the Lord Chancellor Lord Kilmuir, sounded them out one by one. Salisbury, known as *"Bobbety"*, had a problem pronouncing his *R*'s. *"Which is it?"* he asked, *"Wab or Hawald?"*

RAB was deeply shocked when Chief Whip Edward Heath informed him, *"It's Harold."*

It was a crippling blow to his confidence. He could not understand why it had happened. The problem went back a long way. To right wingers in the party he had a reputation as a pre-war appeaser and someone who had been too keen to give India independence. More recently, his neutral approach on taking over as Chancellor of the Exchequer from Labour's Hugh Gaitskell in 1951 had given birth to the word *"Butskellism"* – a word of abuse used by those who had hoped for a more robust Tory approach to economic management. Some just regarded him as *"too clever by half"*.

Chief Whip Heath was certainly not sorry to see Eden depart. Apart from having the heavy responsibility of holding the Tory parliamentary party together, he had been very unhappy about the Suez adventure and was fed-up with having to deal with the jittery Eden who would call him at all hours to seek reassurance in the face of growing press criticism and speculation. Almost simultaneous with Eden's departure, a vacancy occurred in the *News Chronicle's* team in the Parliamentary Press Gallery. John Waddell, the third man in the team, had asked to be given a different job. News editor Tom Steele had to find another reporter to work under both Ian Trethowan, the lobby correspondent and Douglas Brown, the parliamentary sketch writer. He had been impressed by my correct forecast of the Tory leadership contest and my political contacts. He told me the job was mine.

At some stage in the endless circulation war between Fleet Street papers the *News Chronicle* had employed a character named Lobby Lud to tour seaside resorts when people were on their summer holidays, giving away pound notes to those who challenged him with the words, *"You are Lobby Lud and I claim the reward!"*

In the previous summer I had been assigned to accompany him and report on the exchanges. It was now a case of moving on from Lobby Lud… to lobby lad.

CHAPTER FOUR
Parliamentary Press Man

I took my seat in the Parliamentary Press Gallery on the first day that Harold Macmillan entered the Commons Chamber as Prime Minister. He had not had time to ensure that his newly reshuffled ministerial team was working smoothly. There was confusion as to who should be answering which question at the daily Question Time hour. It gave me the opportunity to write a light-hearted mickey-take reflecting badly on the competence of the new administration. To my surprise, no other gallery reporter bothered to do likewise. I received a note of congratulation from Tom Steele, the News Editor. It was to be my daily chore to report Question Time when ministers were grilled by the Opposition – and sometimes by disenchanted members from their own side of the Chamber. It ended at 3.30pm and I then had to rush to the telephone to alert Steele to any stories that had emerged before he attended the Editor's daily four o'clock conference for the final planning of the paper. Steele was always in a tense, impatient mood at that time of day, his ulcers giving him hell. My call to him was the most worrying, least enjoyable part of my new job.

As for Ian Trethowan and Douglas Brown, I could not have chosen two nicer, more helpful and professional people under whom to work. On my first day Ian arranged for me to receive a slim booklet entitled *"Lobby Practice"*. In rather pompous language it spelt out the code of behaviour laid down for those journalists who, like me, had been nominated by their newspapers to enjoy the right to enter the private Members' Lobby immediately outside the Commons Chamber. The numbers of those permitted to do this were controlled by the Sergeant-at-Arms of the Commons. The Lobby rules were basically the same as those followed by any sensible and decent journalist, such as not revealing one's sources without their permission or the collective meetings held by the Lobby. As a result, some, mostly provincial, journalists kidded their naïve editors that they had received individual personal guidance from some unnamed minister or civil servant. I was to learn from Trethowan that the first man to become a Lobby Correspondent was the astute Chief Parliamentary Reporter of *The Daily News* (later to become the *News Chronicle"*). He was Henry Lucy and his reports in the 1870s were so admired that other rival papers were obliged to follow suit.

Fulfilling my role as the *Chronicle's* latest in that line, I wandered down to the famous space outside the Commons chamber to make myself known to MPs. As I stood there, Edward Heath, the Government's Chief Whip, emerged from the Whip's office and I stepped forward to intercept him. Heath had been employed at Brown-Shipley, the merchant bank where my father worked as messenger and catering manager for the board. Heath knew my father well and when I introduced myself he appeared delighted to meet me. He promised always to do his best to help me. That was a good start and Ian, who was entering the Lobby at that moment, was surprised and impressed. Heath was credited with having done a good job in helping to hold the Tory Parliamentary Party together during Suez. Some rebels, however, bore him a grudge for years for what they alleged were bullying and unscrupulous tactics employed by the whips to make them toe the line. I believe that one reason he was so tough with rebels was that he himself had been opposed to the Suez operation but had felt that it was his duty to Eden in his key role as Chief Whip to soldier on rather than quit and cause trouble. By the time I entered the

Lobby the trouble was being caused by a group of right-wing Tory MPs – led by Viscount Hinchingbrook – who were opposed to Britain's withdrawal from the Canal zone and who were known as *"The Suez Rebels"*.

Hovering in the Lobby it was not long before I met up with the few Labour MPs known to me. Arthur Palmer and Hilary Marquand from the Cleveland and Middlesbrough constituencies gave me a warm welcome as did George Thomson, Douglas Jay and Jack Diamond of *Forward*. Reg Sorensen, MP for my local Leyton constituency, was especially pleased to see me as I had become very active in the party. On the Tory side I soon met up with Jocelyn Simon, who had been elected MP for Middlesbrough West in 1951 and within a few months had been appointed as Parliamentary Private Secretary to the Attorney General. He had then become Parliamentary Under Secretary for the Home Office under RAB Butler and in 1958 was to succeed Enoch Powell as Financial Secretary to the Treasury. He was one of the most talented and likeable Tories to enter the Commons in the early 1950s. A barrister by profession, I found him charming, courteous, cultured, erudite and witty. I wrote to congratulate him on his appointment to the Treasury and arranged for him to be guest of honour at a small Lobby luncheon club where he was a great success. Soon afterwards he was made Solicitor General with a Knighthood. As one of my best Tory Commons contacts, however, he did not last long. In 1962, he resigned his seat to become President of the Probate, Divorce and Admiralty Division of the High Court. He was then appointed a Law Lord and in the High Court became an outspoken opponent of changes in the law aimed at making divorce easier.

To widen our circle of contacts and improve our newsgathering, Ian and I were members of a small syndicate. Ian explained on my first day that members of the

Lobby worked in such groups and that the *Daily Herald* men, for example, shared information with the *Daily Telegraph* team. The *News Chronicle,* however, did not want to share information with national newspaper competitors and so had formed a successful syndicate with two hard-working journalists representing leading provincial papers in the Lobby. They were Douglas Haig of the *Birmingham Post* and Trevor Lloyd-Hughes of the *Liverpool Daily Post* who in due course was to become Prime Minister Harold Wilson's Press Secretary at 10 Downing Street. They were a good choice, for each could rely on getting sound information from the numerous MPs whose constituencies were in their papers' circulation areas.

I soon learned that Trevor had a nickname in the Press Gallery. It was *"Tigger"* from A.A. Milne's stories of Winnie the Pooh. Trevor, ever on the track of news, had earned it from his bustling approach to questioning MPs. He would virtually pounce with a bounce on the defenceless politicians as they crossed the Members' Lobby and subject them to a grilling. Hard working Francis Boyd of *The Guardian* also had a nickname – Eeyore. For like the gloomy, thistle-munching donkey in the Pooh tales, he trod a lugubrious path as he toiled for his paper. Both of these experienced characters were very helpful to me during my early Press Gallery days – and perhaps at times regarded me as Winnie, the bear of little brain. Both eventually received well-earned knighthoods.

But if 1957 had started well for me, it was to prove a bad year for the *News Chronicle.* Despite all Curtis' efforts to improve the paper and widen its readership, circulation continued to fall. The scrapping of newsprint rationing that year was a particularly serious blow to the paper. When paper was rationed, advertisers had an arrangement under which their advertisements were shared out fairly evenly among the competing titles. When it ended and newspapers began to carry more pages these advertisers started to give their business to the papers with the largest circulations. To provide the extra pages needed to keep the paper competitive Curtis proposed to the board that the newspaper's price should be raised to three pence. The board was not prepared to take the risk. As the unadventurous directors had also turned down his plan to convert the paper into a broadsheet *Daily Telegraph*-style liberal publication, Curtis resigned. Michael Randall was offered the Editor's post but refused and also left the struggling paper. To the dismay of the staff, Norman Cursley, who had been a cautious, uninspiring assistant editor for some ten years, was promoted to acting editor. I shared the general suspicion that he had been appointed to prepare the paper for the last rites. Curtis took employment with the Aga Khan for whom he founded the East African Newspaper Group based in Nairobi. Randall, eventually, became editor of the *Daily Mail* in 1963, replacing William Hardcastle, a popular journalist who went on to enjoy a successful career in broadcasting. Lord Rothermere, owner of the Mail, when asked by a friend why he had made a change of editors, replied: *"I tried a short, fat one and that didn't work, so now I'm having a long, thin one."*

And, in fact, that did work. Randall, a Labour supporter, set out to raise the Mail's standards of reporting and foreign news coverage and improved it to such an extent that it won the *"Newspaper of the Year"* award in January 1966. Randall's reward was to be sacked the following December, being told by Rothermere that he did not intend to give any reason other than his wish to have yet another new editor.

Randall had shown what a good editor he would have been for the *News Chronicle.* It was much to my regret that, because I was so new to the paper and so junior, I did not get to know him well at the time. In later life, however, I caught up with him in Lewes, Sussex. After working for the *Sunday Times* he had ended up on the *Brighton and Hove Gazette and Mid Sussex Times*. His private life had been a mess, with three broken marriages, and he was drinking heavily. But he could be great company. He knew how to laugh at life and he had a fund of hilarious stories about the ups and downs of Fleet Street, the mind-boggling expense account allowances and monumental binges.

In my exploration of the Houses of Parliament, I would take a walk to the Central Lobby before my Question Time stint at 2.30pm. At that time it was an exciting and bewildering place, crowded with people waiting to lobby MPs on their pet causes and complaints. Amid the buzz of talk, a name would be called. Someone, answering to that name, would push their way through the throng to the desk by the passageway that leads to the inner Members' Lobby. There, if they were lucky, their MP would be waiting but more often than not they would be told that their Member had not been located.

As I loitered in the Members' Lobby I found the Tory MPs to be noticeably tribal. A lot of them wore Old Etonian or Brigade of Guards ties with their sober, well tailored Savile Row suits. They wore hats from Locks and shoes from Lobbs of St James' and smelt of essences blended by Trumpers, the gentlemen's hairdresser in Curzon Street. A lot of them used high-ranking service titles and some had long and complicated names. The longest I can remember was Sir Hugh Vere Huntly Duff Munro-Lucas-Tooth, Baronet. Understandably, such names at times caused confusion. Colonel Sir Walter Bromley Davenport (MP for Knutsford) had gone to address a meeting of the Tory faithful. The Chairman said how pleased and delighted he was to introduce *"Sir Walter Bromley from Davenport"* whereupon his better-informed Vice-Chairman hissed, *"You've got his name wrong!"*

"Oh dear," flustered the Chairman, *"I do apologise! I should of course have said... Sir Walter Davenport from Bromley!"*

Sir Walter, a boisterous ex-Army boxing champion had served as a Tory Whip from 1948-51. On duty one evening to ensure that Tory MPs stayed on for a late vote, he saw someone slinking passed him towards the exit and promptly bellowed in his stentorian Guard's voice, *"You rat!"* His challenge being ignored, the irate Colonel gave the suspected defaulter a hefty kick bringing the man to the floor. The victim recovered his feet and turned out to be the Belgian Ambassador. Sir Walter was sacked from the Whips' office – and his place was taken by the young Edward Heath, receiving his first step up the greasy ladder of government.

Among others with service ranks adding to the length of their names were Major Sir Harry Legge-Bourke and Rear Admiral Morgan Morgan-Giles. Some of the Tory knights of the shires were richer in acres than ready cash. One such horsey, fox-hunting pillar of the establishment, getting towards the end of his life, told his eldest son: "I haven't much to leave you, but I'll give you these three pieces of advice. Never mix port with whisky; never hunt north of the Trent; and never have sexual relations with your wife before breakfast in case something better turns up before lunch."

A sharp fall in Britain's gold and dollar reserves in the late summer of 1957 caused speculation about possible government counter action. Something needed to be done and at a Lobby briefing on September 18, questions about the mounting crisis produced an answer from a minister that led some present to assume that a credit squeeze was imminent. Ian Trethowan handled the development for *The*

Chronicle and no doubt other journalists phoned their offices to report the same. Next day the Chancellor of the Exchequer announced a sharp increase in Bank Rate from five to seven per cent – the highest since 1921. Spending on civil and defence projects was to be limited and banks were asked to restrict advances over the coming twelve months. Almost immediately there was a buzz that the Chancellor's drastic action had been leaked in advance.

I had forged a useful friendship with Sir Leslie Plummer MP, a very close friend of Harold Wilson and a former Chief Executive of Express Newspapers. Within a few days of the Bank Rate rise Plummer beckoned to me in the Members' Lobby and asked what I thought about the rumours of a leak. I replied that, in my opinion, the Lobby, at one of its regular briefings, had been given a clear hint that action was about to be taken to strengthen the pound. I added that, as that was my view as a fairly new boy, it must have been eminently apparent to more experienced journalists at the meeting. Plummer himself was convinced that there had been a leak to the City and was pressing Wilson, as Shadow Chancellor, to raise the matter with the Government. On September 24 Wilson moved into action. He wrote a letter alleging that a leak had led to substantial private gains being made on the Stock Exchange. Macmillan rejected what he regarded as Wilson's *"impudent"* demand for an inquiry, but Wilson, egged on by Plummer, kept up the pressure stating that *prima facie* evidence had been brought to his attention suggesting that the leak emanated from a political source. Then Plummer tabled a parliamentary question on November 12 to the Chancellor in which he widened the attack by asking whether prior information regarding the Bank Rate rise had been given to Oliver Poole, Deputy Chairman of the Tory Party. In a Commons exchange Wilson referred to Poole's vast City interests. Poole, deeply embarrassed, asked Macmillan to set up a formal inquiry to clear his name and the Prime Minister now accepted that need. He announced a Tribunal of Inquiry under Lord Justice Parker. It would have power to cross-examine stockbrokers concerned as to the names of clients who sold after closing time on the day prior to the Bank Rate rise. I felt distinctly queasy – but I need not have worried. Plummer kept quiet about our conversation. The inquiry reported its conclusion on January 21 that there was no justification for allegations that information about the rise was improperly disclosed to any persons. So far as I knew, this was correct, and that it had simply been a case of *"advance guidance"* that prompted some journalists to pick up the scent of the squeeze, and thus the word spread around News desks, City desks and beyond. As Ian Trethowan had been at the Lobby meeting with me it was his job to speak to our office. I merely spoke, in due course, to Plummer. What I did not tell anybody, for nobody asked, was that I knew of someone who gambled on the markets who had indeed received a tip-off on September 18 that a crunch was on its way and they duly made a good profit on the basis of the information. So much for the thoroughness of the inquiry.

Soon after that event I had received my first taste of a Conservative Party political conference. Some highly paid political commentators such as Richard Crossman, who had been wrong about the Tory leadership succession, had started to predict an early general election after Macmillan had taken over. Once again they were wrong, but some uncertainty remained until that party conference. I was to play a small part in clearing the air.

As I had not been to a conference before, some Commons Press Gallery drinking chums thought it would be fun to kid me that I should wear a dinner jacket for evening functions. On the eve of the conference, I donned my D.J.

and strolled into the cocktail bar of the headquarters hotel to be greeted by some ribald comments from the assembled hacks at the bar, all of whom, as usual, were underdressed. *"Hey, waiter!"* said one wit. *"Bring me a large gin and tonic!"*

I bought myself one instead and decided not to go to the trouble of returning to my hotel to change. Then, out of the corner of my eye, I saw a steady stream of men in DJs passing along the side of the bar and entering a room at the back. A quick inquiry revealed that it was the traditional eve of conference dinner of the Tory Party agents – and it was to be addressed by Harold Macmillan himself. When clapping announced that the PM was on his feet I strolled to the doorway. No one challenged me. In my penguin suit I was either an agent or a waiter. Luckily, no one asked me to get them a drink. The important news that Macmillan gave to his audience was that he intended to complete the Government's full term and the tasks for which the party had been elected.

My story was too late for the first edition, but in the morning the *News Chronicle* carried prominently on the front page my scoop and my by-line. When I revealed to those who had tricked me how this had come my way they looked sick. Derek Marks, political correspondent of the *Daily Express* was particularly irritated. He liked to think he had the Tory Party sewn up. That *"left-wing bugger Butler"* had got away with an exclusive annoyed him. We had rowed at the bar more than once about Suez too. They used to say on Fleet Street, *"Never fall out with anyone – they might be your editor next week."* That was advice I should have heeded. But before he would become my editor – on the *Daily Express* – I was to irritate him many more times.

Marks, known as *"Jumbo",* was physically imposing, an overweight man who, despite his size, worked prodigiously hard and with great success. He had a huge expense account – far bigger than anyone else in the Press Gallery- and spent large amounts wining and dining his right-wing Tory friends. His thirst for news and booze was fabled. Sadly, the fact that he suffered from diabetes added to his drink problems. He was particularly successful at getting blow-by-blow accounts of private Tory backbench committees – such as the weekly meeting of the 1922 committee of all Conservative MPs. The men he *"fed and watered"* regularly at the Savoy repaid him with leaks of who said what at such gatherings and anger was growing among the more honourable MPs about this embarrassing problem. One evening, as I stood in the Members' Lobby, a Tory MP for whom I had done a favour strolled in, took me by the arm and walked me outside. At a meeting of the Tory backbench Finance Committee he had just attended, a minister had revealed that the Government was about to put up National Insurance charges. The exclusive on the front page of the *News Chronicle* next morning caused not only Jumbo Marks to explode in red-faced fury. The Chief Whip strongly complained to the Chairman of the 1922 Committee about the leak and it was decided that action must at last be taken. So accurate were the accounts of meetings reported by Marks that a suspicion had grown that the committee rooms were being bugged. It was declared that, in future, such rooms would be searched for devices before meetings were held. To no avail. The problem was not bugs but buggers with no honour who were prepared to regularly embarrass their colleagues in return for costly entertainment or favourable mentions in the *Daily Express.*

At the Labour Party Conference, a week before the Tory jamboree, there had been an important development. The one-time darling of the Left, Nye Bevan, had come to a working relationship with the embattled Hugh Gaitskell on the key issues of nuclear weapons and nationalisation. Harold Wilson who, when at his best, was the most formidable operator on Labour's frontbench in the Commons, decided in the light of this new alliance at the top to stake his claim to be the *"third man"* in the party hierarchy. Wilson had concluded that if Labour were to lose the next general election – which friends like Crossman had led him to believe could be near at hand – the parliamentary party would not choose Bevan as successor to Gaitskell, who surely would have to resign after such a defeat.

Sir Leslie Plummer, who had been asked by Wilson to spread the word about his *"third man"* position, tipped me off. The *News Chronicle* broke the news and my friends in the *Forward* office were particularly interested. They despised Wilson, referring to him contemptuously as *"little Harold, the little man"* or worse. After reading my news item, Douglas Jay said bitterly, *"The little rat never misses a trick – always scurrying for position!"*

Despite my allegiance to the Gaitskellites, I had a growing respect for Wilson as an operator and was so effusive in a Press Gallery report with my praise for one of his performances that I received a stern-faced admonition from Tom Steele. Tom, who looked as though his ulcer was giving him a hard time that morning, made clear that there was no place in the *Chronicle* for such *"emotive"* news reporting. The Tories, too, were not without their internal problems. Both as a journalist and as a person, I found myself continually drawn to MPs who gave trouble to the Whips. So it was that in the 1957-58 period I monitored closely the activities of the Suez rebels who were deeply opposed to the Government's decision to cut its losses and withdraw from the Canal zone. Led by the lofty Viscount Hinchingbrook, they included John Biggs-Davison, Anthony Fell and Patrick Maitland (who later would inherit the earldom of Lauderdale). Apart from their staunch opposition to the humiliating outcome of the whole fiasco, they were outraged by the unscrupulous pressure brought to bear on them by the Tory Whips. Fell, who was to become a friendly neighbour of mine years later, told me that a Whip had tried to involve one of the group with a busty blonde nymphomaniac in order to blackmail him into toeing the Government line. Another was warned that his business interests would be seriously damaged unless he stopped giving trouble. Over and above such personal arm-twisting, it was common for their constituency party chairmen to be warned that, unless they got their MPs to behave more loyally, they would not be invited to any Buckingham Palace garden parties and most certainly would not appear on any Honours Lists for political services. Eventually, Patrick Maitland partially exposed this unhealthy situation that compromised everyone's integrity when he complained publicly about *"extraordinary and unexampled pressures, some of them altogether underhand, to force the Tories into line."*

Victor Montagu, Viscount Hinchingbrook, son of the Earl of Sandwich led the rebels. He was like a character from the 18th century. Tall, immaculately dressed, his fine patrician head rising above a stiff white collar and ramrod back, he looked every inch an aristocrat. He was, in fact, a genuine English eccentric and radical who yearned for the days when Britain was governed by gentlemen. Sadly he lamented that the Tory Party had been damaged by *"letting in the Money Barons"*. Known in Parliament as *"Hinch"*, he represented South Dorset for twenty-one years, succeeding to the earldom in 1962. With seven other Tory rebels he abstained from supporting the Government in a vote of confidence over Suez in May 1957, lambasting the operation as *"catastrophic"* and the subsequent diplomacy as *"entirely unsuccessful"*. After his political career, he settled at one of his family's houses in Mapperton, Dorset, where he created a delightful garden that I would have the pleasure of coming to know and admire.

Having been defeated in the leadership battle by Macmillan, RAB Butler was appointed Home Secretary by him, ushering in a period of humane reform very much to the liking of the *News Chronicle*. He had, in fact, wanted the Foreign Office but Macmillan had decided that Selwyn Lloyd, the despised scapegoat of Suez, should remain in that post to help the Tory Government brazen out the shambles. Lloyd, in fact, had borne the brunt of the attacks over Suez in the Commons Chamber, scenes of uproar unparalleled since World War II, caused by Eden's folly and blatant lying about the collusion. As a lawyer who believed in the rule of law, he was never the same confident politician after that ordeal.

I enjoyed reporting RAB's appearances at the Commons Dispatch Box. He was not a great speech maker, but his words were well chosen and delivered in a quiet, thoughtful manner which impressed me and won the respect of the reformist members of the House. In particular, his efforts to reform the penal system and bring in a prison building programme as part of his policy to humanise the antiquated administration of Britain's jails struck me as deserving support. One of my reports of a speech on prison reform led the *News Chronicle's* front page and I hoped the paper's recognition of its importance had pleased the quiet, reserved politician who had delivered it.

Over a decade before, RAB had produced for the Tory Party an Industrial Charter designed to *"humanise capitalism"*. He had done so in the knowledge that one reason Churchill had lost the '45 general election was that many voters blamed the Tory-dominated coalition governments of the 1930s for the appalling growth in unemployment during those years, with jobless black spots such as Tyneside, Liverpool and South Wales becoming distressed areas. Churchill had given him the job of producing a radical policy shake-up for the Tory Party that helped it to return to power in 1951, with RAB rewarded with the post of Chancellor of the Exchequer. With one of his famous little chuckles, RAB told me on one occasion that when, as Chancellor, he was called by Churchill to 10 Downing Street one mid-morning, he found the old man sitting up in bed, its counterpane littered with newspapers, a glass of brandy in one hand, large cigar in the other, and perched on his bald head, his pet budgerigar. Despite the seriousness of the business discussed, he confessed it was difficult to keep a straight face.

I greatly respected RAB, as did Francis Boyd, whose shrewd assessments of the politician had been formed over a couple of decades as a parliamentary reporter. In the late fifties, as Francis puffed his pipe and drank his Bass at the Press Gallery bar, I soaked up his observations. Over half a century later, I noted with much interest that David Miliband, a leading candidate for the Labour Party leadership in August 2010, declared that his party must learn lessons from RAB's role in policy making in the Tory Party. Warning that Labour under new leadership must engage with the big issues with an openness unlike it had ever seen, Mr Miliband said: "The closest parallel I can think of is the Tories' rethink under R.A. Butler after they lost the 1945 general election."

It was after that defeat that Butler argued successfully for the party accepting much of the Attlee government's reforms, including the setting up of the Welfare State.

Meanwhile, there was a growing smell of burning on the good ship *Chronicle* and some of the younger staff were beginning to jump for safer berths. One evening, Ian Trethowan asked me to have supper with him in the St Stephen's Tavern, opposite the Houses of Parliament. Over our meal he revealed that he had given three months' notice to editor Cursley and would be joining Independent Television News (ITN) whose editor was an ex-*Chronicle* man himself, a short, dapper New Zealander named Geoffrey Cox. After an impressive war record he had become Political Correspondent of the *Chronicle* in 1945 and an efficient assistant editor in '54. In 1956, he had been appointed Editor of ITN and had recruited Trethowan to fill the political spot on the paper. Cox went on to get a Knighthood in 1966 and became Chairman of Tyne-Tees television and then LBC Radio. After breaking the news of his imminent departure for the more promising world of TV, Trethowan complimented me on my work and said he had no doubt that in due course I would get the top political job on the paper. Meanwhile, however, as I had been at the Commons for less than a year, he understood that Cursley intended to replace him with one of the *Chronicle's* most experienced journalists who had knowledge of Whitehall already as the paper's Defence Correspondent. He was David Willis. I could not and did not complain. Smartly dressed and personable, Willis had been a successful reporter in his field but as it turned out, he was not cut out for the daily grind of parliamentary coverage.

The *News Chronicle* had purchased the right to use the respected Gallup Poll system and in July 1958, this revealed a big increase in Macmillan's popularity. The Tories, despite all of their problems, were running level with Labour at 47.5% of sample voters committed to supporting each party. It came as a sharp shock to Labour and my friends at *Forward* told me that it had given Gaitskell the jitters. He knew that defeat at the polls next time would not only be a disaster for the party but also a personal disaster for himself – he would have to resign as Labour leader. An elder statesman who took a great interest in the Gallup polls was Hugh Dalton. I had been introduced to him in a downstairs bar off the Commons Central Lobby by the *Daily Herald's* political correspondent Hugh Pilcher, a gregarious character, larger than life, who shared a room with the *Chronicle* team in the Press Gallery. Pilcher was so dedicated to searching out stories for the Herald that he would be in the Strangers' Bar at the Commons before lunchtime, buying drinks for MPs and stimulating the gossip. Unfortunately, sometimes by evening he was so full of drink himself he was incapable of filing the stories garnered. This tall, gangling man, whose trousers ended well above his ankles, had been so kind, welcoming and helpful to me, that I did my best to repay him by phoning reports in his name to The Herald. One evening, he asked me if I would like to meet Dalton and led me down to a bar not much larger than a broom cupboard that he knew the statesman liked to use. A big man, with a dome-like head and booming voice, Dalton took up much of the available space, but we squeezed ourselves in. So began my friendship with the politician who, as Attlee's Chancellor of the Exchequer, had honourably resigned over a tax change tip-off to a friendly London evening *Star* journalist as he entered the Commons Chamber to deliver a Budget speech. By bad luck, the advance information was published in the paper's stop-press news column before he could announce it to MPs.

Born the son of Canon Dalton, tutor to the Princes at Windsor castle, he was educated at Eton and King's College, Cambridge. Although starting out as a Tory democrat, he became an admirer of the economic approach of John Maynard Keynes and went on to become a key figure in the Labour Party. Influential in policy making, he assisted in the formation of the wartime coalition and, as an admirer of Churchill, helped to push the Labour movement into supporting rearmament in preparation for the inevitable war with Nazi Germany. As Chancellor in the post-war Labour government he strived to bring about a redistribution of wealth in Britain. As MP for a North-East constituency he also endeavoured to bring about a much-needed relocation of industry.

With Hugh Pilcher usually in attendance, I began to meet Dalton regularly in the *"broom cupboard"* bar. His conversation was a gold mine for a young reporter – full of indiscretions laced with shrewd observations on men and matters. He could be wickedly malicious. I was flattered by his friendliness, his openness, interest and trust. I did not know then that he was reputed to have a sexual interest in promising young men in the Labour movement. What I did know was that he had assisted the fledgling careers of Gaitskell, Tony Crosland and James Callaghan. I asked him on one occasion what he thought of Gaitskell and Harold Wilson. He replied that he and Gaitskell had been friends for years and that he had a very high regard for him. On economic and financial issues he rated him head and shoulders above all in the Commons. When it came to dealing with policy problems, however, he thought Gaitskell was inclined to get bogged down in detail. In a later conversation he was to express his concern about Gaitskell's strenuous determination to attack his critics on the Left rather than putting more effort to opposing the Tories. In his view, however, the Left's continuing attacks on Gaitskell were unfair. The Bevanites failed to give him credit for his deeply held beliefs in equality and social justice. As for Harold Wilson, although he was very clever, Dalton thought he lacked strength of character. This weakness had won him a reputation for being untrustworthy. He recalled describing him as *"Nye Bevan's little dog"*. This tag had been picked up by the press, something that he rolled his huge eyes and chuckled to remember. Apart from the fact that I was a young political reporter who supported Labour, he did seem interested in me because of his own links to the LSE and for my connection with the Dover coal-mining community. He had represented the Durham miners of the Bishop Auckland constituency for some twenty-six years. When I told him I sometimes thought of trying to get adopted for the Dover seat in Parliament he replied that, if I wanted to represent miners, I should try for Bishop Auckland and promised to help me if he could.

Dalton was interested in the *Chronicle's* Gallup Polls and as he was not prepared to buy the paper, I undertook to send each poll to him as soon as it was published. When he announced his decision to retire from Parliament in the autumn of 1957 I wrote in the *Chronicle* how *"his boisterous, expansive personality will be missed at Westminster."* In his second volume of memoirs *High Tide and After* he wrote that of the press comments, *"I liked best Arthur Butler of the News Chronicle."* I was very pleased to have pleased him.

What Dalton had said of Wilson came back to me some time later when Leslie Hale MP, who had been closely involved with the Bevanites, told me that Nye Bevan regarded Harold as less than honest and lacking in principle. Bevan took it as an act of personal disloyalty that Wilson had filled the vacancy on Labour's Shadow Cabinet caused by his surprise resignation over South-East Asia defence policy in 1954. Wilson was too ambitious to be trustworthy. In comparison, Bevan regarded Gaitskell, whom he had described as *"a desiccated calculating machine"*, as honest.

At a meeting of the Central London Fabian Society in 1957, the Chairman Tom McKitterick told me that the Fabian Colonial Bureau needed a volunteer to help prepare its journal *Venture*. Would I be interested? I explained I was giving my spare time to *Forward* but promised to call at the bureau to see what needed to be done. Housed in the Fabian headquarters in Dartmouth Street, it was run by the dedicated and formidable Lady Hylda Selwyn-Clark. Less formidable and more relaxed was her able deputy, a genial ex-forestry expert named Jimmy Betts. Usefully, from my point of view, he was the brother of Barbara Castle, the intelligent and outspoken politician on Labour's left wing who was on her way up. I got on well with Jimmy and was soon involved in writing material, mostly about Britain's African colonies, and getting involved in policy issues. Labour's spokesman on colonial affairs was James Callaghan who I thought was doing a good job at the Dispatch Box. When I told him this one day in the Lobby, he quickly made clear to me that he would prefer to be a shadow spokesman on some other issue as there was little interest in colonial problems in his Cardiff constituency. I promised that when next writing on the subject of a shadow cabinet reshuffle I would report that there was a feeling that he should be dealing with one of the big domestic issues, such as housing, which to me was a burning issue. Still, I regarded the colonial freedom battle as important too, so was somewhat disappointed that Callaghan wanted to move on from it.

One of his problems was that he was shadowing an extremely hard-working, well-informed Colonial Secretary called Alan Lennox-Boyd. A formidable performer at the Dispatch Box, he often surprised Callaghan and other opponents with his detailed knowledge of a situation. As Colonial Secretary from 1954–59, he held office at a time of great dispute about the pace of independence from Britain's colonial rule and chose a middle course. This brought him under fire from the right-wing Tories opposed to *"the break-up of The Empire"* and from the official Opposition that was pressing for faster action. As a strong supporter of the independence movement, I regarded him as a dangerous and formidable reactionary, but to give him his due, the Gold Coast, the first colony to go, did so on his watch and he also played a key role in preparing Nigeria for independence too. When a number of Mau Mau detainees were killed by African wardens in the notorious Hola prison camp in Kenya, he offered to resign. Macmillan, however, successfully persuaded him to brazen it out and he did not quit until the 1959 general election, after which he was succeeded by Iain Macleod. He was made Viscount Boyd of Merton and I dubbed him Lord Boyd of Hola. When he later became Managing Director of the brewers Arthur Guinness and Son – having married the wealthy Lady Patricia Guinness – he invited some Lobby Correspondents to visit the firm's famous Dublin brewery. I was not going to go but was persuaded by my bibulous friend, Hugh Pilcher. To my surprise and embarrassment, Lord Boyd placed me on one side of him when we sat down to lunch and was most affable throughout – evidence of his generous and forgiving nature.

Commonwealth and Colonial affairs were about to come more to the fore. In January 1958, following a bitter dispute over the Cabinet's spending plans and, in particular, proposed welfare state expenditure, the Chancellor of the Exchequer, Peter Thorneycroft, resigned together with Enoch Powell, First Secretary to the Treasury, and Nigel Birch, Economic Secretary. With great panache, Macmillan described the politically shattering resignations as *"little local difficulties"* and set off on a tour of the Commonwealth.

The shadow of the Hola massacre hung over the Commons. The camp in Kenya housed terrorists taken prisoner during the Mau Mau rebellion and when a riot broke out over forced labour, eleven of the detainees were beaten to death by prison guards. The Opposition in the Commons blamed the Government and called for an inquiry, which was granted. Then, in a bitter Commons debate, Enoch Powell, who had resigned earlier from the Treasury, made his first big breakthrough as an orator in a searing and eloquent attack on the Government's handling of the affair. MPs rushed to the Chamber to hear him speak, but when I approached him later in the Lobby he turned smartly on his heel and snapped, *"I have nothing more to say!"*

He had won a new respect from liberal Britain – which he would subsequently lose over the issue of race and immigration.

Almost simultaneously, there had been serious rioting in Nyasaland (now Malawi) in which over fifty Africans had been killed and many arrested, including a leading political activist, Dr Hastings Banda. The rioting had been caused by strong black dissatisfaction with the running of the white controlled Central African Federation made up of Nyasaland, Northern Rhodesia (now Zambia) and Southern Rhodesia (now Zimbabwe). The Government set up an inquiry under Mr Justice Devlin and late on a sultry July evening Dingle Foot, an MP who had taken a close interest in the affair, whispered to me in the Lobby, *"Devlin is very bad news for Macmillan."*

To my disappointment, my scoop was not splashed on page one but *"buried"* on page two of the *Chronicle* next morning. On reflection, I concluded that I failed to phone and *"sell it"* to the night editor. Macmillan was so angry with Devlin's report that he delayed its publication for a few days while he had a rival one produced by the Governor of Nyasaland, Sir Robert Armitage and they were then published together. Much of the report bearing Sir Robert's name was, in fact, written by Macmillan's staff in a couple of days as it sought to undo the serious damage to the Government done by Devlin's severe criticisms of the *"police state"* style of administration in Nyasaland.

CHAPTER FIVE
Last Chronicle

The future of the Central African Federation had become a burning issue. In 1956, tough, uncompromising right-winger Roy Welensky had taken over as Prime Minister there. Born of a poor family, he had become an engine driver and at the age of 19 was professional heavyweight boxing champion of Rhodesia. The Federation had been set up in 1953 to provide a thriving economic entity; Northern Rhodesia's mineral wealth and Southern Rhodesia's agricultural and industrial strengths being harnessed to the plentiful labour resources of Nyasaland. It was supposed to be an experiment in White-Black racial partnership and it was assumed that over the years, the African majority would get more political power. Welensky, however, had no intention of handing over any power to the Africans and after much posturing by him and huffing and puffing behind the scenes in Whitehall, the Cabinet set up a Royal Commission in March 1960 to advise on the future of the Federation. As the row over the Federation's future grew, Jim Callaghan would sometimes phone me in the Press Gallery to ask me for up to the minute information from Africa. *"Can you tell me what Welensky has said?"* he would ask.

The Federal Government in fact was very active lobbying in London, employing, among others, a PR firm named *Voice and Vision*, which had a link to the Labour Movement. Welensky and his friends were very anxious to get leading politicians to visit the Federation to be *"softened up"* and to my surprise, I learned one evening from a friend of Nye Bevan that he was seriously thinking of going out to have a look. The story appeared on the *Chronicle's* front page next day and for a few days the subject went quiet. Then John Stonehouse, from my LSE days, came up to me in the Lobby, a broad smile on his handsome face. *"That was a good story you had about Nye going to Rhodesia,"* he gushed.

Before I could respond, he continued, *"Thank Goodness you got to it before he could announce he was going. Now we've managed to stop him. It would have been a terrible mistake. We'd have lost the Africans' trust and he could not have done anything useful!"*

I winced. So much for my scoop. Now I would have to write another story saying Nye had changed his mind.

At the age of thirty-one Stonehouse had entered the Commons for Wednesbury. It was said that when Gaitskell heard he was trying for the seat he exclaimed, *"Over my dead body!"* But Stonehouse, who was active in the Co-operative Movement, used his influence successfully and achieved his ambition to get into Parliament. He dragged with him stories of his financial fiddling as a student body official and reports of more fiscal mismanagement while he was involved with a Co-operative venture in East Africa – a position he had got with the help of the well-known colonial freedom fighter, Fenner Brockway MP He was also far too left wing for Gaitskell's tastes. He was, however, the sort of politician who was going to make news and although I had not known him well at the LSE, I introduced myself to him in the Lobby soon after he arrived in Parliament, reminding him that we had met as students. He seemed genuinely pleased, as he did not know any national newspaper lobby correspondents and said he would be delighted to help me when he could. Although he seemed to me at the LSE to be somewhat overbearing and too self-confident, we shared an idealistic interest in helping the African colonies to independence and in improving their economies. He was very critical of the white-dominated Central African Federation and we often talked about the problem when we met in the Lobby.

One day, he invited my wife Evelyn and me to dinner at his home in a smart part of up-and-coming Islington. We arrived to find that the two other guests were already there – Reg Prentice MP for East Ham North and his wife Joan. Reg, who looked like a countryman with his round, rubicund face, had known Stonehouse at the LSE where he had been two years ahead of me, having joined the school on being demobilised as an artillery officer in 1946. After serving the Transport and General Workers' Union in its legal department, he had only recently become an MP after winning a by-election. It was an important introduction for me and over the next fifteen years we were to become close friends. We all got on well that evening. John's attractive wife Barbara, whom he had married in 1948 when she was only seventeen, was an excellent hostess, despite also having to keep an eye on their well-behaved young children. I remembered seeing her with him at the LSE and had assumed wrongly that she was a student there. They lived in good style and John was already exhibiting a connoisseur's taste for wine.

In due course, a financial problem was to force Stonehouse to sell the Georgian terrace house and move the family to a more modern home in the Home Counties, where I attended a couple of parties and was reunited with Bernard Levin on both occasions. John would often talk about his mother, a leading figure in the Labour Party and Co-operative Movement, who clearly had a great influence on him. In 1954, he had begun his deep involvement in the management of the London Co-operative Society and was to be elected president in 1962, but his efforts to modernise the organisation failed. He blamed communist obstruction. In fighting them, he used some of his own money and this had led to the problems which made him have to sell up and move on from fashionable N1.

Despite the treasury team resignations, the Suez fiasco, the Hola scandal, and other setbacks, *"Supermac"* Macmillan, as he had by now been labelled, seemed to soar above clouds. By May 1959, the fact that Gaitskell had privately aired the view that he thought it probable the Tories would win an autumn general election had filtered back to the office of *Forward*. Gaitskell had carried out a successful tour of Labour's heartland in the North-East. On their return, John Harris, who, as deputy editor of *Forward* had been asked to accompany Gaitskell as his press relations man, was puffed up by the success of the tour. In particular, he was full of praise for a certain T. Dan Smith, a go-getting Tyneside City Councillor and Public Relations man who had big plans for the area and had entertained them well. *"We need more people like him in the Labour Movement!"* said Harris, impressed too easily by the hospitable largesse.

Smith, however, was a crook. Nicknamed *"Mr. Newcastle"*, he operated like a corrupt American-style city mayor, controlling key committees on the Council, in cahoots with an equally corrupt architect and developer named John Poulson.

One Durham County Alderman who was caught up in Poulson's web of corruption was Andrew Cunningham, who enjoyed enormous unparalleled power in the North-East through the Labour Party and the giant General and Municipal Workers' Union. He steered important building contracts to Poulson's firm and received in return free luxury holidays and a sinecure position for his wife, a former teacher and JP.

Poulson was the main client of Smith's PR firm. When in due course the police uncovered a network of bribery over the allocation of publicly financed building contracts Smith, Cunningham and Poulson were jailed.

To be fair to John Harris, the trio of rogues went on to fool many top people, far more experienced and discerning, before the police arrested them in the early 1970s. Cunningham's time in prison did not undermine his tough northern constitution. He celebrated his centenary before his death in June 2010.

In a clever step towards watering down the hereditary element in the House of Lords, Macmillan introduced in 1958 a scheme for Life Peers to be nominated by the Government and Opposition parties. Heading the first list of fourteen men and women was the name of Robert Boothby, a pushy Tory politician who, in my opinion, needed some lessons in morality. Speaking to a respected Tory knight in the Lobby I expressed surprise that Boothby had been awarded such an honour. He smiled knowingly. *"Mac doesn't see it as an honour. He sees it as an insult. Boothby wanted an hereditary title for political services when he failed to get a seat in the Cabinet. Harold's got his own back by making him a 'lifer'."*

I asked what he meant by getting his own back.

"Don't you know?!" he retorted, *"Boothby's been Dorothy Macmillan's lover for years!"*

Noting my look of astonishment he quipped, *"I would have thought a well-informed young chap like you would have known that?"*

When I cross-checked with some other members of the Lobby, I was relieved to discover that they shared my innocence. I had met Dorothy Macmillan at a party for the Press at No. 10. It was difficult to imagine this rather overweight matron *"getting it on"* with such a flamboyant Lothario as Boothby. As the daughter of a Duke she was titled Lady Dorothy – which made *"Life Peer Boothby"* appear even more second rate – despite the grand title he had adopted of Baron Boothby of Buchan and Rattray Head. He was the father of Lady Dorothy's youngest daughter Sarah.

A good speaker with a big outgoing personality, Boothby had entered Parliament in 1924. During the 1930s he enjoyed his best period as an MP, speaking out against the rise of the Nazis in Germany, calling on the Government to build up the RAF and denouncing the Munich agreement in strong terms. Churchill gave him a post in his wartime government as Parliamentary Secretary at the Ministry of Food. Then events took a serious downturn. In 1940, a Commons Select Committee ruled that his conduct in connection with some Czech assets threatened by the Nazis with seizure had been *"contrary to the usage and derogatory to the dignity of the House."* He resigned his post in the Government and took a wartime commission in the RAF. Churchill never offered him a post again. Oddly, however, when Macmillan became Prime Minister, he hoped for a good government job. By then Tory knights of the shires regarded him as a bounder, a bisexual adventurer and a liar. Recklessly, he had a well-known affair with a male cat burglar who introduced him to London's criminal underworld in the 1960s – including the notorious Kray brothers.

What would Lady Dorothy have said if she had known what other locks her lover was picking? The Labour Party had an equally bad case in Parliament in the person of the gay journalist, Tom Driberg, who also had an affair with a member of the Kray gang. Harold Wilson, when Prime Minister, protected Boothby from exposure fearing that, if he did not, the Tories would retaliate tit-for-tat by revealing Driberg's activities. Churchill said Driberg gave buggery a bad name.

As the summer wore on I found a growing dissatisfaction among Labour MPs with Gaitskell's leadership – and this had also spread to normally loyal *Daily Mirror* bigwigs, as I learned from the Mirror men in the Press Gallery. Behind the scenes a serious row was developing between Gaitskell and Bevan over nuclear disarmament, with the party leader insisting on Britain's right to be prepared to use the H-bomb if faced with the threat of war with the Communist bloc. The left-wing nuclear disarmers led by Michael Foot and including the powerful Transport Workers' Union leader Frank Cousins, were pressing for a party campaign to *"ban the bomb"* – and a lot of party workers were in support. So far as the realistic British public were concerned, however, Gaitskell had got it right. A Gallup poll in the *News Chronicle* revealed that only 15% of the public were in favour of unilateral nuclear disarmament. I sent the findings to Dalton whose response was delighted.

On September 7, Macmillan paid the traditional Prime Ministerial visit to Balmoral and used it to inform the Queen that he intended to call a general election. Promptly he did, naming the day as October 8. Another *News Chronicle* Gallup poll on September 22 revealed that the great majority of Labour voters expected the Tories to win. Despite a mood of despondency among Labour supporters, Gaitskell gave confident leadership at the outset. This had an upbeat effect on Labour headquarters and in Leyton, where I was busy campaigning for Reg Sorensen, we believed we were heading for a national victory. Then disaster struck.

On September 29 the *News Chronicle* and others papers gave prominence to a speech in Newcastle by Gaitskell in which he pledged that there would be no increase in income tax under the next Labour government. He had phoned Harold Wilson, his Shadow Chancellor, in advance to clear it with him. We shall never know if Wilson, ever the self-seeking careerist, decided that if such a pledge lost Labour victory it would enhance his prospects of succeeding Gaitskell as leader sooner rather than later. When I read the press reports I felt sick. It seemed to me an appalling campaign blunder that would lead many voters to lose confidence in Labour. Gaitskell had made the mistake of *"doing things on the cheap"*, using John Harris as his personal assistant and PR advisor again. With typical gaucheness, Harris, inexperienced and lacking independent confidence, had either failed to foresee the consequence or to warn against it. Gaitskell had walked into the Tory trap set with the all-too-obvious bait of an accusation that Labour would have to raise taxation to carry out its proposals. Matters then got even worse when Labour's General Secretary, Morgan Phillips, followed up in London by issuing a document in which it was stated that Labour was pledged to cut purchase tax on essential goods. Harold Wilson had promised this on several previous occasions.

The Gallup poll now showed that while Labour was at level pegging with the Tories, the number of *"Don't Knows"* had risen ominously. When the result of the election was announced the Tory majority had increased to 108 over Labour. The 1959 election was the first in which broadcasters sought to provide extensive coverage. Independent Television News, headed by Geoffrey Cox, was well to the forefront and despite some hair-raising problems in trying to ensure fair and balanced TV reporting, came through with flying colours. It was first and alone to cover the moment of high drama when Gaitskell conceded defeat only four hours after the polls had closed. It also marked an important success for my old friend and Lobby mentor Ian Trethowan who, together with Brian Connell, had made up the core presentation team for ITN.

When Harris returned to the *Forward* office he revealed that Gaitskell had still been confident of winning to the end, drawing up a list of his cabinet a few nights before polling day. He had been stunned when he heard the result. As the election approached my friend, Tom McKitterick, joint editor of the esteemed and influential *Political Quarterly,* had decided that in the next issue he would publish articles on the records of the two main parties since 1951. He invited Enoch Powell to write *"Labour in Opposition 1951-59"* and asked me to write the corresponding piece *"The Conservatives in Power 1951 – 59"*. Something of Powell's innate fanaticism was reflected in his comments on Labour's performance. *"It is not a picture of men with fire in their bellies who are spoiling to speak out what is in them,"* he complained, adding, *"An Opposition must have a categorical imperative: 'Do this, and this alone, if you would be saved'"*.

Some months earlier, when Powell had again been bitter in his denunciation of government folly I had intended to question him in the Lobby. But as he stood there alone, thin lipped and brooding, looking even more pallid and constipated than usual, I decided not to risk another snub. After the publication of our two articles, however, I decided to tackle the prickly fellow. I wandered up in the Lobby and after saying that I had enjoyed his piece added that I had written the companion Tory piece.

"Oh you did, did you?" he snapped contemptuously, then turned on his heel and stalked away.

A week after the general election there was a buzz of excitement in the *Forward* office. Douglas Jay, egged on by a bitter and disappointed Gaitskell, had written an article demanding a root and branch change in the party and its policies. He argued that better-off wage earners were regarding Labour as a party associated with a class to which they did not belong. The word nationalisation had become a liability. The article caused a great stir when published on October 16 – and, with my inside knowledge, I had been able to write a piece for the *Chronicle* forecasting that the Gaitskellites were about to drop just such a bombshell. Jay even suggested changing the party's name to *Labour and Radical* or *Labour and Reform.* As a result of the Jay initiative, the Gaitskellites and Bevanites were locked in battle within a few weeks of the election.

More than ever, the Gaitskellites were suspicious of Harold Wilson, believing that he would seek to use the split in the party to his own advantage. My colleagues on *Forward,* and John Harris in particular, busily spread smears about him, alleging that he was plotting to lead a left-wing revolt against Gaitskell and – on a more personal note – that he was having an affair with his private secretary Marcia Williams. My fellow syndicate member Trevor Lloyd-Hughes of the *Liverpool Post* saw a lot of Marcia in his dealings with Wilson, whose Huyton constituency was in his newspaper's circulation area. He told me that she was close to Wilson, well informed and influential and encouraged me to ask her out to lunch. Foolishly – or perhaps, who knows, wisely – I disregarded his advice.

As the rumours of *"the affair"* gathered pace, I found them difficult to believe. Wilson, I thought, was far too ambitious and cautious to take such a risk. As Chairman of the Public Accounts Committee he was one of the few MPs to have a good-sized office to himself and I decided that he was so mistrusted in the parliamentary party, and as Marcia was distrusted by other secretaries, they had grown close in their isolation. To sum up my view: they were as close as two people could be without hopping into bed. I was wrong. There was no on-going affair as John Harris wanted people to believe but, as was to be revealed in due course by Joe

Haines, Wilson's former Press Secretary at No. 10, Marcia admitted on one occasion that she had in fact slept with Wilson a few times during those early years in Opposition. Wilson's foolish and uncharacteristic lack of caution in this matter was to cast a shadow over the remainder of his life, leaving him in a relationship that was to become a serious, weakening distraction during his eventual premiership.

Tall and blue-eyed, Marcia had an attractive appearance marred slightly by her protruding teeth. Well educated, with a university degree, she had got a secretarial job in 1955 in the office of the Labour Party's influential General Secretary, Morgan Phillips. Soon, she was learning from office gossip that a lot of people around her were Gaitskellites who distrusted Harold Wilson. She made it her business to warn him in a series of anonymous letters.

One reason why I had not followed Trevor's tip to take Marcia out to lunch was that I was about to get married and did not want any misunderstandings. Westminster is known as a *"village"* for a reason – when not flinging tomatoes, people gather round the deep well of gossip. I had first seen Evelyn Luetchford when she was six weeks old. I was six. Her parents were close to my mother and father and had come to tea to show off their new baby daughter. We saw each other on and off over the years and about a year after my return to London from Middlesbrough we began to *"date"* regularly. In May 1958, we were married and Evelyn came to live in my flat in Leytonstone.

Meanwhile, my father's health had deteriorated as a result of years of heavy cigarette smoking and my parents were beginning to think about moving out of London to somewhere with cleaner air. Two years earlier, mother had taken me to Hampton Court Palace to visit my grandmother and her employer, the ever-helpful Lina, who showed much interest in my new career. She seemed very depressed and told us how she missed so many of her friends such as Mary MacCarthy, who had died in recent years. Within a year she had followed them and my grandmother returned to live in her Walton Street basement flat.

During the 1959 general election I had spent much of my spare time canvassing on the doorstep for Reg Sorensen. Evelyn often accompanied me, attractive and red-haired, her appearance reflecting the fact that she was the youngest fashion buyer at the luxury London store Harrods. Her cut crystal accent had been polished at one of the finest girls' schools in England, North London Collegiate, which she had attended as a scholarship winner. *"What are you doing in the Labour Party?"* we were often asked by Leyton's voters as we delivered leaflets for Reg.

Soon after being safely returned as MP for the constituency, Reg recommended that I should be appointed Political Education Officer for the local party. I was pleased to take on the job and one of the speakers I invited to address a meeting was the well-known former Labour Minister Arthur Bottomley who, wrongly assuming I was lining him up to take over the seat was very grateful. Reg also included me in a local Labour discussion group that met monthly to talk over political issues. After one of these sessions Reg asked me if I had parliamentary ambitions. I admitted that I had thought about such a move and he confided that when, in due course, he decided to retire, he would be pleased to do what he could to help me take his place. I thanked him for this offer and said that I would certainly prefer to have a London constituency such as Leyton if I were to proceed down the parliamentary route.

Rows over nuclear defence and Gaitskell's efforts to get the party to drop Clause 4 on public ownership from its constitution continued to split the Labour Movement. But in April 1960, I was involved in reporting a Commons defence debate that provided the opportunity for a unifying initiative on the nuclear deterrent. Just before the 1960 Easter recess, Defence Minister Harold Watkinson had announced the Government's decision to abandon the Blue Streak rocket – a key part of Britain's independent nuclear strategy. More than any other political correspondent, I had been following every move in Labour's tortuous wrangling over this. I haunted the committee corridor after party meetings and in all this was assisted by John Strachey.

A former Minister for Food and then War Minister in the Attlee Government, he was a left-wing intellectual and co-founder of the influential Left Book Club. He had played a leading role in the ill-fated, costly scheme aimed at large-scale production of groundnuts in Africa. Mercilessly harried by the right-wing press, for years he was greeted by calls of 'Groundnuts!' from Tory rowdies whenever he rose to speak in the Commons.

Soon after arriving at the Commons, I had introduced myself to Strachey with the words that it was due to him that I had become a Labour supporter while still at school. I told him I had bought a copy of his book *"Why You Should be a Socialist"* – and that had done the trick. He seemed delighted to learn this and from then on I found him extraordinarily helpful. In his open and straightforward assistance to me he seemed almost naïve, over-trusting. On one occasion, when there was to be a crucial meeting of the party's defence policy group in a Commons committee room, he took me upstairs with him and sat me on a bench outside the room, with the promise that he would put me in the picture when it was over. Receiving some questioning looks from some of the other MPs as they entered the room I decided to move down the corridor to look less obvious. At the end Strachey told me all.

I was, therefore, better prepared than the other Press Gallery reporters to judge the importance of the debate that Gaitskell had decided should run only until 7pm, to prevent long speeches by Labour defence rebels. In total only forty minutes were to be allotted to the rank and file MPs – thus gagging defence *"experts"* such as Manny Shinwell. This made backbenchers furious. Then Gaitskell made another tactical error. He decided that as it was to be such a short debate he would not need to attend and so flew off to attend a meeting of the Socialist International in Israel. Nye Bevan's health had deteriorated seriously and so *"third man"* Harold Wilson was put in charge. Quickly, he announced that the Opposition wanted a full day's debate – and this was arranged. George Brown, who, despite his, at times, clumsy bullying, drunkenness and street market manners, could be brilliant on occasion, opened for Labour and made one of the cleverest speeches of his political career. Arguing that Watkinson's announcement had meant that our independent nuclear deterrent no longer existed, he went on to make clear that the Opposition could, therefore, no longer support it. His tactical move, which had got Labour off the hook, sent a wave of relief and delight through the Labour benches. They greeted his words with a loud cheer. Forewarned by MPs such as George Wigg and Sir Leslie Plummer, I was the only gallery reporter to run-down to the Members' Lobby to tie-up the loose ends before phoning my story to the *Chronicle.*

My story led the paper next day, providing far more background detail and assessment of the importance of the occasion than any other paper. Douglas Clark, a leading member of Beaverbrook's political team, was one of those who congratulated me – and his notice of my work was to prove of considerable importance to my career a few years later. Congratulations came, too, from Laurence Thompson, who had replaced David Willis as the *Chronicle's* political editor. He was a very fine writer but no great reporter of day-to-day events and relied heavily on me to cover the field. The son of the famous Thompson who had edited the left wing crusading *Clarion*, he had resigned from the *Chronicle* over its Suez policy but had been persuaded to return – and I regarded myself as lucky to work with such a decent, civilised man.

Following George Brown's unifying initiative, Gaitskell unleashed John Harris to encourage the press to run articles attacking *"irresponsible"* trade unions and *"pacifist"* constituency parties for supporting the Campaign for Nuclear Disarmament. As the Trades Unions became more of a problem for Gaitskell, I smiled as I recalled the adverse reaction to my views on the unions' block vote when I had applied to edit *Forward*. As a result of my continued activity with the Central London Fabian Society, I signed up for a Young Fabian weekend school for those aged under thirty. It was in 1958 and I just qualified. The venue was a Sussex Downs country house inland from Brighton and, on boarding the coach to take us there, I found myself seated next to a young man whom I was to hold in high regard for the rest of my life. His name was Tam Dalyell.

Tam was already something of a celebrity for, having been President of Cambridge University's Conservative Association while studying history and economics at King's College, he had transferred his allegiance to the Labour Party. This would have shocked his ancestors for Tam was a Scottish aristocrat – the tenth baronet – who lived in a turreted mansion in Linlithgow called The Binns (Gaelic for "hills"). Built in the 14th century and enlarged three hundred years later, it was the first stately home in Scotland to be handed over to the National Trust. That was in 1944 when Tam was only twelve and under the arrangement he was able to continue living there, contributing to some of the domestic bills, such as heating for the twenty-three rooms. One of his ancestors, a royalist general known as *"Black Tam o' the Binns"* or *"Bluidy Tam"* had formed the famous cavalry regiment the Royal Scots Greys in 1678, on the orders of King Charles II. Old Etonian Tam joined the regiment as a trooper to carry out his National Service. After losing an armoured car on Salisbury Plain, Tam also lost his hope of becoming an officer. On being demobbed he got a job teaching history and maths at a local school and became increasingly active in the Labour Party.

As we sat together in the coach I found him to be a most agreeable travelling companion. He had a broad, honest face and a fine head that gave intimation of considerable intelligence. Like me, he had been infuriated by the Tory Government's attack on Egypt. Like me, he was looking forward to getting to know better the fascinating Labour politician Richard Crossman who would be chairing the weekend school. In fact, for Tam that weekend sitting at Crossman's feet was to be the start of a life-long personal tie with the man soon to be described in *The Observer* as one of the most brilliant and unpredictable people in British politics.

Crossman's problem, however, was that too many other Labour politicians could not keep up with his high-speed, high-calibre thinking. His intellectual integrity would prompt him to dump an idea on thinking up a better one. This habit won him a reputation for unreliability and the nickname *"Double Crossman"*. He might well have retorted to his critics in the words of John Maynard Keynes: *"When the facts change, I change my mind. What do you do, Sir?"*

Educated at Winchester and Oxford, Crossman became a Fellow of New College and then a full-time tutor with the Workers' Education Association (WEA). During World

War II, he was a leading operator in the propaganda broadcasting campaign aimed at undermining German morale and was recognised as a master of psychological warfare. After the war, he became Labour MP for Coventry and in Parliament began to specialise in foreign affairs. He impressed Hugh Cudlipp, Editor-in-Chief of the *Daily Mirror* and *Sunday Pictorial,* who appointed him as political columnist – a well-paid post that gave him the opportunity to express his opinions to a multi-million readership. Revelling in this highly influential role, he then switched his interest from foreign affairs to the devising of a national pension scheme that was to become an important plank in Labour's 1959 election manifesto. After getting to know Crossman better at the Young Fabian School, I did my best to monitor his influence in the Labour Party on such issues as defence. I was impressed by his ability to break new ground.

Bevan had once said that whereas Gaitskell was intelligent he was not an intellectual like Crossman because he was afraid of ideas. At a *News Chronicle* editorial conference in May 1960, I persuaded the features editor to commission an article from him in which he outlined the Crossman plan for the future. At about that time he sent me a copy of his new Fabian pamphlet on the subject, expressing the hope that I would get it a good show in the paper.

An *Observer* profile of Crossman in June declared that he had just chalked up the two biggest successes of his career. These were a pamphlet challenging the revisionism of Gaitskell's leadership which had led to the suggestion that he might follow Aneurin Bevan as leader of the Labour left; and a policy on the much disputed area of defence policy, which he had produced with George Wigg.

Wigg, who had served in the ranks in the regular Army and had risen to Colonel in the Education Corps in the War, was the best-informed MP on detailed Army matters in the Commons. Culling through copies of Hansard, press cuttings and regimental magazines in his basement flat in Victoria he amassed a great knowledge of the state of the Army. From the regimental journals, for instance, he learned about the movement and disposition of troops that enabled him to ambush ministers at Question Time in the Commons. *"You need to do your homework!"* he would say with a wag of his finger as he admonished journalists who failed to understand what he was up to. George certainly did his homework and it seemed to strengthen his belief in the conspiracy theory of history.

My original MP friends were continually helping me to widen my field of political contacts. I had invited Hilary Marquand to be my guest at a Press Gallery lunch in honour of the veteran Australian politician Sir Robert Menzies, a staunch friend of Britain and a successful Dominion Prime Minister. Marquand knew Menzies and in renewing his acquaintanceship introduced me to the great man. Described as *"a pragmatic conservative with some liberal instincts"* he had formed the Australian Liberal Party in 1944 and five years later had swept Labour from power, to remain Prime Minister until 1966. His period of power was marked by prosperity, high employment and low inflation. His immigration policy was designed to avoid international racial problems by the expedient of keeping immigrants out. A strong monarchist, he was in due course to be appointed Lord Warden of the Cinque Ports – a position of great honour held previously by such national heroes as Churchill and the first Duke of Wellington.

Marquand responded to my hospitality by inviting me and my wife to dinner at his home in Wimbledon where the other guests were the witty barrister Elwyn Jones MP – one day to become Lord Chancellor – and Fred Mulley MP, in due course to serve as Secretary for Defence and eventually to become a business associate and neighbour of mine. I kept in touch with Elwyn Jones and after he had retired as Lord Chancellor in 1979 and was doing the Shadow job, I would sometimes be invited to join him in a glass of whisky in his room at the Lords, where he held court in avuncular style, deploying his impish sense of humour to great effect.

News Chronicle political correspondents had a reputation for balanced reporting and were often invited to broadcast for the BBC's General Overseas Service. I became a regular contributor to 'The Week in Parliament' series and in November 1959 dealt with the controversy that had arisen when Mr W.S. Morrison, who became Viscount Dunrossil on retiring as Speaker of the Commons, accepted another job. I explained that by tradition the Speaker was almost the only man in British politics completely debarred from seeking to promote his own welfare, adding:

"It has always been accepted that he should have no cause to anticipate favours at the end of his service – least of all from the Government or Palace."

I then reported that some MPs were deeply disturbed to learn that Morrison, the much respected Speaker of the previous Parliament, had accepted the post of Governor General of Australia – and accepted it soon after resigning from his post on grounds of poor hearing. Feeling was heightened by the coincidence that the announcement of his Australian appointment came just as the Government was introducing a Bill to bestow on him the traditional pension of £4,000 a year.

Led by forthright MPs Robert Mellish and Charles Pannell, one hundred and fifty-five Labour MPs voted against the Bill in protest. Added to doubts about the constitutional propriety of the situation was the question of whether it was fair that Dunrossil should accept a pension while earning the Governor's salary of £10,000 Australian pounds.

Home Secretary Rab Butler tried to assure the Commons that Dunrossil's decision to retire was not influenced by the prospect of the appointment, which had been made not by the British Government but by the Queen's ministers in Australia. The Bill was passed with a majority of one hundred and forty-five and Opposition Leader Hugh Gaitskell abstained rather than appear to be leading the protest. The affair, which underlined the traditional importance placed on the complete independence and integrity of the Speaker had, I explained to my listeners, won a notable niche in Parliamentary history.

My personal memory of Speaker Morrison is in lighter vein. I heard him say on one occasion that he had recourse to quietly humming *'The Campbells are coming'* in order to keep in step during the Speaker's dignified daily procession through the corridors and lobbies to the Commons chambers.

As with all my Overseas Service broadcasts, the talk was produced by the admirable Robert Finigan, an experienced and patient operator who taught me the brick-by-brick technique of drafting my pieces – so different in style from newspaper reporting where one aimed to make maximum impact with the first sentence. I enjoyed my broadcasting work for the Overseas Service and was sad when it dried up as my reporting became more partisan as political editor of *Reynolds News.* I was sad, too, to lose the small but useful fees.

I recalled my happy experience of broadcasting overseas for the BBC when, in January 2011, it was forced by crisis cuts in the Coalition Government's funding of the World

Service to close five foreign language services and sack 650 staff. Politicians from all sides condemned the cutbacks arguing rightly that they would damage the service's high international reputation and the considerable benefits it brought to Britain, such as important trade deals. Looking ahead, a small light flickered at the end of the tunnel. The BBC said it would reverse some of the cuts in 2014 when the World Service was due to start being paid for from the licence fee rather than from a direct Foreign Office grant.

Among occasional contributors to the *News Chronicle* was Jill Craigie, the film director and journalist wife of Michael Foot. Michael, then out of Parliament, was a close friend of some of the paper's leading writers, such as Cameron and Baistow. Jill, a very attractive woman, had met him when she was making one of her best films, *"The Way We Live"*, a documentary about a bombed-out family's life in post-war Plymouth. Michael was standing as Labour's candidate for Plymouth, Devonport, in the 1945 general election. Michael, according to Jill, had been a *"terrible womaniser"*, but they had a deeply loving, successful marriage. It was to be revealed, however, that in 1951, two years after her marriage to Michael, she was raped by another one-time writer for the *Chronicle* – Arthur Koestler. The attack occurred when she was helping him find somewhere to live. Although she tried to fight Koestler off he had virtually knocked her out and raped her twice. She did not tell Michael at the time as she did not want to upset him. Fearing damaging publicity she also failed to report the assault to the police. It was eventually revealed in a biography of Koestler in 1998 and was confirmed by Jill. Following her death in December 1999, I considered it a great honour to be invited by Michael to attend a memorial meeting to celebrate her life at London's Conway Hall. After pinning up photos of her taking part in CND marches,

Michael described her as *"a William Morris socialist from the start... and bright and burning till the end."*

As for Koestler, I had not known of his link with the *News Chronicle* until one day in the office Willie Forrest saw me reading the first part of his autobiography *"Arrow in the Blue"*. As it covered only the period from his birth in 1905 to his joining the Communist Party in 1931 it had not taken me into the Spanish Civil War on which he had reported, like Forrest, for the *Chronicle*. Willie told me that not only had he known him well – he had been involved in saving Koestler from execution by Franco's troops.

As the months passed in 1960, troubles increased for both the Labour Party and the *News Chronicle*. After long and bitter backroom wrangling amongst Labour's leaders in a futile attempt to get a defence policy acceptable to all, Gaitskell was defeated by the unilateral nuclear disarmers at the Labour Party Conference on October 5. Lambasting them as *"pacifists, neutralists and fellow travellers"* he made his famous commitment that *"some of us will fight and fight and fight again to save the party we love."* As coverage of the conference was shared between the industrial labour correspondents and the paper's political correspondents, I did not attend but was left in London to keep an eye on the Government's activities. With MPs back in London on October 13 the left-wing unilateralist, handsome Tony Greenwood, resigned from the Shadow Cabinet and next day announced that he was prepared to challenge Gaitskell for the leadership. The scheming Harold Wilson was put on the spot by this development. His plan had been to run for the deputy's job in any contest for the leadership.

I found this all very depressing but within a week was to have cause to feel far worse. On the Friday, rumours that the *News Chronicle* was heading for a merger began to circulate strongly around Fleet Street's pubs. As I was due to work on Sunday I had taken the day off and missed the excitement. On the Saturday, one paper reported a possible merger with *The Guardian* but this was denied by Laurence Cadbury. On Sunday, however, as I worked at home on the telephone, rumours of a takeover by the *Daily Mail* began to grow. These were confirmed when *Chronicle* reporter Peter Campling tracked down a printing firm which had been hired by the Mail circulation department to produce leaflets announcing a takeover of the *Chronicle*. When news editor Bill Pattinson received a copy of the leaflet he realised that although the takeover was imminent, it could not happen that day as the leaflet had to be distributed to newsagents due to substitute the Mail to the unsuspecting *Chronicle* subscribers. Like the good newspaperman he was, Bill therefore got on with producing a paper for Monday morning.

At home, cut off from the buzz of rumour, I continued with my phone calls to try to produce at least one good political story for the paper that day. It was a report of the latest developments in Gaitskell's battle against the unilateral disarmers and it was to become the lead story on page one – for the 35,648th consecutive and last morning paper to be published by the Daily News organisation. Leader writer John Ardagh wrote an editorial urging Gaitskell to stand firm. The headline above my name read: *"Last Ditch Plea to Gaitskell"* and the sub-headline read, *"Shadow Cabinet will try to heal rift."* When the *Chronicle* dropped through my letterbox that Monday morning I was pleased with my *"splash"* but did not realise that I was holding a copy of the last issue of the paper. Only the *Daily Telegraph* reported what was about to happen, one of the grubbier incidents in the history of Grub Street. That afternoon, heads of department were called in to Editor

Norman Cursley's office. Grim faced he read a short statement: *"Tomorrow, The News Chronicle will be merged with The Daily Mail and The Star with The Evening News"*.

As for compensation for the staff – there would be only one week's basic pay for each complete year of service. This was adding penury to injury. The normal rate in Fleet Street was one month's pay for each year of service. I had gone down to the Commons at lunchtime and returned to the office to find a highly charged situation. Angry at their betrayal by the flaky Cadburys, the men and women for whom the *Chronicle* had meant so much were gathering in the canteen to be addressed by Tom Baistow, Father of the Union Chapel. Unlike Hugh Gaitskell, however, they were not getting the opportunity *"to fight and fight and fight again"* to save the paper they loved.

Soon television crews and reporters from agencies and other papers were pouring into Bouverie Street and filling *The Feathers* to cover the story. I felt utterly deflated and as I rode home to Leytonstone on the tube I was embarrassed as tears welled in my eyes. When the *Daily Mail* fell through my letterbox the next morning I was faced with a news story that explained: *"The News Chronicle today ceased publication after one hundred and fourteen years and becomes incorporated in the Daily Mail. At the same time the London Evening News is absorbing the Star. This dramatic fusion of newspaper interests is without parallel in the history of the British Press."*

Laurence Cadbury was quoted as saying that in his view, the *News Chronicle* and the *Daily Mail "have so much in common in the integrity of their reporting and honesty of outlook."* His cynical summing up of a deal so singularly unfaithful to the spirit of the paper in his care, of which he was custodian, reflected an appalling disregard for the mismatch in history and traditions of the two papers. It was an arranged marriage of indeed unparalleled unsuitability. James Cameron, who had sadly and reluctantly resigned from the paper a few months before, commented with angry wit, *"The News Chronicle has died from arterial sclerosis – an active circulation impeded by clots."*

The *Chronicle* had had a circulation of over one million. Since the selling price had been increased to two-pence halfpenny in October 1957, however, sales had fallen by 232,000 copies. The *Star* lost 172,5000 copies in the same period but still shifted 700,000 copies a day. The combined financial losses of the *Chronicle* and *Star* in the first nine months of 1960 amounted to £300,000.

At a staff meeting on the Tuesday it was decided to set up an action committee, to try to rescue something from the debris. As the only active member of the political team still around I was asked to join. We were confident that lots of readers would refuse to take the *Daily Mail* with its right-wing Tory policies and well-known history of support for fascism in the run-up to World War II. We believed that quick action could persuade these readers to support a relaunched paper staffed by former *News Chronicle* journalists.

The Canadian press mogul, Roy Thomson, who had bought the *Sunday Times* from Lord Kemsley in 1959, was known to want to enlarge his empire. We hoped he might be up to adding a lookalike *Chronicle* to his stable. We were in favour of him also as it was known that he did not interfere in editorial matters. Thomson agreed to meet a few of us at his office on the Grays Inn Road – in the building where I had worked for Kemsley. It was agreed that Tom Baistow, as Father of the Union Chapel, should lead the delegation and that Richard Moore, a young leader writer and myself should accompany him. In his large executive office Thomson gave us tea – and sympathy. But he calculated that

£3 million would have to be raised from somewhere to launch a revived paper – even though we claimed to have a loyal readership waiting to flock back. Smiling benignly at us he said, *"I didn't come into this business for philanthropic reasons. If you can raise the £3 million come back and see me again."*

Yet some years later, he was to say that his successful bid to take over *The Times* was *"almost an act of philanthropy"*.

Owner of a newspaper empire in Canada, Thomson had appeared on the British media scene in 1953 when he bought the ailing *Scotsman* newspaper. This enabled him to get the franchise for Scotland's commercial TV station in 1956 and that in turn gave him the springboard to buy the Kemsley Group in 1959. Of his entry into commercial television he famously commented: *"It's just like having a licence to print your own money."*

Of the old Kemsley titles he soon sold off the loss-making *Sunday Graphic* and *Empire News* and put Denis Hamilton in charge of the *Sunday Times* which entered a new era of success, helped by the launch of a colour supplement.

Richard Moore, whose son Charles was to become a respected editor and columnist of the *Daily Telegraph*, thought he knew someone who could help – an up-and-coming Liberal MP with a flamboyant style named Jeremy Thorpe. I had met him years before at the English Speaking Union's younger members group based in Charles Street, Mayfair. He and Baistow had a meeting with him and he was certainly anxious to see the continuation of a popular daily liberal paper. He also seemed confident, initially, that the sum could be raised. He was wrong. As for Thomson, before long he had scooped up *The Times* and for someone who did not get into publishing to be a deep-pocketed benefactor, it must have been painful to shell out the enormous sums he did to keep that paper afloat.

Meanwhile, following his thumbs down, I made myself busy in the Commons. My MP friends, especially those with links to the media, such as George Thomson and Douglas Jay were sympathetic. Sir Leslie Plummer, a close friend of Sidney Bernstein, left-wing boss of Granada Television, said that if I had not got a new job lined up he would suggest to Bernstein that he should make me an offer. It was said that he had chosen to operate his Granada TV station in Manchester after studying a rain fall map, on the assumption that where it fell heavily, the local people were more likely to stay indoors and provide him with a captive audience. A life-long Labour supporter, he was a close friend of Michael Foot. I thanked Leslie for his offer of help and went in search of some MPs to get an early day Commons motion tabled about the death of the *Chronicle* and the state of the Press.

Tom Baistow had told me that it was time for a new Royal Commission on the Press to be set up by the Government. Tom Driberg, the left-wing journalist MP who had given evidence to the 1946 Royal Commission, agreed when I approached him. He said he would call for such a move and did so, stressing the damage done to the public interest by the further concentration of newspaper ownership. In the past I had been wary of dealing with Driberg who had a reputation for being self-seeking, untrustworthy and unscrupulous. But my dealings with him on this issue paid off. A Royal Commission was set up and within a couple of weeks I was to find myself a colleague of the tricky fellow.

I quickly received an offer from Bernstein to go to work in his Granada team in Manchester. Almost simultaneously, however, George Thomson told me that there was about to be a vacancy for political editor of the Labour Co-operative Sunday paper *Reynolds News*. He said my name had been recommended to the editor Billy Richardson and if I was interested I should telephone the managing editor Eric Wright. The Granada television offer had been tempting, especially as I had done a lot of broadcasting on parliamentary developments for the BBC World Service and had enjoyed it. The *Reynolds News* opening, however, appealed to me much more. I was greatly enjoying my life as a political reporter and apart from enabling me to continue with that, the Reynolds post would help me to establish myself as a leading Labourite journalist. I phoned Eric Wright to say I would l like the job and he was pleased when I agreed to do so at less than my not very generous *News Chronicle* salary. In return, he said that, although the current political editor Ivan Yates was not due to leave for a month or so, I could join the paper the following week.

CHAPTER SIX

Last Reynolds

My appointment as political editor of *Reynolds News* was well received by George Thomson, Douglas Jay and my other friends at *Forward* who were anxious that this key post should be filled by a Gaitskellite. Ivan Yates, who was about to retire from the job, had been a firm supporter of Gaitskell but editor Billy Richardson, like many in the Co-operative Movement, was a supporter of the Campaign for Nuclear Disarmament and the Gaitskellites had feared that the vacancy might be filled by a left-wing unilateralist. That would certainly have suited not only the editor but also the great majority of the paper's readers.

The weekly column written by Yates had not pleased them as it peddled the Gaitskellite line – and readers were deserting the paper. Upon studying the situation, I decided to use the column basically to attack the Tories and to make friendly comments whenever possible about Labour politicians on both sides of the widening party divide. In particular, I planned to give a boost in my news stories and the column to the members of the Labour Co-op group of MPs in the Commons, who had been neglected for years by their movement's Sunday paper. As for news reporting, I was confident that with my extra experience and wider contacts I could improve on Yates' output.

Still depressed by the death of the *News Chronicle*, I was determined to do my best to help *Reynolds* survive – and this determination made me realise that I was a journalist before a politician. If I could help the paper hold on to its mostly left-wing, unilateralist readership by muffling the Gaitskellite drum then I would do so. As with the *Chronicle*, however, my arrival on the paper was a signal that its days were numbered. The first issue of *Reynolds* had appeared on the streets in May 1850. George William MacArthur Reynolds had launched the paper to support the Chartist Movement's demand for long-overdue political reform. After a bruising battle, the Chartist goals of adult suffrage and equal political rights were eventually won. The paper was also a staunch ally of trade unionism as it struggled to become established and it supported the Co-operatives in the struggles against greedy private traders and bad employers. In due course, the Co-operative Movement came to own the paper. Always involved in world affairs, it thundered against Napoleon III and went on to play a leading role in the fight against the fascists – Franco, Mussolini and Hitler.

Few readers appeared to regret the departure of the civilised, charming Gaitskellite Ivan Yates. He had succeeded the up-and-coming Anthony Howard who went on to become one of Britain's leading political commentators. But the name that kept cropping up over the next year or two at party conferences was that of Gordon Schaffer. This old-style Socialist had been responsible for the paper's political coverage for more than a quarter of a century. His friends were on the extreme left of the Labour Party, such as Aneurin Bevan, and in the Communist Party, such as miners' leader Arthur Horner. Largely due to his influence, *Reynolds News,* together with *Tribune* and *The New Statesman*, were targeted for attack at the 1952 Labour Party Conference by Hugh Gaitskell. Schaffer himself was singled out for attack by the future party leader. Within a few years the board of management of *Reynolds*, faced with falling circulation and advertising, decided that Schaffer's extreme brand of Socialism was partly to blame and gave him his marching orders. His colleagues on the paper threatened to strike in his support. Realising that even one week's stoppage could do serious damage to the paper, Schaffer resigned.

Whenever I attended party conferences and meetings as the *Reynolds News* political editor, readers of the paper would say, *"I hope you do as well as Gordon Schaffer."*

No one ever mentioned Ivan Yates or Anthony Howard who had done such excellent work. When the news reached Great Aunt Nell's house in Dover that I had joined the paper, my uncles Alf and Charlie gave a cheer and proudly announced, *"We've got a Gordon Schaffer in the family!"*

To them, *Reynolds* was the Sunday version of the communist *Daily Worker*, later to become *The Morning Star*. I knew there was no way I could fulfil their hopeful expectations. I was to see more of them in the future, however, as due to my father's worsening problems with his lungs, my parents had moved from London in search of cleaner air to the village of West Hougham, up in the hills between Dover and Folkestone. Alf, a genial giant, six feet three inches tall and all muscle, had become a local hero. When the coal mine where he laboured had flooded and swirling water had threatened to bring down part of the roof, he had used his great strength to support it until new props could be put in place. Minerals in the water stained his body brownish yellow as he stood like Atlas, the flood up to his chest, and he bore the tidemark of honour on his skin until he died.

My background, with its upstairs / downstairs links with service in great houses and the toil of the coal mines, was in stark contrast to that of Anthony Howard – yet there were several similarities in our careers. Five years my junior, he had been born the son of a curate of smart St Mary's Abbot's, Kensington – later to become a Canon of Guildford. While I went to Wanstead High School he enjoyed a privileged private education at Westminster from where he went on to Oxford. Then came Suez – and as I, a captain in the front line Emergency Reserve, decided to risk a court martial by deciding to refuse to be mustered for this appalling, illegal act of aggression – he risked court martial as a National Service second lieutenant in the Royal Fusiliers by openly opposing the invasion. His first regular job as a journalist after that was with *Reynolds News* – although he never became as involved as I did with the Co-operative Movement and its Labour–Co-op MPs.

Despite these parallels, I did not get to know him until after 1964 when he became Whitehall Correspondent of the *Sunday Times*. His announced role – to break open the traditional secrecy of the corridors of power – not only annoyed Harold Wilson but irritated members of the Lobby in the Parliamentary Press gallery. I shared his contempt for some of the stuffy, indolent Lobby members, sheltering behind their restrictive rules, and had already clashed with them. But I was not happy by mounting reports that he had let down helpful civil servants and MPs by deliberately breeching confidences. He was, in fact, at that stage a ruthless, ambitious young man and his mode of operations soon cost him his Whitehall job. He left the *Sunday Times* to become Chief North America Correspondent of *The Observer* and never looked back, becoming one of Britain's best known political journalists and broadcasters, although never embedded in the Parliamentary Press Gallery.

Pioneer House, near the seedy King's Cross end of the Gray's Inn Road, was the location for the depressing headquarters of *Reynolds News*. It was owned by the Co-operative Society. The area was run down, home to prostitutes, down-and-outs and greasy spoon cafes. Traffic whirled about as if anxious to escape. The Victorians had developed it as their monument to steam travel, King's Cross railway station standing side by side with the St

Pancras terminus. Rising above the 1950's squalor was architect Gilbert Scott's gothic palace – the Midland Grand Hotel with its domed entrance hall, sweeping main staircase and ornate staterooms. Our office was drab in contrast. On my first morning I had a brief meeting with Editor Billy Richardson whose florid complexion reflected his love of good wine. Then I was left in the hands of the man who really ran the paper, Managing Editor Eric Wright, a roly-poly figure of fizzing energy, totally dedicated to the survival of the struggling paper. While Billy Richardson contented himself with writing the weekly leading articles, lunching well with left-wing contacts and then snoozing off the booze, Eric appeared to relax only at Saturday lunchtime. Then, with the paper virtually complete, he would take a few colleagues to a nearby Italian restaurant for a hearty meal before returning to the office to start planning next week's edition. I quickly made friends with the hard-working industrial Labour correspondent, Charles Timeaus, one of the best reporters in his field. Well informed and in possession of good judgement, the easy-going Charles helped to educate me over many a pint and pub lunch in the mysteries of the trade union movement. At that stage I had never even attended a Labour Party conference and had a lot to learn.

Three Labour MPs had weekly columns in the paper but were rarely seen around the office. They were Tom Driberg, Douglas Jay and Hugh Delargy. Driberg had been a great catch for the paper when he was sacked by the *Daily Express* in 1946 after producing the most successful gossip column of that time, under the *nom de plume* of William Hickey. A left winger who coupled a strong social conscience with the most appalling social snobbery, he was elected to Labour's National Executive Committee for the first time in 1949 and held his seat on that body until the

1970s, for much of the early period largely on the strength of his *Reynolds News* column. By Buggin's Law, he did a year's stint as party chairman. His column, however, far from having a strong political content, was mostly devoted to Tom's progress as a *bon viveur*. There were recommendations for restaurants and dishes and attacks on such unacceptable social practices as the use of paper table napkins. His promiscuity at a time when homosexual acts were still illegal meant he continually risked prosecution, *"cottaging"* as he did in public lavatories. As someone said, *"his proclivities were confined almost entirely to the lower decks"*, making him vulnerable to blackmail. He was an active high churchman and seemed to enjoy the dressing up and swinging of the incense. He was also a double agent during the Cold War, seemingly savouring both the intrigue and the money. The Czechs paid him for information and gave him the code name *"Crocodile"*. It emerged eventually that the Russians used him too, under the code name *"Lepage"*. At the same time he was providing information for Britain's security service MI5. Among his friends he included Guy Burgess, the diplomat who defected to Moscow.

Driberg lived in a fine small Georgian mansion at Bradwell in Essex —a luxury that kept him short of cash and reluctant to buy a round of drinks at the bar. His financial problems also meant that when, as often happened, he got a big exclusive news story, he would almost always sell it to a high-paying national newspaper rather than give the benefit of it to the struggling *Reynolds*. Some years later, when forced by money worries to put Bradwell on the market, I took him to lunch at the Coq d'Or restaurant in Stratton Street and told him I was thinking of trying to raise enough money to buy it as I had always admired the property. He explained the problems of living in such a high maintenance pile. I took his advice and abandoned the idea.

Douglas Jay, the right-wing Labour MP and confidant of Gaitskell, whom I had got to know at *Forward,* wrote a sharp weekly column on financial and economic issues under a pseudonym. Cadaverous and unkempt, usually wearing a wrinkled blue suit, he had great success with the opposite sex who were presumably attracted by his intellect rather than his looks. He was certainly not hooking them with big spending either, as I was to find out. A *"Little Englander",* strongly opposed to Britain's involvement with the European Common Market, he even had a dislike of foreign food. If he had to travel to the Continent he would take sandwiches to avoid having to sample local cuisine. Such habits could be an embarrassment to his travelling companions. In the early 1960s, he went on an official Labour Party visit to India with George Thomson and John Strachey. On arrival, they found that lunch was being served in the top class hotel where they were staying. Jay, however, who had not bothered to adjust his watch to local time, declared that it was breakfast he needed and ordered bacon and eggs. The surprised Maitre d'hotel explained that they were unable to produce such a dish at that hour. To the dismay of Strachy and Thomson, Jay then behaved like a boorish blimp, accusing the hotel of being substandard.

The third MP columnist on the paper was Hugh Delargy, a delightful and mellow Irishman who wrote about anything that took his fancy. In response to the fact that so many Tory MPs continued to use their service ranks more than ten years after the war, he retained the title of Captain. A few other Labour MPs had done likewise, such as Colonel George Wigg and Colonel Marcus Lipton. One of Delargy's pet themes was the need for Britain to have an Ombudsman. Whenever he was short of an idea he would return to the subject and his readers were greatly relieved when the Government eventually appointed one. Delargy immediately claimed the credit.

Meanwhile, as I settled in at *Reynolds*, awaiting Ivan Yate's departure, events took a serious turn for the Parliamentary Labour Party at Westminster. On 29 October, Harold Wilson announced his intention to stand against Gaitskell for the party leadership. Wilson's hand had been forced by left wing Tony Greenwood's challenge to Gaitskell earlier in the month. *"The little rat has been smoked out!"* snapped Douglas Jay.

Supporting Wilson in a challenge for the deputy leadership was a former engineering union shop steward, Fred Lee, with whom I was to become very friendly in due course. Fred was a shrewd and genial Lancastrian who had moved into the left wing of the Labour Party through membership of the Amalgamated Engineering Union. He won a Manchester area seat in 1945 and was made Parliamentary Secretary, Minister of Labour in 1950. He had a keen interest in technology stemming from his time as an engineer's turner and chairman of the works committee at Metropolitan Vickers Ltd. I believed him when he told me that it was he who had originated the phrase *"the white heat of the technological revolution"* used to such good effect by Harold Wilson in the run-up to the 1964 general election campaign. I think he was disappointed that Wilson never gave him public credit for that, but he was rewarded in other ways.

Although they were both defeated, Wilson had staked his claim as the leader of the left – for Nye Bevan had died, mourned by no one more deeply than Michael Foot who was chosen to replace him in the safe Labour seat of Ebbw Vale. The by-election was set for November and the impending return of Foot to the Commons created great excitement among left-wingers following their failure to topple Gaitskell from the leadership. Eric Wright asked me to go to Ebbw Vale to report on the contest – and so I met Foot for the first time and began a friendship that was to last for well over forty years. He had been out of Parliament since losing his Plymouth Devonport seat in 1955.

It was cold and wet when I arrived in the Welsh coal-mining constituency one November evening. Entering the small hotel's dining room next morning I found Foot already there, halfway through breakfast, a newspaper in front of him. The chill damp weather was not good for his weak chest and he coughed and looked far from robust. I had a feeling he would not wish to be disturbed and decided to introduce myself later that morning. I already knew his wife, Jill Craigie, who had been a contributor to the *News Chronicle*. When I made myself known at the local Labour Party office Foot shook my hand and warmly said, *"It's always good to meet someone from Reynolds."* He kindly said that he remembered my work for the *News Chronicle* and described its death as a disgrace. Jill had got to know the South Wales mining communities in 1948 when she had made a documentary film about life in a local village. As Michael's wife she had also known Aneurin Bevan. Indeed, on one occasion when travelling with her in a car Bevan had tried to fondle her. Pulling away from the would–be Welsh Casanova, she indignantly exclaimed, *"What would you say if a policeman saw you?"*

Eyeing the lovely Jill, Nye replied, *"I would say, 'Officer, can you blame me'?"*

Jill had an edgy relationship with Barbara Castle and was said to dislike her. Although they had disagreements over policy, the problem could have started with the rumour that before she met Michael he had had an affair with the good-looking Barbara, who, as a young woman, was certainly very sexy. When I danced with her at a Leyton Labour Party fundraising ball in about 1959 I recall that, lithe and sinuous, she used her thighs to good effect. After Jill's death in 1999, Baroness Castle, as she had by then become, said:

"I don't think she disliked me very much, although she disagreed with 'In Place of Strife'," Barbara's plan for reform of the trade unions.

At Foot's morning by-election press conference I met a cheerful young chap in a scruffy raincoat from Barnsley who was reporting for *The Guardian*. He was friendly and helpful and took me to a pub where he had already discovered the best beer. We got on well together and expressed the hope that we would meet up again one day. We never did – which was my loss for he was Michael Parkinson who, after his career as a newspaper columnist, would eventually become one of the most famous TV and radio presenters and interviewers in Britain. When I met him he was in his mid-twenties and already exhibiting an infectious zest for life. I had the feeling that wherever he was he would be having a good time and helping create one for those in his company.

We wandered around the town together with Foot, the vivacious Jill and their shaggy dog – one of a number they had over the years. Despite being one of the finest orators of his time, while I was there he never attracted more than about fifty to the evening meeting – in contrast to the packed halls that would listen spellbound to the silver-tongued Nye Bevan. But then I doubt whether the locals knew how funny and entertaining Foot could be. What I discovered when I tried to report him, however, was that at times he became so carried away with his oratory that he failed to finish a sentence, leaving it hanging in the air, incomplete, but with its point made. When I have told this to people who have listened to his speeches they have been surprised – almost unbelieving. The fact is that they had been so entranced by his argument and dramatic delivery they had not noticed.

By contrast, Tony Benn, who at that time was beginning his political career, is a brilliant orator who completes perfectly every thought he expresses. Michael and Tony differed in another important respect. As a young politician, Michael had preferred freedom to the responsibility of office, not even trying for a place on Labour's National Executive Committee. Cultivated, erudite and humane, Michael was nevertheless often wrong on policy in my view – but always very likeable. He had been raised in a non-conformist West Country family, from whom he derived his decency and sense of public service. He developed into a fine essayist and political pamphleteer. His favourite work was as a literary reviewer and he was an authority on Hazlitt and Swift.

In my report on the Ebbw Vale campaign I said that on the day that pit-scarred constituency stopped sending Labour MPs to Westminster there would surely be a fuel-shortage in Hell. For a number of reasons, however, I forecast that Labour's huge majority might be cut by nearly half. In the week when Gaitskell had held the Labour leadership by a clear but hardly overwhelming victory against challenger Harold Wilson, I reported that Nye Bevan's esteemed one-time agent, Archie Lush, was on record as saying that the late member for Ebbw Vale had no respect for Gaitskell as leader and if alive would have contested the leadership.

On the same page, Ivan Yates in his last column for the paper, argued that not only had Wilson won the backing of less than half the number of MPs who voted for Gaitskell – but that those who supported him were mostly elderly or out-and-out unilateralists. To Yates, the most heartening feature of the election was the high number of younger MPs who had voted for Gaitskell. If Dora Gaitskell's influence over her husband at the time of the Suez War had been unhelpful, it was about to become a serious problem for the Labour Party during his battles with the Left over Clause Four of the party's constitution and nuclear disarmament. Totally opposed to any compromise with the Left, she never relaxed in her relentless efforts to convince him that he must crush the Bevanites, and she carried out her own bitter personal feud against the consorts of some of the leading figures on the Left. Thin lipped and vindictive to the extreme, she hated Wilson in particular for standing against her husband for the leadership. Although she received her life peerage after Wilson had become Labour leader, she always asserted that Harold Macmillan, as Prime Minister, had recommended her for a seat in the Lords.

Perhaps Hugh Gaitskell sometimes gave way to her on political matters because he felt guilty about his endless womanising. Perhaps he sometimes went in search of a quieter life with other women to escape from her obsessive and virulent interference in political affairs. I sometimes wondered how she felt when he went waltzing off on the dance floor with the best looking young women at Labour's conferences. She could recall, however, that they lived together for four blissful years before they married, following the break-up of her first marriage to a doctor in 1933.

Back in dreary Pioneer House, it was time for me to take over from Yates. I had asked him why he had not attended the end of week Government briefings given to the Lobby and he said he thought they would be a waste of time for a Sunday paper journalist. I was not so sure. I had seen a room full of political journalists miss a point more than once and decided I could spare an hour on a Thursday afternoon to sit in and listen. I decided to raise the matter with the Secretary of the Lobby, a stiff, dour Scot named Harry Boyne, who had been political correspondent of the *Daily Telegraph* since 1957, and before that for the *Glasgow Herald*. He had some good qualities – such as loyalty to his colleagues on the *Telegraph*. This he exhibited publicly when he joined the picket line outside the old office in Fleet Street during an industrial dispute and handed a letter of protest to the shocked proprietor, Lord Hartwell. As a journalist, however, he was unadventurous and pedestrian and at Westminster was mostly on the side of the establishment. He seemed surprised when I told him I would like to attend the Thursday Lobby briefing and dismissed me rather curtly with the words, *"Lobby briefings are not open to the Sunday press."* To which I retorted, *"James Margach of the Sunday Times attends them, as you well know."*

Boyne then showed some of the hypocrisy that normally was concealed behind his façade as a fair-to-all fellow. Jimmy Margach, he explained, attended as a representative of one of the Thomson group provincial papers, for which, it was understood by all, he was in reality far too grand to write by then. It was the type of phoney little arrangement that he should have found unacceptable. I gave him the most disdainful look I could muster and said he would hear from me again.

As it happened, the *Sunday Telegraph* was just being launched in February 1961 and the charming and courteous Ian Waller had moved from the *Glasgow Herald* to become its political correspondent. I had much respect for Ian, a reporter of great integrity, and on phoning to congratulate him I told him of my experience with Boyne. Would he support me, I asked, if I told Boyne that we – and perhaps some other Sunday journalists – would hold our own meetings on a Thursday and invite ministers to attend. Ian was quick to say he would indeed. I phoned Boyne and broke the news; he was as curt as ever. I sensed he did not like me. He said, however, that he would consult and let me know. When he rang back it was to tell me that the *"Sundays"* were to be allowed in. I imagine he liked me even less after that.

Our Battle with the Boyne had appealed to Ian, who had something quixotic in his nature and loved to tilt at creaky windmills. He took a leading role in the successful campaign to give women the right to stand at the bar at El Vino's, the Fleet Street wine dive noted at the time for its stuffiness. There was a near riot when women journalists and secretaries assisted by Ian invaded the bar one lunchtime and he was barred from the premises for a while after.

Margach, who had never had the integrity to demand the right of the *Sunday Times* to attend the meetings and had connived with Boyne in bending the rules now started to attend the briefings as a Sunday paper representative. Others, like Wilfred Sendall of the *Sunday Express* did likewise. Then, when the weekly journals, such as *The New Statesman* and *The Spectator,* asked for the same right, who was the first to stand up at a meeting and oppose their request for parity? Wilfred Sendall! Margach and Sendall had something in common. Both used stories for their papers originally written by Trevor Lloyd-Hughes, the hard-working political correspondent of the *Liverpool Post.* They had been published in his paper the day before – usually in his Saturday column. Sendall paid for them. Margach, merely bought Saturday's edition of the *Post* and lifted the material. On Sundays, political correspondents looking for stories for Monday's papers would often follow up the Sendall/Margach reports, thus giving further exposure to the nuggets buried in Lloyd-Hugh's provincial Saturday column.

As 1960 drew to a close, there was a build-up of press attacks on Macmillan, and Harold Evans, the P.M.'s advisor on public relations noted in his journal (later published) *"there is certainly a phase of doubt"*. Summing up the situation in his admirable memoirs *"Downing Street Diary"*, Harold wrote that Fleet Street was in a carping mood at the beginning of 1961 and quotes at length my *Reynolds News* column as reporting:

"Some disgruntled Party members believe that 1961 may be the last full calendar year they will have to put up with the whims and wiles of the man many now call MacTarnish."

He concluded that to an extent *"these rumblings reflected the absence of major political excitements."*

It was about this time that I met my first Russian spy. The Strangers' Bar at the Commons had become a favourite watering hole of Communist bloc agents in London. They were taken in as guests of MPs, mostly left wing Labour but also by a few Tories involved in East-West trade. I was drinking there one day when my host was called away and another MP asked me to join him and his guest, a smartly dressed, good-looking young man who, from his appearance, could have been the product of an English public school, as could have been his accent. Then he held out his hand and introduced himself – *"Michael Lyubimov"*. He had recently arrived in London to take on the cover role of Second Secretary in the Press Department. As I was to discover eventually, however, his real work was to get inside the Conservative Party for information of use to the KGB intelligence service, and to recruit agents. The Labour left wing was a natural hunting ground for Eastern bloc agents but having a taste for the high life, he preferred socialising with Tory MPs and journalists. He gave me his card and asked if I could spare the time to lunch with him. Within a few weeks we were sitting opposite each other in a smart, discreet London restaurant. We continued to meet for lunch regularly during my time with *Reynolds* and although he was to admit years later that he succeeded in recruiting some journalists as agents, he never tried it with me. He did invite me to take part in a Mediterranean cruise with other journalists, but I politely declined. In my naivety, I thought that I might persuade this affable man, who so obviously loved London life, to defect to Britain. We talked about current political developments and personalities, their policies and prospects. One day, discussing Gaitskell, he asked to my surprise, *"Is it true he likes dancing?"*

I confirmed that it was so, and wondered afterwards to what use that revelation would be put. He had been led to believe that if anything were to happen to Gaitskell, George Brown would become Labour leader. I told him that view was widely held but that, in my opinion, Harold Wilson would follow. He was surprised and clearly intrigued by this statement. Years later, in his retirement, he revealed that the KGB had some hopes that Wilson would prove helpful as he rose up the ranks, because he had connections with the Eastern bloc dating from when he was President of the Board of Trade in Attlee's Cabinet. They concluded eventually, however, that the wily Mr Wilson was unrecruitable. Nevertheless, in Lyubimov's opinion, British counter-intelligence was justified in keeping tabs on him when he became Prime Minister because someone who had dealt so extensively with the Eastern bloc should have been under observation.

Whenever we met after that, he would return to the question of the Labour leadership and press me on my view about Wilson's prospects. I stuck to my opinion and he would then ask me about Wilson's position on defence issues in the light of the support he had received from the nuclear disarmers in the leadership battle. The KGB was beginning to assess the possibility of having a CND sympathiser as leader of the Labour Party. If they began to believe that, they might think it worth paying someone to push Gaitskell under a bus! I pointed out to Lyubimov that to win the party leadership, Wilson would have to get the support of the bulk of MPs who believed in the nuclear deterrent and that on becoming party leader, he would no longer have to rely on the left wingers he used to get there.

Meanwhile, Lyubimov was living it up with the Tories, attending celebrity-studded parties hosted by the right-wing journalist Peregrine Worsthorne where he met ministers such as Trade Minister Reginald Maudling; and dining with up-and-coming MPs such as Peter Walker and Nicholas Scott. Over thirty years later, when Scott was facing deselection as MP for Kensington and Chelsea, the by then retired KGB Colonel Lyubimov was to enter the fray in his inimitable jokey fashion by publicly endorsing the embattled Tory knight as a true British patriot. He admitted that in the 1960s he had made repeated attempts to recruit Scott – then a Young Conservative tipped as a high flyer – by wining and dining him in London. *"But Nick was always true to Britain,"* noted Lyubimov, *"even when I tried to persuade him that Soviet ways were better."*

As I always met Lyubimov openly and went on several occasions to parties and recitals at the Soviet Embassy, I assumed that the British intelligence service was aware of this link and not bothered by it. In fact, perhaps because they were understaffed, they were not. Lyubimov's activities did not escape their notice, however, and after being followed by British intelligence agents for some time they eventually pounced on him as he was attempting to recruit a man in a West End pub. He was expelled from the country in 1965 on the grounds that his activities contravened his diplomatic status. Back in Moscow, he wrote the KGB's guide on how to spy in London. Always an elegant dresser, he advised his Russian readers to take care in choosing their clothes. An English gentleman, he cautioned, never wore brown. It was about that time that the formidable right-wing Labour MP, Dr Edith Summerskill, who had the discomfort of sitting on Labour's National Executive Committee with left winger Ian Mikardo, would refer to him, not by name, but with disdain as *"the man in the brown suit."*

Despite my best efforts, I got very little useful information from cagey, clever Lyubimov. In order not to be under any obligation to him I always hosted alternative lunches, so he was a drain on my limited expense account. But I confess that I enjoyed his company and thus had no regrets.

When Michael Foot re-entered the Commons as MP for Ebbw Vale, he was to find the atmosphere in the deeply divided Parliamentary Labour Party bitter and poisonous. Gaitskell's uncompromising stand on the issue of nuclear weaponry was beginning to make middle-of-the-roaders uneasy. Irritation quickly turned to anger and anger to blows. I had been taken to the Commons Strangers' Bar by right winger and shadow minister Fred Peart, whose father, a big name in local government, I had known in the North-East. Easy-going Fred enjoyed a pint but as we stood at the bar an extreme left-wing MP, Will Griffiths, who was already *"under the influence"* and in combative mood, started to argue angrily with him. Not liking something Fred had said he suddenly lurched forward and swung a punch. Fred, a skilled boxer, ducked and as Griffiths lost his balance the blow caught the side of my head. As he was not aiming at me and was very unsteady there was no injury inflicted beyond some spilt beer and the drunken Griffiths was helped out of the bar. In common with other journalists, I found Fred good company. A graduate of Durham University, which he had represented at boxing and football, he had served as an artillery officer in the war. Like his father, he was keenly interested in education and was Opposition Spokesman on Education and Science before being moved to shadow agriculture in 1961. With his amiable, convivial style he got on well with the farmers and was a popular choice when appointed Minister of Agriculture when Labour won power in 1964.

Following Labour's defeat in the 1959 general election, in due course, *Forward* was closed down having failed to win the hoped for readership from the party's rank and file. Roy Roebuck, former Labour MP, barrister and experienced journalist, told me years later that when he was involved in the printing of *Forward* in Manchester, he had to deal closely with deputy editor John Harris and found him to be "lazy and incompetent". With the demise of the journal Harris became Parliamentary Party press and liaison officer and in that role was soon adding fuel to the flames of the bitter internecine conflict on the Labour benches.

Instead of representing the whole PLP, Harris was operating as Gaitskell's personal PR man, continually *"stirring it up"*. It was Harris more than any other who spread smears about Wilson and peddled the story that he was having a heavy affair with Marcia Williams. Whatever Wilson and Marcia might have been up to – and it was certainly not very much – one thing is certain: that one of the most active womanisers in the PLP was Gaitskell himself. Harris, being so close to the party leader, must have known about his constant philandering. At a dinner party one evening at the home of George Thomson a high ranking

American diplomat told of his astonishment when Gaitskell, who was flying with him to Scandinavia, set about *"picking up"* a pretty air hostess. One of the jobs of a cockney member of the *Daily Mirror* staff deputed to help Gaitskell as he travelled round the country was to find attractive young members of the party to dance with him. But a far more serious situation was to be brought to my notice in due course – a situation that could have lost Labour the next general election.

It was in this depressing setting that I began my work as the political editor of *Reynolds News*. My aim was to provide a potential political lead story for the paper virtually every week – and in three out of every four weeks I did that. As I also covered the diplomatic and defence fields for the paper the task of getting the lead was made easier. With the column I sought, whenever possible, to look forward rather than to chew over the events of the past week and to use it to attack the Tories rather than stir up the running row in the Labour Party.

One of my problems was that my strongly Gaitskellite friends, who had helped me get the *Reynolds News* job, were expecting me to continue in the Yates' tradition of attacking the left and belittling Wilson. Looking at the Labour scene, however, I had reached the conclusion that, if Gaitskell *were* to be run over by a bus, the majority of the Parliamentary Party would vote for Wilson as the man most likely to unify the Labour Movement and win the next election. Deputy Leader George Brown, although capable of flashes of brilliance, was too fond of drink and too much of a bully to be acceptable to many. Thanks partly to the influence of John Harris, however, nearly all in the media had been persuaded that Wilson had no hope of winning the leadership and that Brown, or some other right-winger, would get the job if, and when, a vacancy occurred.

Throughout the early months of 1961, leading members of the Labour Party struggled to thrash out an acceptable policy on defence. It was Richard Crossman's turn to be party chairman and in this key role he worked hard to bridge the gap between the triumphant unilateralists and Gaitskell. The leftish Union of Shop, Distributive and Allied Workers had a close relationship with the Co-operative Movement and so with *Reynolds News*. The Union President Walter Paddley, a shrewd and amiable man, backed Crossman's efforts for compromise as a means of persuading USDAW to move away from unilateralism. Billy Richardson, who was in close contact with Padley, invited me to join them for lunch in a restaurant off Charlotte Street and most of the time was spent in discussing the party's defence problem – and in particular the damaging personal feud between Gaitskell and Frank Cousins, the trade unionist standard bearer of the unilateralist cause. Cousins was not a man easily persuaded to compromise and such was Gaitskell's deep distrust of him that there was no hope of them reaching agreement. To make the personal problem more intractable, Dora Gaitskell had now developed an aggressive detestation of Cousin's wife. Soon after the lunch with Padley, Richardson arranged for me to join him and Cousins for lunch in the same restaurant. Perhaps he thought that, as I had sympathised with Padley's efforts to achieve a compromise, I might be persuaded to sympathise with Cousins, too. It was not to be.

However, in March I no doubt pleased Cousins by using my *Reynold's* column to attack the Labour leadership's decision to expel from the Parliamentary Labour Party the newly returned Michael Foot and four other unilateralist MPs who had voted against the Government's Defence Estimates. Fearful that any vote against such estimates would be misconstrued by the public as votes against any defence of Britain, the Shadow Cabinet had persuaded the PLP to agree that it should not oppose them. Despite this, twenty-four rebelled against this decision on one vote – a demonstration that received little publicity in the press. But, as I wrote in my column, *"because party decisions must be obeyed, Mr Gaitskell was obliged to warn against a repetition."*

It was a safe bet that a few would ignore this, in the light of the previous autumn's party conference decision, and take the path to martyrdom. The press gave the small revolt next to no publicity. The expulsion of the five rebels, however, resulted in screaming headlines proclaiming a new Labour crisis. I criticised the Shadow Cabinet for a clumsily handled business and expressed the fear that the affair might adversely affect the result of a by-election due in the Labour-held seat of Small Heath, Birmingham, the following Thursday. In 1959, Labour's majority had fallen to 4,931 in a straight fight with the Tories. Now the resurgent Liberals had re-entered the field. Labour, however, had adopted an excellent candidate named Denis Howell – in due course to be known not only as Minister for Sport but as the *"Minister for Weather"* when he famously made the rain fall in a drought. Denis was a local man with a fine record of service to Birmingham, both on the Council and as MP for the All Saints Division, where his defeat in 1959 was one of the big shocks of that general election. A strong pro-Gaitskellite and multilateralist on defence, he was helped in his campaign by many young people sporting nuclear disarmament badges. Howell won comfortably – and some Gaitskellites were quick to claim that the expulsion of the five rebel MPs had helped bring this about by showing Gaitskell to be a strong leader. They were entitled to their view.

At the Co-operative Party conference the following month, a resolution was passed reaffirming the unilateralist stand taken the previous year. In the leader column of *Reynolds News* Billy Richardson deplored the fact that the duration and intensity of the defence debate was stultifying Labour in other directions. He called for a sense of balance. This was no doubt appreciated by Richard Crossman who, in offering fraternal greeting to the Co-operative Party conference as Labour chairman, paid tribute to *Reynolds News* as the only newspaper owned and controlled within the movement. He declared, *"For years Reynolds News has been fighting valiantly against the tide that swept away the News Chronicle and lost us the Daily Herald as a genuine Labour newspaper."*

He feared that, *"apart from the so-called quality papers, ordinary people might, within five years, find that the only choice they had in their daily and weekly reading was between a Beaverbrook product and one controlled by Cecil King."*

My encouragement of Tom Driberg to call for another Royal Commission on the Press after the death of the *News Chronicle* had not been in vain. When soon after that black day for Fleet Street the *Daily Mirror* took over *Odhams* and the *Daily Herald,* Prime Minister Macmillan decided that he would have to respond positively, after all, to the growing demand for a top-level inquiry into the newspaper business. Lord Shawcross, who had been Attorney General during the Attlee Government, was appointed to chair the Royal Commission. Giving evidence to the inquiry, newspaper proprietors blamed the death of the *Chronicle* on poor top management. Roy Thomson revealed that he had considered taking over the paper at one time – but that was in response to an approach made to him before it became known that the paper was going out of business. He said he had wanted to take it over but, when all the pros and cons had been examined, the stark fact stood out that if he could not make a success of it and had to close it, he would be faced with a redundancy problem amounting to two or three million pounds. In fact, when it came to redundancy payments, due to a shareholder's legal challenge to the paper's compensation scheme, young journalists like me with little service in the Cadbury stable got virtually nothing.

The Royal Commission wasted little time and reported in September 1962, concluding that different, more consistent management and editorial policy may have saved the *News Chronicle,* which had a circulation of over a million and many more readers than that. On the wider front, the report covered the problem of a growth in concentration of ownership, trade union practices which hampered efficient management and the need to reform the toothless Press Council. Although Shawcross had become something of a joke in political circles, nicknamed before his peerage as Sir Shortly Floorcross, I thought his Commission had done a good quick job and in my personal dealings with him, I always found him helpful and courteous.

As the summer of 1961 wore on, some of the material in my weekly column – such as the criticism of the expulsion of the five rebel MPs – was becoming a source of irritation to Gaitskell. I had arranged, through John Harris, to have regular private meetings with the Labour leader and one afternoon Harris confronted me rather huffily in the Members' Lobby to say Hugh wanted to have a word. When I entered the room allocated to the Leader of the Opposition I felt a distinct chill in the air. Gaitskell lost no time in making it known that he was disappointed with some of my comments and seemed to be insinuating that I must have unilateralist leanings to have written as I did about the expulsions. He was also displeased that I had drawn attention to an increase in young members of the Communist Party at a time when the Young Socialists were struggling to maintain members. I had done so to underline the need for the Labour Party to produce policies to satisfy the idealising of young people. *"Did he think I was a fellow traveller?"* I wondered. Then came an irritable reference to the fact that I had given some praise, at this difficult time, to the work on various committees by the man who had challenged him for the leadership some six months before – Harold Wilson. Perhaps I should have said that I thought Wilson would replace him if he were run over by the proverbial bus? But in his highly-strung, stressed-out state he would have had apoplexy had I done so. I stood my ground, but not very forcefully, and left the room in a somewhat shell-shocked state.

John Harris had clearly put in the poison and there had been no acknowledgement of the fact that, week after week, I had been providing strong anti-Tory stories and reports helpful to Labour and the Co-operative Party. I arrived home still shaken and depressed and decided to write immediately to Gaitskell to explain how, as a supporter of his, I saw my role as the political editor of the struggling last national newspaper in the Labour movement's fold. I also took the opportunity to point out that, with regard to the unilateralist issue, it was very much in my personal interest that we should have a strong nuclear deterrent as I was an officer in the Army's poorly equipped front line reserve and could be called up for service without a general proclamation. I added, with a drip of sarcasm, that, although he had never served in the armed forces, I was sure he would understand the seriousness of that position.

The letter helped to ease the situation. I received a short reply in which Gaitskell thanked me for my explanation – and suggested that I might find it useful to have lunch with his close colleague and mine, Douglas Jay, to talk matters over further. Soon after I received a call from Douglas, who sounded a trifle embarrassed, and a lunch was arranged. Educated at Winchester with Gaitskell and Crossman and then at New College, Oxford, he had a razor-sharp mind. He had been City Editor of the *Daily Herald* before serving with distinction as a civil servant during the war. Entering Parliament, he had been appointed a Treasury Minister by Prime Minister Attlee. In opposition, he had never trusted Wilson and found George Brown's style unacceptable. On the social side he was notoriously thrifty and greatly enjoyed the company of women. He had married his bright and attractive wife Peggy in 1933, having twin daughters and two sons, the elder of whom, Peter, married James Callaghan's daughter and was to be appointed Ambassador to Washington by his father-in-law. I had great respect for his intellect and writing ability but knew well his reputation for parsimony. It came as no great surprise, therefore, when he suggested that we should eat in the soulless King's Cross Station cafeteria – a short walk from the *Reynolds News* office. On the appointed day he picked me up in the reporters' room after handing in his weekly column. He was in his usual crumpled, dandruff-flecked suit, his sparse hair ill combed. As we set off, I asked myself how it was that someone so physically unprepossessing could have been so successful at attracting bright, attractive women. A tireless womaniser, he had warned his young wife-to-be, the formidable Peggy, that he considered monogamy *"a sin"*.

In the utilitarian cafeteria he handed me a menu listing various fry-ups, pastas and puddings. Then the old skinflint lived up to his reputation. Eyeing me across the narrow table in a distinctly challenging manner, he said, *"I'm not very hungry today. I think I'll just have a bowl of soup."*

I paused, bringing the light of relief to his eyes when I replied, *"A bowl of soup Douglas – that will suit me fine. Tomato, please."*

"Two tomato soups with rolls – and a jug of water please!" he ordered triumphantly. And so we settled down to our one-course chat. I explained to him how I saw my role and he agreed that I had a problem. He explained for his part that Gaitskell was being put under constant exhausting pressure and that I must make allowance for this and try not to add to his problems in my efforts to keep *Reynolds* afloat. Then I moved the talk on to the issue of Britain's entry into the European Common Market that was beginning to loom as the next big political issue to confront the Labour leadership.

In my regular talks with Gaitskell I had never been led to doubt that he was in favour of British entry. Moreover, virtually all his closest colleagues were strongly pro-European – Roy Jenkins, Tony Crosland, William Rogers, George Thomson, Jack Diamond, and so on... Douglas was the great exception – and in this respect linked up with Labour's anti-Common Market brigade led by formidable fighters such as Michael Foot and Barbara Castle. In the course of our short talk I was left with the clear impression that Douglas did not assume his boss would be on his side of the battle.

By the early summer of 1961, the question of Common Market entry had in fact begun to rise on the political horizon and the scene was being set for another policy row within the Labour Party. Under pressure from pro and anti-marketeers, Gaitskell warned his friends of the danger of trying to commit the party to a detailed policy. It was generally assumed, however, that he would be broadly in favour of the principle of entry and Harold Wilson's friends were forecasting another major battle between him and the

Left on this issue. Wilson himself had chaired a sub-committee of the party's National Executive Committee on the question of whether entry would be of economic advantage to Britain. Leslie Plummer had much pleasure in tipping me off that Wilson had cleverly got his committee to agree that, on the economic front, there was nothing in it either way. Like a spider, Wilson had spun his web and now waited for Gaitskell to become entangled in it. Wilson had no intention of losing the support of the Left on the issue of Europe and of offering Gaitskell help through his committee's report. He assumed that, despite the report, Gaitskell, in line with the views of most of his close friends, would come out in favour of joining the Common Market and suffer another humiliating defeat on this issue at the party conference.

My responsibilities at *Reynolds* included the coverage of defence issues and when in June 1961 Iraq made aggressive moves towards its neighbour Kuwait, and Britain responded to an urgent request for aid from the ruler of the oil-rich kingdom, I found myself reporting on developments. In a shade temperature of 120 degrees, Royal Marine Commandos, a squadron of Centurion tanks and RAF Hunter jets had been quickly deployed and British and U.S. warships were moving towards the danger zone. It was Saturday July 1. I decided to phone the Admiralty to ask about naval deployment. I announced myself as *"Arthur Butler, Reynolds"* and asked for the information department. A man with a crisp public school accent took the call. *"Intelligence!"* he snapped.

"Arthur Butler, Reynolds," I said again. *"Could you let me have the latest on naval ship movements in connection with the Kuwait operation?"*

"Hold on a moment, I'll get the cables," he replied.

That, I thought, was unusually good service. He came back on the phone and started to read the information to me. Then he paused.

"I think you'd better go on the scrambler," he said. I gulped.

"OK," I concurred.

After a short burst of scrambled noise he came back to me.

"Got what you need?" he asked. I gulped again.

"I'm sorry," I replied, *"my scrambler's not working."*

With a note of impatience in his voice he said, *"Right, I'll read them again."*

This time with no scrambler, I completed my notes. I thanked him and hung up. I walked into Eric Wright's office in a slight daze and told him we had the navy's secret battle plan. Naval *"Intelligence"* had presumably assumed I was some high-ranking fellow named *"Arthur Butler-Reynolds"*. Eric and I laughed and agreed that nothing should be reported, not even the security breach by the Admiralty. A few days later I met Dr Charles Hill, the Minister responsible for Government information in the Commons, and told him – without naming the department involved – that there had been a serious security breach and suggested he take steps to ensure that in future all callers were thoroughly checked out and put through to the correct person.

Hill, with the title of Chancellor of the Duchy of Lancaster, had been given the job of coordinating the Government Information Services in Harold Macmillan's reshuffle in January 1957 following the Suez debacle. Hill had first achieved fame as the Radio Doctor, his gravelly voice disturbing our breakfasts with advice on bowel movements and the help that could be provided by *"the little black-coated workers"* that he called prunes.

Some fourteen months later I became involved in more serious circumstances in the aftermath of the Kuwait operation. On a Friday at the end of August 1962, Trevor Lloyd-Hughes, in return for some information I had given him, told me that George Wigg, the Commons expert on Army affairs, had given him a story that his paper the *Liverpool Post* would be carrying the next day. The Labour MP's grave criticisms of the previous year's British Army operation in Kuwait had been supported by official inquiries. In fact, it had been established that the British Army troops could have suffered heavy casualties if attacked early in the operation because they were severely vulnerable to heat exhaustion in the baking temperature. Wigg, who had learned of the Army inquiry, had been granted a private interview for the following Tuesday with War Under-Secretary James Ramsden to discuss his misgivings in advance of a Commons adjournment debate at the end of that week. It would take place in the light of Army investigations that had revealed that much of the troops' personal equipment was unsuitable for hot desert conditions. Moreover, the Army investigators had concluded that it was unwise to send men into the desert before being properly conditioned to the heat. The Government had tried to cover up the blunders and Wigg feared that unless the truth was exposed British troops would again be sent ill equipped for such a battle zone. Some forty years later they were to be − sent into Iraq by Tony Blair's Labour Government. George Wigg surely turned in his grave. Under the banner headline *"Desert War Blunder" Reynolds News* carried the story as its front-page lead on Sunday. I had phoned Wigg to ask for a statement but, although confirming the story off the record, he declined to give me a quote. I was puzzled by this reticence but learned in due course that Wigg had been granted the meeting with

Ramsden on the understanding that it was to be kept secret. Wigg had assumed that no one would notice if the story were carried only in the *Liverpool Post's* Saturday edition.

As I had forecast, Wigg visited the War Office on the Tuesday and gave the Under Secretary details of the points he intended to raise in his end of day Commons adjournment debate on the Friday. Nothing was said about my report of the previous Sunday. On the eve of the debate Army Minister John Profumo phoned Wigg at home to go over matters again – but made no reference to my news story or to some misleading letters he had received from two Commanding Officers suggesting that there had been no problem. Wigg was therefore very angry when, in the course of the debate next day, Profumo failed to deal with some of the issues he had raised privately. Moreover, the Minister revealed the existence of the officers' letters and went on to imply that my story in *Reynolds News* had originated from Wigg, who had, in fact been embarrassed by the splash that had caused considerable annoyance in the War Ministry. John Profumo felt badly let down. Wigg knew he was at fault – but he was a proud man and could not forgive Profumo for implying he had broken his word, for not dealing with the key issues as he saw them and for using the letters as a red herring. He was determined to make the dapper forty-seven-year-old Minister suffer. In the following year he did just that – in what became known as the Profumo affair, a scandal that was to seriously damage the Macmillan Government.

Following his 1959 general election victory, Macmillan had been riding high. Vicky, the left-wing cartoonist, had scornfully depicted him as *"Macwonder"* or *"Super Mac"* but to his horror he began to discover that Macmillan's political successes were making these nicknames appear appropriate and well earned. He had to drop them. By the summer of 1961, however, Macmillan, like Gaitskell, was faced with a split in his party on the question of Britain's application to join the European Economic Community.

On July 30' I predicted in *Reynolds News* that the Prime Minister would face a small but fierce revolt by right-wing Tory MPs when he announced to the Commons in the coming week that Britain was about to open negotiations to join the six-nation Common Market. Due to the efficiency of the Government whips the revolt was even smaller than I had expected but it was also fiercer. Anthony Fell, the young right-wing Tory MP for Yarmouth, whom I had got to know some years before as an outspoken Suez rebel, accused the Prime Minister of making a shocking statement full of political double-talk and branded him *"a national disaster"*. Fell, together with the five Labour MPs from whom the Whip had been withdrawn, voted against the Government. A handful of Tory critics abstained and as the official Labour Party also abstained, Macmillan won an easy Commons victory. On August 10' Britain formerly applied for membership of the EEC. Fell, who had grown to bitterly dislike Edward Heath because of his heavy-handed disciplinary activity as Chief Whip during the Suez debacle, now had even more cause to curse him in his role as the Government's most dedicated Common Marketeer. He eventually played an active role in losing Heath the leadership of the Tory Party and was awarded with a knighthood by Margaret Thatcher. Years later, he and I would recall these events over drinks in my house for we became close neighbours.

Heath had been given the task of handling our case for entry into the EEC and as he haggled over the terms, debate about it in Britain became more heated. The Canadian Lord Beaverbrook, a great campaigner for stronger Commonwealth trading links, was strongly opposed to

Heath's efforts and urged his editors to conduct a relentless anti-Market fight. They were to encourage the Tory rebels and the growing anti-market faction in the Labour Party – and he believed he had in his hand *a "secret weapon"* powerful enough to ensure that Gaitskell, after some uncomfortable fence sitting, would desert his close pro-Europe friends and come out against joining. I was not to find out until January 1963 just what that secret weapon was. There is no doubt in my mind, however, that he made sure that it was brought to Gaitskell's attention in the summer of 1962 – and before the Labour Party Conference was due to make its decision on the issue in the October. It was vital to Beaverbrook's campaign that Labour should not support Common Market membership and it was tactically important, therefore, that Gaitskell should be warned in advance of the consequences to him personally and his party's general election prospects if it decided to support the Government's pro-Europe line.

In the face of Beaverbrook's demands Gaitskell's problem was how to account for a sudden decision to oppose Common Market membership. At the eleventh hour he was provided with the solution.

On Sunday September 9, *Reynolds News,* under the headline *"Market Sensation",* led with my report that at a meeting the day before Commonwealth Labour leaders – five of them Prime Ministers – had flatly rejected the Common Market terms the Government had so far negotiated. I wrote, *"Their bombshell – after talks with Mr Gaitskell – means a head-on clash with the Government, which is determined not to revise these terms.*

"Unless Mr Macmillan gives way, the Labour Party, with the blessing of the Commonwealth, will be forced to oppose Britain's entry into Europe and demand a general election."

The meeting, between Commonwealth and European socialist leaders at Labour headquarters in London, had issued a statement declaring: *"We cannot regard the provisional outline agreements so far reached at Brussels as safeguarding the relation of Britain with the Commonwealth and as adequately fulfilling the Prime Minister's pledge."*

That pledge, given on August 2, was not to ask Parliament to support entry if it would injure Britain's relations with, and influence in, the Commonwealth. Gaitskell, in a separate statement said, *"If the Government propose to go into the Common Market on terms which the Labour Party regard as wholly unacceptable we should then ask for a general election."*

The TUC, at its September conference, sat on the fence over the issue and the Labour Conference was expected to unite on a demand for a general election to be held before agreement was reached with the *"Common Market Six"*. On October 3, however, Gaitskell, in his conference speech, stunned his pro-Market friends. Following the line laid down by Harold Wilson's committee that on economic grounds the arguments for and against were evenly balanced, he declared with great emotion that, politically, a federal Europe would be the end of an independent Britain and of the Commonwealth – *"the end of a thousand years of history."* Lord Beaverbrook could not have been more satisfied if he had written the speech himself.

Labour's anti-marketeers gave their leader a loud standing ovation. The pro-Europeans looked sick and Bill Rodgers, one of the most loyal Gaitskellites, was so angry and upset he refused to rise from his chair. Jack Diamond, one of Gaitskell's most ardent supporters who had played a leading role in setting up the Labour Common Market Committee to campaign for EEC membership, was devastated. A week later, at the Conservative Party

Conference at Llandudno, the Tory anti-marketeers were soundly defeated. I, meanwhile, had made an important personal decision. From what I had heard of the plans to transform the broadsheet *Reynolds* into a breezy tabloid – the *Sunday Citizen* – I had concluded that politics would no longer be the *raison d'etre* of the paper. Despite my personal efforts on that front, the amount of space devoted to politics had certainly not boosted the circulation in the past two years. It had fallen from under 400,000 to around 300,000 a week. I did not relish the prospect of working for a tabloid. Moreover, despite the ample space provided for my stories and weekly column in *Reynolds* I was finding the Sunday paper routine increasingly frustrating. I wanted to return to the excitement of daily journalism and this seemed a good time to make the break.

The last issue of *Reynolds News* was published on Sunday September 16. Just as a report by me had been the lead story in the last issue of the *News Chronicle* two years before, so a report by me provided the splash for that goodbye issue of *Reynolds.* Under a six column headline *"Paperhanger Mac"* it dealt with the Prime Minister's attempt to cover up his failure to win over the large majority of Commonwealth leaders to his Common Market proposals. Next to it, across two columns and running the length of the page, was a blurb advertising the highlights that Eric Wright hoped would thrill readers in the first issue of the *Sunday Citizen* the following weekend. They included *"The Truth about Z-Cars"* –TV's popular police serial; a new line-up of women columnists; sports pages; and competitions providing *"chances to make dreams come true"...* but of the reporting of the political scene there was no mention. I was dismayed and sure that such a recipe would not appeal to the radical old paper's traditional readers – in fact, that the Editor's dream of increased circulation would not come true.

In his last column for *Reynolds*, Tom Driberg, while pointing out that it was right to demand a general election on the Common Market issue, argued that there were formidable difficulties about having an election on one issue, especially one on which both main parties were internally divided. *"There remains the device of the referendum,"* he went on – opening up a subject of which we were soon to hear much more. His columns had too often been trivial and snobby, but this was one of the best he had written.

When the first edition of the red top *Sunday Citizen* arrived in the office the following Saturday evening I tried to look enthusiastic as Eric Wright proudly waved a copy in the air. But I felt as though I had swallowed a heavy weight. As soon as possible I left the office and walked around the block. Tears trickled down my cheek for the first time since I had wept for the *News Chronicle*. Sometime later, Cyril Hamnett, chairman of the Co-op press that had published *Reynolds*, revealed that he too had shed a tear over the demise of the paper. Next day I wrote my letter of resignation, giving three months notice, which I handed to Eric Wright on the Tuesday. I thanked him sincerely for having given me the opportunity to work for such a great campaigning paper and explained that I now felt the need to return to some form of daily journalism. I had decided to act quickly knowing that sales of the new paper would initially be higher than those of *Reynolds* and so I could not be accused of deserting a sinking ship.

My fears for the longer term, however, were well justified and before long the readership began to fall until it had slumped to 230,000 by 1965. It had become a far more serious drain on the finances of the Co-op Press than

Reynolds had ever been and it was closed down two years later. It was hard-working Eric Wright's turn to shed a tear. Billy Richardson, whose easy-going arm's length approach to the arduous job of editing a struggling paper had contributed to the death of *Reynolds* was to receive a Knighthood from Prime Minister Harold Wilson a week before the closure of its unsuccessful successor the *Sunday Citizen*. It must be rare for an editor to receive such an honour for helping to kill off his paper by neglect. The tone of his left-ish leading articles had been very acceptable to Wilson however, during his manoeuvring to oust Gaitskell as Labour leader.

Eric Wright was distinctly unhappy about my resignation and no doubt interpreted it as a vote of no confidence in the newborn *Sunday Citizen*. When he asked me if I had another job lined up I admitted that I had not, but I was confident that I would find one within three months. Depressed by the fact that two great radical papers had sunk with me aboard within such a short period, I thought that perhaps it was time for me to leave the world of newspapers and try to get into television news. I recalled that Bernstein had been interested in employing me when the *Chronicle* died but, deciding that I did not wish to be based in Manchester, I turned my thoughts towards Independent Television News. Ian Trethowan, who had been so helpful to me when he led the *News Chronicle's* parliamentary team, was by now well established at ITN. At the Conservative Party Conference at Llandudno in early October I approached him with my problem. Typically, he put himself out to assist. He said he knew ITN was intending to recruit someone soon to join the news team and he would have a word with his boss, Editor and Chief Executive Geoffrey Cox, to let him know of my interest. Two days later, at the end of conference business, Cox met me on Llandudno pier. The 52-year-old New

Zealander had established a revolutionary style of news coverage, including incisive, probing interviews with top politicians to replace the stuffy, reverential questioning of the past. He had already recruited and trained a team of other youngish journalists, including Ian and Robin Day. Having won a Rhodes Scholarship to Oxford he had joined the *News Chronicle* on graduating and had reported on the Spanish Civil War before joining the *Daily Express*. Commissioned in the New Zealand Army in World War II, he worked as a senior intelligence officer before returning to the *News Chronicle* in 1945 as political correspondent, becoming assistant editor nine years later. He had left to edit Independent Television News in 1956 soon after I joined the paper, and so had not got to know me.

Briefed by Ian for our meeting, he was sympathetic about *Reynolds* rolling over but as we talked about that chapter in my career I realised that with his problems of achieving political balance in his news reports he would presumably not be keen to take on someone who, for the past two years, had been lambasting the government week after week. He had won a reputation for being fair and non-partisan and was anxious to protect that. He explained that there had indeed been a vacancy, but it had been decided to introduce a regional touch to the news team. It had been proposed, therefore, that a young chap named Alastair Burnet should be recruited. It was the same clever young Oxford graduate whose TV style was to earn him the nickname of the *"Simpering Scot"* and who, in due course, was to edit *The Economist* and the *Daily Express* – and to receive a Knighthood. I told Cox I appreciated his desire to bring in a regional flavour and thanked him for finding time to see me. He wished me luck and we parted. He went on to launch *The News at Ten* in 1967 and was knighted the previous year. As for Ian Trethowan, he went on to become

Managing Director of BBC Radio, then Head of BBC Television and finally, at the age of 54, Director General of the BBC, succeeding Charles Curran. Considerate and reserved in manner, he was a conservative with a small "c" and in that respect was perhaps not the ideal person to be political correspondent of the *News Chronicle*. I held him in very high regard, however, and his reports on politics were always scrupulously fair.

As the weeks passed, I began to spend more of my time applying for posts on left-ish radical daily papers and eventually the Sunday press. There were no vacancies for senior political correspondents. My Labour MP friends were understanding about my desire to find a new job as they were not impressed by the *Sunday Citizen*. Members of the Labour Co-operative group in the Commons were particularly sorry about my impending departure. They included such politicians as Albert "Bert" Oram, a conscientious, mild left-winger and early advocate of British membership of the Common Market who was to become Parliamentary Secretary for Overseas Development in 1964. Another very friendly member of the group was George Darling, a former journalist and BBC industrial correspondent, who had been appointed by Gaitskell to serve under Douglas Jay shadowing Board of Trade ministers. His special interest was consumer protection and Wilson made him a Minister of State at Trade in 1964. They told me later that they had never received such coverage in *Reynolds* until I arrived there and Oram, as chairman of the Co-op group of MPs had expressed their thanks by inviting me to attend their regular group meetings at the Commons. I was the first and, as it turned out, the last political reporter to be granted that facility.

The early sixties were a time of fast-growing interest in consumerism and playing up to that, I led *Reynolds* one

Christmas with a report headlined *"Shoddy Goods Fight"* about the Labour Co-op MPs introducing a Private Member's Bill to provide safeguards against dangerous appliances and misleading labelling. I also gave publicity to a consumer protection bill introduced by Co-op MP Bob Edwards, the doughty left-wing General Secretary of the Chemical Workers Union. An ardent pro-marketeer, his passion for a united Europe stemmed from his experience as an officer in the Republican Army in the Spanish Civil War. While fighting in Spain he met George Orwell but did not hold him in very high regard, suspecting he was more interested in operating as a journalist than as *"a true anti-Fascist fighter."*

As Christmas approached, I began to regret that I had not got myself the promise of a new job before giving in my notice to Eric Wright. To add to my impending financial problem, my wife and I had decided to move from our rented flat in Leytonstone and to buy a house. I was attracted to South London as there was a good late night train service from Blackfriars station near Fleet Street, much used by journalists after a heavy night in the Press Club – or even in the office. We had found a property in leafy Dulwich and were due to move in at the beginning of January.

Chapter Seven
In The Black Lybianka

It could have been the *"Last Chance Saloon"*. With imminent unemployment staring me in the face, I was drinking in mid-December in the Press Gallery bar when Douglas Clark, political editor of the *Daily Express* moved in beside me offering a prospective gamble. He said he had just heard that I was looking for a new job and would I be interested in joining the Express? If he had asked me the week after I had given my notice to the *Sunday Citizen* I would have replied, *"Thanks for the offer, Douglas – but no."*

Although I admired the professionalism and élan of the Express, the tone of its political coverage had often revolted me and I had always said that I would not work for Beaverbrook. Faced with a serious financial problem, however, I asked Douglas what the job amounted to. He revealed that he was moving to the *Sunday Express* early in the New Year and that his number two, Ian Aitken, was due to take over, leaving a vacancy at the lower level for a lobby correspondent. A third member of the team, Charles Douglas-Home, nephew of Foreign Secretary Lord Home, specialised as a diplomatic correspondent but also helped out on the political front. Clark said that he had been impressed by my work on the *News Chronicle* and *Reynolds News* and that Beaverbrook had shown an interest in some of my exclusives. He added, also, that in his opinion Aitken would not stay in the job for long and that top billing might come my way. Aitken, in fact, an experienced *Express* reporter, had come from true left-wing stock for whom it might be assumed reporting politics for Beaverbrook would be anathema also. His father George, a Scottish engineering worker, was an early member of the Communist Party and, like my friend, Bob Edwards MP, had fought against Franco's fascists in the Spanish Civil War. He had broken with the communists in 1939 and joined the Labour Party in 1945, becoming research officer for the Amalgamated Engineering Union.

Douglas asked me to think over the offer and phone him the following Monday. I had not bothered to ask about the salary as I knew it had to be better than the *Sunday Citizen* pittance. Evelyn looked very relieved when I broke the news that evening. My main consideration was to be able to continue working as a political reporter and I reassured myself that if I found working for Beaverbrook unbearable I could look around for a job on another paper – and that would be easier to get with by-lines in the hugely successful Express to my name. I told Douglas on Monday that I would like the job and on Tuesday he bought me a large gin and tonic at the Press Gallery bar to celebrate my decision. He said he would arrange for me to be interviewed by the editor Roger Wood, but that would be a mere formality as he was recommending me after consultation with Lord Beaverbrook.

Two days before Christmas, I walked through the door of the spectacular black glass building in Fleet Street that housed the offices of Beaverbrook's newspaper empire. The *Daily Express* brashly called itself the *"World's greatest,"* selling around four million copies a day. The cocky, confident staff almost took pride in the fact that the Duke of Edinburgh had described their flagship as *"a bloody awful paper"*. Their substantial salaries bolstered by generous expense accounts and their daily operations abundantly resourced, they looked down on their competitors like Balliol men with an effortless assumption of conscious superiority. From 1957 until 1962, the paper had been edited by the urbane, experienced Edward Pickering, better known as *"Pick"*, who had successfully succeeded the legendary Arthur Christiansen. Beaverbrook, who fired the famous *"Chris"* out of short-sighted jealousy, had then repeated his mistake by dismissing *"Pick"* after he had continued to increase the paper's circulation for five years. It was a turning point. From then on, editors were to come and go in quick succession.

On entering the headquarters of Beaverbrook Newspapers, nicknamed *"The Black Lybianka"* I had found myself in a dazzling art deco hall, concocted from moulded plaster enriched by gilding. Golden panels designed by Eric Aumonier paid tribute to the British Empire – the Empire which Beaverbrook regarded as the most important institution in the world. On the far side of the foyer from the glass front door, metal serpents flanked a flight of stairs that led to the offices. The whole setting was lit so as to heighten the dramatic effect. There could have been no greater contrast to the run-down dingy office of the *Sunday Citizen*. I was dazzled. Possessing a well-thumbed copy of Evelyn Waugh's novel *"Scoop"*, I recognised it as the Byzantine vestibule that had stunned the hero William Boot on his visit to press baron Lord Copper, clearly based on Beaverbrook.

The Express was enjoying a boom in sales with a circulation of well over four million. There was an excited buzz of pre-Christmas festivity in the air. Roger Wood, who had a reputation for disorderly behaviour and schoolboy pranks, was sober and business-like as it was not yet lunchtime. He asked me what I earned on the *Sunday Citizen* and offered me a small increase more redolent of Scrooge than the Spirit of Christmas Present. I agreed to start in the first week of January.

Two days before I joined the Beaverbrook stable we moved to our new home in Dulwich. As I approached, I saw a familiar figure standing outside on the pavement. It was Peter Chambers who had been at Kemsley House during my time there and had moved to the *Daily Express* as a feature writer. *"Hello Peter,"* I exclaimed, *"What are you doing here?"*

"You won't believe it," he grimaced," *Some bloody fool has decided we should have a piece on a young up-and-coming couple moving house. So I phoned Harrods removals department and they told me they were moving just such a pair into this place today."*

It was my turn to grimace.

"I'm half of that couple," I said apologetically, adding, *"and as I'm joining the Express this week I suppose I can't tell you to bugger off?!"*

So the Butlers' move to a maisonette in Dulwich provided reading for the Express' millions of readers the next day.

I had got my new job in my last week with the *Sunday Citizen.* But after I had informed Eric Wright he put it around the office that I had obviously planned to join the Express from the start and had revealed my move only at the last minute to avoid embarrassment. On December 16 I had my last lead story for his already troubled tabloid. It was a report that Macmillan planned to offer France a share in the development of the nuclear Skybolt missile if President de Gaulle agreed that Britain could join the Common Market.

I was sad that Eric had taken my departure so badly as I admired his energy and strenuous efforts to keep the paper afloat. I was also deeply indebted to him for rescuing me when the *News Chronicle* sank. As I stepped aboard the *Daily Express,* Douglas Clark, a wartime naval officer, was there to greet me. He led me into a congested glass cubicle in the reporters' room that was supposed to provide privacy for the political team. There he introduced me to Ian Aitken and Charles Douglas-Home, who comprised the rest of the Lobby and diplomatic correspondents' team. The *Daily Express* and *Daily Sketch* were the only national newspapers on which the political editor was also responsible for covering the diplomatic field. Indeed, on the Express, the political team were known in the office as *"the dips"*. This put them at a distinct disadvantage when competing against rivals such as the *Daily Mail*.

As Parliament was enjoying its Christmas recess, Douglas took me to the Savoy Grill for a leisurely *"new boy's"* lunch. There, over potted shrimps and Irish stew, he briefed me on the *Daily Express* scene and explained that in recent years the editors had changed with bewildering frequency. Recalling that circulation had reached a record height of 4.3 million sales under Pickering, he explained that *"Pick"* had been replaced by his deputy Robert Edwards and had been given a directorship to soften the blow. He added, however, that despite his circulation success, *"Pick"*, a cautious and calculating man, had found it so difficult to take decisions at times that he would walk away from an editorial discussion and *"get lost"* in the office. Decisions were made with or without him. Robert Edwards who took over next pushed the sales even higher but was unpopular with some key people on the staff and was soon in turn replaced by his deputy, Roger Wood. In Douglas' opinion, Wood would not be editor for long himself. He was right.

Douglas then turned to the political scene and touched on the competence of Gaitskell as Labour leader. *"There's something you should know old boy, about that situation,"* he confided, leaning forward and lowering his voice. *"We've got a dossier on him. Beaverbrook's had him watched. We know all about his affair with Ann Fleming. Their meetings in London and at Golden Eye have been recorded... and we've got pics, too. If Gaitskell hadn't come out against the Common Market the Old Man intended to unload the lot at the next general election."*

The comely, highly sexed Ann, while married to her second husband Esmond Rothermere, owner of the *Daily Mail*, had embarked on a roaring affair with Ian Fleming, then foreign editor of the *Sunday Times*. He had named his estate in Jamaica *"Golden Eye"* after the code name of one of his wartime operations in Naval Intelligence. Like his creation James Bond, Fleming was a fast-living, womanising gambler. He regarded women as a lesser breed to be used and abused. A sadist, he enjoyed flagellation and other such sex games – and Ann became bound up in it all. In 1948, she became pregnant by him, but the baby died. They married in 1952 after she had divorced Rothermere and she then encouraged Fleming to write the first of his smash series of James Bond novels – *"Casino Royale"*. After some four years they drifted apart and she became involved with a number of men including Hugh Gaitskell whom she met at a dinner party in about 1956. One of London's most colourful and busy society figures, she introduced Gaitskell to her great friend Beaverbrook two years later. She told him that the Labour leader, whom she described as *"Heavenly Hugh"*, had a great interest in wine, women and song. Six months later, the Gaitskells and Ann were guests at a party thrown by Beaverbrook. Gaitskell reported later that he had found the "Old Man" *"less prejudiced, irresponsible and evil than he used to be."* If he had known that his host was about to compile a dossier on his affair with Ann he would have had second thoughts about the improvement in his character. The torrid romance, in fact, was no secret to some close members of Gaitskell's circle. He would borrow Tony Crosland's flat for their passionate encounters. It has been reported that Ann had enjoyed being whipped by Fleming during their sado-masochistic relationship. One might wonder if she introduced Gaitskell to such diversions?

Sitting at the lunch table in the Savoy I was stunned by Douglas Clark's revelation. The thought that Labour's hopes of winning the next general election could be scuppered by the disclosure of such reckless dissipation made me very angry. If Beaverbrook had hoped to use his dossier as a means of persuading the Labour leader to oppose Britain's entry into the Common Market he had presumably taken steps to ensure that Gaitskell knew of it existence. Is that why he had come out so suddenly and so vehemently against Common Market membership at the party conference, shocking his very close pro-European friends such as Jack Diamond, Bill Rogers and George Thomson? *"Might Beaverbrook still unload the stuff at election time?"* I asked, almost choking on my food.

"I don't think so old boy," replied Douglas. *"Not now."*

He was right again – but for a reason neither of us could have foreseen. It struck me, however, that if one old press lord had all this damaging information, surely others in Fleet Street opposed to a Labour election victory must know about it too.

Events moved quickly. Early in January, Gaitskell was taken into the Middlesex Hospital apparently suffering from pleurisy and pericarditis. Doctors then diagnosed a severe virus infection of the heart and lungs – but there was uncertainty about the exact nature of the illness. It was then realised that he had an obscure disease named lupus disseminata, which attacks the body's organs. It was rare in Europe. On January 18 1963, he died at the age of 56. On duty at the *Daily Express*, I helped to write an obituary and then phoned some of his closest friends and colleagues to gather their reactions. They included his loyal Chief Whip Herbert Bowden, who was shattered when I gave him the news. Some of these friends suspected that he might have picked up the disease on one of his recent visits to the Eastern Bloc. His doctor asked to see someone in MI5 and Arthur Martin, head of Russian Counter-espionage, met with him and asked Peter Wright, an assistant director, to see whether the chemical and microbiological laboratory at Porton Down could throw any light on the matter.

As Wright revealed in his memoirs *"Spy Catcher"*, MI5 had been told by a Russian defector that *"the KGB had been planning a high-level political assassination in Europe in order to get their man into the top place."* In view of Gaitskell's proclivity for sexual adventure, and remembering how Soviet spy Michael Lyubimov had been so interested in the Labour leader's penchant for dancing and socialising, I concluded that there was a very real possibility that the Russians had provided *"Heavenly Hugh"* with some female company during his Eastern Bloc visit and had poison administered. If they had carried out enough soundings with Labour MPs they would have known, as I did, that in the event of Gaitskell's death the man likely to succeed him was Harold Wilson, the politician they wanted to lead the Labour Party. His friendly links with the Eastern Bloc encouraged them to think he would be easy to deal with and they hoped he would be sympathetic to unilateral nuclear disarmament in Britain.

Wilson won the leadership election. While most Lobby correspondents tipped deputy leader George Brown, the *Daily Express* got it right. Brown's campaign team resorted to strong-arm tactics that, coupled with their champion's reputation for drunkenness and bullying, lost them the votes of Gaitskellites – including key stalwarts like Herbert

Bowden. George Wigg, Richard Crossman and Leslie Plummer ran a clever, low-key campaign for Wilson that won the day. Gaitskell must have turned in his grave as the man he distrusted and had tried to discredit took his place as leader of the party. MI5 never found conclusive evidence that he had been assassinated.

Despite the courage and honesty Gaitskell had shown in tackling big issues, he had been totally irresponsible in his private life. To satisfy his sexual appetite he had taken unforgivable risks with the electoral prospects of the great movement that he had been given the honour to lead. As time went on it seemed to me, too, that for all his intelligence and social conscience, he did not really understand what made the Labour Party tick. Out of touch with so many of its grass-roots members, he continually struggled to drive the party up paths that too many activists did not wish to take. When some of his more heavy-handed right-wing colleagues urged him to expel rebels he bowed to their demands, despite the misgivings of his more liberal and civilised friends. When it came to producing policies his advisor, Hugh Dalton, was right to complain that he got too bogged down in detail. His pedantry and haggling over the little stuff often left his colleagues exhausted and despairing. He exhausted himself by his continual battles with the Left and his hedonistic private life. And, as Dalton also observed, he did not pay enough attention to fighting the Tories.

When Parliament resumed after the Christmas recess I felt rather uneasy as I made my way towards the Members' Lobby. How would my friends in the Labour Party react to my sudden membership of Beaverbrook's payroll? My worst fears were confirmed as I opened the swing door and Denis Healey pushed passed me. *"I thought you were one of us,"* he commented gruffly as he hurried away down the corridor. My heart sank. He was not one of my close contacts but I wondered whether I should hurry after him and explain. Then it was too late. He had gone – and I never did get around to telling him how it had happened.

In fact, I was merely following in a long line of left-wingers who had chosen to work for *"that Beaver"*. Michael Foot, as a one-time editor of the *Evening Standard* was the most famous. Robert Edwards, recently sacked as editor of the *Daily Express,* had worked for the left-wing weekly *Tribune* – as had my new colleague Ian Aitken. Terence Lancaster, the Foreign Editor, also had a left-wing background. Beaverbrook liked to employ such people, not only because it pleased his wicked mind to think that he had subverted them with gold, but also because he believed they were on the whole better, sharper political journalists than those on the Right.

Meanwhile, events were moving on the Common Market front. On January 17 France had said that the negotiations on Britain's entry should be suspended indefinitely and on January 27 our negotiator Edward Heath was informed in Brussels by the Six that no agreement could be reached. When the breakdown was announced to the Commons, Douglas Clark did a little jig in the Press Gallery and then exclaimed, *"How can I do justice to this?"*

"How about starting with 'It's Stone Cold Dead in the Market'?" (The name of a popular calypso at that time) I replied.

"That's great old boy!" he chortled, *"I knew you'd make a real Express man!"*

To be a real Express man, however, one had to be inducted into the expenses racket. At the end of my first week Douglas had handed me an expenses claim form and asked me to show it to him before sending it in to the news editor, likeable Keith Howard.

"That won't do, old boy!" he observed in a concerned voice, as he overlooked the modest total, *"You're not on Reynolds News now..."*

Running his eyes down the frugal entries he prompted, *"What about the taxis to and from the Commons? And what about entertaining your contacts? You must have bought someone lunch or dinner this week? But you'll need to produce a receipt. Produce some expenditure for every story you've filed and if it was used... charge more!"*

He went on to explain, *"We have certain standards for 'exes' here, old boy. If you let the side down you won't be loved!"*

When we had finished rewriting the form my *"exes"* had been boosted considerably.

The racket was encouraged by Beaverbrook's big spending approach to newsgathering. As he had told the Royal Commission on the press: *"I run the Daily Express for influence, not for profit."*

Some Foreign Correspondents were able to invest their salaries and live off their exes. There is a story of one who, when covering a Middle East desert war, put in a bill for transport that was so unusually large that it was queried by the Foreign Editor. Back came the explanation: *"Hired racing camel. It died of exhaustion. Total cost includes burial."*

No one played the great expenses game with more panache and success than Brian *"Vino"* Vine. I believe he was one of the few ex-*News Chronicle* reporters who, like me, went on to work for both Beaverbrook and Associated Newspapers. On the *Chronicle*, always well dressed, he produced lively copy for the paper's limping version of a gossip column. Arriving on the *Daily Express* however, he blossomed into the *"Bertie Wooster"* type character that made him well known in smart bars on both sides of the

160

Atlantic. His suits were tailored in Savile Row, his hats made by Locks of St James' and, to add to the effect, he sported a monocle (plain glass). His voice, already becoming loud and fruity on the *Chronicle*, now boomed in an exultation of the joy of good living. His waistline expanded, his face shone with a rosy glow. One ex-*Daily Express* man recalled that soon after joining the paper as a young reporter he was sent on a story by Vine. A week later, Vine shouted at him across the office and waved an expenses sheet in the air. Bellowing *"Follow me!"* he marched up Fleet Street to El Vino's wine bar. There, at 11.30 a.m. he ordered champagne and laid the expenses sheet on the bar. To the young reporter's surprise, Vine had pencilled in a figure three times his original claim. Vine explained, *"It's called 'Playing the Game' old boy. If you get a lot in the paper, make 'em pay."*

When working as Express bureau chief in New York, however, Vine overplayed his hand. Having run the office for a dozen years from 1969, his high lifestyle caught the attention of the *"New Yorker"* magazine. It carried a profile of him, describing his costly estate on Shelter Island where he entertained in grand style; his 32-ft powerboat; and his racehorses. The article was brought to the attention of Lord Matthews, the rough diamond who had become proprietor of the *Daily Express*. Matthews, a one-time bricklayer with a liking for whelks, is reported as exclaiming, *"Blimey! He's living better than I am! Bring him back at once!"*

Life at the New York office was not, however, without risks. Despatched with a colleague to Cuba in the early days of the Castro takeover, Vine was suspected of being a spy by Havana's notorious security police. They knocked at his hotel door at four in the morning which earned them a sharp rebuke for calling at such an uncivilised hour. Then, as he sat in the police van, wearing his monogrammed silk pyjamas and dressing gown en route for the security squad's HQ, the full danger of the situation began to dawn on him. Turning to a colleague he said, *"If these swine are going to torture us, you can go first!"*

The quirky John Junor, known as the *"Sage of Auchtermuchty"*, who for many years successfully edited the *Sunday Express* never questioned my expenses when I worked for him part-time for a period. Douglas Clark had moved from the *Daily* to the *Sunday Express* and had then been taken seriously ill – and I had been asked to work for Junor on a Saturday to help cover the political field. It was there that I got to know Alan Watkins of the political team, a convivial *bon viveur* who introduced me to the delights of Montrachet at El Vino's on Saturday lunchtimes. The glorious Burgundy was rated by some connoisseurs as the greatest of all dry white wines. It did not come cheap. Alan knew how to play the expenses game. He told the story too, however, of a *Sunday Express* reporter who broke the code. Frugally, he had listed a half carafe of rosé wine on his expenses form.

"No one in their right mind orders half-carafes!" exploded Junor in pop-eyed disbelief. *"And only pooves drink rosé!"* he added as an extra admonishment.

Having read law at Cambridge, Alan decided that it would be more fun to be a journalist than working as a barrister. He wrote an article for the journal *Socialist Commentary* that caught the eye of John Junor. It dealt with Parliament's pompous and heavy-handed treatment of Junor in summoning him to appear at the Commons to apologise to the House for an article criticising the conduct of MPs. As it was sympathetic to Junor he offered Alan a job and when I caught up with him, he was assistant political correspondent and helping to produce the *Crossbencher* diary column.

I enjoyed his often rather boisterous company and was agreeably surprised to discover that he had a Labour Party background – an allegiance that did not survive the disastrous Kinnock episode or the Blair-Mandelson New Labour era. By then he had moved on to write much-read political columns for consecutively the *Spectator, New Statesman, The Observer* and *The Independent on Sunday*. I enjoyed his elegant, erudite writing and shrewd judgements but suspected that due to a certain indolence and heavy drinking (mostly champagne) he had not renewed the good contacts he had built up from the 1960s to the 1980s. There were continual references to the days of Wilson, Callaghan and Heath. Alan had also been distracted from his coverage of politics by reporting on rugby football and writing on wine – perhaps to help pay for his expensive clubland life. By the time of his death at the age of 77, in May 2010, I had long since lost touch with him.

I had scarcely had time to learn how to write up my expenses form at the *Daily Express* when there was a sudden change at the top. Roger Wood, who had hired me, was fired as editor and Robert *"Bob"* Edwards returned to take his place. After originally being sacked as editor, Edwards had asked Beaverbrook if he could be appointed editor of the group's *Evening Citizen* in Glasgow. Beaverbrook agreed. A year later, the Old Man, having realised his mistake in appointing Wood, restored Edwards to his old job. After only two months with the paper I was already serving my second editor. With the "second coming" of Edwards there was much excited speculation about the fate of certain individuals who had led the rejoicing at his sacking. The name mentioned most was that of Terence Lancaster, the Foreign Editor, who had thrown a party to celebrate the event. Edwards, however, did not immediately seek revenge as expected. Lancaster, for the time being, stayed put on his comfortable perch. The denizens of the Black Lybianka thought Edwards had been surprisingly forgiving – and others who had rejoiced with Lancaster breathed sighs of relief.

Within the group's London political team, however, changes had been made. Douglas Clark, having moved to the *Sunday Express,* had handed over to Ian Aitken, whose easy-going relaxed style was in marked contrast to that of his bustling predecessor. So began my most enjoyable, but all too short, period in journalism. Ian, Charles Douglas-Home and I worked very well together as a tip-top team of friends and colleagues. Ian, two years older than me, had covered troubles in many parts of the world for the Express. In Cuba at the time of the revolution, he had been imprisoned for a while by Fidel Castro's police. He had also covered the Algerian War, his life often in danger during that vicious conflict. After graduating from Oxford and serving in the Royal Navy he had joined the staff of the left-wing weekly *Tribune,* mouthpiece of the followers of Aneurin Bevan. Ian always remained a Bevanite and a close friend of Michael Foot. Despite his left-wing background he had married into the Scottish land-owning Mackie family.

Charles was the son of Major the Hon. Henry Douglas-Home, younger brother of Alec, the fourteenth Earl of Home, who at that time was Foreign Secretary. Left lame and pain-wracked from a horse-riding fall, Henry had served with distinction as an officer in charge of public relations for Scottish Command in the war. In 1931, he married Lady Margaret Spencer, youngest daughter of the sixth Earl Spencer, and a relation of Princess Diana. Charles was one of their three children. The marriage was dissolved in 1947. Perhaps partly to ease his pain, Henry was a heavy drinker and had been in trouble with the police over a drink-drive incident.

Henry's brother William, the playwright, had also had trouble with the law – military law. As a young officer in the Buffs (Royal East Kent Regiment), he had been court-martialled in World War II, cashiered and sentenced to a year's hard labour for refusing, in the name of humanity, to attack Le Havre in 1944. His aim had been to save the lives of thousands of French civilians after the British high command had refused a German request to let them out of the town before the battle for possession commenced.

I liked Charles as soon as I met him on my first morning on the Express. He was a very boyish looking twenty-five with a relaxed, amiable manner. Beneath this easy-going surface, however, was a young aristocrat of great courage, energy and dedication. I was to discover that he had been a King's scholar at Eton and had been commissioned in the Royal Scots Greys in 1956. In 1958, he had served as aide-de-camp to the Governor of Kenya Sir Evelyn Baring and on returning to Britain in 1959 had joined the *Scottish Daily Express* as a general reporter. Soon after, he was sent to the *Daily Express* in London, to be deputy to the paper's highly successful defence and science correspondent, the famous Harry Chapman Pincher. Some eighteen months later, he joined Douglas Clark's political and diplomatic team.

Charlie, like his father, had enjoyed his drink too much and in his mid twenties was warned that he must stop as it was seriously damaging his health. He told us, however, that he was allowed to drink champagne *"in moderation"*. So that is what we drank – and *"Champagne Charlie"* was his nickname! To Charlie's great embarrassment, however, we discovered another nickname he had earned in Kenya. One evening, he unwisely brought into the Parliamentary Press Gallery bar two *"debbie"* girls he had known while serving in the colony. One mischievously revealed that he had been known to the girls out there as *"Close Clinch Charlie"*. As

Ian and I roared with delight our embarrassed friend hustled his guests to the exit before more of his past could be disclosed.

Charlie's great relaxation was fox hunting. In the season his well-worn riding boots and hat would litter the back of his mucky mini. Like his father, Charlie was a hard, fearless rider and was often too reckless for his own good, breaking and straining limbs. When in a wheelchair twenty years later suffering from cancer he would joke that it was a result of falling off a horse too often. Sometimes, he would drop me off at Victoria Station on a Friday evening on his way to stay with his brother Robin and his wife, the beautiful model Sandra, at their home in Hampshire. Robin, an occasional gossip columnist for the *Daily Express*, had for a time earned a living as a nightclub pianist. He had idolised the American singer Peggy Lee – a great favourite of mine – and had followed her around Europe on one of her tours. He had also been engaged to Princess Margaretha of Sweden, but her father had wisely put an end to the affair on the not unrealistic grounds that Robin did not earn enough to support her in the required style. Like his father, Robin also had a drink problem – and he was a womaniser.

Sandra was only eighteen when she married him and as she needed to continue working to pay the bills, he looked for fun elsewhere while she graced the catwalks. When the 26-year-old Nicolette, Marchioness of Londonderry, spent a weekend with them he was discovered by Sandra having sex with "Nico" in her car. About the time their son Sholto was born, when Sandra was twenty-two, the Marchioness gave birth to a daughter, Cosima – whom she revealed two years later to be fathered by Robin, not the Marquess. Sometimes Charlie, looking frayed at the edges, would return to the office after a weekend with Robin and Sandra saying how they had rowed for much of the time while the baby never stopped crying.

Sometimes, the tall debonair Robin would stroll into our glass booth in the office to chat with Charlie and exchange gossip. One day in early March, the talk was of an item in a column written by Robin for a glossy magazine entitled *Queen*. In it he had asked a question about the identity of two men using official cars who had been visiting a certain lady on the same day. The piece, published the previous summer, was headed: *"Sentences I'd like to hear the end of."* It continued: *"Called in MI5 because every time the chauffeur-driven Zis drew up at her front door, out of the back door into a chauffeur-driven Humber slipped..."*

This was the first printed reference to what was to become known as *"The Profumo Affair"*.

The man in the official Zis car was Captain Eugene Ivanov, Naval Attaché at the Russian Embassy; the man boarding the Humber was the Secretary of State for War John Profumo; and the lady was Miss Christine Keeler, a shapely *"model"* who moved in high places. By March, rumours had been circulating for weeks about the extraordinary situation and one of the MPs most determined to bring the affair into the open was George Wigg, still smarting from Profumo's performance in the Kuwait debate and, in particular, the implied rebuke that he had broken his word by originating the *Reynolds News* report of the near military disaster in the desert. At about that time, Wigg had received a hint that Profumo was involved in a sex scandal – but at first could not believe that the minister could be such a fool as to allow himself to become a security risk. He wondered whether he should seek a private meeting with the minister, but, in view of his perceived idea of Profumo's conduct towards him, he decided instead to raise the matter on the floor of the Commons where he would be protected by the tradition of Parliamentary privilege.

Events, meanwhile, were moving fast. On the *Daily Express* the buzz was that Christine Keeler had been speaking openly about her relationship with Profumo and the Russian, who had hurried back to Moscow in January. Early in March, it was expected that one or two Sunday papers would break the news. Keeler, who had sold her story to the *Sunday Pictorial*, had left the country, even though she was a key witness in the case of a West Indian, John Edgecombe, who had taken a shot at her out of jealousy over her relationship with another West Indian, one *"Lucky Gordon"*.

Every day, Express news editor Keith Howard pestered us to find out more about the possibility of some development on the affair in the Commons. I was getting fed up with the situation as this type of sleaze story was what I most detested. Then George Wigg decided he could wait no longer. He saw his opportunity in the fact that a debate was due to take place on the outcome of another "security" scandal – the Vassal Case. In October the previous year, while I was on the *Sunday Citizen,* William Vassal, an Admiralty Clerk, had been convicted of spying for the Russians and jailed for eighteen years. Although only a junior official he had access to top-secret files concerning the development of nuclear weapons, radar and tactics. He had confessed that he had been lured into a Soviet homosexual *"honey trap"* as a first blackmail step to being recruited as a Russian agent while serving in the British embassy in Moscow. Vassal, who had then become an assistant in London to the private secretary of the Civil Lord of the Admiralty, the honest and upright Thomas Galbraith, had sought to involve the minister in a friendship which had led to an exchange of letters, some beginning *"My dear*

Vassal". The letters concerned mundane matters such as the provision of office furniture but unscrupulous elements in the press, led by the *Sunday Express* had started a smear campaign aimed at leaving the impression that a homosexual relationship had existed which could have left the minister open to blackmail. Despite some half-hearted efforts by Eric Wright to get me to follow up the witch-hunt I refused to write on the issue, believing Galbraith to have been no more than kind-hearted. He was, in fact, cleared in an inquiry of any improper relationship with the spy. Macmillan, furious at the reporting of certain journalists, had set up an inquiry chaired by Lord Radcliffe. The outcome was that the Press itself appeared to have been put on trial and two journalists who refused to disclose their sources of information were jailed. It was largely due to the hammering the Press received over the Vassal case that editors were being cautious in reporting the Profumo rumours. It was also due to the minister's vindication by the Radcliffe inquiry that Macmillan did not take them seriously, suspecting that they were concocted by the media in revenge for their drubbing.

Although the Express, like other papers, was too cautious to print the whispers, the newsroom, under pressure from Beaverbrook, kept up its demands for titbits of information and Ian, Charlie and I were getting increasingly frustrated. Then late one afternoon in mid-March, Charlie came into our Press Gallery room flushed from a good lunch and pent up excitement. *"Guess what chaps?"* he asked. *"I've got it from a good source – Profumo's offered his resignation and it's been refused!"*

Ian clambered to his feet exclaiming *"That's a great story!"*

Then, after a moment's thought, he added ruefully, *"But I'm afraid we can't use it as we can't give the reason. The lawyers will never let it through."*

I had been sitting silent at my desk pondering the implications of Charlie's revelation. Then I interjected, *"Yes, we can use it. We can say he's offered his resignation 'for personal reasons' – because he wants to devote more time to his family."*

Ian and Charlie laughed and I grabbed a sheet of paper and started to write. Ian sat down behind his typewriter as I dictated the introduction. Charlie then chipped in with some useful facts about a dispute over defence reorganisation and economies and we padded out the story with more facts about Profumo's career. When we had run out of ideas Ian took the story from his typewriter with a flourish. *"I've put all our names on it!"* he said, as he headed for the phone box.

"I should hope so!" I thought – but with no real hope that the three names would appear above the story. In fact, I envisaged it being used as a single column centre page *"fizzing stick of dynamite",* above the front-page fold – so there would be no room for three by-lines. That would be the sophisticated way to display it, I thought. But, in fact, unbeknown to the three of us, the *Express* was now in a position to rise to an even higher level of inky flair.

On the same day, the trial had begun at the Old Bailey of John Edgecombe, the West Indian who had taken a shot at Christine Keeler. However, the prosecution announced as the hearing began that Keeler had disappeared and the case would have to proceed without her. As night news editor Peter Johnson was placing the Keeler court story on the front-page, our Profumo resignation story fell into his lap. It was a lucky coincidence of which to dream. Under the headline *"War Minister Shock"* we got the splash and separated from that lead story by one column was a picture of Keeler headlined *"Vanished"* and the account of the opening of the Edgecombe trial. Ian, Charlie and I moved to the Press bar for a celebratory drink, not realising what had happened at the office. We waited in excited anticipation for the first edition of the Express to arrive in the hands of our competitors and to see the rush to the phones as news editors called on their political teams to follow up. Profumo and his lovely, dignified wife, the actress Valerie Hobson, had been out that night and when they arrived back at their London home they found the front door blocked by reporters, press photographers and TV camera.

"Is it true you've offered to resign?" they shouted at the stunned minister and the bewildered Valerie. Although our story led the front page it carried one by-line only – the name of Ian Aitken. He had done a good job typing it but – more important – he was taking the personal risk if the story could be found libellous. The Attorney General was called in to go through it line by line, but he could find no grounds for a libel case. Indeed, far from besmirching Profumo, it made him out to be a decent chap, putting aside his career and ambitions for the good of Britain's defence and his wife. I had, in fact, always found Profumo a courteous and civilised man to deal with and would not have wished to harm him.

Harold Evans, Macmillan's public relations adviser, reveals in his published diary for March 1963 that the first inkling the PM's office had of the *Express* report that Profumo had offered his resignation was from Douglas Haig of the *Birmingham Post* who had phoned at about nine that night to say he believed *"one of the public prints"* was about to run such a story. Expecting my name to be on the report with Ian's, I had been anxious to give my old fellow syndicate member Douglas early warning so that he would not be rung up late by his news desk. I had not expected him to ring Downing Street. Evans recalls that he told Douglas *"confidentially"* that it was not true. Called later by the Government Chief Whip, he advised against Whitehall denying the report on the record *"for all the obvious reasons"* and because it had already been done non-attributably. In his view, a direct on-the-record denial could only come from Profumo – when he got home after speaking in the Army Estimates debate earlier that night.

Macmillan was furious with the *Express* and phoned Beaverbrook at Cherkley, his country estate, to complain. Deviously, Beaverbrook replied that he was an old man and no one at the newspaper took any notice of him. As soon as Macmillan ended the angry call, however, that same old man phoned the editor to congratulate him on the front page.

Naturally, our competitors thought the front-page coup had been planned in advance. Our rivals in the press gallery found it hard to believe that a simple serendipitous coincidence had led to the layout of the virtual juxtaposition of our story and the court case. To the people of Fleet Street, Members of Parliament, denizens of Whitehall and others of the informed inner circle, it carried the obvious message of the Profumo – Keeler link. To the millions of Express readers around the country, however, no such message was conveyed as Fleet Street had been too scared to give them any clues in advance. To the great British public the Profumo affair continued to remain an amazingly well-kept secret. Keeler was to tell the *Daily Express* that Ivanov was indeed her *"friend"* at the same time she was going out with Profumo and that she did see each of them on the same day on at least two occasions.

On the night of March 21, George Wigg took the lid off the wriggling Profumo can of worms in the Radcliffe inquiry debate. I watched from the Press Gallery as, protected by Parliamentary privilege, he declared: *"There is not an Honourable Member in the House, nor a journalist in the Press Gallery, nor do I believe there is a person in the Public gallery who, in the last few days, has not heard rumour upon rumour involving a member of the Government Front Bench."*

He then went on to ask the Home Secretary to make a statement about this rumour, relating to Christine Keeler and another *"model"* named Mandy Rice Davies and a shooting by a West Indian. Wigg was followed by Barbara Castle, whose husband Ted was a senior journalist on the *Daily Mirror* and who would have briefed her on what the Press knew. Referring to the disappearance of Keeler, she now demanded: *"If accusations are made that there are people in high places who do not know and who are not informing the police, is it not a matter of public interest?"*

Macmillan was awakened from his sleep by his law officers and Chief Whip, Martin Redmayne, to be told that in their view Profumo should make a personal statement before the Commons adjourned for the weekend. Profumo too was roused and told to return to Westminster to discuss the situation. Macmillan and his key ministers believed his denials. Just after 11 o'clock on the Friday morning he told the Commons he was on friendly terms with Keeler but that there was no impropriety whatsoever in his acquaintanceship with her. The Press knew better and so the pressure continued from the news desk to provide the paper with something more it could run. Ian, Charlie and I were more aggravated than ever. Our story had failed to blow open the wretched business as we had hoped. Despite more damaging developments Profumo carried on at the War Office. Then, at last, on June 4 he wrote to the PM confessing he had lied to the Commons about his relationship with Keeler and tendered his resignation.

Profumo, descended from an aristocratic Italian family – barons of the old kingdom of Sardinia – had been appointed Secretary of State for War in 1960. One of his main tasks was to build up a regular volunteer force following the abolition of conscription. From my position as a captain in the Army Emergency Reserve I was not impressed, for we were ill-equipped and under-trained. Others, however, applauded his success in building up the reserve forces. In dealing with him as a lobby correspondent I found him approachable and charming. Following his resignation, he spent the last forty years of his life trying to make amends for his folly by charitable work in the East End of London.

He had met Keeler in 1961 at a weekend party at Cliveden, the great country house in Buckinghamshire, owned by Lord Astor. Stephen Ward, a society osteopath, who was friendly with a number of call girls, had taken Keeler there as he had a cottage on the estate. One of his clients as an osteopath was, incidentally, Hugh Gaitskell. The hot-blooded Profumo first saw her when she famously stepped naked from the swimming pool. She left Cliveden that weekend with Yevgeny Ivanov, the Soviet attaché and friend of Ward. Profumo foolishly phoned her and so began an affair that lasted several months.

Sleepy MI5 failed to learn of the affair until tipped off by Ward, the man who would pay the highest price of anyone involved, taking his own life as blame and recrimination were flung about. Profumo, on being warned of the Ivanov link, ended the liaison. Macmillan had been left badly shaken, his credibility seriously undermined by the slipshod way in which the affair had been handled at Government level. His reputation as PM never recovered. I found it ironic that two of the journalists who had helped to bring all this about were the nephews of Foreign Secretary, Lord

Home, the man who was to replace Macmillan in the autumn.

I had heard in the Lobby that some insiders thought the Chief Whip had handled matters badly by calling Profumo in at 2 a.m. to answer the charge levied by the Labour MPs. Profumo had been taking sleeping pills since the media had been besieging his house and he arrived at the Commons befuddled and only half-awake. Some took the view that in such circumstances it was hardly surprising that he failed to tell the truth. Some years later at a party I met the Tory peer Lord Aldington who had been deputy chairman of the Conservative Party in 1963. He confirmed that Profumo had offered to resign at the height of the crisis. He was told that was not necessary. Aldington added that he had no doubt at the time that Profumo was lying and said as much to Chief Whip, Martin Redmayne, at a meeting called to discuss the problem. The pompous Redmayne red-faced with indignation, barked, *"Are you really saying the minister is lying?"*

"Yes," replied Aldington, *"I am."*

"Then you had better leave the room!" spluttered the quivering Chief Whip.

Aldington left and when Profumo finally resigned Redmayne never acknowledged he was right or apologised for his reaction. On the contrary, Aldington told me that Redmayne treated him with considerable animosity after Profumo's downfall. As for Macmillan, Aldington confirmed my view that the PM had been wrong-footed by the Vassal/Galbraith affair, which the Press had got badly wrong, and had assumed that they were wrong again about Profumo.

Labour politicians had been revelling in the Tory discomfort over the Profumo scandal and were enjoying a twenty per cent lead in the Gallup Poll. Harold Wilson was so confident of victory in the next general election that he had been busy drawing up the structure for his first administration. At the top there would be a new Minister of Economic Planning, followed by a Minister of Science and Higher Education, with the traditionally all-powerful Treasury downgraded to second-tier status. Fred Lee, closely involved in updating the Gaitskellite policy for science, told me that *"Science and Technology"* had become the buzzwords. I was glad to hear it, for in the previous year I had encouraged *Reynolds News* to devote more space to the importance of these subjects and in July 1962, had led the paper with a report of a major row looming over the Government's neglect of scientific research and development. I reported that in a 12-page policy booklet about to be published, Labour would hit out at ministers for not understanding that the era of electronic computers, automation, new chemicals and atomic energy was, in fact, a new revolutionary age. Labour, I forecast, would demand a properly staffed Science Ministry; more cash for research; more coordination and control of projects; a big Government-aided drive to produce more scientists; and action to stop the drift of trained men to America – the *"brain drain"*.

The following week, Austen Albu, a Labour spokesman on science under Gaitskell and a governor of the Imperial College of Science and Technology, thanked me for writing the report and bemoaned the fact that so little attention was paid to science and technology by the Press. I had also reported the fact that two prominent Conservative MPs had criticised the Government in a Tory journal for failing to ensure that industry's techniques and products were kept up to date. They were former Supply Minister Aubrey Jones and Basil de Ferrante, Parliamentary Private Secretary to the Home Office Minister of State. Jones had derided the establishment of the Minister of Science in 1959 as little more than giving a new title to the Lord President of the Council, Lord Hailsham. Another writer had ridiculed the Science Minister's set-up – no ministry, a staff of less than sixty and an annual budget of only £106,000. Having drawn attention to Lord Hailsham's pathetic tin-pot portfolio, I decided that I should go to see it for myself.

His Lordship, the rumbustious former chairman of the Tory Party, welcomed me into his small office in Richmond Terrace, off Whitehall. He seemed to be bursting out of his cramped quarters and talked freely. It was the beginning for me of a most rewarding friendship.

Macmillan appeared to regard Hailsham as a *"fireman"*, switching him from job to job as emergencies arose. With Tory Party morale at a low ebb after the Suez fiasco, he had been made Party Chairman to raise the spirits of the constituency workers and restore the party's fortunes. His hand bell-ringing act at the following party conference was designed to be part of that process. But when coupled with his decision to take a dip from the beach in a voluminous pair of trunks, which he aptly and earthily described as *"bum bags"*, the combined operation made him look a clown in the eyes of many journalists who could not take him seriously from then on – rather the Boris Johnson of his day. That was a big mistake, for as Party Chairman, he went on to play a key role in the Tory general election victory of 1959 – assisted by Gaitskell's disastrous taxation pledges. He then became Minister for Science and Technology and Lord Privy Seal, and despite being starved of resources, enjoyed the challenge. The scientific community rewarded his efforts, in due course, by conferring on him a Fellowship of the Royal Society.

Meanwhile, Macmillan had loaded him with other responsibilities, the most newsworthy of which was Minister for the North-East following bad publicity for the Government over the poverty and unemployment in that area which led to headlines about *"the North-South Divide"*. The fact that, by mistake, he left his usual bowler hat in London, and accepted the offer of a cloth cap on arrival in Newcastle, gave the press a field day and gave rise to unjust accusations of gimmickry. Apart from admittedly talking himself into jobs by forthright contributions to cabinet discussions, Hailsham was at times puzzled by the number of special assignments he was given by Macmillan – including Minister for Sport and Minister in Charge of the Test Ban Treaty talks. I believe that one unusual factor that linked the two men in the PM's mind was that they had both been cuckolded by their wives. Macmillan's wife Dorothy had been involved in a long affair with Robert Boothby and Hailsham, an officer in the Rifle Brigade, returned to London from Middle East duties in 1942 to discover that his wife, Natalie, was having an affair with a Free French officer. After their divorce, he went on to enjoy a very happy second marriage.

Following a successful Commons debate on science in July, Wilson was convinced that he should underline the party's relevance to the modern age by making Labour and Science the theme of his keynote speech to the party conference in September. Charlie Douglas-Home had never attended a Labour Party Conference so I agreed to hold the fort in London while he accompanied Ian Aitken to Scarborough where it was being held. Wilson's speech, in which he used Fred Lee's phrase about forging policies in *"the white heat"* of the technological revolution, was a resounding success.

Richard Crossman, who had worked closely with Wilson on developing the science policy, was surprised when he included in the speech a proposal for the modernising of apprenticeships. Wilson, in fact, had been listening again to Fred Lee, the only experienced, technically minded trade union member of the shadow cabinet, who had been arguing for some time that the apprenticeship system should be brought up to date. When I met Fred soon after the conference he was delighted that Wilson had used his idea and that it had gone down so well with the trade unions. Wilson also claimed credit for the proposal for a *"University of the Air"*, although distinguished educationist Michael Young, later Lord Young of Dartington and father of Toby Young, the writer, had aired the idea of an *"Open University"* a year earlier.

No matter where the ideas and phrases came from, Wilson had moulded them together in a *tour de force* which won Labour important new converts. When Ian and Charlie returned from Scarborough, I was to meet one at first hand. *"He's been converted by Harold!"* chortled Ian.

"Yep," agreed Charlie, who confessed that he had been bowled over by Wilson's performance.

A new Member of Parliament on the Labour benches who was to take a great interest in the development of science and technology was none other than Tam Dalyell. He had entered the Commons in 1962 as MP for West Lothian at the age of 29. We had a warm reunion when I saw him crossing the Members' Lobby, and recalled our first meeting at the Young Fabian Weekend School. The link he had forged then with Richard Crossman was to become much stronger still within a couple of weeks.

Throughout the summer of 1963, there was a buzz of speculation about how long Macmillan would continue as leader and who would succeed him. There was a growing belief that he might retire before the Tory Party conference to enable his successor to settle in before any general election the following year. Leslie Plummer told me that the man Wilson thought would provide the most serious threat was Reginald Maudling, reasonably young, highly intelligent, and experienced. The best outcome for Labour, in Wilson's view, would be for the aging, tired Macmillan to soldier on. I agreed with that but said that, in my view, the easy-going Maudling had not got a large enough following in the parliamentary party, especially among the more serious MPs – or enough determination to take over the leadership. Perhaps Rab Butler would be chosen at last, but I had a suspicion that he was still not acceptable to a lot of Tory knights in the shires.

The Conservative Party Conference, to be held in Blackpool, was looming fast. It was due to start on a Wednesday following a two-day local government conference in the same hall. Unbeknown to the wide world, Macmillan had a meeting with Hailsham on the Monday in which he told him, in strict privacy, that he planned to retire before Christmas. He added that he wished Hailsham to succeed him, which would involve him disclaiming his peerage and fighting a by-election to gain the necessary seat in the Commons. By Wednesday, however, all had changed. Faced suddenly with the need for an operation for an enlarged prostate, Macmillan announced his decision to resign from the premiership. When the conference delegates heard the news there was bedlam in Blackpool, summed up in a brilliant *Daily Express* headline *"Tower of Babel"* alongside a cartoon of the famous Blackpool Tower. The two front-runner candidates were immediately identified as Rab Butler and Reggie Maudling – and Hailsham thought Rab would win. Then, to his surprise, Foreign Secretary Lord Home told Hailsham that he was being pressed to stand and disclaim his peerage. On hearing this, Hailsham announced his own intention to do the same and join the contest. The *Daily Express* headline was *"Enter Mr Hogg"*

–the family name to which Hailsham would revert on relinquishing his title. It turned out to be a noisy, boisterous entry, with a bibulous Randolph Churchill conducting an ill-judged American-style campaign on his behalf.

Early on, Reggie Maudling sounded me out in the Imperial Hotel lobby about the betting and his prospects. Not wishing to depress him, I said a lot would depend on his address to the conference and then added truthfully that I knew he was the contender Harold Wilson feared the most. *"Really?"* asked Reggie. *"Is that true?"*

I assured him it was and thought I noticed a slight swagger as he ambled off to write his speech. Despite his intelligence, however, Reggie often failed to rise to big occasions. Crucially, he failed to do so at Blackpool. I kept out of his way after hearing his speech in case he asked for my opinion.

On Tuesday morning, I was standing at the back of the conference hall when the bulky figure of John Morrison, chairman of the 1922 Committee of all Tory MPs, moved passed me and stopped beside a backbencher. I moved close and realised he was taking soundings. The names of Rab, Reggie and Quintin Hailsham/Hogg were aired, without the MP naming a preference. Then, after a short pause, Morrison asked, *"What about Alec? What if Alec were to run?"*

On hearing this, the MP became less indecisive.

"Ah well," he replied. *"If Alec were to run that would be a different matter."*

Morrison moved on and I followed him around the hall, listening, as he gently pushed Lord Home's name at MP after MP. By the end of the morning I was convinced that a quiet but heavyweight campaign had been launched to put Douglas-Home, Charlie's uncle, into No 10. I reported my findings to Ian who was impressed. By late afternoon, however, Ian reported that the Express newsroom had learned that Lord Beaverbrook was now convinced that Rab Butler would win. To make matters worse, he had been influenced by freelance writer Henry Fairlie, who in recent times had been transformed from an incisive, well informed political commentator into a thoroughly unreliable character, usually deeply in debt with a private life in chaos.

A former leader writer on *The Times*, he made his name as a brilliant political columnist on *The Spectator* before joining the *Daily Mail* and then the *Daily Express,* where his expense account became a legend. At his peak, he had enjoyed the reputation of having an unequalled understanding of the workings of the Tory Party – and it was our misfortune that Beaverbrook believed that still to be the case. Alas, Fairlie's judgement had been shot to pieces by his riotous living. By 1965, his Fleet Street career ended in a deluge of tax bills and legal suits and he decamped to America.

The *Daily Express* led with Fairlie's *"Butler for Leader"* report and our account of the influential build-up of support for Home was spiked. By the following Monday, Home's name was much to the fore. Macmillan, ill and worn out but still a realist, did not push his support for Hailsham. By the weekend, after the soundings had been assessed and on Macmillan's advice, the Queen sent for Home and invited him to form an administration. Charlie's uncle became Prime Minister and on disclaiming his peerage ruled at No. 10 as Sir Alec Douglas-Home. Hailsham also disclaimed his peerage and, as MP for St Marylebone, continued as Minister for Science and Lord President of the Council in the name of Quintin Hogg. Reversing that process of social downslide, John Morrison, the chairman of the 1922 Committee who had helped Home get to Downing Street, became the first Lord Margadale in 1964, after twenty-two years as MP for Salisbury. Noted for his sound judgement, he went on to predict in 1972 that Margaret Thatcher would be the next leader of the Tory Party – three years before it happened.

It was during the Tory leadership battle that I had the good fortune to get to know Ian Gilmour, the charming, progressive intellectual who was campaigning enthusiastically for Quintin. Ian (Eton, Balliol and the Guards) had joined Quintin's chambers on being called to the Bar in 1952. In 1962, he had been elected to Parliament for Norfolk Central. I knew him by repute as the owner, and for a time, Editor, of *The Spectator*. Under his control, it had became much more lively and had employed Bernard Levin who produced the most entertaining weekly political column in British journalism, outraging the Tory establishment. Charlie Douglas-Home introduced me to him as the leadership battle raged in Blackpool. I found the tall, gangling aristocrat very likeable. Over a drink he urged me not to persist with the view that Home would win the contest as it would encourage too many *"undecided buggers"* to jump on the bandwagon. When Quintin returned to the Commons in December, he appointed Ian as his Parliamentary Private Secretary and it was in that capacity that he invited me to lunch at a smart Italian restaurant in the Brompton Road, to get my views on the political scene. He was intrigued by my opinion that Labour had a better chance of winning the coming general election under the unifying hand of Harold Wilson than it would have done under Hugh Gaitskell, whose extra-marital sex life would almost certainly have been exposed by one of the Tory newspapers. When Ted Heath regained power for the Tories in 1970, Ian was to be appointed Defence Under-Secretary and then promoted to Secretary of State just before Wilson won the 1974 election.

Owing to Douglas Clark's illness, I was doing a Saturday stint for the *Sunday Express* at the time and on the Friday evening, as a *Daily Express* man, had seen editor John Junor visit Rab Butler at the St Ermine's Hotel in an eleventh hour bid to persuade him to fight for the leadership. Harold Macmillan's departure from office had not only been welcomed by him – it had saved him his editor's job. In the spring, he had clashed with Beaverbrook over his antipathy to Macmillan following the jailing of the two journalists who had refused to disclose their sources to the Vassal case tribunal. Beaverbrook accepted his resignation but while he was working out his six months' notice Macmillan had quit and his breach with the boss was healed.

An ex-liberal with a Scottish Presbyterian working class background, Junor believed that the *Sunday Express* *"should be a newspaper which made people feel better, not worse, on a Sunday – that it should be a paper of optimism."*

His successful formula never changed much and certainly seemed to make Beaverbrook feel better on a Sunday. Junor once said that he had never taken on anyone he did not personally like. As I was not a full-time staff man but only on loan from the *Daily Express* I was not sure whether that rule applied to me. As it was, we got on without disagreement, but I felt that I was never really on his wavelength.

Junor went on to edit the *Sunday Express* for a total of thirty-two years and continued writing his highly opinionated weekly column until 1990. He then stunned Fleet Street by moving with his column to the rival *Mail on Sunday*.

Meanwhile, Beaverbrook was reported as being very annoyed with Henry Fairlie – and intent on making some recompense to his political team who had got the Tory leadership story right but had been ignored. One day, I received a message from the Editor to say that Beaverbrook had invited me for Sunday lunch at his country estate Cherkley, set amidst some of Surrey's most beautiful countryside. His chauffeur would pick me up at Dulwich and drive me there and back.

Arriving at the mansion at precisely the agreed time, I was ushered into the richly furnished reception room where I was soon joined by the wrinkled and asthmatic *"Old Man"*. He lost no time in having me served one of his famous rum cocktails while he explained that he had also invited his great nephew Jonathan Aitken to join us. However, Jonathan, who was an undergraduate at Oxford reading history, had telephoned to apologise for the fact that he would not be able to attend. I sensed that Beaverbrook was irritated. Jonathan eventually caught up with me when he arrived at the Commons as a promising and handsome young Tory MP in 1973. Although he saw a lot of his great uncle, Beaverbrook left him no money. Perhaps it was partly the lack of private funds that eventually got him into trouble and led to his downfall and imprisonment.

Beaverbrook quickly moved on from Jonathan's absence to ask about the drama of the Tory leadership change. He was impressed that we got on to the right track at Blackpool so quickly and I explained how I had followed John Morrison around the conference hall as he peddled Alec Home's name. He chuckled, *"Didn't anybody ever tell you, young man that it's rude to eavesdrop?"*

He was obviously delighted, however, that I had got the situation right from the start – but never mentioned his own mistake of pushing the name of Rab Butler. As we talked, his good looking new wife came into the room, picked up a book and glided out. Half Greek, she had formerly been Lady Dunn, widow and third wife of the industrialist Sir

James Dunn, his late friend and fellow Canadian. On his death she inherited fifteen million dollars. Beaverbrook's mistress by the 1960's, she married him in the June preceding my visit. She was fifty-three and he was eighty-four.

We talked about the current state of the Tory Party and he asked me if I had read his book on the political intrigues of an earlier era – *"The Decline and Fall of Lloyd George"*. Beaverbrook himself had played no small part in this fascinating period of political history between 1921 and 1923 when a Prime Minister, riding the crest of the wave, was suddenly dismissed from office. When I confessed that I had not read it, he said he would arrange for me to receive a copy. *"And what are we paying you Mr Butler?"* he asked.

When I told him, he reached for his Dictaphone to inform the editor that I was to receive an immediate – and in my opinion long overdue – increase.

Over lunch he got on to one of his favourite topics – the state of affairs in South Africa. How did I see the future there? My crystal ball was a bit foggy that day. I said I feared that without drastic electoral reform it would end in awful bloodshed. He looked put out and changed the subject. What did I do with my spare time? I mentioned, among other things, watching films. *"Films,"* he repeated.

Did I like Westerns? I said I thought some of the finest films ever made had been Westerns – *"Stage Coach"*, *"High Noon"*, *"Shane"*, *"Destry Rides Again"*… The Old Man's face cracked into a smile of approval.

"Yer like 'Destry'? It's my favourite film! Lost count of the times I've seen it."

In fact, he had his own copy and his favourite bit was when Marlene Dietrich sits on the bar of the rowdy saloon, long legs sheathed in sexy net stockings and rasps *"See what the boys in the backroom will have…"*

It is said that the term *"back room boys"* used to describe the boffins in the war, came from Beaverbrook, then Minister of Aircraft Production, inspired by the song. It has also been rumoured that he once offered Marlene £1000 to spend the night with him in a London hotel. It was certainly not beyond him and in keeping with his womanising ways.

Brought together by our mutual admiration of *"Destry"*, we moved outside on to the terrace and sitting on well-worn wicker chairs enjoyed the autumn sunlight and view of the estate. Told a year before that he had cancer of the bladder, he knew it was his autumn, too. As we savoured the beauty of the setting, he pointed to the great trees bathed in golden light and to my surprise brought up the subject of his son, Max. Max Aitken, wartime RAF fighter ace, speedboat fanatic and handsome playboy, would in due course take over from the ailing Old Man. What worried Beaverbrook, who seemed preoccupied that day by the prospect of death, was, in his words, that Max had *"no soul"* when it came to the preservation of the Cherkley parkland. He feared that he would cut down the trees and sell them off for timber.

The following May, a great celebration dinner was held in London to mark Beaverbrook's 85th birthday. Many of the guests knew he was dying, but he used the occasion to joke stoically about his fast failing health. After referring to his apprenticeship in life, he concluded with the words: *"It is time to become an apprentice once more. I have not settled in which direction, but somewhere, sometime, soon."*

He died at his beloved Cherkley two weeks later. Max Aitken took over – and confirmed Bob Edwards in his editorship of the *Daily Express*. Despite his father's fears, Max, in fact, preserved the woodlands. Decades later I revisited the estate as a tourist and was pleased to admire them again. Then, early in 2010, I learned that the Beaverbrook Foundation, having failed to make a commercial success of running the estate as a visitor attraction, had put it up for sale.

Ian Aitken, who had a real affection for Beaverbrook, was saddened by his death and uneasy that Max, a true blue Conservative, was taking control. Under his maverick, mischievous father, the paper had espoused a number of anti-Tory cases. Along with Labour's left wing, it had opposed entry into the Common Market. Moreover, it was not anti-trade union and supported a high-wage economy and full employment. A large proportion of its readers voted Labour. We wondered how soon change would come.

Meanwhile, as Ian had done more than his share of travelling, he was happy for me to go on some of the foreign trips that came our way when ministers went abroad for negotiations. I had never been abroad for the *News Chronicle* or *Reynolds News* and my first trip for the *Express* was to Paris, city of youthful larks. In contrast to past visits, however, this was in luxury. Douglas Clark was also covering the story for the *Sunday Express* and we were both booked into the Hotel Bristol, a highly expensive establishment much favoured by executives from our respective papers. On our first night, Douglas told me over dinner that when the post-war Labour Government's Foreign Secretary, Ernest Bevin, had stayed there and had been asked if he was ready to order dinner he had commanded, *"Steak, frites and a bottle of Newts!"*

The rugged old trade union boss could never quite pronounce *Nuits Saint George*. His boots, too, had caused some embarrassment. Following usual procedure, he put them outside his bedroom door at night to be cleaned. They were so well worn and shabby, however, that the boot boy assumed they were done with and threw them away.

188

Next day, late in the morning, Douglas led me into the Crillon Hotel where my mother had so often stayed with Lina some forty years before. There, in the grand long cocktail bar, I was to meet the legendary Sam White, columnist of the London *Evening Standard*. Stationed, as always at that hour, at one end near a doorway, he was waiting hopefully for people like us to walk in. Nearby stood a telephone labelled *"Sam White only"*. Douglas introduced me to the famous Aussie, one of Beaverbrook's favourite and most respected employees. The bulky, hard-drinking Sam could produce with equal ease the most titillating gossip stories and accurate well-judged reports on the French political scene. In his lively weekly column he gave the impression that Paris circulated around him. I suppose it could be said that if you maintained a static position on the Place de la Concorde it rather did. He was one of the first to get it right about de Gaulle returning to power and about his surprise decision to get out of Algeria. I remember him with gratitude that, on hearing I was going to Greece on holiday, he advised me to stay overnight at Delphi and to absorb there the real mystery and beauty of the ancient oracle of Apollo at the site. Then suddenly, after several rounds of drinks, Sam looked at his watch, bade us a warm goodbye and left with surprising agility through the nearby door. Douglas gave a low chuckle. *"He never buys a drink if he can avoid it,"* he explained. *"I'll pick up the bill. The barman knows the ropes. Just hope he hadn't been drinking too long before we arrived!"*

Another assignment took me for the first time to New York City and the United Nations Buildings. I felt a thrill of excitement as I walked along the teeming streets, as steam rose from the subways and the swarm of battered black and yellow cabs produced a continual buzz. Like many well-read visitors to the city I went in search of the ghosts of

Dorothy Parker and Thurber in the Algonquin Hotel. Disregarding warnings about muggers, I wandered alone through the green oasis of Central Park. I marvelled at the soaring sun-touched Empire State Building and told myself that here was a city of real opportunity. Had I been ten years younger I might have stayed to try my luck.

With Sir Alec Douglas-Home now leading the Tories towards a general election due the following year, ministers were asked to look for issues that would give the party a modern reformist appearance – and hopefully win support from the majority of voters. At the Department of Trade, the dust was blown off a file marked R.P.M. While at *Reynolds News* I had drawn attention to the fact that a report advocating abolition of Resale Price Maintenance was in the filing tray of the then Minister for Trade, Reggie Maudling. I forecast rightly that Reggie, who liked a peaceful life, would decide to leave it pending. Now, however, Edward Heath was in charge of Trade and he was not the man to shirk a fight. He proposed a bill to abolish RPM and persuaded Sir Alec that it would be a popular move with voters.

Standing in the Lobby one evening prior to Beaverbrook's death, I was pleased to see the new MP and minister Quintin Hogg. He was clearly excited about something and I soon learned from him that a battle had been raging in Cabinet over Heath's proposal and that he, one of the *"old guard"* as he described them, was opposed to such a move. My exclusive report of the Cabinet clash led the *Daily Express* next day and I assumed that Beaverbrook would favour abolition. I was wrong. He showed great interest in the story. I was congratulated on the scoop and the *Daily Express* immediately launched a campaign against abolition on the ground that it was a threat to small shopkeepers and helped the growth of supermarket chains. It was to be the Old Man's last big campaign and helped to stoke up revolt by Tory backbenchers. Angry protests at a meeting of the Tory 1922 Committee in January 1964 gave me the lead again in the paper. I reported, too, that there was evidence of more unease and scepticism among senior ministers.

Quintin Hogg observed later that the move to abolish RPM, without adequate consultation, without a mandate and forced through Parliament with tiny majorities, was a significant factor in the Tories losing the 1964 general election. Supermarket bosses and others in the business of selling cut-price goods were jubilant, however, at the impending removal of restrictions and shares in chains such as Tesco and Associated British Foods rose on the Stock Exchange. In line with these developments, the system of price fixing for newspapers came to an end in 1964.

CHAPTER EIGHT

Friends in Power

As the general election approached I began to feel uneasy. How Tory-biased would the *Daily Express* be? Would pressure be put on the political team to angle stories against Labour? Then Ian Aitken announced that he was resigning to join the political team on the *Guardian*. He had decided, as a deeply committed Labour supporter, that he could not face what he assumed would be the blatant pro-Tory coverage of the election and the even more blatant anti-Government bias if Labour won. He went on to enjoy a distinguished career on the *Guardian* and was much liked and respected. It was rather sad, however, that despite his many important exclusives and fine writing, the one scoop attributed to him time and time again was the Profumo resignation story where his main contribution had been to type the exclusive produced by Charlie Douglas-Home and for which I had produced the formula that enabled the *Express* to use it without risk of a libel action.

During his time at the *Guardian*, Ian was involved in an extraordinary incident concerning his glass eye. While on the Express he had undergone a serious eye operation and had worn a glass one ever since. During James Callaghan's premiership, Ian accompanied him to talks with President Carter in Guadeloupe, and while he was swimming in the Caribbean it fell out and settled onto the sandy seabed. Ian and his friends searched to no avail. Two days later, wearing a black eye patch, he heard someone shout, *"Have any of you guys lost an eye?"*

A tourist, swimming near the seabed, had seen it winking through the waves.

Despite my considerable contribution to the work of the political team, Bob Edwards appointed Foreign Editor Terry Lancaster to replace Ian. I was still a relative new boy whereas Lancaster was a senior seasoned operator on the paper who knew a lot about foreign affairs and had been active politically. Running an efficient foreign desk he was a key figure on the paper, controlling a large team of correspondents all over the world. His organisation of the coverage of President John F. Kennedy's assassination had been particularly successful and in 1957 he had won acclaim for flying to Moscow to interview Nikita Khrushchev after the Russian leader's historic speech breaking with the bloodstained regime of Stalin.

Terry was very likeable – witty, generous and big hearted. After his comfortable well-ordered life running the foreign desk, however, he seemed anxious initially at the prospect of the daily grind of covering Parliament with all the pressures that went with being political editor. I tried to reassure him and said the only real competition was from Walter Terry, the scoop-hunting political correspondent of the *Daily Mail*. Then the election was upon us and, as it turned out, the best story run by the paper was an interview given by R.A. Butler, then Foreign Secretary, which was seriously embarrassing to the Tory Party. It was conducted in a train by George Gale, the paper's boozy gravel-voiced special correspondent, whose bluff knock-about exterior concealed a highly intelligent Tory radical. Asked by George – better known as *"George G.Ale"* – how the election was going, Butler replied: *"Very close. We're running neck and neck. I'll be surprised if there's much in it, say twenty seats either way. But things might start slipping away in the last few days."*

"Slipping away?" queried the incredulous George.

"Yes," replied Rab, *"they won't slip towards us."*

There were more delicious indiscretions and the big question in the office was, *"Did Butler realise the interview was on the record?"*

George assured us that he did. The published interview was a sensation – and *Lunchtime O'Gale* was feted as never before in the Fleet Street hostelries. In due course he went on to edit *The Spectator*. Rab was right. As a result of the general election on October 15 Labour scraped home with only 200,000 more votes than the Tories and a majority over them of 317 to 304 seats in the Commons. Labour had suffered from a massive increase in the Liberal vote although, due to our electoral system, the number of Liberal seats had risen from six to only nine. Labour was left with a tiny overall majority of four. Alec Douglas-Home had done surprisingly well. It seemed to me, however, that if any of the other contenders in the Tory leadership race – Rab, Reggie or Quintin – had won, Labour would have lost the election. The Tories certainly got one more vote than I had expected. Despite his admiration for Wilson's science and technology theme speech at the party conference, Charlie decided, after all, that for family reasons he must support uncle Alec and the Tories.

Hard-core Gaitskellites claimed that if Gaitskell had been leading the party Labour would have won with a much bigger majority. I doubt that. Indeed, it is highly likely that someone hostile to Labour, who knew of his affair with Ann Fleming, and other adventures, would have ensured that this was disclosed in a newspaper during the campaign, thus causing Labour to lose the election.

Prime Minister Harold Wilson called a meeting of Lobby journalists and together with Terry Lancaster I went to 10 Downing Street to hear what the victorious Labour leader had to say. To my disappointment, he said very little of importance. Instead, he used the occasion to score some cheap points off the Tories. I was irritated by the reception he received from some fawning reporters who not long before had regarded him with some loathing. I decided to try to get some useful information and asked a question about his social policy. Wilson brushed it aside as something not to be dealt with that evening. I had started to *"go off"* the new Prime Minister at a very early stage.

A new paper was represented at Number 10 that evening. During the election, the decent but dreary Labour supporting *Daily Herald* had appeared for the last time to be succeeded by *The Sun* – more breezy and independent and described as the first daily born of the age in which we live. I welcomed its arrival as a decent left-of-centre addition. No one could have foreseen then, how, in due course, it would come to have such a downgrading effect on the standards of the Press and wield such influence.

One of the new Labour MPs who had entered parliament at the general election was Peter Shore, member for Bethnal Green and Stepney. I had got to know him well while at *Reynolds News* when he was head of Labour's research department. I did my best to give him publicity for policies based on that work but was uneasy when I learned that the earnest, lanky young man was an active member of CND and had taken part in the Aldermaston marches with Michael Foot, for whom he had great respect. Like me, he had had problems with Gaitskell – but for different reasons. Shore's opposition to Britain's membership of the Common Market, however, had helped him to heal the rift with the Labour leader and in due course he came to oppose unilateral nuclear disarmament. He also became close to Harold Wilson over the development of Labour's economic policy and after the general election, quickly became joint Parliamentary Private Secretary to the Prime Minister. I regarded him as an honest and courageous politician and was pleased when he was made a minister and entered the Cabinet in 1967.

Another new Labour MP was a certain Robert Maxwell who owned a small publishing empire with Pergamon Press at its centre. He specialised in scientific topics, pirating articles that appeared in Russian and East European science journals. A controversial figure even then, he had earned a bad reputation for unscrupulous methods. Despite this, he had impressed Richard Crossman when he was involved in developing Labour's science policy and was asked to form a group of specialists to help with the work. As he appeared to know his way around the financial world and gave evidence of having a knack with money, he was appointed chairman of the Labour Party's National Fund Raising Foundation in 1960. Brimming with self-confidence and speaking in a bombastic style, he had quickly become unpopular in the Commons and had started to receive a bad press. He was, however, a friend of *Express* editor, Bob Edwards, and one day I was called in to the editor's room to be asked if I knew him. I confessed that I had not had much to do with him personally and added that he had not made a very good start in the House. Edwards nodded. *"That's what I understand,"* he said, and went on to ask me if I could try to get him moving on the right lines. *"Take him out to lunch. Go to the Savoy. Give him some good advice."*

I agreed to do so and not long after I was sitting face to face with Maxwell in the Savoy Grill. I thought I was a fast eater but he ate at high speed and quickly emptied his glass. His voracious appetite would become well known. I had taken the trouble to find out more about his background and was surprised to discover that he had been born Jan Ludwig Hoch in 1923 to poor Jewish parents in Czechoslovakia. He had changed his name on escaping to England from the Nazi onslaught on his country in 1938 and in 1940 had joined the

British Army. Partly on the strength of his language skills, but also by displaying courage and determination, he had been commissioned and had reached the rank of Captain. He had also been awarded the Military Cross. After the war, he had used his linguistic skills to start his publishing company. He was clearly an extraordinary person.

As we settled into our lunch, I warned him, as diplomatically as possible, of the pitfalls of the Commons' chamber. I stressed how important it was, especially for new members, to abide by the conventions, no matter how cobwebbed and stuffy they appeared. I soon realised that he was not taking it in and certainly was not interested in convention. We moved on to other topics. He seemed fascinated by my experiences of the Labour Movement and asked me if I would write a biography of Hugh Gaitskell that he would publish. I had already met some freelance journalists, however, who had written for him and never been paid. I thanked him for the offer but said that would not be possible as the *Daily Express* did not allow members of its staff to write for other publishers. I was to receive more offers to work for him in the years ahead but was never so foolish or so desperate to accept. To my embarrassment, he would sometimes make a fuss of me in the Members' Lobby and in the Central Lobby introduced me to his French wife Betty and children as *"an important political journalist"* who would work for him one day. My attempt to guide him on how to behave in parliament, however, had no effect. His brash behaviour annoyed MPs on all sides of the house.

Still, foolishly impressed by his boastful claims to financial and management skills, MPs then appointed him Chairman of the Commons Catering Committee in the hope that he could stem the annual loss on food and drink. The

Commons was justifiably proud of its well-stocked wine cellar, replete with great vintages built up over the years. Maxwell decided that to show a profit for the department he would sell off these liquid assets, buying much of them himself at extremely favourable prices. At the end of the year he was able to proclaim that he had indeed turned the account books around – and there was even some grudging applause from those who did not know how this had been achieved. Some wag even renamed the Commons *"Maxwell House"*. Then it came out. There would only be coffee to drink soon. The Treasury refused to accept his accounts, indignantly pointing out that he had improperly disposed of capital assets in the form of wine stocks to boost the income on current account. Forced to give up the Catering Committee chairmanship, he continued unabashed down a dubious path of cheating and fraud.

Before his eviction from his Buckingham constituency by the voters in 1970, I walked into the Commons Strangers' Bar one day to be met by Frank Barlow, the shrewd cockney secretary of the Parliamentary Labour Party. Greeting me warmly, he noted with some surprise, *"You're wearing a Queen's tie – I didn't know you served with the regiment?"*

I explained that I did part of my national Service with the Queen's Royal Regiment and added that there must be a few more ex-members of the Second of Foot in the Commons. Frank, who had been a colour sergeant in the regiment, said that was so and reeled off a few names. *"And there's Robert Maxwell,"* I interjected. *"He won the M.C."*

Frank stiffened. His tanned face looked stern.

"Maxwell!" he spat out. *"When that man enters this bar I walk out. We don't shoot our prisoners in the Queens!"*

What had happened? According to a later, more detailed account that I came to read, he was attacking a German town with his platoon and summoned the local Nazi mayor to warn him that unless the small number of German troops sheltering there surrendered immediately the place would be destroyed. The mayor returned to announce that the German soldiers had agreed to Maxwell's demand. As the victorious Queen's men moved out of cover, however, a German tank opened fire. Furious at what he regarded as the mayor's betrayal, Maxwell shot him on the spot. Only a month earlier Maxwell had been awarded the Military Cross by Field Marshall Bernard Montgomery for bravery during a night attack.

Despite being proud of their platoon commander's success, some of his men were clearly deeply dismayed by his callous disregard for the rules of warfare. If Frank Barlow felt unable to be in the same bar with him twenty years later, how was it that his fellow officers were prepared to drink with him in the mess? And what of the role of his commanding officer in this affair? If non-commissioned officers and other ranks knew what had happened, the facts must have reached the commanding officer. The Queen's, the second oldest infantry regiment in the British Army, was founded in the reign of Charles II to garrison the Tangier territory which was part of the dowry of his Queen, Catherine of Braganza. It had a proud history. Perhaps the C.O. took the view that by acting to punish Maxwell, he would have drawn attention to a war crime that would have sullied his regiment's reputation. That would have been very damaging to morale. Maxwell got away with it.

Captain Bob, as he came to be known, was to get away with far worse as a crooked financial operator before his bloated body was recovered from the sea off the Canary Islands in November 1991. In the 1970s, a Board of Trade inquiry was to declare Maxwell a person who could not be relied on to exercise proper stewardship of a publicly quoted company. Despite that, the great confidence trickster went on to build up a precarious paper empire, borrowing from undiscriminating banks to repay other foolish banks. By the time of his death at the age of sixty-eight, his business faced imminent collapse while he faced personal ruin. By then I had turned down several offers of employment from him. When I read the news I wondered if he had faked accidental drowning to avoid disgrace, throwing himself over the side of the luxurious yacht named for his daughter, *The Lady Ghislane*. Before that, as owner of the *Mirror Group*, he had robbed hundreds of journalists and other employees by plundering the company's pension fund to help keep afloat. His yacht should have flown the Skull and Crossbones.

Someone who was finding it increasingly hard to *"get away with it"* was *Express* political editor Terry Lancaster. Faced with the intense daily pressure and the shot and shell encountered in the frontline of political news gathering, he was beginning to go to pieces. He needed time off. Edwards asked me to fill in. Then I was informed that he would not be coming back. Edwards said he would like me to continue as acting political editor until a decision could be taken about filling this key job on the paper. I received a modest increase in salary. Some old hands on the *Express* who had been watching the situation recalled a Bible story often quoted by Lord Beaverbrook and referred to in his papers' leading articles. It concerned King David of Israel who, wishing to enjoy Bathsheba, the beautiful wife of one of his military commanders, Uriah the Hittite, had placed that warrior in the forefront of battle so that he would be slaughtered. It struck them that if Bob Edwards had wanted revenge on Lancaster for organising that celebration party when he was first sacked, he had adopted a similar strategy. By taking him from his comfortable foreign desk post to sending him to the frontline in Parliament, he had sent him over the edge, and brought about his breakdown. In due course, however, Edwards rescued Lancaster from oblivion and reinstated him as political editor of a Sunday paper where the pressure was almost nonexistent and where he flourished once more in his old expansive style.

Before Lancaster moved on, Charlie Douglas-Home had also left the team – but in happier circumstances. On the recommendation of Alun Gwynne-Jones, Defence Correspondent of *The Times*, he was appointed to replace him in January 1965. Charlie had got the job in a roundabout way. Wilson's big idea on the foreign affairs and defence front was to appoint a first ever Minister for Disarmament – a sop to the unilateral left wing. I got the inside story from George Thomson who had been made a Foreign Office Minister of State. Wilson's choice for this new post was the highly respected Kenneth Younger who had served as a Foreign Office minister in the Attlee government and had later become Director of the Royal Institute of International Affairs – Chatham House. Younger, however, greatly disliked and distrusted Wilson and turned down the offer. To most people, the obvious candidate for the post was Philip Noel-Baker, a former Attlee Cabinet Minister and prominent campaigner for disarmament who had been awarded the Nobel Peace Prize in 1959. The saintly Noel-Baker wanted the job, but Wilson thought he was too old and idealistic. George Wigg then suggested Alun Gwynne-Jones, a realistic ex-regular Army officer for whose work on *The Times* he had a high regard. Gwynne-Jones accepted the post and the peerage that went with it, becoming Foreign Office Minister of State with special responsibility for disarmament. To the amused surprise of some of his colleagues, he adopted the high-sounding title of Lord Chalfont.

I was saddened by Charlie's departure, but we continued meeting up for lunch with Ian Aitken and when he married

Jessica in 1966, we were guests at the reception in the Royal College of Music. Charlie's mother, Lady Margaret, was an accomplished pianist and was involved with the institution. Charlie's brother Robin inherited their mother's talent at the keyboard. Jessica was a painter and stage designer, working for the National and West End theatres. She held exhibitions in London of her work and later on became a successful author.

While still in charge of the political team, Terry Lancaster asked me to look for a replacement for Charlie as I had better knowledge than he of the talent in the Parliamentary Press Gallery. I had been impressed by the appearance and intelligence of a young man named Stewart Steven who had been working as a reporter for *Central Press Features* and then the *Western Daily Press*. I asked him if he would be interested in joining the Express team as third man. He was very interested indeed and I arranged for him to be interviewed by Terry, who was equally impressed and agreed to take him on. So began the Fleet Street career of the man who was to become editor of the *Mail on Sunday* and the London *Evening Standard*.

Stewart had been born Stefan Cohn in Hamburg in 1935, the son of a German-Jewish businessman and had been brought to London when a year old as his parents escaped Nazi persecution. In Britain, the family name was changed to "Steven" as his father sought to re-establish his successful "Import-Export" business. In line with this, the young Stewart received the best cricket coaching available to help make him a good Englishman. At Mayfield College, in Sussex, he shone at the sport. Academically, he did not do so well. He decided to become a journalist and joined the *Oxford Mail*. I was delighted that Terry had taken my advice and employed him. His main job was to cover the diplomatic front and I told him jokingly that as a true cricketing Englishman he would get on well with the Foreign Office types.

For Bob Edwards, however, time was running out as editor. He and Max Aitken had never got on. Bob, for one thing, was viewed with suspicion by his new boss as being far too left wing. So, although the paper was doing well, he was replaced by Derek Marks, who had been switched from the *Evening Standard* to be his assistant editor shortly before. Working still as acting political editor, my heart sank at the news. When Marks had been political correspondent of the *Daily Express* and I had been on the *News Chronicle*, we had shared a mutual dislike not helped when the practical joke played on me at the Tory conference had backfired into a scoop. Now I recalled the advice about not falling out with anybody for they were sure to end up as your editor. Moreover, I also remembered that due to his bulk he was nicknamed *Jumbo* – and according to the old saw, "elephants never forget."

Eric Raybould, Bob's earthy, experienced deputy, who had no doubt hoped to replace him, came to find me in the news room and asked if I would join in a farewell drink, or two, for Bob at El Vino's. It had all happened so suddenly that very few were there. A year later Bob would re-emerge as editor of the left-ish Sunday *People* following the death of its veteran editor, Sam Campbell, to whom I had applied for a job when leaving *Reynolds News.* He had not needed a political correspondent but it was here that Bob Edwards – who, due to his unsinkable nature, became known as "Bob Upwards" – would give Terry Lancaster a second chance in the form of that post. He picked him up, brushed him down and appointed him political columnist of the paper. Resuscitated in that more gentle environment he went on to become a journalistic adjunct to Prime Minister Wilson's *"Kitchen Cabinet"* and would spend much time at Number

10. After that, he became an adviser to his friend Betty Boothroyd when she was elected Speaker of the Commons.

Beaverbrook, I decided, had been right to worry about his son Max taking over. He proved to be hopeless at running the business and had none of his father's journalistic flair. In appointing Marks as editor he had shown bad judgement off the bat, but he had wanted a dedicated Tory team player in charge of the paper. Marks certainly knew the political scene – but not much else. Aitken should have given the job to David English, the desperately ambitious foreign editor but probably did not trust him because of his sharp manner of dressing and his radical views. English was promoted to associate editor and Stewart Steven then left my team to become foreign editor. I was delighted that Stewart had received this promotion, fully justifying my original recommendation that he should be taken on the staff.

Eric Raybould would also have been a better choice than Marks, who was suffering from diabetes and yet drinking too heavily to provide steady leadership. It became a Fleet Street joke that he was *"drunk in charge of a newspaper"*. Eric, a stalwart number two who had a mastery of the craft of producing a daily paper, had asked me, as part of his self-improvement programme, to help him understand the political world by arranging lunches with some leading politicians. Chomping on his cigar, this burly, blunt, tough-looking man reminded me of a character in a Hollywood gangster movie, Jimmy Cagney, or Edward G. Robinson. I remember he got on very well with George Brown over a heavy lunch at his favourite Soho restaurant *"L'Etoile"*. If he or English had been appointed editor I like to think I would have been appointed political editor.

Meanwhile, with Labour in power, many of my close contacts had been given appointments at all levels of government. In the cabinet, George Brown had the key role of First Secretary of State at the newly created Department of Economic Affairs, which was to be the powerhouse of Labour's drive to modernise Britain's industrial base; James Callaghan, who had been coached by Douglas Jay in basic economics, had become Chancellor of the Exchequer; Douglas himself had been made President of the Board of Trade; Fred Lee was Minister for Power; Fred Peart became *"Fred the Farmers' Friend"* as Minister for Agriculture; another in this "Government of Freds", Fred Mulley, was appointed Minister of State for the Army; Barbara Castle, my memorable dancing partner, became Minister for Overseas Development; George Wigg was Paymaster General – to be known as *"Spymaster General"* – with the job of working at 10 Downing Street covering a number of subjects, including security; and Richard Crossman had become Minister for Housing and Local Government.

Apart from Douglas Jay, my other friends from *Forward* had also received good posts. Accountant Jack Diamond, appropriately, had become Chief Secretary to the Treasury; and George Thomson had been made Minister of State at the Foreign Office. John Stonehouse, regarded by Wilson as having commercial flair and experience – qualities in short supply in Labour's ranks – had been appointed Parliamentary Secretary to the Ministry of Aviation under Minister Roy Jenkins.

Among the new MPs entering Parliament was Alf Morris who, as a student officer, had put Stonehouse out of business for fiddling the books when running student tours abroad. Alf, MP for Wythenshawe, Manchester, quickly became Parliamentary Private Secretary to Fred Peart and soon after that, one of my closest, long-lasting friends in Parliament. Another PPS appointment was that given to Tam Dalyell by Richard Crossman, for whom he was to operate as a loyal, unpaid aide for several years.

Another appointment announced by Wilson came as a pleasant surprise. Trevor Lloyd-Hughes, the hard-working political correspondent of the *Liverpool Post* and valuable member of my Lobby syndicate, had been made Press Secretary at Number 10. As his newspaper covered Wilson's Huyton constituency, they had got to know each other very well and Wilson rightly had a high regard for Trevor's ability and trustworthiness. In view of our long-standing syndicate link, I hoped Trevor would always help me out whenever I had inquiries.

Denis Healey, whom I admired from a distance, had been appointed Secretary of State for Defence. Despite my confidence in him and his Army Minister, Fred Mulley, I decided to carry out my earlier decision and resign from the Army Emergency Reserve. Operating as Captain Adjutant of an Ordnance Corps vehicle company, I had become increasingly frustrated with the Tory mismanagement of the defence services in general and the reserve army in particular. After being awarded the Emergency Reserve Decoration, I quit.

In my opinion, the man most out of his depth in the new Cabinet was Callaghan. As the economy was in poor shape I found this alarming. When the economic crisis struck in November he was said to have lost his nerve. Clearly, if Chancellor Jim did not have the ability to get the economy right in the short term, George Brown would be severely handicapped in trying to get his longer term economic plan successfully off the ground. When I mentioned my concern to George Wigg in the Lobby he muttered, *"You've put your finger on it."*

Apparently he had little confidence in Callaghan either.

Why then had Wilson, knowing of Callaghan's lack of ability in this field, given him such a key job? Presumably it was because the cunning Callaghan, by clever manoeuvring, had got himself into the position that Wilson had held in the days of Gaitskell and Bevan – third man in the Parliamentary Labour Party hierarchy. He and his followers, therefore, had to be appeased as part of the general balancing act.

One face was missing from Wilson's planned Cabinet line-up. Patrick Gordon Walker, his choice for Foreign Secretary, had managed to lose his seat in Smethwick where he had enjoyed a 3,544 majority, after a lacklustre campaign in which he had sought to play down the sensitive and growing local race problem. He was attacked by the Tories as the man who had led Labour's opposition to the Government's Commonwealth Immigrants Bill. This earnest, rather solemn, Oxford academic was said to have the puzzled look of a don who had strayed into politics and wondered what he was doing there. He certainly lacked the common touch. Although as a close friend of Gaitskell he had wrongly forecast that Wilson, if elected leader, would be a prisoner of the unilateralists, the Prime Minister was determined to get him back into the Commons. He decided to create a vacancy in a safe Labour seat – Leyton, where for years I had been an active member of the constituency Labour Party. My friend, the Rev. Reg Sorensen, had held the seat with a comfortable majority of 7,926. Wilson put pressure on him to resign from the Commons and accept a seat in the Lords. Reg, under protest, agreed. A peerage was the last thing the unworldly man wanted. He had intended to soldier on as a conscientious, much respected constituency servant for at least another full parliament. He had also hinted to me a few years before that if, in due course, I wanted to succeed him he would do what he could to help. He made it known locally that he was very reluctant to resign the seat – but at Wilson's insistence he sadly announced his retirement.

Leyton Labour stalwarts thought the whole affair stank and resented having an outsider foisted upon them. Soon candidate Gordon Walker was to be seen tramping the grey streets, a glum, embarrassed look on his face, followed by a rather pompous John Harris in his new role as Transport House Press Chief. When not knocking on doors, Walker conducted his campaign from the back of a van. It was reported that *"his voice echoed forlornly from the loud speaker and no one in Leyton listened."* He was getting bad advice from Harris. My Labour Co-op MP friend, Bob Edwards, who offered to take his car and loudspeaker to Leyton to help, was told by the over-confident Harris that would not be required. He told party headquarters the result was in the bag. When the result was declared the Tories had won by 205 votes. Gordon Walker had lost two good Labour seats in three months. Wilson was stunned. His wafer thin majority in the Commons had been reduced to three. I was appalled by the result – and was worried about Reg's financial situation for he had given too much of his small Commons salary to good causes to have been able to save much. On entering the Lords, he was made a Government Whip to help him with money problems. The kindly, forgiving preacher was not the stuff that Whips are made of. He was sad and uncomfortable.

Although I had moved away from Leyton I had continued to toy with the thought that perhaps, when Reg decided to retire, I would try to get adopted as Labour candidate. The loss of the seat to the Tories had now closed off that avenue for a few years. Moreover, although I was still well remembered there in the local party, now, instead of being employed by *Reynolds*, I was on the *Express* – a position that would make me much less acceptable to some key constituency figures. There was also the fact that I was enjoying the full and exciting life of a political journalist and had begun to be much less active in the Labour Party. I was, in truth, more a journalist than a party politician – a fact I had once before acknowledged on joining *Reynolds* and deciding my priority during Labour's bitter internecine war. I would never again entertain the thought of trying to become a MP.

I discussed the Leyton disaster in detail with George Wigg who was appointed chairman of a committee set up to improve and coordinate party policy. Like me, he had little confidence in the ability of John Harris and wanted him removed as head of party publicity. Publicity, however, was hardly George's strong point either and so he was duly replaced as chairman by the more adroit Richard Crossman.

As acting political editor I arranged a meeting with some new ministers in their offices. Some produced stories. Dick Crossman, for example, at Housing and Local Government, expressed his concern at the inadequacies of the local rating system that was not providing sufficient funds for what needed to be done. It was also inequitable. He was considering new forms of raising money, including the possibility of local sales taxes. This made a good page lead for the Express.

Fred Lee, Minister of Power, told me of plans for handling the important discovery of North Sea Oil and Gas. On the Tory front, I decided to improve my links with some key people over lunches and to host at the famous Savoy Grill for most of these. It was much used by top Fleet Street journalists who mingled at the tables with politicians, well-heeled City types and stars of stage and screen. Winston Churchill had a favourite table and during the war had taken his Cabinet there for lunch. Tucking into the salmon trout, Iain Macleod, the brainy moderniser who had resigned from the Government in protest at the choice of Sir Alec Douglas-Home as Prime Minister, was still rankling about the way the selection developed. After Home's selection, Macleod had hit out publicly at the secrecy involved in what he had caustically described as the *"magic circle"* system for producing a new Tory leader. In February, however, under growing pressure, Sir Alec had announced that in future the party leader would be elected by all Tory MPs in a secret ballot conducted by the chairman of the 1922 Committee.

Macleod was in no doubt that his criticisms had helped to bring about this important reform. In fact, soon after Douglas-Home became PM, the leftish Tory MP Humphrey Berkeley wrote to ask him whether he would set up a proper system for electing the party leader. Home asked Berkeley to produce a plan, the one he subsequently accepted and which would operate whether or not the party was holding office.

Macleod had been a Butler supporter and believed that if Rab had been chosen the Tories would have won the general election. He blamed the Tory Chief Whip Martin Redmayne who was responsible for polling the MPs, and the Lord Chancellor, Lord Dilhorne, whose job it was to sound out members of the Cabinet. When I told him how I had stumbled on 1922 Chairman John Morrison pushing Lord Home's name so quickly he nodded and said, *"That adds up."*

He admitted sadly that his popular Parliamentary Private Secretary Reggie Bennet MP, who had his ear close to the ground at Blackpool, warned him early on that Home was emerging as likeliest candidate to take over from Macmillan. *"I didn't believe it was possible,"* lamented Macleod, *"so I didn't act on his advice."*

He was pleased that he had just been made President of the Young Conservatives' organisation but added ruefully that with Douglas-Home leading the party the image was not conducive to luring young people to join up.

Many, including myself, regarded Macleod as the sharpest, most formidable of the post-war generation of top Tory politicians, such as Maudling, Heath and Enoch Powell. He had a high intelligence and the means of deploying it through his gifts of oratory and a barbed wit. But he had a liberal, radical and compassionate approach to Toryism that caused him to be distrusted by right-wingers who, in the words of Lord Salisbury, found him *"too clever by half"*. One of the finest bridge players in Britain, he had made a living from gambling as a young man. He repaid my hospitality by inviting me to enjoyable drinks parties at his flat in Chelsea.

I also lunched Quintin Hogg at a famous old restaurant, the Coq d'Or in Stratton Street, near Green Park, to where he cycled from his Putney home. He had bought a Moulton bicycle in 1960 and would arrive in bowler hat and cycle clips, chaining the bike to the restaurant's railings. He was always good value. Lunching with me on another day at the Savoy, Edward Heath talked mostly about the case for Britain entering the Common market. With Beaverbrook dead, he hoped the *Daily Express* would be less strident in its opposition. But he feared Harold Wilson, in his opportunistic manner, would kick the issue around like a football in any direction that suited him best at the time. He then reciprocated by inviting me to lunch at his newly occupied apartment at Albany, the exclusive set of residences in a handsome Georgian building set back from Piccadilly. A fine musician, he was playing the piano when I arrived and was relaxed and friendly as he ushered me into the living room. I was impressed by his taste for low-key, masculine décor and noted that, like me, he was a collector of Rowlandson's prints of members of the London volunteer regiments, raised as a Home Guard during the Napoleonic Wars. He was a most attentive, impeccable host.

Heath's cool, uncluttered style of décor that I admired at Albany did not survive in his later homes. As he added to his possessions his residences became more warm and homely. I was saddened to learn in November 2010 that the future of his handsome Georgian house *"Arundells"* in the cathedral close at Salisbury, that he had intended to become a museum displaying his personal effects relating to politics, music, sailing and the army, had become the subject of controversy. Five years after his death at the age of eighty-nine, the trustees of the charitable trust he had set up decided there was not a financially sound future for the museum. They wanted to close it to the public – 13,000 had visited in 2010 – sell the house where Heath had lived for the last twenty years of his life, and give the proceeds to causes the former Prime Minister had supported. The plan was opposed by a group wanting to preserve *"Arundells"* for the nation by using volunteers to run the museum. The Charity Commission was reported as promising a public consultation if it approved the sale of the house. I wished I had visited when Heath lived there in somewhat lonely splendour towards the end of his remarkable life. Friends who did call on him say he was as ever a welcoming host who lost no time in opening a bottle of champagne. On 1 May 2011 it was reported that the Commission had authorised the sale. A spokesman for the Friends of *"Arundells"* warned: *"We will fight this contemptible deal to sell off our heritage every step of the way."*

On the Friday before the Whitsun holiday weekend, I went to Conservative Central office for a private meeting with Tory Party Chairman, Edward du Cann. Over coffee I received a relaxed briefing from the suave forty-one-year-old West Country MP, who had served as Minister of State, Board of Trade. Then, remembering Ian Macleod's worries about attracting young people to a party led by an elderly aristocrat, I asked about recruitment. Du Cann replied that I should understand that there was growing unhappiness at constituency level with Sir Alec's leadership and this made it difficult for him as party chairman. I wished him an enjoyable Whit recess and returned to the office.

I had not expected such a good story and realised that if it appeared under my name the next day that staff at Central Office would realise that the information had come from du Cann. My problem was that I was due to fly to Portugal on the Saturday for a week's holiday. I wrote my report about the unhappiness in the Tory constituency parties and its implications and dictated it to Stewart Steven, who had not yet been switched to the foreign desk. To my delight I read it, word for word as I had written it, while I lounged on an Algarve beach the following Tuesday. It had been the front-page lead story with a by-line for Stewart. Du Cann should be in the clear. I thought he had been seriously disloyal to the man who had appointed him. As for Sir Alec, being the gentleman he was, he would not wish to retain the Tory leadership if he was led to believe he was not wanted. Clearly, du Cann wanted to get rid of him.

Some weeks later I had lunch with Ian Aitken and Charlie Douglas-Home at the Gay Hussar in Soho. Charlie was enjoying his new job as Defence Correspondent of *The Times* and revealed that, on taking up the appointment, he had been called in for questioning by MI5. They knew that when he was on the Express he had lunch meetings with the Russian spy Michael Lyubimov. They wanted to know more about their discussions and whether Charlie had continued to meet other Soviet agents after Lyubimov had been ordered to leave Britain. It struck me that if they knew of Charlie's meetings with the convivial Russian, they presumably knew of mine, also. If that was the case, it would seem they did not regard my meetings with

Lyubimov as a problem. Since his departure, and in order to have one Eastern bloc embassy contact, I had been lunching occasionally with a Hungarian diplomat Kalmain Docze whom I had met at a Labour Party conference. Presumably, MI5 would know about that, too.

As lunch was breaking up Charlie revealed that Uncle Alec had just moved to new accommodation – a flat in an ugly windswept development in Stag Place, Victoria. Helpfully, Charlie gave us his uncle's new phone number. Back at the Commons, I quickly learned that Ted Heath was throwing a party at Albany that evening for the team of Tory MPs he had led in the line-by-line committee stage battle over the Finance Bill implementing Callaghan's complex March budget. Heath had organised his Finance Committee members with military precision and because the Budget and Bill were so complicated, they had given Labour a very hard time. *"They will be impressed by his smart digs,"* I thought, remembering my recent lunch there.

So I wrote a story about Heath taking the opportunity to roll out the carpet in high society style – and was told that Derek Marks had put it on the front page. I walked down into the Members' Lobby, which was empty, and was about to leave when Sir Frederic Bennett, wealthy barrister Tory MP for Torquay and close friend and confidant of Reggie Maudling, entered and came straight up to me. *"Something's up,"* he said. *"Can we have a drink?"*

I took him into Annie's bar, used by the Press but empty that warm summer evening.

"There's a rumour," he blurted out as we sat down in the back room, *"that Alec's going to resign."*

"I'm not really surprised," I commented, *"after all the grumbling from the constituencies."*

"Well, Reggie hadn't expected it to happen so soon," he went on in a worried, despairing tone.

"It's good timing for Heath," I added. *"You know about the party he's throwing for his Finance Bill team tonight?"*

Freddie nodded. I thanked him for the tip and excused myself to go off to confirm it from other sources. Clearly, unlike Heath, Maudling, in his usual laid-back way, was not ready for a leadership election. His friends like Freddy Bennett hoped that if the Press were to report that Alec was about to quit enough Tories would persuade him to change his mind at the eleventh hour. Some senior Tories suspected that financier Freddy was a bad influence on Maudling, but if Sir Alec were to draw back from the brink he would have served Maudling well by gaining more time to prepare. I returned to the Members' Lobby. It was still empty. Then I heard a rustling in the undergrowth in the direction of the Tory Whips' office and Chief Whip, Willie Whitelaw, suddenly emerged, face flustered. *"It's being said Alec's about to resign,"* I said to him as he hurried past.

"Don't believe it Arthur," he replied. *"There's nothing in it."*

Well, he should know I thought. Moreover, I had always found him truthful. That was my mistake. He was lying through his teeth. I hurried up to the Press Gallery and wondered about using the phone number Charlie had given me at lunch. I also wondered whether any other journalists had heard what was going round. Ian Aitken was in the cafeteria having supper. With a reference to the Guardian's political editor Francis Boyd he joked, *"I trust he's having better than this. He's gone to dinner at Sir Alec's new flat."*

That put an end to any thought I had of phoning the Tory leader at home. Time was ticking on. I decided to consult Derek Marks before filing a story for the second edition. I phoned the Express and after what seemed a long wait Marks came to the phone. I gave him the information I had – including Whitelaw's denial. *"I can phone over a story about the rumour, if you can put me through to Copy?"* I suggested.

"No, replied Marks. *"Leave it to me."*

His speech was slurred. He had consumed a lot of drink – but that was not uncommon. And, as much as I disliked him, I knew he had better Tory contacts than any other journalist in London.

As there was no vote that night, the Commons had emptied and I went home. When I picked up the *Express* next morning the only political story on the front page was my account of Heath's party. Wilfred Sendall, who was due to join the Express as political editor the following week, had asked me to have lunch with him that day at his favourite restaurant in a hotel in St. James. He had been political correspondent for the *Sunday Express* but finding it too stressful had moved to the *News of the World.* He congratulated me on my exclusive on Heath's party but showed no great interest when I told him of the resignation rumour. *"He could go in the autumn,"* is all he had to say.

As I arrived back at the Commons Press Gallery I found Stewart Steven in a state of great excitement.

"Sir Alec's resigned!" he burbled. *"Can you phone the news desk?"*

Derek Marks said nothing to me about the previous night's exchange. Had he been so drunk he had forgotten? Or was he so ashamed that he had let both me and the paper down that he could not bring himself to refer to it? The incident confirmed that I had nothing helpful to expect of him. To Marks' dismay, Heath, the dedicated campaigner for Common Market membership, won the ensuing election for the Tory Party leadership.

Future Tory leader Margaret Thatcher was among those MPs taken by surprise by Sir Alec's decision to quit. As she did not frequent the Commons bars or smoking room she had been unaware of the pressure building up on him and said later that if his loyal supporters had known they might have persuaded him to soldier on. This possibility was clearly in the mind of rubber-bones Whitelaw when he misled me in the Lobby. A staunch Heath man, he wanted a change at the top. Knowing of Heath's organisational ability and Maudling's lack of it, he guessed that the latter would be beaten in the first-ever ballot for the Tory leadership by Conservative MPs. If the Express had carried even a speculative report by me, it is likely that enough constituency party chairmen would have phoned their MPs urging them to intervene. Freddy Bennett had been badly let down by the Express. It emerged later that Whitelaw had told Sir Alec of the pressure in the party for him to step down with the words *"You can stay and be criticised or resign and be a hero."*

When it had become known to me that Marks intended to bring the ageing, garrulous Sendall in as political editor I began to think of making a move. On duty one Sunday, I read in the *Sunday Times* a small item forecasting that in the coming week John Harris was to be appointed Press Liaison Officer for the Parliamentary Labour Party. He was currently in charge of the Press Office at Labour Party HQ in Transport House, and his appointment was to be rubber-stamped at a meeting of Labour's National Executive Committee on Wednesday.

"That would be just the job for me!" I thought, and phoned George Wigg. He confirmed that the report was true and I asked him why the vacancy had not been advertised, as I would have applied for the job. Wigg detested Harris, who had done so much to undermine Wilson. I could almost see the malevolent glint in his eyes as, after a short pause, he said, *"Thanks for the call, and leave it with me."*

When the National Executive met, Harold Wilson announced that he wanted the appointment deferred. He detested Harris even more than Wigg. Then to my great embarrassment, there was a buzz in the Parliamentary Press Gallery that I had applied for the job. Stewart Steven asked me with surprise if it was true and I confirmed that it was. I could just imagine what Derek Marks would say when the news got back to him. Unbeknown to me, however, my intervention had started other wheels turning. Dick Crossman, on hearing of the postponed appointment, decided that the man best suited to fill the vacancy was a journalist who had worked for a time as his researcher and member of the political staff of the *Daily Mirror* – a certain Gerald Kaufman. Kaufman had been assistant General Secretary of the Fabian Society in the mid-fifties and it was through the Society that I had met him. When I was on the *News Chronicle*, he had sought my advice about getting on to the political team of a national paper and had bought me lunch at Bush House. He had done an excellent, diagnostic job as political correspondent of the *New Statesman* from 1964-65 and I had the highest regard for his intellect. Crossman got his way. But now that Harris was out of the running Wilson decided that the job, while retaining its title, should become much more associated with his personal requirements at Number 10 – such as assistance with speech writing. Trevor Lloyd-Hughes broke the news to me. I was disappointed not to get the job – but pleased that it had gone to someone whose work and intelligence I admired. I had no idea, then, what a lucky escape it had been for me.

My intervention had been lucky, also, for both Harris and Kaufman. The former decided to throw in his lot with the fast-rising Gaitskellite Roy Jenkins, who eventually got Harris a peerage and a Ministerial post in the Home Office. Distrusted by members of Wilson's kitchen cabinet, he would have had a rotten time at Number 10. As for Kaufman, he never looked back, becoming a key member of Wilson's Downing Street team which in due course helped him take over a safe Labour seat at Manchester Gorton. In 1974, he was given a job in the Government as Parliamentary Under Secretary of State for the Environment and later was promoted to Minister of State for Industry. Eventually, he received a knighthood.

One of the problems for anyone working in Number 10 was the extraordinary power and influence of Wilson's personal and political secretary Mrs Marcia Williams. Because Wilson had allegedly been foolish enough to sleep with her a few times before becoming leader of the party, he seemed unable to control her. Indeed, there were times when she made his life hell with her demands. Regarding it as one of her jobs to protect Wilson, who had a nagging sense of insecurity, she had decided that something must be done to win over Walter Terry, who had been lampooning the PM in his weekly political column in the *Daily Mail*. Terry had drawn a parallel between Wilson and Walter Mitty, the dreamer and fantasist in the 1930's novel by James Thurber. He suggested that, like Mitty, Wilson had lost touch with reality. Walter's sharp jibes had got under Wilson's skin.

One evening, as I sat drinking with Walter in the Press Gallery, someone from the Number 10 Press Office ushered in Marcia and asked if they could sit with us. She was at her most vivacious. As the drink flowed and the evening wore on I became rather uneasy. Marcia and Walter were getting on all too well. My instinct was right. I was witnessing the Start of the Affair. Shortly after, while lunching an MP in *La Capannina,* an Italian restaurant in Soho, I saw Walter and Marcia at a table at the other end of the room.

Soon they were being seen together more often. I swore. How were we to compete with Walter when he was having such an affair with the woman who was not only the Prime Minister's personal secretary but his close confidante and influential adviser? In fact, as Marcia was to reveal, she fell in love with Walter in 1967. Her marriage to Edmund Williams, an aeronautical engineer, had been dissolved in 1960.

Walter's output of well-informed exclusives increased. I told Sendall of the problem, but he seemed incapable of taking any action. Then Max Aitken invited the political team to lunch in his private dining room in the *Daily Express* building. Soon after we were seated he looked across at Sendall and asked, *"What can you tell us about the Wilson-Marcia business, Wilfred?"*

Sendall burbled for a while and when he paused I leaned forward and said bluntly to Max: *"So far as we're concerned, Sir, Marcia's involved in something far more serious. She's sleeping with Walter Terry of the Mail."*

I had hoped Max would want some action taken. I had forgotten that in Fleet Street dog doesn't eat dog. If Sendall was prepared to be awakened at night by the news desk wanting a Terry scoop followed up I was not. At one of my regular lunches with Trevor Lloyd-Hughes I told him what I knew and asked him to speak to Wilson and try to put an end to the affair. I pointed out that as Terry was married there was a risk of blackmail – and a subsequent security risk. Trevor looked embarrassed. He said he knew what I was talking about but that it would be very difficult to interfere. When nothing happened, I tackled Wilson's Parliamentary Private Secretary, my old friend Harold Davies. Harold knew about it, too, and was very angry that Marcia was so involved with someone on the detested Tory *Mail – "of all bloody papers!"* he spluttered.

He said he'd like to stop it and would see what he could do.

"Marcia's wearing Harold out with her goings on," added Davies, rolling his eyes in despair.

Despite his strong feelings, still nothing happened. I then tackled Fred Peart, who by then had become Leader of the Commons. He looked suitably perturbed but stressed the difficulty of trying to raise the matter with Wilson. His wariness was understandable in the light of the opinion of George Caunt, a Parliamentary Labour Party official, who became a member of Wilson's No. 10 staff. He complained bitterly that Marcia had far too much influence over the Prime Minister and made everyone's life in the office a misery by her hysterical behaviour.

The nearest any minister had got to pointing a finger in Cabinet at the culprit responsible for leaking information from No. 10 was when Wilson, at a meeting in August 1966, referred to the danger of leaks to the Press during another crisis for Sterling. Talk of a possible devaluation was in the air. Tony Crosland, Education Minister, chipped in with the comment that they all knew that most of them sprung either from No. 10 or from the DEA (Department of Economic Affairs). Soon after, on the eve of the Labour Party Conference, I was to discover just how personally irresponsible Wilson could be with sensitive information. I had taken to lunch Henry James, the charming hard-working number two in the Downing Street Press Office. Over coffee, he informed me that there was a state of meltdown at No. 10 as Wilson believed that James Callaghan, Chancellor of the Exchequer, was plotting to overthrow him and was in talks with certain other ministers to bring this about. Way back in July, Wilson had suspected that Roy Jenkins was involved in a plot against him as the Sterling crisis worsened. Encouraged in his paranoia by Marcia Williams, he believed the plan was to make Callaghan Prime Minister with Jenkins as his Chancellor and, if necessary, to seek to form a coalition government. He even believed in his fantasy world that this was being hatched at a country house party attended by Jenkins and hosted by Gaitskell's one-time mistress, the ever-busy socialite Ann Fleming. Always anxious to keep his links with Russia warm, he had chosen to attend a trade fair in Moscow that weekend and spoke scathingly of Ministers who went whoring after society hostesses.

Henry did not enlarge on the latest plot panic, but it was clear to me that it was about economic policy and the pound. Unbeknown to me, however, Wilson believed Callaghan, as Chancellor, had decided that, in the teeth of his opposition, the pound must be devalued and that in this he had the support of key members of the Government, including Jenkins and George Brown. Callaghan was attending a conference abroad and was due to return to London at the weekend. Wilson, who had directed Henry to give me the information, clearly expected that the *Daily Express* would give the story a big show on the front page the next day –as delegates assembled for the Conference. The fact that sterling was in a weak state and would be weakened further by the publication of such a report did not concern the scheming little man. It did concern me and I made the decision not to write the story or to inform my office. The more I thought about it, in fact, the more irresponsible Wilson's move appeared. The PM, however, was determined to find an outlet for his conspiracy complex. The next morning, at the conference headquarters hotel, disappointed by the *Express*, he sidled in next to Sunday paper journalist Tony Shrimsley in the gents' toilets and told him what Henry James had been instructed to tell me. Next day, when I turned up for Sunday duty at the office, the news editor passed me a cutting and asked me to follow it up. It was a copy of Shrimsley's weekly political column and there, buried away on an inside page, was the yarn. When I asked Shrimsley about it later he told me what had happened and said he thought it *"smelt a bit"* – and not just because of where he heard it. I still had no intention of writing it up as a story for the *Express* that Sunday but, instead, offered to write a feature describing how, while the hard-working Chancellor was doing his best for Britain abroad, 10 Downing Street was undermining him with destabilising and unbelievable talk that he was planning a "palace revolution". I had long since ceased to have any warm feelings for Callaghan, whom, in some ways I actually despised, but I was content to do him a favour in the interests of sterling. Moreover, I had by now developed an even greater contempt for Wilson.

This was strengthened by the ridiculous development in the Parliamentary Press Gallery – the formation of what became known as *"The White Commonwealth"*. This short but disgraceful chapter in the history of the Lobby was the result of an attempt to manipulate the Press dreamed up by a lackey of Wilson who did not understand the camaraderie that existed among some journalists. Due to that bond, the White Commonwealth was not destined to last long.

Difficulties between some political correspondents and ministers had begun to grow soon after Wilson had won a brilliant general election campaign in March 1966, transforming Labour's majority in the Commons from a pathetic two to a handsome ninety-six. Hardly had the new Labour Government settled in when the country found itself facing a major crisis in the form of a seamen's strike that threatened to cripple the economy. The National Union of Seamen, whose members were poorly paid and often worked in appalling conditions, was demanding a wage rise of seventeen per cent, hopelessly well above the three and a half per cent norm set by the Government.

Rumours began to spread from Whitehall that the Communist Party was behind the strike – but there was no evidence that the union was run by communists. Nevertheless, when communist activity on the fringes became apparent Wilson chose the moment to denounce the *"tightly-knit group of politically motivated men"* whom he accused of holding the country to ransom. On June 22, the Government introduced Emergency Powers. At a Lobby meeting, Wilson was closely questioned about his accusation. It became clear that some journalists, including my colleague Wilfred Sendall, regarded it as an unjustified smear on the leaders of the strike. I did not ask any questions at the meeting but was unhappy at Wilson's choice of words and was not surprised when it was followed by reports in sections of the media that the Government was blaming communists for the strike. Typically, Harry Boyne of the *Daily Telegraph,* whose short hand was better than his judgement, lapped up every word of Wilson's and regurgitated them in a long front-page report.

John Prescott, who was to become Deputy Prime Minister under Tony Blair, and a former seaman, played a leading role in the industrial action as an adviser to the National Union of Seamen. He attended union meetings that were bugged by MI5 and was said to have been one of the *"politically motivated men"*. He wrote a pamphlet attacking the Government's handling of the dispute and believed Wilson had been misled by his advisers. He has said there was very little communist involvement in the stoppage. Wilson had invoked Emergency Powers during the 47-day strike fearing that Britain would be seriously hit by a shortage of oil and food.

George Wigg complained of irresponsibility in sections of the media and claimed that this was due to the fact that

Parliamentary Lobby standards had slumped, because the Lobby had become too large.

Soon after, as I was walking through one of the Press Gallery floors, I saw a group of my colleagues being hustled into a television room accompanied by a minister, Margaret Herbison, Minister of Social Security. I asked Sendall if he knew such a meeting had been held and he said he did not. Wigg's wish for a smaller Lobby was being made to come true. While I could not blame journalists such as Walter Terry or Francis Boyd of the *Guardian* for playing the No. 10 game, I was appalled that officers of the Lobby such as Victor Knight of the *Daily Mirror* and Harry Boyne of the *Daily Telegraph* were involved, thus undermining the institution they were supposed to defend. By discreet inquiries I soon discovered that, apart from the *Daily Express, The Times,* the BBC and the communist *Morning Star* were also being excluded. I suggested to Sendall that he should expose the No. 10 ploy in an article but he declined. I then decided to have a word with David Wood, the thoughtful, normally well-informed political correspondent of *The Times,* who, I found to my surprise, did not know of the development. He had a weekly column which appeared on a Monday and I suggested he should use it to expose the special briefings for Wilson's trusties. He did so. The result? He was invited by No. 10 to join the Lobby-within-the-Lobby – and he accepted, to my intense irritation. However, I had a laugh at David's expense. Members of the *"White Commonwealth"*, as the group had become known, were invited to a reception at Downing Street. I phoned Fleet Street's own journal, *The U.K. Press Gazette* and tipped them off, suggesting they should post a photographer outside No.10. The picture they published on their front page was of a journalist, appropriately pulling on a pair of white gloves, as he stepped out of the famous doorway. It was David Wood. David did not hold it against me and said on some later occasion that when he retired as political correspondent of *The Times* he would have liked me to take his place.

Wilson tried to persuade the Editor of *The Times* to remove the decent, painstaking David from his political correspondent's job. He was not successful.

The name *"White Commonwealth"* was an allusion to the custom of the old white dominions, such as Australia and Canada, to side with Wilson on such issues as his handling of the Rhodesian crisis in face of criticisms from new African Commonwealth members. It was fun sniping from the sidelines at Wilson's bunch of goody journalists – but it was not that tactic that brought the experiment to an early end. The fact was that some members of the White Commonwealth were distinctly embarrassed by its existence and would happily leak to me the contents of briefings given to them at secret meetings by Wilson and his ministers. Francis Boyd, the experienced and distinguished political correspondent of the *Guardian*, who thought the new development was disgraceful, was my best source. Most of the material was not very newsworthy background material – but I had an advantage over the White Commonwealth members because I could attribute the information they received. The best story involved Denis Healey, who from 1964 did a good, intelligent job as Defence Secretary for six years. He had a number of differences with Wilson on defence issues during that time and after one such private row, Wilson foolishly criticised Healey in a briefing to the "goodies". Francis duly passed on this information to me that evening over a drink in the Press Gallery bar and next morning the *Daily Express* carried an exclusive report to the effect that the Prime Minister had attacked his Defence Secretary over a policy issue at a briefing for handpicked journalists at Downing Street. That was the last nail in the coffin of the *"White Commonwealth"*. It died unlamented.

As for the BBC's exclusion from the stooges' club, accusation and counter-accusation about its alleged political bias has continued over the decades. While serving as Postmaster General, Edward Short took me into the Commons Strangers' Bar one evening to leak that Wilson was about to appoint Lord 'Charlie' Hill, the former Tory minister and propagandist, as chairman of the BBC. Hill had just retired as chairman of the Independent Television Authority and Short presumably feared that the move, if announced, would cause uproar in the Labour Party. He was right about that. Michael Foot described it as the most extraordinary appointment since the Roman Emperor Caligula gave his horse a seat in the Senate. But Wilson got away with it. As Richard Crossman observed, Hill had run the ITV to please the politicians, making sure their treatment of news and current affairs did not offend the establishment. As he had avoided all the irritating things that the BBC did, he was being given the opportunity to discipline the great public service broadcaster famed for its independence.

One Lobby-type institution which did not split during the White Commonwealth episode was the Guinea Club which lunched monthly and often had ministers to speak as guests of honour. Its name was derived from the fact that a guinea had been the original price of the excellent three-course meal served in a private Commons dining room. One such guest of honour was Jennie Lee, widow of Aneurin Bevan, who in 1967 had been promoted to Minister of State with special responsibility for the Arts within the Education and Science Department. She appeared to enjoy the occasion and said that if any of us ever wanted to have a word, her door would always be open. What an invitation, and one I decided to take up – apparently the only one to do so. As she was reputed to detest *"the Tory Press",* was often arrogant and had a sharp tongue, many journalists gave her a wide berth. To me in her ministerial office that day she could not have been more charming and helpful. I departed with the news that she was intending to set up an Open University. She told me that Nye would have been delighted with the founding of such an institution, as he had been a great supporter of further education through such bodies as the Workers' Education Association. He had, in fact, expressed the view in the mid-1950s that it would be wonderful if television could be harnessed in some way to provide regular tuition for those seeking to improve themselves.

Although I represented the *Daily Express* I found her friendly and accessible –but perhaps that was because she knew that I had also worked for *Reynolds News.* My exclusive received due prominence in the *Express* next day. She may have been over sixty then but the sexy Jennie, a coalminer's daughter, still retained her smouldering good looks. And holding a ministerial position did not stop her from having an affair with a civil servant twelve years younger than herself. She was also said to have flirted with Arnold Goodman, the gross wheeler-dealer solicitor, whom she appointed chairman of the Arts Council. When the Open University was successfully launched, Harold Wilson took the credit and it is often said that it was his most important accomplishment as Prime Minister.

I enjoyed the gatherings of the Guinea Club, and then became involved in setting up a lunch club of a very different type. It began because of my close friendship with Leslie Hale, Labour MP for Oldham, who had the well-established reputation for being the fastest and wittiest speaker in the Commons. An original member of the *"Keep Left Group",* in 1947 he had joined with Crossman, Foot, Wigg and others in signing a pamphlet *"Keep Left"* which criticised the Attlee government on two main issues. Firstly, it accused it of being too anti-Russian. Secondly, it complained that it had failed to have a national economic plan under the control of a Minister of Economic Affairs – an idea to be resurrected in due course by Harold Wilson. Leslie, a clever solicitor and *bon viveur* had become a staunch and leading Bevanite. I first got to talk to him in a train taking us both home to Dulwich where he also lived in a large crumbling Victorian house with an impeccably tended garden and vegetable plot that tumbled down to the railway line. He invited me there for a Sunday morning drink where I met his charming wife Dorothy, son Bill and daughter Lesley. I saw the many oil portraits he had painted of his hero Nye Bevan in an ongoing struggle to get a good likeness. One of his closest friends was the painter and lithographer James Fitton who also lived in Dulwich, in a cottage by the duck pond, and whom I was to get to know very well too.

Leslie had contributed to policy-making on the Left. As a solicitor, he had been involved in providing free legal advice to Africans accused in Kenya of involvement with the Mau Mau terrorist organisation – being shunned for this by white settlers in the colony's hotels, clubs and restaurants. He had also been a dedicated Commons backbencher, specialising in long funny speeches late at night when, with other members of a small group called *"The Midnight Hags"*, he would harass Tory government ministers and delay legislation. Always generous with free legal advice to Labour colleagues in the Commons, he was owed a lot of favours. Thus, when Labour won power in 1964 he expected a good position in the Wilson administration. He got nothing – some said because the Prime Minister feared his drinking habits could cause problems. Deeply disappointed, he then became disillusioned with the Government's handling of various issues and in particular with one affecting his constituents.

On a Friday afternoon in 1967, Alf Morris MP bumped into Leslie in the Commons and noted that he was deeply distraught. When Alf asked him what was wrong Leslie declared angrily that he had had enough, and was not returning to the Commons again. His Private Member's Bill to have byssinosis recognised as an industrial disease had been killed off by Minister for Pensions and National Insurance, Margaret Herbison. It was of great importance to Hale's cotton workers in Oldham. The bill had been talked out after Herbison had said the Government could not accept it. Hale, already disappointed and disillusioned, resigned his seat. Alf in due course, as Minister for the Disabled, brought about recognition of and compensation for byssinosis in the Social Security Act of 1975. Leslie rejoiced.

At the age of sixty-four, having served in the Commons for twenty-two years, he announced his resignation in March, forcing a by-election at a bad time for Wilson. Life in the House had meant much to him. Cut off from it he became increasingly despondent – to the point where I became worried for his health. Knowing how he enjoyed convivial company over a good lunch, I asked if I could arrange a get-together with one of his old friends.

He said he would like to see Ian Aitken again and so the three of us met at the *"Gay Hussar"* restaurant in Greek Street, Soho. A favourite meeting place for leading members of the Labour left, it was run by Victor Sassie, a considerable character who had been born in Barrow-in-Furness of Italian stock but had adopted a middle-European style and accent after visiting Budapest in 1932. His colourful establishment had been named after Hungary's horse soldiers rather than the colourful characters who trip down Old Compton Street these days (or "Old Queen Street" as I believe it is known). There he supervised the cooking and serving of Hungarian-type dishes ranging from wild cherry soup and pressed boar's head to goulash, smoked goose and carp.

The lunch with Ian Aitken was a great success, with Leslie recapturing some of his old entertaining form. We met again a month or two later, joined on that occasion by Charlie Douglas-Home, by then well dug in at *The Times*, Michael Foot was added for the third lunch and James Fitton and left-wing MP Ian Mikardo for the fourth, entailing a move upstairs away from the red-plush banquettes to a private room at the top of the building. The Leslie Hale luncheon club was beginning to grow. Ian Mikardo, distrusted by many in the Labour Party, was good company on such social occasions. Genial, witty and an amusing gravel-voiced raconteur, he was bookmaker for the House of Commons. Always ready to quote a price on any election connected with Westminster from a general election contest to the Chairmanship of the Tory 1922 Committee, *"Mik"* was not helped by his appearance. It led people to suspect that he was conspiring, even when his only thought was which horse would come in first at Goodwood. Churchill once remarked unkindly, *"I'm told he's not as nice as he looks!"*

Clever and articulate, he was chosen as prospective Labour candidate for Reading in 1944 and started to give the party leadership real trouble when at that year's Labour conference he moved a successful resolution calling for wholesale nationalisation. Herbert Morrison, in a fury, told him he had lost Labour the coming general election but not for the first time got it wrong. Labour won with a huge majority and young *"Mik"* captured Tory-held Reading.

A good organiser, he developed a method of tracking down friendly voters and getting them to the polling station, which famously became known as *The Reading System.* Not even that, however, could help him survive Gaitskell's inept handling of the 1959 election and he lost his seat. Five years later he returned to the Commons as MP for Poplar. Yet, despite his ability, Wilson did not offer him a government post, as there was a mutual distrust. Instead, he became a highly effective chairman of the Select Committee on Nationalised Industries. He also became a nagging critic of aspects of economic policy and of the Government's policy on Vietnam, where he called for a strong anti-American stance.

At an early lunch club meeting he revealed how impoverished members of his family, on arriving in London from Eastern Europe in the nineteenth century, were told they were in New York by the swindling agent who had arranged their passage. They lived in a cellar in the East End for months before discovering the truth. His mother had come from the Ukraine and his first language as a child was Yiddish. As a standard bearer of the Left, he served on Labour's National Executive Committee for years and I received interesting evidence of how he was distrusted by the right wing when I took him as my guest to a Guinea Club lunch. The guest speaker was Denis Healey. At the end, a self-important political correspondent of a Labour-supporting newspaper accused me of ruining the event as Healey was not prepared to say anything of interest on Lobby terms with *"Mik"* sitting at the table.

Royal Academician James Fitton was another *Hale* club member with good stories to tell of his early life. Arriving in London from the North-West, he was walking along the Thames embankment near the Houses of Parliament when he recognised a figure coming towards him. It was J.R.

Clynes, one of the top men in the Labour Government of Ramsey MacDonald – a man James had known through his involvement with the Labour Party at home in Oldham. They shook hands and when Clynes learned that James had just arrived in the city to seek his fortune and had nowhere to sleep he invited him to stay at his official residence. Clynes in fact, was Lord Privy Seal and then Home Secretary. James moved in and began to enjoy being on the fringe of political life of London. One afternoon, Clynes said he was due to attend a party that evening at the home of the famous science fiction writer H.G. Wells, who had been an active Fabian Socialist. He said he could take a guest and asked would James like to go? He gave him the address and explained to his provincial friend that, on his arrival, the door would be opened by a butler who would take his coat and escort him to the reception room. James arrived on time, gave his coat to the man at the door and walked into the room where the party was already underway. Receiving a tap on his shoulder he turned to see the butler. *"I'm Wells!"* the man announced. *"And who are you?"*

James, who shared Leslie Hale's dim view of Wilson, told us of the Prime Minister's attempt to become involved with the famous *"match stick man"* artist L.S. Lowry. James, one of his great friends in the North-West, had been planning with my old *Reynolds News* colleague Hugh Delargy MP to invite the popular painter to dinner at the Commons. Sitting next to Harold Wilson at a Royal Academy dinner, James mentioned his plan when Lowry's name cropped up. The Prime Minster immediately suggested that the dinner be held at Downing Street. He said he would need only about two week's notice and if Lowry gave him a month's notice he could choose almost any day. Wilson, clearly, was not a busy host at No. 10. James was uneasy, suspecting that Wilson, as with the Beatles, was hoping that some of the painter's popularity would rub off on him. He undertook to write to Lowry, however, and after a month, receiving no reply, feared he had offended his old friend. Months later, he met Lowry in London and as they were walking up Bond Street to visit a gallery, James decided to tackle him on the subject. *"Did you get that letter from me about Harold Wilson's invitation?"* he asked.

Lowry, who had a habit of veering to the left even as he walked, was a pace ahead of James and after a few more strides retorted, more in sorrow than disgust, *"Yes, Jim. I did. And I wouldn't have thought it of you – I wouldn't have thought it of you!"*

Another addition to the club on Leslie's recommendation was Archie Gordon, editor of the BBC's Radio Documentaries and Talks Department, who had got to know him when he produced *The Week in Westminster* from 1946-66. He was to inherit the title of Fifth Marquess of Aberdeen and Temair and then sat on the crossbench in the Lords. He was interested in painting and greatly enjoyed the company of James Fitton. A naturally courteous man, he had been noted for his strict impartiality during his time covering Parliament and was liked and respected by MPs of all parties. Our lunches gave him scope to deploy his lively sense of humour.

Harold Davies, Parliamentary Private Secretary to the Prime Minister from 1967-70 was another addition. An exuberant roly-poly character, he had been a close friend of Nye Bevan and as a schoolmaster had shared his hero's interest in furthering adult education. Wilson had made him Pensions Ministry Parliamentary Secretary in 1964 and the following year had sent him on a secret Vietnam peace-seeking initiative to Hanoi as he had a long interest in the Far East and personal links with the Ho Chi Minh government. Self-important officials at the Foreign office were furious at being bypassed and decided to wreck the mission by leaking it to the press before Davies arrived in Hanoi. They hoped to annoy the Vietnam government by giving the impression it was a Wilson publicity stunt. The mission was unsuccessful.

Typical of the good stories told at the table about politicians was one involving former Tory Lord Chancellor, the swarthy-faced Lord Kilmur, better known as David Maxwell-Fyfe. Leslie Hale recounted how, following World War II, a team of prosecutors was being assembled for the Nuremburg Trials of Nazi war criminals. Someone suggested lawyer Maxwell-Fyfe who was tracked down to the smart Adelphi Hotel in Liverpool, where he served as Recorder. A phone call was put through. "Is a Mr Maxwell-Fyfe there?'

"No Sir," replied the waiter.

The caller insisted, "I'm sure he is."

"What does he look like," asked the waiter.

"He looks like a Caucasian assassin," said the caller.

"Ah yes, sir, in that case the gentleman is here."

With so many characters around the lunch table there seemed no need to introduce more. Yet more came. Stewart Steven, now Foreign Editor of the Express, had known Leslie before I recruited him to the paper and added a somewhat brassy note to the occasions. Alf Morris, well-liked by Leslie also joined. Then Ian Aitken suggested his MP brother-in-law John Mackie, a wealthy successful farmer who had been another close friend to Nye Bevan and had advised him when he got into pig farming. A tall, heavily built Scot with a wry sense of humour, he had served as Parliamentary Under Secretary at Agriculture under Fred Peart. Despite his wealth, I noted that John was always careful not to pay a penny more than was necessary when it came to the bill. He once said with feeling, *"The more I see of politicians, the more I like farming."*

He retired from the Commons in 1974. He continued to attend the club, however, and when it became clear to me that he was bored and would like a job on a public body, preferably connected with the land, I mentioned this to Fred Peart, Leader of the Lords, over a drink in the Commons Strangers' Bar in 1975. Fred, a leading anti-European, who had a difference with John on this front, did not appear very interested at first but when I recalled John's work for the party over the years, he said he would put in a good word. In 1976, *"out of the blue"*, John was appointed Chairman of the Forestry Commission. He held the job for three years and in 1981 became a life peer as Lord John-Mackie.

The club was paying off as a source of patronage – and there were to be more developments, not all good. Meanwhile, I operated as unelected secretary of the increasingly lively get-togethers.

Soon after I began reporting from the Parliamentary Press Gallery, I noticed that agitation was building up on the Labour benches about what was described as the inadequate pay for MPs. The Tories, mostly enjoying extra private incomes from the City, business, law, pensions or the land, were on the whole far less concerned by the issue.

One young MP playing a leading role in building up pressure for a new deal on salaries was Roy Mason, a former coal miner from Yorkshire. When I first dealt with him he was busily engaged in gathering names for a Commons motion. He looked to me like the sort of man who got things done. Clever and ambitious, Roy had won a trade union scholarship to the London School of Economics, one of the top three academic institutions in the country, at a time when less than five per cent of the population went to university. He had entered the Commons as MP for

236

Barnsley in 1953 aged twenty-nine. I decided he had a bright future. In 1960, he became a Labour frontbench spokesman and entered the government following Harold Wilson's 1964 general election victory. Although up-and-coming MPs like Roy, who got ministerial posts, received salary increases, Wilson faced growing pressure from within the Parliamentary Labour Party to deal with the rumbling pay issue –and there was certainly cause for grievance.

It was risky for an MP to be seen clamouring for more pay as such action could lead to unpopularity with voters, especially those on low incomes. It could also be an irritation to party leaders. Roy, however, and his supporters, had known they had a good case – and as he was to show throughout his career he was not short of courage, even earning himself top place on the IRA hit list after serving as a tough Northern Ireland Secretary.

He and his campaigners did not object to me reporting on their agitation. As I did so I reflected that I was earning comfortably more than if I had succeeded in entering Parliament as an MP.

Faced with a succession of economic crises, however, Prime Minister Wilson found it necessary to resort to national appeals for wage restraint. He dared not give MPs the pay rise they were due. Instead, he decided, typically, to employ a less straightforward tactic. He asked a respected senior member of the Cabinet, Edward Short, to devise a system of expenses for MPs that would provide them with some of the extra money they were demanding. At that time expenses were virtually nonexistent in Parliament – unlike in Fleet Street. At Short's suggestion, funds were also provided to help cover the expenses of running the office of the Leader of the Opposition.

The minister produced the required scheme and when it was accepted I reported that it had become known as *Short*

Money. Moreover, MPs were left in no doubt that the extra cash, provided supposedly to help them do their jobs, was in fact in lieu of a pay rise. We were on the slippery slope. Soon *Short Money* became big money. That slope, with various hair-raising additions to the expenses trough by later Labour and Tory governments, eventually transported former Labour MP David Chaytor to jail for a sentence of eighteen months on January 7 2011, convicted for falsely claiming parliamentary expenses of over £20,000. Some other politicians, accused of robbing the taxpayers they were elected to protect, were awaiting their turn to face a judge on similar charges.

I had been in at the beginning of what was to develop over the next forty years – due to the failure of governments and greed of some politicians – into the Great Expenses Scandal. It had been maturing steadily decade after decade, and when eventually uncovered by the *Daily Telegraph* in 2009 produced a stench akin to an over-ripe, maggot-ridden cheese.

When Roy Mason and his colleagues began their campaign for an overdue fair deal on pay they could never have foreseen that it would end in payments for duck houses, moat cleaning, pornography – and a money-making racket in MPs' second homes.

By coincidence, the first sitting MP to be convicted of fraud – in January 2011, for dishonestly claiming over £14,000 in expenses – sat for the constituency once represented by Roy Mason, Barnsley Central. He was Eric Illsley, who had been suspended from the Labour Party when he was charged, shortly after retaining the gritty Yorkshire seat in the May general election. I had welcomed him as Roy's successor when he first arrived at the Commons, a personable, fresh-faced, keen new Leeds University educated member in 1987. But he was not exactly Roy's *'cup of tea'* – and thanks to Roy, the town retained an honourable link with Parliament through its distinguished resident Lord Mason of Barnsley.

CHAPTER NINE
Browned Off

After three years of dithering over the future of the pound, the time for the Government to announce an inevitable devaluation had arrived. It was November 1967, and with devaluation came the resignation of James Callaghan who, predictably, had failed as Chancellor of the Exchequer. Wilson, who had been credited with opposing devaluation, was saying, towards the end, that he had an open mind. He gave Callaghan a second chance, arranging for him to swap jobs with Home Secretary, Roy Jenkins. With Jenkins went John Harris who, despite his early failure, had proved to be a successful image builder for his boss. He had gone to work for him after my intervention had prevented him from getting the Parliamentary Labour Party liaison officer job – and what a good turn that had been. He and Jenkins became the closest of confidants. The fact that they were both inclined to snobbishness helped them to bond. Harris even publicly signalled his worship of Jenkins by aping his foppish mannerisms and peculiarities of speech, such as the contrived failure to pronounce his r's, transforming his favourite tipple claret into *"clawet"*. Despite Harris' efforts to appear a gent in the Jenkins' mould, it took him a long time to learn that it was not done to tuck one's shirt into one's underpants, thus revealing tired elastic above the trouser waistline. This solecism and his attempt to be a Jenkins' clone made him a joke among political journalists. One of those was Walter Terry, with whom he lunched regularly and whom he would often tip off. One such "leak" was a report that Jenkins was considering the introduction of identity cards – which reveals how long civil servants at the

Home Office have sought to foist that totalitarian project on their ministers.

Ever since my time on the *News Chronicle* I had taken a close interest in the problem of the future of the Rhodesian Federation. I had watched with growing anger as Tory imperialists had tried to hamper progress towards black majority rule when Iain Macleod was Colonial Secretary. Douglas Clark, who later recruited me to the *Daily Express*, wrote at Beaverbrook's command, a searing, savage attack on Macleod and his colonial policy – an article laced with bitter invective aimed at seriously damaging his career. I have never seen a more vicious attack on a politician – and at the time, as someone who respected Macleod, I was strengthened in my view that I could never work for Beaverbrook. Perhaps, as with politicians, struggling political reporters should never say *"never"*.

A year after Labour had won the 1964 general election, Ian Smith had gained power in Southern Rhodesia. The fighter pilot ace wounded in the Battle of Britain was making it clear that he would proclaim independence for his country if Harold Wilson opposed his plan to continue with white minority rule. His middle class white supporters lived an existence similar to that enjoyed by families in the Home Counties around London – an endless round of tennis, golf, bridge and cocktail parties. One wit described Southern Rhodesia as *"Surrey with a lunatic fringe on top"*.

Covering the Commonwealth Conference in London in June 1965, I led the *Daily Express* with a report of a split over Rhodesia when a group of African leaders banded together in an effort to force Wilson to adopt a tough timetable for ending white control. Wilson, his back to the wall, insisted that the problem was essentially one for Britain and Rhodesia to settle alone. On October 11, I led the paper again with a report of urgent talks between Wilson and Tory leaders following a visit to London by Ian Smith. The Commonwealth Secretary Arthur Bottomley, I reported, had appealed to Smith not to take the law into his own hands but to agree to a special conference right away to discuss the independence issue.

On October 14, the Express chose to lead again with a report by me that Wilson was flying to Balmoral to discuss with the Queen the role of the Crown in the growing Rhodesian crisis.

'If all else fails,' I wrote, *'an intervention by the Queen – on the advice of the Government – is now seen as a real possibility in Whitehall. It would be the last card.*

'Government sources believe it might prove decisive in persuading Rhodesians to draw back from an illegal independence grab – for there is no Commonwealth people with stronger regard for the Crown.'

My old friend Arthur Bottomley was giving me useful guidance. Then Wilson, to Arthur's dismay, made the tactical error on 29 October of announcing that Britain would not intervene with military force to bring the defiant Smith to heel. It was as if he had given the Rhodesian leader the green light. The following month Smith announced his Unilateral Declaration of Independence (UDI). Wilson, in typical Walter Mitty style, announced bombastically that his campaign of economic sanctions against Rhodesia would bring Smith down *"in weeks, not months"*. Some hope!

As negotiations dragged on, it was decided to offer Smith talks on a Royal Navy vessel off Gibraltar in December 1966. Just before they were due to be held I bumped into Arthur Bottomley in the Commons Members' Lobby. By then Minister for Overseas Development, he had great hopes for the outcome of this sea-borne operation. Wilson had been informed by British Intelligence that Smith was not happy at sea. Wilson's advisers hoped that on board ship

Smith would be uncomfortable, disorientated and not at his best – making it easier for Wilson to get the better of him. It sounded dubious and somewhat barmy to me, but as Bottomley had not said I should not use the information I wrote it for the Express. Wilson and Smith, with their advisers, met on the Royal Navy cruiser *Tiger* and according to plan, sailed down the choppy Mediterranean. Some of the Rhodesians suffered from seasickness and communication suffered, too. Wilson, moreover, failed to get the better of Smith.

Arthur Bottomley lost his government post in 1967. He had been nicknamed *"Topless Bottomley"* following a number of gaffs. Arriving on an official visit to Zambia he declared his great pleasure at being in Gambia and went on to talk of his joy at representing the great Queen in London. He referred to the bewildered Zambians as *"these noble creatures."* Born in Walthamstow in 1907 and raised in the East End of London, he always retained his cockney twang and at one time had hopes of representing an East London constituency. I had been introduced to him by Reg Sorensen and after Arthur lost his marginal Rochester and Chatham seat in 1959 I invited him, in my capacity as Political Education Officer, to give a talk to the Leyton constituency Labour Party about his experiences in the Attlee government as a minister in the Dominions Office. Arthur was delighted and, as Reg was getting on in years, thought I was trying to help him to succeed our mutual friend as MP for Leyton. As I had hopes of succeeding Reg myself he could not have been more wrong – but he always treated me with gratitude and when he fought and won a by-election at Middlesbrough East in 1962, I was able to assist him with my first-hand knowledge of the town and key people there. He was very proud of his Commonwealth links, especially with India and Burma, and Wilson made him Shadow

Commonwealth spokesman in 1963 and Commonwealth Secretary the following year. He had a deep distrust of Ian Smith, however, and complained to me about Wilson's failure to adopt his proposal for crippling sanctions against Rhodesia in the early stage of the independence dispute. Denied a peerage by Labour leader Michael Foot, who wanted younger men in the Lords, he was put there by Margaret Thatcher in 1984.

A black mark on his record as Commonwealth Secretary was his involvement, at an early stage, in the shameful expulsion of the population of the Chagos Islands to make way for an American military base. An appalling violation of international law, it is one of the most disgraceful chapters in British colonial history. In 1964, the Tory Government had reached agreement with Washington to help with the setting up of US defence facilities in the Indian Ocean. As part of this scheme, the Chagos Islands were detached from the British colony of Mauritius in 1965 and renamed British Indian Ocean Territory. By 1967, the expulsion of the islanders had begun, with plantation workers being shipped to Mauritius and refused permission to return home. By 1973, the last of the islanders were expelled and it would take over thirty years before they won the right to return home after a series of court battles.

In 1968, the idea was revived of having more talks with Ian Smith aboard a naval vessel. On October 8' the *Daily Express* led with my report that the summit would be held again off Gibraltar. On Downing Street guidance, I described how Wilson and Smith would be accommodated on separate Commando vessels, would exchange visits and sail once more down the Med, possibly putting in at Malta if the talks were prolonged. I recalled that Wilson had told the Labour Party conference the previous week that any resumption of the talks would be within the context of the six points presented to Smith in December 1966 when they had met on the cruiser *"Tiger"*. I recalled also that a large group of left-wing Labour MPs were ready to oppose any settlement that gave Smith as much as the six proposals and there was a fear that Wilson was no longer firm on the key principle of no independence before majority rule.

I was assigned to cover the talks and with other members of the press corps was housed in the pleasant Rock Hotel. Wilson and his party, including Marcia Williams, were accommodated aboard the 11,000-ton Royal Navy assault ship *"Fearless"* where the talks were to take place. Smith and his party were aboard the guided missile destroyer *"Kent"*. On the first evening I filed a report revealing that Wilson had decided not to adopt the browbeating tactic used on the *"Tiger"* of insisting that Smith should arrive with power to settle on the spot. That tactic, used in a vain attempt to force a split between Smith and his right wing, was no longer necessary as the Rhodesian leader was now in clear command in Salisbury. Wilson's team included my friends George Thomson, who had been appointed Commonwealth Secretary, and Harold Davies, the Prime Minister's Parliamentary Private Secretary.

At the last minute it was wisely decided after all not to cruise along the Med to ensure steadier stomachs and better communications. On Friday October 11, the *Daily Express* led with my report that in a dramatic move to settle major differences, Wilson and Smith had plumped for private man-to-man talks without ministers or advisers. The development followed five hours of discussion around a long table in the wardroom of *"Fearless"* where the going had been tough. The main stumbling block was Smith's insistence that there could be no African majority rule in his lifetime.

Meanwhile, I had been fascinated and disturbed by a troublesome sideshow – the blatant ongoing shenanigans between Marcia and Walter Terry. She had successfully escaped publicity when she had given birth to a son by Walter the previous August. On the first full day in Gibraltar I had lunched with Walter and a few other journalists. Marcia joined us. A car trip around the Rock had been organised for the afternoon but at the last minute Walter declined to join us. On the sightseeing tour I spotted Walter with Marcia admiring the view from a secluded corner. The following evening Marcia, who was accommodated on *"Fearless"*, arrived at our hotel with Gerald Kaufman. In due course she and Walter left the dining room separately to meet up in his bedroom. Being seasoned journalists we stayed up late drinking the bar dry. Kaufman stayed with us, sipping soft drinks. Eventually we went to bed leaving him to wait for Marcia to finish her tryst before escorting her back to the ship. I could only think, *"What a humiliating chore for such an intelligent man!"* That was certainly not the type of job I thought I had applied for – thankfully without success. By Monday evening, October 14, with the talks broken off and Wilson and Smith back in their home capitals, the role of the Privy Council in Rhodesian affairs had emerged as a new sticking point. Under the headline *"Where Rhodesia Talks Jammed,"* I led the paper again, reporting that at a time when leading Commonwealth states were removing the role of the Privy Council from their constitutions, Britain was insisting that an independent Rhodesia must accept that body as the final judge.

Wilson's Attorney General, my contact, the charming and erudite Sir Elwyn Jones, was arguing that the PC must be the final court of appeal in all constitutional disputes and in appeals against Rhodesian court judgements. Smith retorted that Rhodesia would not be truly independent if the

PC could overrule its parliament and courts. Although progress had been made on four of the six principles, Britain was insistent that the PC's role was a vital safeguard for the first two principles, dealing with *"unimpeded advance"* towards African majority rule and with guarantees against retrogressive amendment of the constitution.

By Wednesday 16 October, however, I led the paper again with a report of another shift by Wilson who was now said to be ready to negotiate on an alternative to the proposal for a Privy Council watchdog. That alternative was said to be a treaty of guarantee, possibly underwritten by the Commonwealth – an idea originally put up by the ex-Tory Premier Sir Alec Douglas-Home. George Thomson, who dropped his title of Commonwealth Secretary to become Minister without Portfolio, had the job of dealing with any matters arising from the talks on *"Fearless"*. George, who remained a member of the Cabinet, lost his title as Wilson had decided to merge the Foreign & Commonwealth Offices and had put Michael Stewart in as head of the new combined department.

On my return to Westminster from Gibraltar, I decided to take a more drastic step to halt the flow of information from Marcia to Walter. I had been particularly annoyed by his exclusive account of the sacking of my friend Douglas Jay from his post as President of the Board of Trade the previous year. It had been a humiliating affair for Douglas who was on holiday on Dartmoor at the time. Wilson, on holiday in the Scilly Isles, had summoned Douglas to a meeting in the stationmaster's office at Plymouth railway station where he was told his services were no longer required. Douglas has been too forthright in his views about the damaging effect on the nation's economy if Britain joined the Common Market. In February 1967, I had reported in a front page lead story that at a private meeting with Labour MPs he had alleged that if Britain went in, the cost of living would rise by 4%, not the 2.5-3% forecast. He had argued that Britain's interests would be served best by free trade in food and curbs on some imports of manufactured goods. Coming from the President of the Board of Trade this opinion was a gift to the anti-Common Marketeers in the Labour Movement. Douglas, who had never liked or trusted Wilson, had nevertheless served him well as a hard-working, competent minister. His strong opposition to Britain's application to join the Common Market was clearly an important factor in his sacking. A few months later President de Gaulle of France said *"Non!"* to Britain's membership.

In the light of his treatment of Douglas it is worth recalling that when Wilson asked George Thomson to handle the negotiations for joining, George had pointed out that this could be a problem as he was a firm believer in the importance of Britain's ties with the Commonwealth. Wilson, playing one of his double games, had replied that it was for that reason that he had decided to ask George to deal with the European Economic Community.

Studying the Marcia Williams–Walter Terry situation, it seemed to me to raise an issue of national security. Walter was a married man, which could provide someone with the idea of blackmail – information in return for silence. In view of my friendly relationship with *"Spymaster"* George Wigg I could have raised the problem with him if he had still been in office – but he had lost his job in 1967. In fact, in the mid 60s Wigg had decided to look into Marcia's private life and its implications for the Government. He did so as part of his brief to prevent the Government from getting involved in scandals like the Profumo affair. He did not like Marcia's behaviour – and presumably, she did not like him much either.

Having decided against approaching Wigg, I nevertheless deployed a Wigg-style tactic. One of my favourite Tory MPs was Neil Marten. As his anti-Common Market stance was in line with *Daily Express* policy, I talked to him a lot and so decided to ask for his assistance. A war hero of the Special Operations Executive, he had parachuted into France to work with the Maquis résistance movement and had been awarded the Croix de Guerre three times for his exploits and cool courage. He had served briefly as Parliamentary Secretary, Ministry of Aviation from 1962-64 and had then become one of the Tory Party's most vociferous anti-Common Marketeers. I made sure his views received ample publicity in the columns of the Express.

Neil was often to be found standing in the Members' Lobby and on a suitable occasion I explained to him the problem of the Walter–Marcia pillow talk and aired my belief that there was a tangible security aspect. Would he be willing, I asked, to table a parliamentary question to the Prime Minster asking whether he was satisfied with the security arrangements at No. 10? Then, in a supplementary question, would he, under the protection of parliamentary privilege, refer specifically to the liaison? His cool blue eyes twinkled and he grinned in anticipation at the prospect. He said he would – but I then had to disappoint him by adding that my plan was to inform No. 10 that I had made such an arrangement and would only proceed with it if Terry continued to receive exclusive information from Marcia. Neil agreed to do nothing until I gave him the go-ahead. I lost no time in informing a contact at No. 10 of the plan. There was a sharp intake of breath. I waited for the next Terry scoop that might have come from his mistress. It never came. The parliamentary question was never tabled. Meanwhile, by early 1969, Marcia Williams was pregnant again. The birth of their second boy was hushed up again and, like his elder brother, he was named Terry-Williams.

Walter had married a fellow journalist in 1950 and had two sons and a daughter by her, but the death of one of the boys in childhood appeared to me, at the time, to have damaged the marriage. The long-affair with Marcia left it in a hopeless mess. A shrewd Derbyshire man of no great education, he was outstanding as a political reporter in the Macmillan and Wilson years. His success may have been helped by the fact that he was a detached non-party man who was cynical of politicians of all parties, milking them for information and treating them with little respect. Of his many scoops the story that won him most fame was given to him by his boss Lord Rothermere. His lordship had lunched with the famously indiscreet RAB Butler in July 1962 and had gleaned that Prime Minister Harold Macmillan was planning a cabinet reshuffle. Walter merely reported what he was told by Rothermere and got the credit.

Soon after his involvement with Marcia he passed on to her a Commons rumour that, while Wilson was in Moscow, his Chancellor James Callaghan was involved in a plot to replace him. He then got a scoop on Wilson's devaluation of the pound in 1967 not because his lover had leaked it but because she refused to talk to him for a few days during the latest sterling crisis. He rightly guessed that she was avoiding the risk of being blamed for passing on such explosive information. I liked and respected Walter and found him to be good company, but he was not one for sharing his thoughts.

My dismay over Wilson's attempts to curb the freedom to report the bungling of his dysfunctional government – that involved me in the successful break-up of the *"White Commonwealth"* lobby group – reached a new height over his serious mishandling of the *"D Notice"* affair. It began with an exclusive report by the *Daily Express'* well-informed defence correspondent Harry Chapman Pincher on February 21 1967, concerning government security vetting of Post Office cables. Wilson alleged that the report was both a breach of two *"D Notices"* and a breach of the *"D Notice convention"* on procedure. The Defence, or *"D Notice"* system, aimed at protecting State security, had been agreed between the Government and the Press. A badly advised Wilson had decided to refer the Chapman Pincher case to the Services, Press and Broadcasting Committee that had the responsibility for issuing the notices. He was stalled, however, by two developments. Firstly, Tory leader Edward Heath made an appeal for a committee of backbench MP Privy Councillors to make an inquiry, following briefings in which I was involved concerning such questions as whether the matter was covered by D Notices and whether they should apply. Secondly, Mr Lee Howard, editor of the *Daily Mirror,* who sat on the D Notice Committee, resigned in a letter to Colonel *"Sammy"* Lohan, the committee's secretary, complaining that use of the committee to conduct an inquiry would be a gross abuse of its functions. In his view, the D Notice committee existed solely to provide a link between the Government and the voluntary acceptance by the Press of the need to restrain publication of certain information in the national interest. He added that he knew of no D Notice that would have any direct bearing on the Pincher story and declared:

"The D Notice committee is not an instrument of censorship but a voluntary body."

Embarrassed by these developments, Wilson sought a way out by announcing that he was setting up a committee of Privy Councillors under Lord Radcliffe, a distinguished 67-year-old lawyer, to investigate questions arising from the Pincher article. Reporting the move, I pointed out in the front-page splash story that it amounted to a major change of view by the Prime Minister. The affair then took a turn for the worse for the rattled Wilson. Lord Radcliffe's findings acquitted the *Daily Express*. Refusing to accept this, the Prime Minister had a White Paper on security problems published instead. In the face of Wilson's inept and outrageous handling of the issue, the normally supportive *Daily Mirror* virtually declared war on him.

In common with most people who had dealings with George Brown, my relationship with Labour's deputy leader was like a ride on a roller coaster – but with more downs than ups. The son of a Lambeth lorry driver, George was a volatile colourful character all too often well-oiled. The expression *"tired and emotional"* could have been invented for him. When Wilson won power for Labour in 1964, he held the key post of Secretary of State for Economic Affairs and when his economic plan collapsed due to Callaghan's incompetence as Chancellor of the Exchequer, he became Foreign Secretary. During his four years in the Government he resigned, or threatened to, on at least eight occasions, giving reasons as varied as control of economic policy to rows with his long-suffering wife, Sophie. George Thomson told me that when working under Brown at the Foreign Office he tore up at least one of his resignation letters before Brown could deliver it – for which service Brown, when sober, thanked him next day. In July 1966, Brown, as Secretary of State for Economic Affairs, had resigned over the handling of the sterling crisis that resulted in the collapse of his grand strategy for boosting Britain's economy, known as the *"National Plan"*. Although news of his resignation became public, he withdrew it late that night after an angry confrontation with Wilson and key Cabinet members. A clear sign that he had lost out to Callaghan in the Cabinet battle over control of the economy came on the evening of

Wednesday July 27 when Brown made a disastrous speech in the Commons on winding up an important two-day economic debate. MPs I spoke to in the Lobby after the vote, which the Government won comfortably, thought it sad that a man of such ability had flopped on such a major Commons occasion. Astonished Labour MPs assumed that this must be the end of Brown as a political force His pathetic performance had destroyed what prestige he still had left after the farce of his resignation announced and then withdrawn.

Two days later, I had to report that he had arrived for a TV interview on the state of the economy two hours late. The original programme had been cancelled and replaced by a short interview just before midnight. In my lead story for the Express I wrote that it must have seemed to most people who watched to mark the end of his career as a major political figure. Brown's excuse for his lateness? *"I forgot,"* he mumbled apologetically. There were to be more dramas before his final departure from government. One evening in March 1968, Evelyn and I were dining at the Carlton Towers with our close friends Gerald Thomas, director of the cult *"Carry On"* films and his wife, Evelyn's best friend Barbara. I was called to the phone to be told of Brown's latest resignation threat – this time as Foreign Secretary. The cause was his liquor-fuelled complaint that Wilson had failed to consult him over a decision to call an emergency Bank Holiday, suspending trading in foreign currency and gold to avoid devaluation. Such a move required a meeting of the Privy Council in which the Queen and Brown, as Deputy Prime Minister, would normally have been involved. But Wilson could not at first track him down and was then told he had been drinking heavily and went ahead without him. When Brown tried to find him to withdraw his resignation, the Prime Minster deliberately kept out of his way.

On Saturday March 16 the *Daily Express* splashed my report that George had finally quit. I wrote:

'The resignation came at 10.30p.m. after twenty-four hours of 'Will he, won't he?' speculation which Mr Brown ignored by staying all day in the top floor flat of his official residence in Carlton gardens.'

I added:

'What was eventually revealed was a deep and bitter breach with the Prime Minister – in particular over the events of Thursday night and early yesterday morning when Mr Wilson, through a Privy Council meeting held by the Queen, set in motion the crisis measures to protect the dollar and the pound.

'In his resignation letter Mr Brown said that these events 'brought to a head a really serious issue which has been troubling him for some time – the way this Government is run and the manner in which we reach decisions.

'He was furious that while the Chancellor Mr Roy Jenkins and Economics Minister Mr Peter Shore attended the PC with Mr Wilson, he, as Foreign Secretary and Deputy PM was not even consulted.'

Wilson, in his defence, insisted that *"unsuccessful efforts were made to get in touch with you at a critical phase."*

I reported, however, that Brown's friends claimed that neither his private secretary nor the Foreign Office switchboard knew of any *"serious effort"* to get hold of him.

At the root of the running relationship problem was the stark fact that Brown had loathed and distrusted Wilson for well over a decade. Although his tempestuous and erratic behaviour had produced many good stories, I was greatly relieved to see him depart. I was thoroughly browned off with Mr Brown.

He could be a tricky person to entertain at a lunch or dinner table. Once, when the *Daily Express* invited him to lunch during a party conference in Brighton, he was being embarrassingly rude to his wife Sophie, so to distract the offensive bully I chipped in with a harmless question about party policy. With an ugly scowl he then turned and rebuked me sharply for being so impolite as to raise such a matter when he was our guest. On another occasion, at a lunch hosted by an industrial company, he jumped up from the table and stormed out shouting that he had been insulted because someone had asked for his views on the Common Market.

One had to be careful, also, in interpreting his speeches. During his short spell as Minister for Economic Affairs he made a speech, in December '65, on the situation in the labour market that I decided was of some significance. I phoned the press office in his department as a safeguard to ask if my interpretation was correct. The press officer assured me that I was absolutely right and said he had expected more calls but that mine was the only one so far. The *Daily Express* led with my report next day. Under the headline *"Brown's Bombshell"* it stated that he had issued a startling warning that Britain may have to accept shortages caused by strikes if his incomes policy was to work. Although he had not actually mentioned strikes in his speech to the Women's Consultative Council, he clearly had them in mind when he declared:

'If the policy is to be pressed home and is to have the impact required, there may be difficulties and hardship for the public.

'The acceptance of this – and the temporary interference with supplies – may be the contribution the general public

can make to the result we all desire: price stability and an end to the dreary round of inflation.'

Following what had turned out to be my exclusive interpretation of his speech, I was told later that day that George Brown had called a briefing at his department for political and industrial correspondents. I went along hoping for a pat on the back. Instead, I discovered that he had called it to denounce me for what he described as a false and mischievous account of what he had said. I phoned his press office later to be assured again, privately, that my interpretation had been correct, but Wilson had been annoyed that Brown had gone so far and had insisted on a refutation of my report.

One of the most extraordinary incidents involving Brown as Foreign Secretary was described by Government Minister Lord Chalfont, who witnessed it. The President of Austria was hosting a magnificent reception for ministers and officials attending a conference in Vienna. As the orchestra began to play, Brown turned to a figure in a scarlet robe standing nearby and asked, *"Madame, may I have this waltz?"*

Haughtily the person replied, *"There are three reasons why I will not dance with you Mr Brown. First, this is not a waltz, it is the National Anthem of Austria. Second, you are drunk. Third, you have made a terrible mistake as I am the Cardinal Archbishop of Vienna!"*

Despite my relief when he quit the Government and accepted a peerage, I had to admit that his downfall, although involving some hilarious episodes, had been sad to watch. There was evidence that on a good day George Brown could produce a flash of political genius. Jack Diamond, who had one of the sharpest brains in the Government and served with distinction as Chief Secretary to the Treasury, told me that he had a high regard for

George when he was sober and that often, when the Cabinet was bogged down on an issue, it was George who would come up with the solution. That was praise indeed from the man whom Tony Benn was to describe as *"probably the best minister in the Government."*

George did not enjoy sitting in the House of Lords and continued to seek solace in the bottle. His wife Sophie put up with his drunken, boorish behaviour and appalling rudeness until 1982 when he abandoned her to live with his secretary. He died of sclerosis of the liver in 1985. Life was easier and more enjoyable with his fast talking MP brother Ron. Some seven years younger than George, he had a similar voice and the same habit of addressing people as *"brother"*.

He entered Parliament in 1964 for Shoreditch and Finsbury and had links with Dulwich where I was living, which made a talking point when we met up in the Commons Strangers' bar. He was Chairman of the Governors of the College of God's Gift in Dulwich, a foundation set up by the famous Elizabethan actor-manager Edward Alleyn. It owned much valuable land in the village. Over a beer one Friday lunchtime in 1969, he tipped me off that there was a serious subsidence problem in our development. Having had a baby girl, Caroline, in May 1966, Evelyn and I were looking to move anyway so decided that was the moment. We still wanted, however, to stay in the neighbourhood.

In 1982, Ron, a passionate European, was one of the 26 moderate Labour MPs who left the party to join the new Social Democrat Party of which I had become an early member. He lost his seat in the general election the following year.

Political problems over Commonwealth immigration into Britain and race discrimination were capturing the headlines in the spring of 1968. *Daily Express* editor Derek Marks was fascinated by the issues and by the utterances on racial issues of the fanatical Tory MP Enoch Powell. One Friday evening he told me he was clearing the feature page to run a complete speech by Powell that I had brought to his notice. The following Monday, I asked Powell in the Members' Lobby if he was pleased with the coverage we had given him. Looking more constipated and bad tempered than usual he snapped, *"I think the Express should pay me a fee for using my speech as a feature article. Tell Derek Marks I look forward to receiving a cheque…"*

No cheque was forthcoming from Marks who, on learning of the request, retorted, *"What an ungrateful, money-grubbing bugger!"*

Instead of earning him a cheque, Powell's continued use of inflammatory language to draw attention to the need to curb immigration earned him the sack from Tory leader Edward Heath's Shadow Cabinet. The occasion came in April and took the form of an address to the annual general meeting of the West Midlands Area Conservative Political Centre in Birmingham. Attacking the Government's Race Relations Bill as the means of showing that the immigrant communities could organise to consolidate their members, to agitate and campaign against their fellow citizens, he declared:

"As I look ahead, I am filled with foreboding. Like the Roman, I seem to see 'the River Tiber foaming with much blood'."

Unlike most of his speeches, this notorious *"river of blood"* outburst was delivered on a Saturday and so I did not have to report it. It fell to the Sunday papers to deliver the shock to Edward Heath and Shadow Cabinet members such as Quintin Hogg. Powell had boasted in an interview that he deliberately included one startling assertion in every speech to attract enough attention to give him such a power base in the Tory Party that Heath could never sack him from the Shadow Cabinet. He was wrong in that forecast. Heath sacked him that Sunday evening.

The issue came alive in the Commons the following Tuesday, April 24, in a debate on the Race Relations Bill when Quintin Hogg revealed that if Heath had not acted against Powell he would have resigned from the Shadow Cabinet himself, in protest. I reported that it was one of Quintin's finest parliamentary performances and sent him a note of congratulation – to which, with his customary courtesy, he replied with thanks. From my soundings in the Lobby I was able to report that if the resignation issue had arisen Quintin would have had the backing of other Shadow Ministers such as Iain Macleod, Sir Edward Boyle and Robert Carr.

As MPs debated the immigration issue, hundreds of dockworkers marched on Parliament in support of Powell. He told a delegation from St. Katherine's and West India Docks, *"I had to say something – it's like watching the country digging its own gave."*

Despite his earlier boast, he claimed that he knew he was going to get the sack. The dockers would have been less pleased with Powell if they had known that when he was Health Minister in Macmillan's Government he had actively encouraged the influx of Afro-Caribbean immigrants into Britain. Alarmed by the growing number of black and Asian people in their constituencies a small group of Tory MPs from the Midlands had gone in a deputation to raise the issue with him. He defended his position at that time by arguing that he needed such immigrants to staff his hospitals.

A week later, watching Home Secretary James Callaghan being interviewed by Robin Day in a BBC television

"Panorama" programme, I spotted him make a serious error on Government immigration policy. In a front page lead story the following morning, I reported that millions of viewers heard him say that the Government had a scheme for assisted passages for immigrant families wanting to return home to their countries. I added,

'What Mr Callaghan did not make clear, however, was that the scheme – which has been operating for some years – applies only to those unable to support themselves in Britain.

'The Social Security Ministry and the Home Office confirmed the restricted nature of the scheme last night – but no doubt too late to stop a flood of applications from immigrants. These are likely to come from coloured families who are able to make ends meet in Britain but have not got the several hundred pounds in the bank needed to get them home to the West Indies, Pakistan, India or other distant countries.'

I forecast big trouble for Callaghan in the Commons and with the immigrant communities. The following month, under the banner headline ***Out! Out! It's a total rout!*** I reported that *'defeat and rejection, shattering and humiliating, hit Labour in yesterday's borough elections – and to round off Harold Wilson's day of disaster, London produced a Tory landslide.'*

An exuberant Quintin Hogg shouted at Cabinet Minister Tony Benn during a TV confrontation, *"Get out! You're no longer wanted. The message is 'Get out'."*

It was to be over a year, however, before voters were to be given the opportunity to vote Labour out of office in a general election. Meanwhile, by-election and other disasters gave strength to the *"Wilson-must-go"* campaign and little Harold sought to divert attention and boost confidence with yet another Cabinet reshuffle and the introduction of an inner Cabinet. A new role for Transport Minister Barbara Castle was central to this reorganisation in his view. She was to take over the all-important and tricky job of relations with Labour's paymasters, the trade unions. Richard Crossman, who was privy to the plan, was told that he could give her a hint that something big was coming her way. Crossman was also given the go-ahead to raise the curtain on the change from a Mark One to a Mark Two Government in a speech he was due to make at Basildon. He tipped off the BBC and ITV that he was going to say something important and, pleased that he had got the message over to the journalists in the hall, returned home as soon as possible. As he recounts in his memoirs, he was just settling down when *"Arthur Butler of the Express rang up. He was worried at the difference between the press release with its last sentence about a Mark Two Wilson Government and the Press Association report which omitted it."* Crossman recalls that I asked, *"Did you omit that last sentence from your press release?"*

Crossman replied *"No"* and then answered two questions. When later, other puzzled political reporters started to phone him, he asked the Press Association to correct the report sent in by their man at the meeting who had not bothered to report the important last line.

On the day of the reshuffle, Barbara Castle arrived in her office soon after 9 a.m. full of high expectation. Tom Taylor, treasurer of her local Blackburn constituency party was in the office and she told him excitedly that she was expecting a call from 10 Downing Street. When Marcia Williams eventually phoned to put her through to Wilson Barbara told Tom (later to be Lord Taylor of Blackburn) that he could stay in the room. Suddenly he saw her stiffen, her face contorted with rage. She screamed down the phone that the post of Employment Secretary that he had offered her was *"unacceptable"*. Angrily she reminded Wilson that she had supported him through thick and thin and had expected to be appointed Foreign Secretary. His offer, she added bitterly, was *"intolerable"*. A shocked Wilson explained that it was not possible to offer her the Foreign Office as it had been given to someone else. Barbara insisted that she was not accepting Employment. She slammed down the phone. Her husband Ted then arrived to find her shaking with fury. Gently he pleaded with her to think again. If the Foreign Secretary job was no longer open he advised that she should take Employment and ask Harold to also name her as First Secretary of State. She thought it through and called No. 10 back. She asked Marcia to connect her to Harold and said she would accept the post with the added pip. He immediately agreed. What with Marcia and Barbara, Wilson certainly had his work cut out with the ladies.

Ted Castle, a sensible fellow, no doubt gave his fiery wife other good advice over the years. There was considerable surprise, however, when he was made a Life Peer in 1974. Apparently it was not because of his London local government experience or his work on the Labour-supporting *Daily Mirror*. There was a much more down-to-earth explanation. When Labour returned to power, Barbara, now putting on a weak woman act, explained to Wilson that she needed her husband around at Westminster in the evenings so that he could drive her home at the end of the day. Wilson obliged by putting Ted into the Lords. Her request would have rung a bell with the Prime Minster as, years before, not wanting to call an official driver late at night after a long ministerial meeting, he had decided that it was necessary to get his son Giles out of bed to drive Barbara home to her cottage in the Chilterns.

On the foreign news front, there had been growing interest in political developments in Czechoslovakia in the first half of 1968 and in my diplomatic correspondent role, I had discussed these with a good contact at the Czech embassy. We were witnessing the *"Prague Spring"*. Alexander Dubcek, who had become first secretary of the Czech Communist Party in January, was pushing for reforms in an attempt to deliver *"socialism with a human face"*. The majority of the Czech people, fed up with the economic failures of the rigid communist system, were behind him. My contact at the embassy was optimistic. But in Moscow there was growing anger and constant attempts at interference. Finally, on a warm summer's day in August, as Prague swarmed with visitors enjoying the sights of the historic city, Russia struck. Soviet tanks, armoured vehicles and troops entered the Czech capital. Hundreds of people gathered outside the offices of the Communist Party where Dubcek and his colleagues had been in session, carrying national flags and singing the National Anthem. They were quickly swept aside by overwhelming numbers of Russian troops and soon Dubcek was under armed guard. He had never believed Russia would invade. His belief had been reflected in the relaxed atmosphere of the London embassy where the invasion came as an appalling shock. Throughout that August day my friend at the embassy updated me with *"insider"* news from Prague, which I passed on to a grateful *Daily Express* foreign desk. The Prague Spring had run its course, its delicate blooms crushed by Russian boots. The Dubcek men in London, including my man, were soon recalled for other duties.

The highest honour that can befall an MP is to be selected Speaker of the House of Commons. The most dishonourable act an MP can commit in Parliament is to lie deliberately to the Commons. A minister found to have done this should resign. Selwyn Lloyd, as Foreign Secretary during the assault on Suez, denied that Britain and France had instigated Israel's attack on Egypt – that there had been collusion. In the opinion of the Labour and Liberal parties there was no doubt that he had lied – and lied on the gravest issue of all – Britain's commitment to war. Lloyd nevertheless went on to become Speaker. Many MPs were unhappy when he was proposed for this distinguished post – and the unanimity tradition was broken when fifty-three Labour MPs and two Tories voted against him in the *"election"* in 1971. Others abstained. Moreover, his parliamentary seat, which by tradition is not contested – was challenged by both Labour and Liberal candidates in the two general elections in 1974. This was very damaging to the traditional aura of neutrality surrounding the Speaker and I felt strongly that Lloyd should have declined the invitation to stand for this immensely important office. In fact, much of his career in office was tangled in controversy, but being endowed with a thick skin and lacking in imagination, he soldiered on stolidly out of loyalty to his leader and party through a hail of brickbats that would have downed most men. Eventually he was sacked suddenly and ignominiously as Chancellor of the Exchequer by Harold Macmillan and so appeared to have reached the nadir of his career in public life. The fact that he was then picked up, brushed down and elected Speaker is a reflection of how short memories can be in Parliament – and how forgiving it can be too. On my frequent visits as a guest to the hall of Gray's Inn I have studied the portrait of Lloyd in his Speaker's wig and have wondered whether his brothers in law, the busy barristers, have thought, like me, that it has the haunted look of a guilty, unhappy man.

Lloyd, however, did behave with dignity and propriety once elected to the Speaker's chair. The same cannot be said for Dr Horace King, Labour's nominee for the post following the death of the respected Speaker Sir Harry Hylton Foster in September 1965. Reporting the situation for the *Daily Express* I explained that Harold Wilson had hoped to get a Liberal MP to take the job as the Government had a majority of only three in the Commons and could not spare a backbencher and the loss of a precious vote. Wilson failed in his ploy, King took the job and Labour's majority was reduced to two. Stooped and sallow faced, King had a drink problem and there were times when, wig askew, he almost fell out of the Speaker's chair. He was also sexually over-active and had the offensive habit of touching up female staff. He was invited as guest of honour to the Press Gallery annual dinner. He was very much the worse for drink as we sat down to eat and I watched as occasionally his head fell forward into his plate. The chairman would give him a discreet nudge and Dr King would sit up with a slight start. A moment or two later the lady on his right would also give a start as his hand touched her knee below the table cloth.

I then learned from one of the Government whips that the police at the Commons had reported that a middle-aged secretary had been seen leaving the Speaker's quarters regularly late at night. It was assumed Dr King was enjoying some rumpty-tumpty. There was a risk of scandal. The powers that be had it put politely but firmly to the randy doctor that he should give serious consideration to taking a wife. Soon after he followed that advice.

George Thomas, Speaker from 1976-83 and probably the best known and most popular with the public in the twentieth century, had another problem in that he was actively homosexual and entirely anxious about being revealed as such. We became friendly soon after I entered the Press Gallery for the *News Chronicle* and as he was a great gossip he was a useful contact. Born to very poor parents in Port Talbot, Wales, in 1909, he had suffered at the hands of a brutal father who was often drunk and made life miserable for the family. His unhappy mother had done her best to protect him and was a major influence in his life. He called her *"Mam"* and he would often refer to her when we talked together. The other great influence in his life was the Methodist church. While working as a teacher he had become a part-time Methodist lay preacher and a teetotaller, so unlike some of my other regular contacts he did not meet me in the many bars in the Palace of Westminster. He would often sit next to me on the only bench in the Members' Lobby where journalists were allowed to perch. Putting his hand on my knee he would say in his lilting Welsh voice, *"Oh you're a lovely boy, Arthur. You must come to Cardiff and have tea with my old Mam."*

In 1964, Wilson, whom he had supported, made him a junior Home Office Minister and this was followed by a move to the Commonwealth Office as Minister of State. One of his favourite stories of that period related to a visit he made to a tribal meeting in Africa. As a Methodist preacher he was invited to give a sermon. The chief in charge thanked him for his *"Christian message"* and added, *"It was wonderful, and though Mr Thomas is a white man I am sure that inside his heart's as black as ours."*

After one of his knee patting exercises in the Members' Lobby, I invited George to lunch at Kettner's Restaurant in Soho, a favourite haunt of *Daily Express* journalists. Sipping tonic water, he was in a very gossipy, indiscreet mood. He gave me several good stories, more suitable for a column than a news page – but unfortunately I had none such to fill. He gave me a warm and affectionate handshake as we parted and I returned to the Press Gallery. Late that afternoon I received a phone call from the News Editor

Keith Howard. He sounded harassed and desperate. There was a shortage of stories – could I help?

I pictured a grumpy Editor, Derek Marks, breathing down his neck. I had a rule not to write anything given to me by a minister on the same day he had lunched with me. Foolishly, I decided to break the rule to help Howard. I cobbled together a report and half-way through it included an item about a Cabinet split over an immigration issue. The Express certainly was short of material that night for I learned at 10p.m. that the paper was leading with my report. I should have been told a *"re-written version"* of my report. To my horror, when I picked up the paper from the doormat next morning the clever *"splash"* sub-editor had winkled out my small Cabinet split item and made that the lead of the report. Two days later, I received an icy note from George. It was known that he had lunched with me and his knuckles had been rapped by an angry Harold Wilson. George, with justice, accused me of letting him down. He said he was deeply disappointed. I wrote back with a sincere apology and felt deeply ashamed. George never patted my knee or called me his lovely boy again.

After serving as Secretary of State for Wales, a post that boosted his natural vanity, he went on to become Speaker during the next Labour Government in 1976. He had served as Deputy Speaker for two years under the colourless Selwyn Lloyd and his promotion brought a welcome spark of life to parliamentary proceedings. His mellifluous Welsh voice was refreshing and his ability to defuse an explosive situation in the chamber with a touch of wit and guile enabled him to keep *"Order!"* in the closely balanced house. Left-wingers on the Labour benches, however, accused him of being pro-Tory – and the fact that he had originally been one of them made their criticism all the more bitter. His prim sharpness in dealing with their rowdiness earned him the title of *"malicious old maid"*. He became even more unpopular when, after his retirement, Prime Minister Margaret Thatcher played up to his love of Establishment pomp by giving him a viscountcy – an hereditary title. Remembering his support in the early days for abolition of the House of Lords, I was shocked by his acceptance of the peerage – even though he had no offspring to sustain it. His published memoirs too, created an angry stir. Just as he had been so uninhibited in his gossip with me, so he blatantly revealed in the book information he had gathered in his role as Speaker during private sessions with senior MPs who had assumed that traditional confidentiality applied. When some of these MPs boycotted the launch party for the book, George told me that he was very upset – and I found it hard to restrain myself from reminding him how angry he had been with me when I wrongly abused his confidence years before.

Michael Foot was appalled by George's breach of the vital convention that the Speaker should never reveal private discussions held during his period of office. He feared that this would lead to a lack of confidence in the Speaker and make it more difficult for those subsequently holding the office to have such exchanges with MPs. The spite in George's nature, often revealed to me in his stories, was now exposed to the general public by his autobiography. In particular, he unleashed a tirade against his neighbouring MP in Cardiff for many years – former Prime Minister Jim Callaghan. I imagine much of it was justified.

What did not surprise me, after his affectionate approaches, was the eventual revelation of his homosexuality. That came from his friend and one-time fellow Labour MP Leo Abse, who, some years after George's death, disclosed that he had been haunted by the fear of being *"outed"* and having his penchant for seedy *"porno"* cinemas exposed and that he was indeed blackmailed on several occasions. It was Abse who introduced the legislation to legalise homosexuality. Maybe he was motivated by the suffering he saw George endure? Still, most people who knew him would have drawn their own conclusions about the proclivities of the exuberant bachelor and these did not prevent him from being asked to read the lesson at the wedding of Prince Charles and Lady Diana Spencer. He also had an especially close relationship with the Queen Mother, who was famously partial to gay company.

Another hand which, like that of George, came to rest occasionally on my knee was that of Lord Gavin Farringdon, a well-known homosexual whose languid, limp-wristed manner belied a tough core. It was said that he was the only peer ever to address a startled House of Lords as *'my dears'*. I got to know him through the Fabian Society. A kindly, caring man who had inherited his title and estates from the first Lord Farringdon in 1934, Gavin served on the Fabian executive committee for over thirty years and chaired its Colonial Bureau for six. He was a generous host to Fabians at his fashionable house in London's Brompton Square, where I greatly admired his fine collection of pictures and tasteful décor. I was so taken by the scheme in his loo that I copied it in my maisonette in Dulwich. He also entertained Fabians at his fine eighteenth century country mansion, Buscot Park in Oxfordshire, and was said to encourage young men to take a dip, naked, in the pool – a habit which provided a juicy item for the much read *Crossbencher* political column in the *Sunday Express*. I avoided Buscot but eventually got there with a Royal Academy tour party in 2010 and saw the pictures, *objets d'art*, furniture and ceramics and, at a safe distance in time, the pool. Gavin died in 1977, aged 74.

The eccentric, quixotic eighth Earl of Arran, a friend of Gavin, who had introduced a bill in the Lords to reform the law on homosexuality, then persuaded the peers to vote for his Preservation of Badgers Bill. Congratulated by Lord Gage, he replied that he was disappointed to get fewer votes for that measure than for the bill to legalise homosexuality a few years earlier. "That's not surprising," commented Gage. "There are no badgers in the House of Lords."

The preservers of badgers were even more outnumbered there by well-known practitioners of buggery when notorious homosexuals such as Tom Driberg and Robert Boothby received life peerages. And, of course, the gay ex-Speaker George Thomas ended his career there as Viscount Tonypandy – or 'Torypandy', as some of his one-time left-wing friends renamed him in disgust.

Of the Speakers I have known personally the one I most liked and respected was Bernard 'Jack' Weatherill, well remembered for his determination to defend the rights of backbench MPs. He had been elected to Parliament for north-east Croydon in 1964 and I introduced myself to him early the following year as I thought the *Daily Express* would be interested in his efforts to help small businesses. I found him approachable, helpful and grateful for the publicity I was able to get him for his efforts and other causes. His own business was tailoring – the high-class brand synonymous with Savile Row. Always impeccably turned out himself, he ran the family business in that famous street and always carried a tailor's thimble in his pocket. It was, he explained, to remind him of his background and "to keep me humble." He was reminded of his background when first elected to the Commons. While standing in a cloakroom he overheard one Tory knight of the shires say to another, "My God, what is this place coming to? They've got my tailor in here now!"

On checking his background I discovered that during World War II he had served in the 19th King George V's Own Lancers – the successor Indian Army regiment to that in which Caroline Offley Shore's husband had served before and during the First World War. During one of our chats I told him of my thwarted ambition to join the Indian Army. He commiserated with my disappointment but thought that 1946-47 would not have been a good time for a young officer to be in India.

I was delighted when, on winning office in 1970, Edward Heath gave him a job in the Government Whips' Office. He had assisted Heath to set up a Small Business Bureau when the party was the Opposition and had been duly rewarded by the new Prime Minister. Humphrey Atkins was Deputy Chief Whip and when he was promoted to Chief Whip in 1973 Jack replaced him as Deputy. I found him a helpful source of guidance in his Whips' Office base.

On taking over the Tory leadership from Heath, Margaret Thatcher kept Jack in his job –and after winning the 1979 general election she switched him to the post of Deputy Speaker. There he was when George Thomas announced in 1981 that he intended to retire at the next general election. Word got around that Mrs Thatcher did not think modest, courteous Jack was a strong enough character to fill the vacancy but, in June 1983, he was unanimously elected to the chair. Chosen again in June 1987, he continued as Speaker until his retirement in 1992, noted for his good judgement, restraint and natural liberalism that extended from a general defence of human rights to the particular defence of the rights of backbenchers. His determination to be fair to all was misconstrued by some on the Tory benches who, in a whispering campaign, alleged he was favouring Opposition MPs. He helped to improve the public image of the Commons Chamber by assisting in bringing about the vote in favour of introducing television coverage in October 1989. For years I had been dismayed by the radio broadcasts of its proceedings. They gave a wrong impression of the general work of the chamber by concentrating on big occasions, when it was crowded with members of the yahboo brigade giving vent to their partisan animal noises. Jack Weatherill believed that if the chamber were televised rowdy MPs would behave better. After some setbacks he achieved his aim. Although I twitched when pushy Robin Day claimed credit for the development, I was pleased that Jack's judgement proved correct and TV cameras did seem to inspire improved behaviour in the chamber.

Raised to the peerage in 1992, Jack sat on the Crossbenches and in due course became Convenor of the Crossbench peers. I visited him sometimes in the pokey room he occupied in this role, occasionally offering to provide briefings for his flock on issues in which I was involved.

One evening early in 1969, I received a phone call from Louis Kirby, the lively assistant editor of the *Daily Sketch,* whom I had known and liked when he had worked in the Parliamentary Press Gallery for the *Daily Mail.* He asked me if I would consider joining the *Sketch* as political editor and we arranged to meet for a drink to discuss the offer further. Joe Tobin, tough little ex-wartime paratroops major and East London character had decided to quit Fleet Street for a quieter life as a political consultant to industry and his departure would create a vacancy at the top of the *Sketch's* political team. I had never thought that tabloid journalism was for me. I enjoyed reporting more in depth; I liked the fine detail of a situation. But I was not happy on the Express and believed that I had repaid the paper for taking me on after the death of *Reynolds.* I asked for a week to consider the offer and Kirby helpfully agreed.

I had been getting increasingly restless on the *Daily Express* for some months. I could not complain about the amount of space and by-lines I was getting in the paper as I was producing more front page lead stories and exclusives than political editor Wilfred Sendall. My salary and perks, however, did not reflect the fact that I was virtually carrying the political team. Sendall was showing his age and what I needed was an assurance that when he went I would be promoted to political editor. Kirby had provided me with the opportunity to raise the subject.

I decided that if Derek Marks would give me an assurance about succeeding Sendall I would decline the offer from the *Sketch*. Marks was in hospital due to a worsening of his diabetes. He asked me to visit him and, propped up on his pillows in the hospital ward, he did his best to dissuade me from leaving the paper by painting a gloomy picture of the future of the *Sketch*. He insisted, however, that he could not give me the assurance I would be promoted. My pride would not allow me to be passed over again because of my known Labour Party affiliations. I gave my notice to the ailing editor. In fact, the *Daily Sketch* was more solid in its support of the Tory cause than the *Express*. Its readership was basically staunch Conservative whereas a high proportion of *Express* readers voted Labour. As for the future of the *Sketch*, Lou Kirby had told me that the proprietor, Lord Rothermere, was investing more money in the paper. This was taken as evidence that he believed it had a future. Morale was high. In contrast, morale on the *Express* was sinking. The circulation had been falling and Marks, due to his illness, heavy drinking and overwhelming interest in politics, was incapable of providing coherent leadership and a lively balanced paper. Within two years of my departure Max Aitken was to ask him to retire. In his five years as editor the *Express* had lost 600,000 in circulation. He was replaced by Ian McColl, editor of the paper's Scottish edition, a puritanical Scot out of touch with London trends and fashions, having spent thirty years in the Glasgow office. Marks, who continued to write for the paper, died of his illness in 1975 at the age of fifty-four.

The man who should have been appointed editor was, at the time of my departure, a fizzing and increasingly frustrated assistant editor. He was David English, the clever chancer who, after a successful stint as head of the paper's New York office, had followed Terence Lancaster as Foreign Editor. On his promotion to assistant editor my protégé Stewart Steven had replaced him as head of the foreign desk. Harold Keeble, a highly regarded *Express* executive and brilliant lay-out designer, had been so impressed by English that he had sent a memo to Aitken saying, *"Never let this man leave the Express!"*

Aitken then passed on this opinion to Marks who roared angrily, *"Who's the Editor of this paper? Keeble or me?"*

Foolishly, Aitken disregarded Keeble's good advice.

Soon after I had given my three-months' notice to Marks the *U.K. Press Gazette* reported in February that I was to join the *Daily Sketch* in April. In a prominent position at the top of its first news page it carried a full faced picture of me and a quote from *Sketch* editor, Howard French, saying that I would head the paper's political team whose other members were Rodney Foster and John Hunt. As I began to work out my notice the battle within the Labour movement over Employment Minister Barbara Castle's trade union reform and anti-strike plan provided me with more headline stories. Despite its title *"In Place of Strife"*, Barbara's White Paper was causing a lot of trouble in the Labour Party from the Cabinet downwards. In my view it was typical of the devious untrustworthy Callaghan that he supported the plan as Home Secretary in Cabinet but voted against it with his trade union buddies at a meeting of Labour's National Executive Committee.

I reported that some of Callaghan's cabinet colleagues were recalling that there was a time when Ministers who could not accept the doctrine of collective responsibility resigned from the Government. I thought Liberal Leader Jeremy Thorpe summed up the situation pithily when he said, *"For once my scruples and sense of chivalry are aroused in support of the Red Queen – Mrs Barbara Castle.*

"Does the doctrine of collective responsibility now mean that you support a colleague against your convictions in public at the price of holding on to office, whilst reserving the right to stab that colleague in the back in private on the same issue?"

Callaghan had a long-standing personal dislike of Barbara who was far too left wing and sharp-tongued for his taste. In a mid-March speech, Wilson had warned that he intended to act against the strikes crippling key industries. In what I described as the bitterest speech delivered by any minister on the issue, I added in my report that *"It must end all doubt about his personal determination to legislate on Mrs Castle's anti-strike proposals."*

I then contrasted Wilson's failure to tackle the two-faced Callaghan on the issue with his rebuke for Postmaster General John Stonehouse who had said candidly and publicly that the country was fighting for economic survival. I had been told that Wilson reminded him that Ministers should not speak publicly on other departments' subjects without seeking advance clearance.

I thought Stonehouse had been doing a competent job at the Post Office and had enjoyed his hospitality at a couple of lunches at Post Office headquarters at which Bernard Levin had been the only other journalist guest I recognised. I was intrigued that the Stonehouse-Levin connection, first forged at the LSE, still continued. What was not evident in 1969 was that Stonehouse, as reported by Harry Chapman Pincher, an expert on espionage, had forged a sinister link with the Soviet bloc after being caught in a honey trap during a visit to Czechoslovakia. Faced with the threat of blackmail regarding the sexual indiscretion, he had agreed to provide information for the Czech Government and this was not revealed to Whitehall until 1969, when members of the Czech intelligence service who defected to the Americans let the pussy out of the bag. Given a code name, he had become an important spy for both the Czechs and Russians, serving as he did firstly as Aviation Minister with knowledge of vital aeronautical developments, and then as Post and Telecommunications Minister whose remit included projects at GCHQ, the radio-interception agency based near Cheltenham.

Some of my friends and I had known for years about Stonehouse's dishonest and corrupt practices dating back to his student days. Wilson must have known of them too but decided to give him a Government job, in view of the need to have such a key Labour-Co-operative movement member in office, and also because of his commercial experience. Wilson, in any case, was not too fussy about promoting rogues and rascals. What is unforgivable is that some of the inept members of Britain's security agency MI5 had failed to keep a close eye on him in view of his past record. They were duly shocked when informed by America's CIA of the spying allegations and when they passed their information to Wilson, he reluctantly agreed that Stonehouse should be questioned at No. 10. Stonehouse, of course, denied the allegations and as Wilson took the view that Soviet bloc defectors' allegations were not reliable he was allowed to stay on in his post – where he remained until Labour's defeat in the 1970 general election.

My last front page lead for the *Express* before I left to join the *Sketch* was carried on April 2. It linked an attack on the Wilson Cabinet by Independent Labour MP Desmond Donnelly and an attack on Callaghan by Trade Minister Anthony Crosland, which Labour's Director of Publicity, popular and respected Percy Clark, attempted to censor. Donnelly, in typically colourful language, accused Cabinet ministers of being *"hangers on"* –their thoughts centred on the cash they would lose if they forced Wilson to resign. He claimed he knew of Ministers who had bought large houses with hefty mortgages who would be in financial difficulties if they lost their jobs following a move to force Wilson out of office.

Next to my report was another based on official Government figures revealing that the pound had fallen in value at the average annual rate of four per cent since Labour came to power. The following Friday evening I held my farewell drinks party for *Express* colleagues in a nearby pub. Derek Marks, out of hospital but in poor condition, wished me well in a short, boozy speech. In it, to my stunned disbelief, he accused me, semi-jokingly, of waiting until Sendall had gone to bed late at night before filing stories handed to me by my left-wing buddies. I looked across the room at Sendall who averted his gaze. He had obviously complained to Marks who, nevertheless, had been prepared to publish my midnight dispatches. I comforted myself with the thought that, without my support, Sendall would have to work much harder in future to avoid the sack. Stewart Steven, political reporter Squire Barraclough and leader writer John Thomson, all of whom owed their jobs on the paper to my recruiting, were three of the last to leave the room. As they all died young and long before me, perhaps I had not done them a good service in involving them in the stress and strain of Fleet Street. Thomson, a roly-poly forthright right-winger and ex-military policeman, whom I had poached from the *Scotsman* to help strengthen our Tory contacts, was only fifty-nine when he died.

Arriving home to my new bungalow in Dulwich, I poured myself a large drink and slumped in a chair. I was really depressed. I had enjoyed much of my time on the *Express* – especially the early days with Ian and Charlie – and had not wanted it to end in the way it had. And I was distinctly worried about the prospect of moving to the tabloid *Daily Sketch*.

CHAPTER TEN

Last Sketch

Compared to the glitz and glamour of the *Daily Express* building, the offices of the *Daily Sketch* in Tudor Street were drab and uninspiring. But inside the dreary edifice there was no shortage of good, lively journalists – and there had been a renewed feeling of optimism. Editor Howard French had managed to get the Sketch circulation moving up to over 900,000 but just before I joined sales had again started to fall.

The paper had for a time struggled along under a different name – the *Daily Graphic*, which Lord Rothermere had purchased from Lord Kemsley in 1952. Earlier, it had existed as the *Daily Sketch*. When sales dropped towards the million in 1962, Rothermere had fired editor Colin Valdar and replaced him with French, a less colourful journalist but a hard-working, more businesslike character. With his trim moustache, military bearing and right-wing views he reminded me of Oswald Mosley and I learned that before the war he had indeed been a member of that notorious old fascist's Black Shirt League. When Auberon Waugh had been offered a job as a political reporter a few years before I joined the paper he did not take to French at the interview. He got the impression that he was being offered the post more for his contacts than for his journalistic skills. Unimpressed by the paper and noting its dwindling circulation, he declined the offer.

On my first day, French took me to lunch at one of his favourite restaurants – The Ivy. He appeared upbeat and clearly expected a lot from me, impressed by the many times my by-line had appeared on Express front page lead stories. He did not know how often my stories had been helped by the clever lay-out techniques of the paper's superb and unflappable splash-sub-editor, Peter Hedley.

Then came another *"celebration"* lunch. To my great delight, Douglas Brown, who had been so helpful when I had joined him as a member of the *News Chronicle's* parliamentary team, phoned to invite me to a meal where we would be joined by Bill Pattinson, the popular, highly respected last news editor of the paper. He and Douglas, who had known each other as young reporters in pre-war Dorset, had recently helped to launch *The Port,* a newspaper covering the docks industry. They had read of my new appointment and wanted to congratulate me. I was moved by this as I thought very highly of them both. They stood me a great lunch and gave me one of the proudest days of my life. Bill, together with former *News Chronicle* court reporter, George Glenton, had written a very readable account of the life and death of the paper entitled *"The Last Chronicle of Bouverie Street"*. On the dust cover was a replica of the last *Chronicle's* front page with my by-line on the lead story about the latest round in Labour's battle over unilateral nuclear disarmament.

Recounting my activities on that last day of publication, Bill had generously described me as *"a prolific political fact seeker"*. Bill had got one of his early scoops when reporting for the *Dorset County Chronicle* in the 1930s. Arriving at the scene of a motorcycle crash, Bill recognised the machine as belonging to a certain Aircraftsman Shaw – better known as the famous desert war hero Lawrence of Arabia. In World War II, Bill became something of a hero himself earning two Mentions in Dispatches as a Lieutenant Commander in the Royal Navy.

The *Sketch* could afford a team of only three to cover both Parliament and the Foreign Office, putting us at a disadvantage in competing with other national papers. I had expected Rodney Foster to specialise as our diplomatic correspondent, but this was not to his taste as he greatly enjoyed covering Parliament. To my disappointment, this pleasant and conscientious young man decided to leave to join the BBC's parliamentary team where he went on to enjoy a long and successful career. He was replaced by Maureen Tomison who, apart from covering the diplomatic front, was one of the first women to work for a national paper on the parliamentary front. John Hunt, a very likeable, hard-working and reliable reporter, whom I had got to know when working for *Reynolds News* covered the parliamentary debates. I made the Lobby my personal responsibility, aided by Maureen when diplomatic news was thin.

There was no shortage of political news. In late April 1969, left-wing Labour MPs faced Wilson with one of the most serious revolts since he came to power – refusing to support a vote of confidence on a Budget proposal to raise Selective Employment Tax. Then Social Security Minister Richard Crossman led pro-Wilson ministers in a counter attack, publicly hitting back at the growing number of Labour MPs campaigning for the Prime Minister's resignation. Crossman made his speech, appropriately at a pub named *The Good Companions.* I reported in a front page lead story that a growing number of rebel MPs wanted wily Home Secretary Jim Callaghan to replace Wilson, following his attempt to avert a split with the trade unions over Mrs Castle's anti-strike proposals.

As the Government was rocked by revolt in the Commons, violence flared between Protestants and Catholics in Belfast prompting Eire's Prime Minister, Jack Lynch, to call for a United Nations peacekeeping force to be sent to Northern Ireland. I reported in my front-page lead story for the paper on April 22 that he claimed that the presence of British troops in Ulster was inflaming an explosive situation. Home Secretary Callaghan told MPs in the Commons the aim was to avert civil war. Premier of the province, Capt. Terence O'Neill, had asked for military assistance. I reported that he would be pressed by Whitehall to speed up constitutional reforms but added that Downing Street knew that, if he moved towards one vote for one man in local elections, it could bring down his government and thereby increase the possibility of civil war. In the event, O'Neill resigned saying a new leader, unhampered by personal animosities, might have a better chance of success.

Within a week I had particular pleasure in reporting that *"Mr Wilson shook rebel MPs last night by appointing 'sock-it-to-'em' cockney Bob Mellish as his new Chief Whip."*

Bob, who had been switched from his post as Minister of Public Buildings and Works where he had been secretly killing off the pestilent pigeons in Trafalgar Square, was one of my best contacts at Westminster. I hoped he would continue to be helpful – and I was not disappointed. He changed jobs with soft-spoken John Silkin who had lost the support of the bulk of Labour MPs by operating, under Wilson's orders, a loose and sometimes erratic system of discipline.

Bob, born the son of a dockworker in Deptford, had grown up in a poverty-stricken slum. He never lost his cockney accent or earthy working-class style and possessed a cheery, infectious sense of humour. A dedicated Roman Catholic, he had been appointed a Knight of the Order of St Gregory the Great in 1959 for his work for the church and Roman Catholic schools and had been delighted when I gave him a friendly write-up in *Reynolds News* on this achievement. I had also been helpful when he was accused of accepting hospitality from a doubtful source. He had told me early on that his great ambition as an MP was to improve the quality of working-class housing – one of my own pet causes – and Wilson gave him the opportunity by appointing him as junior housing minister from 1964–67 under Richard Crossman. He had learned how to administer discipline as a captain in the Royal Engineers Dockworkers Battalion during the war and now, with his bluff and sometimes bullying manner, he was all set to apply his experience in his role as Chief Whip. His appointment came on the eve of a party row over the need to crack down on the Selective Employment Tax rebels.

More front page lead stories followed in quick succession as opposition among Labour MPs to Barbara Castle's trade union reform Bill stoked up the *"Wilson must go!"* campaign. Mellish added to the consternation by telling the weekly Parliamentary Labour Party meeting that if the Bill were to be defeated in the Commons, Wilson would have to call a general election.

As the leadership crisis rumbled on, Chancellor Roy Jenkins cut short talks in Washington and flew back to London, his MP supporters spreading the word that he would be prepared to serve under a Prime Minister Callaghan. The previous year, Jenkins had forced Wilson to apologise after the paranoiac Premier had complained in Cabinet that the Government's troubles over leaking stemmed from *"the ambitions of one member of this Cabinet to sit in my place."* Certainly, in the form of John Harris, Jenkins employed one of the most assiduous leakers in Whitehall.

The Chancellor, however, had his own problems with Labour MPs. A series of tough economy measures he had introduced to bolster the pound had included a twenty-five per cent increase in charges for dentures and spectacles. Outraged MPs found it unbelievable that the extra charges had been announced during local election week. On Friday,

May 9, I reported massive Tory wins in the battle for the town halls.

The battle over the trade union reform Bill ended the following month with another ignominious defeat for the Government. Wilson and Barbara Castle, I reported, had scrapped the measure which had proposed fines for unofficial strikers in return for *"a solemn and binding undertaking"* from the TUC that wildcats would be dealt with along lines it had previously put forward. The climb down brought an angry reaction from the Confederation of British Industry. I felt sorry for Barbara. As always, she had fought with persistence, determination and courage. Her junior ministers and civil servants had responded with confidence to her inspiring leadership and intelligence. This time, however, she had failed to win through. In the end, she had been let down by the man who had encouraged her to take on the fight – Harold Wilson.

The ruthless Australian media tycoon, Rupert Murdoch, who had bought the scandal-mongering *News of the World* Sunday paper, needed a daily journal to enable his machinery to operate at full efficiency all week. He made an offer for the *Daily Sketch* and as the paper was not doing well was surprised when Lord Rothermere, who had plans of his own, turned down his offer. Then another ailing daily caught Murdoch's eye. The *Sun* had risen out of the ashes of the Labour Movement's struggling *Daily Herald* in 1964. Decent but not very lively, it had failed to attract young readers and by 1969, its circulation had fallen to around 800,000. The IPC Group which owned this now sinking Sun was ready to sell – and Murdoch bought it for a mere £800,000, roughly a pound for every paying reader.

To bring about the transformation he had in mind, he hired as editor an ambitious former *Daily Mirror* man – Larry Lamb. Lamb had noted that the Mirror had been losing touch with many of its traditional readers. On the false assumption it had a captive readership, the paper had decided to get a better class of advertising by attracting a better class of reader. It began to run educational features, explaining the various issues of the day. The old *Daily Mirror* man yawned and yearned for fun and titillation. Murdoch and Lamb were the dynamic duo to provide it. On 17 November 1969 they relaunched the *Sun* as a saucy tabloid that in due course, was to have the devastating effect of lowering standards throughout the national media. As launch time approached, Howard French and our team at the *Daily Sketch* waited with some trepidation. How much of a threat would it be? My personal anxiety centred on the Sun's political coverage. Lamb had recruited a bright young scoop-hunting journalist named Anthony Shrimsley – the brother of his deputy editor Bernard. Surely he would have produced an eye-catching exclusive for the first issue? We need not have worried. When it eventually appeared that night it gave little hint of the great success it was to become. Instead of an important political scoop, the left of centre tabloid contained a run-of-the-mill interview with Prime Minister Harold Wilson whom it intended to support in the next general election. With a sigh of relief I went home to Dulwich while Murdoch hosted a costly launch party for media bigwigs and advertisers. It was organised by his PR consultant, young blade John Addey, whom I was to get to know all too well in due course.

Unspectacular it might have looked that first night, but within a few days the *Sun's* heady mixture of sex, sensation and sport had sent its circulation soaring – largely at the expense of the *Mirror*. Within a year it was selling some 1.7 million copies a day. In the same period the *Mirror* had lost well over half a million disgruntled readers. By the time the first bare-breasted *Page 3 girls* exposed themselves in

November 1970, the *Mirror* had decided there was no profitable future in trying to educate its readers. The *Sketch,* however, did not panic and clung to its decent, family newspaper style.

I got on well with Tony Shrimsley and we often drank together in the Press Gallery bar. His assistant was a fresh-faced good-looking man named Frank Johnson. He was good company, with a sharp cockney wit and a gift for phrasemaking. I did not foresee, however, that he would develop into one of the most amusing parliamentary sketch writers since World War II and a highly successful columnist – talents that would elevate him to the deputy editorship of the *Sunday Telegraph* and the editorship of the *Spectator* magazine from 1995 to 1999. In his early days in the Press Gallery, when in his mid-twenties, he was noted more as a light-hearted charmer of women, often inviting the better-looking ones to accompany him to the cinema where he apparently spent much of his spare time. He knew a lot about films but was to develop a great liking and knowledge of opera and ballet. In developing an appreciation of fine music he followed in the footsteps of Bernard Levin who had preceded him as the wittiest writer on Parliament. I suspect that Bernard's success in outrageously breaking down the old inhibitions stifling parliamentary reporting inspired the young Frank to follow suit. Typical of his debunking style was his comment on the description of Roy Jenkins as *"a miner's son"* in a by-election campaign leaflet. *"True, certainly,"* wrote Frank, *"but only in the way it is true to describe Mrs Jacqueline Onassis as the widow of a Greek merchant seaman. It simply does not do justice to Mr Jenkins' position in café society."*

Frank certainly came to know a lot about café society and those smart social circles he came to describe as *"the chattering classes".* The son of an East End pastry cook, he was to travel a long way up society's ladder. We shared a birthday and when we marked this with a drink in the Press Gallery bar, I told him we also shared a "pastry" background. My grandmother, I boasted, had been one of the finest pastry cooks in London in the early years of the century. *"I bet my Gran could teach your old man a trick or two,"* I joked.

"My dad was too busy making pastry for good working-class people to be bothered competing with her fussy offerings for the toffs!" retorted Frank.

I kept in touch with him for a few years after leaving journalism and we had an occasional drink at party conferences. He had told me once that his ambition was to be a Fleet Street editor. He never made it, dying of cancer in December 2006 at the age of 63.

In that same month that saw the launch of the new *Sun*, I came closer to Alf Morris, Labour MP for Wythenshawe, who was about to emerge as one of the most important reformers to enter Parliament since the war. I had originally got to know Alf well because of my friendship with Fred Peart. Within a few days of entering Parliament in 1964, Alf had been asked by Fred, then Minister of Agriculture, to be his Parliamentary Private Secretary. Two of the most decent and likeable men in the Commons had teamed up. Both were deeply worried about the prospect of Britain joining the European Common Market and the damaging effect this would have on our Commonwealth trading partners – especially Australia and New Zealand. Fred sent Alf on missions to both countries to discuss the looming problem and issues of trade in agricultural products. Due to the anti-Common Market stance of the *Daily Express* I made it my business to keep in close touch with their activities. Then, in 1967, a Commons vote was held on whether Britain should move towards membership of the Common Market and Fred, as a member of the Cabinet, had to vote reluctantly with the Government. Alf, having more freedom, had sought certain guarantees about Commonwealth trade and, failing to get them, abstained on the vote. His failure to support the Government meant that he had to resign as Fred's PPS. With great delight I was able to report that Fred, out of loyalty to Alf and what he stood for, had decided not to appoint another PPS —and that Alf had announced he would try to assist Fred as his *"Parliamentary Private Friend"*.

The following year, Fred replaced Richard Crossman as Lord President of the Council and Leader of the House of Commons – and in his new role promptly reappointed Alf as his official parliamentary aide. It was while holding this post that Alf, in the autumn of 1969, won first place in the annual ballot for Private Members' Bills. As PPS's were unpaid and not full members of the Government Alf was entitled to enter the ballot and having won, he had first call on parliamentary time allotted for backbenchers' bills and, provided he did not choose something totally controversial, stood an excellent chance of getting his measure on to the Statute Book.

Meeting him in the Members' Lobby, I congratulated him on his success and asked what subject he had in mind for his bill. Brought up in the slums of Manchester, the son of a First World War disabled ex-serviceman, Alf had seen at first hand the problem faced by people suffering from a severe disability. He was determined to do something to make their lives easier. This was his opportunity. He quickly made contact with disability organisations asking for suggestions and was overwhelmed by the response. Richard Crossman, as Secretary of State for Social Services, was responsible for this neglected area and so Alf sought him out to get his views. Crossman, who was bogged down in his massive National Superannuation and Social Insurance Bill, was testily unhelpful. He curtly told Alf that if there had been a need for such a bill he would have introduced it himself. Moreover, he made clear that in his view there was no hope of getting such a measure through Parliament.

To my everlasting shame, I also failed to give Alf encouragement when he told me of his intention and asked me for my views. I replied that, while I thought his plan was admirable, such a bill would do little to further his own career, as it would receive very little publicity from the media. I explained that in my experience from years in Fleet Street, editors would not want to depress their readers first thing in the morning with reports about the needs of disabled people. He looked disappointed. However, unlike those politicians who aim to get maximum personal publicity from private members' legislation, Alf was not to be put off by such a doleful forecast. On November 26, the First Reading of his Chronically Sick and Disabled Persons' Bill took place in the Commons. It was officially supported by some of my friends from both sides of the House, such as George Darling, Jack Ashley and Neil Marten. Behind the scenes other friends such as Fred Peart, Leader of the House, and Bob Mellish, Chief Whip, gave important assistance. As for myself, I promised Alf I would do my very best to get news of its progress into the *Sketch*.

In the early 1970s, it was estimated that several million men, women and children suffered from some form of physical or mental disability. In 1970, however, there were only 235,000 people registered as disabled with local authorities. No one knew how many handicapped and impaired people were hidden away in the backstreets of our communities. Voluntary organisations were warning that there were at least a million − *"the missing million"*.

Alf's bill aimed to ensure that all these disabled people were located and that help was provided to help them solve the problems of earning a living, obtaining aids and equipment, education, leisure facilities and travel. Moving the Second Reading in the Commons on 5 December 1969, Alf explained that what most disabled people wanted more than anything else was to lessen their dependence on other people; to live their own lives as normally as possible in their own homes, with their own families; and to have the opportunity to contribute to industry and society as fully as their abilities allowed. The bill set out to provide specific services based on rights rather than charity. It was welcomed on all sides of the Commons. Nevertheless, some ministers whose departments were affected were irritated by Alf's initiative.

The Minister of State for Education, twitching about the financial implications of the clause on dyslexia, claimed that the condition did not exist. Alf quickly replied that if he was right then the clause would not cost his department anything. He was, nevertheless, carrying an enormous burden of administration and was not helped by such foot-dragging in Whitehall. Meanwhile, letters from all over Britain continued to pour in – over a thousand in two days. As for media interest, I could not have been more wrong in my original forecast. I should have known better, for I was aware of how journalists held Alf in fond regard. The bill's progress received wide and regular coverage.

Then Alf started to receive vitally important help from Duncan Guthrie, the extraordinary and dedicated Director of the Central Council for the Disabled who provided much needed secretarial and administrative assistance. Over six feet tall and possessing a commanding presence, he had served with courage and distinction with the Special Forces in World War II. He had fought with the Finnish guerrilla resistance against the Russians during their invasion of Finland in 1939 and had then parachuted behind enemy lines in France and Burma. During a drop in a remote area of Burma, he suffered an ankle injury that left him permanently lame. After the war, he joined the Arts Council but then became involved in charity work, founding the Polio Research Fund.

With his assistance, Alf's bill made good progress and impressed by the support it was receiving, the Government announced in February 1970 that it was making provision for financial support too. After clearing the Commons, the bill was introduced into the House of Lords by Lord Longford where it was welcomed on all sides. But time was running out and there loomed the prospect of a general election.

Meanwhile, at the *Daily Sketch* the circulation had started to dip again and by early 1970, had dropped below 800,000. Howard French scratched around for subjects to interest the declining readership and asked me to get an interview with Enoch Powell, whose speeches continued to attract much publicity. Following his sacking from the Shadow Cabinet, increasing numbers of the public regarded him as a man of unswerving integrity who would stick to his guns no matter what the consequences. On the hot issue of immigration they were not aware that as Health Minister, he had told Macmillan's Cabinet that he could afford to stand up to the nurses in a pay dispute because he could bring in all the nurses he needed from the West Indies. Powell, not the honest die-hard many thought him to be, changed his views on two other major issues. Having at one time strongly supported the policy for retaining British military bases East of Suez, he had come out in favour of pulling out of South East Asia while Tory leader Edward Heath believed in the importance of Britain staying in Singapore.

More dramatically, he had done a major U-turn on the issue of Britain joining the Common Market, delighting the Tory right-wing anti-Europe brigade by arguing the case against membership in a Commons debate in February 1970. In the Commons debate in May 1967, on the Wilson Government's application for entry to the EEC, as a member of Heath's Shadow Cabinet, Powell had voted in support of the application.

He appeared to me to be prepared to do or say anything to embarrass Heath and grab a headline. I regarded him as a cynical opportunist and was not overjoyed at the prospect of having to sit in a room with him for an hour or so at his London terraced house, under the glare of his fanatical eyes, scribbling in shorthand his impatient replies to my questions. According to his close acquaintances, his generally aloof behaviour was due very much to shyness rather than to a sense of superiority. He had married his secretary when he was forty and it was said that she had made him more approachable. Apparently, they enjoyed reading poetry together. She opened the door when I arrived. On entering their living room I saw no hint of the humorous, kindly man some made him out to be. He was tense and stony faced, wearing even indoors one of his thick three piece suits.

At the end of the interview he demanded – I thought rather rudely – to see my report before it was published. Howard French swallowed the insult and agreed to Powell's terms. I laughed it off by saying that Powell might have changed his mind on another major issue in the short time since I had left his house. As it turned out, he made no changes to the piece and perhaps it helped to persuade a few more right-wing readers to continue buying the Sketch. How would they have reacted if they had been told that their hero Powell had, at one time, been bisexual? My Kennington neighbour and friend, the leftish gay Canon at St Paul's Cathedral, Eric *"The Cleric"* James, revealed after Powell's death that one of his early love poems had been written to a man. Powell had asked Eric not to make this known until after his death. If Powell was unsure about, or was repressing, his sexuality as a young man, this might explain his buttoned-up behaviour.

Powell was not the only Tory MP thoroughly fed up with Edward Heath's style of leadership. One of the more disenchanted was the decorated war hero Airey Neave, the member for Abingdon. He was a man of cold courage who, following his famous escape from the Nazi prisoner-of-war camp in grim Colditz Castle, commanded at great risk a team of agents operating in occupied Europe. As a barrister he had been involved after the war in the Nuremburg trials of the Nazi war criminals, operating as Assistant Secretary of the International Military Tribunal. He had no gift for rhetoric, however, and was not a good public speaker.

We often talked together in the Members' Lobby and I succeeded in getting him helpful publicity for some of his campaigns. One that I reported on for the *Daily Express* was to win compensation for special prisoners held in the notorious Nazi Sachsenhausen camp whose claim had been denied by Foreign Office bureaucrats supported in their unfeeling obstinacy by Foreign Secretary George Brown. In such matters, Airey could be almost quixotic in his single-handed challenge to apparently hopeless odds. To our great delight, his Sachsenhausen campaign was eventually successful and we enjoyed a victory drink in a Commons bar. Airey's compassionate but unsuccessful fight to win freedom for the imprisoned Nazi war criminal Rudolph Hess, held in Spandau prison, was less well supported by the Express but with typical gritty determination he kept up the struggle for years.

One evening in the autumn of 1969, I was doing a last trawl of the Lobby before heading for the Press Gallery bar when Airey entered looking flushed and angry. Seeing me he came across and as he started to speak I could tell he had been drinking. He clearly wanted to let off steam and when he asked me to join him for dinner in the Members' Dining Room I was pleased to accept. Over the food and wine he had a good grumble about various Heath policies but what had infuriated him in a personal capacity was the fact that, when attending a public function at Harwell in Airey's Abingdon constituency, Heath had rudely failed to acknowledge him, a gauche snub for which he would never be forgiven. Airey made clear that he had no confidence in Heath and feared he would lead the party to defeat in the next general election. Then he stunned me with a question I had not expected. *"What chance do you think I'd have if I ran for the leadership?"* he asked.

I liked and admired him greatly but I had never regarded him as a potential leader of the party – or even as someone who might harbour such ambitions. I said as much as he eyed me across the table. I added that, although I knew he was held in high respect on the Tory benches, I doubted whether many of his colleagues had thought of him as a prospective chief. Had he mentioned this idea to any of his friends in the House, I asked. He replied that he had talked to some about the need to find a challenger for the leadership but no one was prepared to take on the task. So here he was, thinking about taking on another, clearly hopeless fight, driven as always by the inner conviction that it was the right course to take. Anxious that he should not be humiliated, I suggested that if he was really serious, he should make wider soundings so as to judge what support he could expect. I asked him to keep me informed of developments. I had been as diplomatic as possible and hoped that my reaction had not disappointed him. He never raised the subject with me again. If he had challenged Heath he would certainly have had the tireless support of his charming, intelligent wife Diana. Like him, she had been in top-secret intelligence operations during the war – so secret, in fact, that neither knew the other was involved until they lost a mutual agent.

Airey, I was to learn, had a grudge against Heath that went much further back than the snub he had suffered at Abingdon. In the 1950s, when Heath was deputy Chief Whip, he had delivered a crushing judgement to Airey who had just suffered a heart attack while serving as a junior minister. Heath, with unfeeling bluntness, informed him that, so far as office was concerned, his political career had come to an end.

At Downing Street there had been a change at the Press Office; my old friend Trevor Lloyd-Hughes was moving out as Wilson's press secretary to be replaced by another friend from the Parliamentary Press Gallery, the gritty Labour supporter Joe Haines, for whom I had always had great respect and liking. Trevor, who had done a good straightforward job in his daily dealings with the media, had been lifted out of the trenches to become Chief Information Adviser to the Government with a coordinating role. Joe had been political correspondent for the seemly *Sun* since 1964. We were both soon to witness a hilarious incident involving US President Richard Nixon. Aptly named *"Tricky Dicky"*, he was returning to Washington after visiting another morally dubious national leader, the odious fascist-style Romanian President Ceausescu. Wilson had persuaded Nixon to stop off at the US Air Force base at Mildenhall, Suffolk, to provide an opportunity for a brief exchange of views. The press corps was invited to attend and as I arrived at the airfield, I noticed with interest that the American flag was flying higher than the Union Jack. That will make a line in the story, I thought. Then matters got worse – or, from my point of view – even better. Nixon's plane landed and out rushed the White House press officers to distribute the news release prepared for the occasion. As I read it I could not contain my glee. Nixon, we were informed, had come to meet British Prime Minister Harold Macmillan. Somewhere along the line, the White House officials had missed out on a change of Tory Prime Ministers and then a complete party change over to a Labour Government. Joe Haines had immediately spotted the unbelievable error and informed Nixon's press officer, Ron Ziegler. Embarrassed officials came scurrying around to retrieve their news release from the journalists. They were too late to get mine. For, on seeing the news release, I had made a dash for a *Daily Sketch* motorcycle despatch rider who was soon on his way back to London to provide the paper with an amusing picture exclusive and our readers with a chuckle. In his very readable book *"Glimmer of Twilight"*, Joe gives a slightly different version. He states that Ziegler announced over the loudspeaker the presence of *"the British Prime Minster Harold Macmillan"*. I did not hear that announcement. Wilson's attempt to build up his reputation as an international statesman by hobnobbing with Nixon had blown up in his face. Apparently, all his hyper-activity since winning power in 1964 had gone unnoticed in the President's busy press office in Washington.

In early October, I was surprised when another friend and contact, Richard *"Dick"* Marsh, announced that he was quitting the government. His Transport Minister's post was being downgraded in another Cabinet shake-up linked to Wilson's liking for *"supremos"*. Two were being appointed. Tony Crosland at 51 was made overlord of Local Government and the Regions, with Transport and Housing included in his empire. Tony Wedgwood Benn (44) was upgraded from Technology Minister to overlord of Industry, taking over Power and key Board of Trade responsibilities. At only 41, Dick Marsh had been the youngest member of the Cabinet and, as I described it, had brought a *"whiz-kid"* image to Wilson's team when he was made Power Minister in 1966. Some had tipped him as a future Labour leader, but the wonder boy had irritated some of his Cabinet colleagues by taking an independent line on too many occasions – and appearing too often not to have read his Cabinet papers before meetings. I was invited to his *"ousting party"* at his home in Eltham that night. Dick said he was staggered by his dismissal.

As a result of the reshuffle, my friend and contact Fred Mulley was moved from Foreign Office Minister of State to Transport Minister under Crosland. His involvement in transport was to bring us into a close alliance in the years ahead. Another even closer friend, George Thomson, became the Cabinet's *"Mr Europe"* with the title Chancellor of the Duchy of Lancaster – despite his strong belief in the importance of the Commonwealth. Although pleased for George, I was sorry that his Cabinet title had been taken from dear old Fred Lee, who, at 63, had been sacked after years of loyalty and useful service to Wilson. He had been very proud of the title as a Lancastrian and had sought to operate as Minister for the North.

Tony Crosland's steady rise in the government seemed significant to me in terms of future party policy. He had been virtually the only successful theorist on the Gaitskellite wing, propounding a democratic Socialist approach for the solution of Britain's economic and social problems. Gaitskell, who had produced very little in writing, had leaned heavily for inspiration on Crosland's most important book *"The Future of Socialism"*.

The reshuffle was followed by a bumpy Tory Party conference for Ted Heath. He suffered a humiliating defeat when delegates voted to bring back hanging for murder. Then, on the immigration issue, he was shaken when his stand against Enoch Powell's calls for tougher action was saved by only 395 votes. In a typically robust speech Quintin Hogg, as Shadow Home Secretary, challenged Powell's followers to stand by party policy, but nearly a thousand rebelled against the official line. Walking with me to the conference hall that morning Quintin divulged that if Heath won the coming general election he expected to be appointed Lord Chancellor, thus achieving his great ambition to follow in his father's footsteps.

As my first anniversary with the *Daily Sketch* approached there were two developments in Fleet Street that were to have a big effect on my career. Our sister paper, the group's flagship the *Daily Mail* was having serious circulation problems, having dropped below the important two million sales mark. Meanwhile, back at the *Daily Express* the slick, thrusting assistant editor David English had become so frustrated that he decided he could wait no longer to replace Marks in the editor's chair. At the age of 38 he was offered the editorship of the Sketch – and, to the dismay of Max Aitken, he accepted. Old-fashioned French was given an administrative job within the group and English moved into his office, coiffed and kitted out like a male model. He was, in fact, returning to the paper having served as features editor before becoming foreign correspondent of the *Sunday Dispatch* and then New York Correspondent for the *Daily Express.* At the outset of his career he had worked for a time for *Reynolds News* and, according to what I was told there, had got himself into serious trouble, seeking to prove slackness in security by stealing a Royal Mail bag from Paddington Station. Hauled before a magistrate and threatened with the possibility of a custodial sentence the fresh-faced young English lied his way out of the jam by blurting out in a tone of distress, *"I'm getting married in the morning!"* In fact, the ceremony had to be brought forward two months to authenticate the statement. Roy Greenslade, in his readable and well-researched book *"Press Gang"* – the best account I know of Fleet Street in my time – has reported that English was dubbed the Artful Dodger and that seemed to me an apt description. I recall the anger swirling around the *Express* foreign desk on the day his by-line appeared above the last edition of the paper's report of the assassination of President Kennedy in November 1963. English was in New York on the day of the killing and the paper's respected Washington correspondent Ross Mark had written the first report. English, however, scenting glory, caught a plane to Dallas, scene of the murder, and on arrival phoned the *Express* to insist that the dateline on the last edition should be changed to read, *"From David English, Dallas."* Later in life he was to claim to have witnessed the shooting. The politician who has reminded me most of David English is slippery, smiling Tony Blair – another Artful Dodger.

Boyish in appearance, English had a gift for enthusing his staff and on arrival at the *Sketch* quickly set about meeting key members of the team one by one over lunch. Within a week, I was face to face with him across a table in a restaurant in Panton Street. He loved gossip and was eager to pick my brains. We started by having two things in common. We had both been part of the last glory days of the *Daily Express* when it was enjoying a circulation of some three and a half million; and we had both felt frustrated by Max Aitken's failure to give us the jobs we believed we deserved. I had been unable to interest Howard French in publishing a weekly political column for airing gossip about parliamentary personalities. I raised the subject with English as we tucked into our roast lamb.

He showed some interest so I produced a dummy within a week and he gave me the go-ahead. My problem then was that when he was short of news, he would take the best item from the column late in the day to provide a lead for a news page, leaving me to scramble around last minute to fill the gap.

Morale was given a much-needed boost by the arrival of this lively, energetic character. He attracted bright, up-and-coming writers to the team, notably Jean Rook, whose catty comments won her the title *"First Bitch of Fleet Street"* and provided Private Eye with the model for the imaginary crude columnist *"Glenda Slagg"*. She shared with English a love of stunts, such as appearing in a cage with lions. Her vituperative descriptions of top people and celebrities included an attack on Prince Philip in which she called him a *"hawk-nosed, slit mouthed tetchy old devil."* As for the Queen, Rook wrote in one column that she needed to pluck her eyebrows.

Big, blonde and busty, she did much to liven up the office and the clatter of her chunky jewellery almost drowned out that of the typewriters. Despite her brazen, confident manner, however, Jean had a running problem in deciding on topics for her column. She would often be seen in a state of almost nervous collapse, her mass of hair awry, scurrying into English's office to confess that she did not know what to write about. He would sit her down with a cup of coffee and recall news stories of the last few days until finally deciding which would make the best items for her to kick around. Sometimes he would suggest a phrase or two. When she had departed at last to type her piece, he would look as exhausted as if he had just given birth. He was, in fact, very good at spotting and projecting talking points.

Jean eventually joined the *Daily Express* where she spent nearly twenty years becoming the highest paid woman journalist in Britain.

General election fever was mounting as summer approached. I had been surprised by Labour's good results in the spring local elections, although the gains were partly due to the recapture of seats lost in previous contests when Wilson's Government had been justifiably unpopular. No doubt the replacement of calamity Callaghan by a competent Chancellor in the shape of Roy Jenkins was helping to restore confidence in the administration. Intellect had replaced indecision. I was puzzled, however, by Labour's good showing in the opinion polls, including that of the *Daily Express*. Would Wilson be encouraged to go to the real-life polls? I had a feeling that if he called an election he would lose. Then a Gallup poll in mid-May gave Labour a 7.5% lead.

There was a strong buzz at Westminster that Wilson was indeed about to dissolve Parliament and go to the country. I phoned Joe Haines at Downing Street airing my suspicion that Wilson could have been mislead by the opinion polls into misjudging the actual mood of the country. I thought I could tell from Joe's voice that he was uneasy. The election was called for June 18 –the anniversary of the Battle of Waterloo.

What had annoyed me particularly about Wilson's scuttle to the hustings was his cynical readiness to abandon important legislation that had taken much time to prepare and debate in Parliament. Crossman's much-needed new deal for pensioners, the national Superannuation and Social Insurance Bill, was one of the measures that would be lost. More personal to me, Alf Morris' vital new deal for the disabled, the Chronically Sick and Disabled Persons Bill, appeared to be threatened with the scrap heap. On the advice of members of the government supporting the measure, Wilson, however, agreed that it should be given priority and it scraped though its last stage to reach the Statute Book on May 29 – the very last day of that Parliament. It must have been painful for Crossman, who had warned Alf that his Bill would not succeed, to see it become law while his own important pensions measure, over which he had sweated blood, was callously dumped by the Prime Minister.

Although the opinion polls continued to show the Tories trailing as the campaign gathered momentum, I continued to have a gut feeling that they would win in the end. Thanks to the prudent finance of Chancellor Roy Jenkins, the economy was for once in fairly good shape, but his policies had not pleased everyone and in 1968, he had introduced an unpopular high tax regime. Perhaps my main reason for believing in a Conservative win, however, was the fact that for the first time in my voting life, I myself had decided to support the Tories. Increasingly disenchanted with Wilson's opportunist style of government, for me his abandonment of so much useful legislation in favour of an unnecessary election had been the last straw. In contrast, Heath appeared to me to be a man of moral courage and integrity.

If I felt like that, I reasoned, surely many others must be preparing to withdraw support for Labour and to vote for him too. My view of the situation puzzled David English, but it meant that the paper's forecasts of the possible outcome were more cautious than most. Enoch Powell, encouraged by opinion polls showing him to be one of the most popular politicians in the country, endeavoured to overshadow Heath during the campaign, accusing him of being an appeaser on the issue of immigration. His poisonous intervention confirmed me in my decision to vote Conservative for Ted.

On the eve of polling I reported the highly significant result of a private poll carried out for Tory Central Office by Opinion Research Centre. It revealed that half of Britain's voters believed that the country was heading for economic trouble and only one in four accepted Labour's sunshine view of the situation. It followed a warning from Heath's supporters that a Labour victory could mean another devaluation of the pound. As the Government's own statistics unveiled a picture of rising prices, falling production and rising unemployment, Heath sought to stir up a housewives' revolt. I observed that the Tories' private poll could be a pointer to an eleventh hour movement of opinion. So it was. Heath won with a majority of thirty-one seats. The *Daily Sketch,* loyal as ever to the Tory cause, had urged readers to vote Conservative.

Thanks to some helpful guidance from Quintin Hogg, the *Sketch* did better than any other national paper in forecasting the make-up of Heath's first cabinet. He achieved his dream of becoming Lord Chancellor and pointed me in the direction of some other key posts, such as Alec Douglas-Home as Foreign Secretary and Iain Macleod as Chancellor of the Exchequer. Within a few weeks of taking office Macleod was to die – his sudden death from a heart attack coming as a tragic and serious blow to the new government.

Quintin's joyous acceptance of the Lord Chancellor's post meant resigning his Commons seat for St Marylebone and entering the House of Lords as Lord Hailsham (once again). It was as Lord Hailsham then that he attended as a guest at one of the regular Guinea Club lunches. As we took our drinks before sitting down, I introduced him to Tony Shrimsley of the *Sun* who, surprisingly, had never met him before. He revealed to the two of us that the Government was looking at the possibility of building London's next airport at Maplin Sands on the East coast. When I asked him if we could report it he gave a little grin and said, *"I don't see why not?"* As a Londoner, troubled by the steady growth of air traffic over the capital and the inability of the over-large Heathrow airport to cope, I was sorry that the Heath Government's Maplin plan was eventually abandoned.

Soon after the Tories' election victory, David English made it known that he thought the Sketch should publish an interview with Prime Minister Edward Heath. I suggested that he might like to conduct it himself as a means of getting to know Ted, whom he had never met. I made the arrangements and it went very well, taking place at No. 10. I accompanied English and no doubt looked suitably embarrassed when Ted praised my political reporting. He had the reputation for being peremptory and lacking warmth but I had never found him so. On this occasion he could not have been more relaxed, friendly and forthcoming. He thanked English for the support he had received from the *Sketch* during the election and the interview got underway. I was impressed by the Prime Minister's attitude to the persistent problem of unemployment. He had been influenced by the views of his old boss Harold Macmillan, a politician haunted by memories of the appalling misery caused to his constituents in Stockton-on-Tees during the depression of the 1930s. Like Macmillan, he had been strongly influenced by his experience as an officer commanding men at the front in a world war, believing that by their joint efforts and the social contract formed between them they could achieve a better, fairer society in which mass unemployment would be abandoned as a means of controlling the economy. Optimistically, he believed the way ahead and the goal of full employment lay in achieving consensus by collective discussions between government, industry and the trade unions.

Again like Macmillan, Heath was clearly prepared to face the risk of modest inflation to boost the economy in order to prevent a return to unemployment on a serious scale. I underlined the economic importance of this to English after leaving No. 10 – yet not foreseeing what a key issue this was to become within the Tory Party within the next few years.

English appeared to have been impressed by Heath and by my friendly relationship with him. It was typical of his approach to news, however, that in the taxi ride back to the office he raised with me the question of Heath's sexuality. The press had made much of the fact that Number Ten was now occupied by a bachelor. English asked me if I thought he was homosexual. I replied that I thought possibly, yes, but that he had subjugated his emotions in the interest of his political career. What about his close friendship with the concert pianist Moura Lympany? Ted and Moura shared common interests in music, food and wine. She was to become a regular guest at No.10 and Chequers and helped him choose the grand piano he installed in Downing Street. There was the inevitable rumour that they were having an affair. However, when Tory MP Sir Tufton Beamish had asked her whether she would marry him to help him become Prime Minister she had said *"No"*. She was, in fact, in love with someone else. Tufton, lampooned by *Private Eye* as *"Sir Tufton Bufton"* had a stuffy, military appearance and was an influential member of the executive of the Tory 1922 Committee. We often gossiped and he had told me that people were saying the fact Ted was a bachelor could damage his prospects of winning votes – especially from women. Tufton had tried to help him in his forthright, blimpish manner.

Nearly forty years later, and after his death, a report appeared alleging that Heath had been actively gay as a young man, and that, together with other Tory MPs had been warned. I have found this hard to believe. In my experience, he would not have taken any such risk that might endanger his political career. He was ambitious and took great pains to build up a *"persona"* that would make him acceptable to the top people in the Tory Party – and perhaps, at some stage, a potential leader of the party, and in time, the country.

Linking his decision to keep his sexuality under control with his endeavours to lose his lower-middle class background and convert himself into a Tory gentleman of taste and refinement, one can come to a better understanding of his defensive, shell-like reserve. In this respect, one can see a certain parallel with Enoch Powell. As to Heath's attitude to women, I like the account of his attendance at a public dinner where he appeared to be ignoring the woman seated next to him. A friend passed him a folded note that said, *"Ted, you must talk to the lady on your left."*

Heath scribbled on the scrap of paper, *"I have."*

And passed it back.

In December 1970, together with other Lobby journalists, I accompanied Heath to Washington for his first talks as Prime Minister with President Richard Milhous Nixon. Despite the fact he had been given some bad times by the American media, he ensured that the British journalists with Heath were made warmly welcome on visiting the White House. His press officers, perhaps to make up for the Mildenhall muddle, were efficient, helpful and hospitable, arranging for us to tour the White House and inviting us to an evening reception there. At that event Nixon made a very clever and amusing speech, rather in the style of the American comedian Jack Benny.

Nixon had welcomed Heath in grand style with flags and fanfares. There was an exuberant rendering of *"Rule*

Britannia" as he greeted the Prime Minister in winter sunshine on the White House lawn. I reported that Britain's bid to join the Common Market was to be a major subject of discussion, with Heath anxious to reassure the President that by joining the European Economic Community, Britain would not harm American interests. At a glittering banquet, Heath stressed that the special relationship, however, was not an exclusive one and covered *"friends and allies."*

Nixon conveyed the impression that he was delighted that Heath had won the election. Washington journalists to whom I spoke confirmed that the White House–Downing Street relationship had a closeness not seen for years. I reported that Heath had forged a better personal relationship with Nixon than Wilson had enjoyed and was restoring the old easy, two-way communication with the White House. In dealing with Nixon, Heath was faced with a very talented and clever man – but a man whose bitter experiences had left him twisted inside and not strong on integrity. As a poor boy who had made it to the pinnacle of American and world society, he had always nursed a deep suspicion and resentment of the wealthy and privileged – especially the East Coast establishment. Robbed of the presidency in 1960 by rich and handsome John F. Kennedy, he had then lost the contest for the governorship of California in 1962. Bitterly, he had told the American press that they would not have him *"to kick around anymore"*. But this tough, indomitable man had bounced back once again, and after disappointments and setbacks that would have prompted most men to quit the political arena, he eventually won the presidency in 1968. There followed, under his leadership, some surprisingly liberal reforms, including desegregation of schools. In 1972, he was to stamp his name on the international field of history by being the first US President to visit China. He also did much to bring the disastrous

Vietnam War to an end. In due course, however, he would be remembered for the ignominy of being the only President forced to resign from office as he became entangled in the Watergate scandal.

On the home front, Tony Barber had been appointed by Heath as Chancellor of the Exchequer following the shock death of Iain Macleod. One of Heath's closest colleagues, he had been party chairman in the run-up to the general election and by improving party organisation had played a major role in the Tory victory. His immediate reward was to be made Chancellor of the Duchy of Lancaster with the key responsibility of handling Britain's Common Market entry talks. Now, as Chancellor of the Exchequer, he was very much dominated by Heath and agreed with his view that it was worth taking the risk of making a dash for growth by pumping money into the economy. Unfortunately, it did not succeed. Encouraged by Heath, he greatly expanded the money supply to produce the *"Barber Boom"* of 1970-72 which fuelled inflation and led to wage demands and threats of strikes.

I found Tony Barber approachable, relaxed and friendly. He was popular with his colleagues in the Commons and had the reputation of being a thoroughly nice, decent man. When he entertained me with other Lobby journalists at No. 11 Downing Street I found that, like Heath, he was a good, attentive, host, continually circulating among his guests. What a contrast to Wilson who, in my experience tended to allow himself to be bogged down by stooges and sycophants in a corner while his wife Mary stood shyly in a corner and Marcia Williams, with what looked like a costly coiffure, paraded around.

Always in search of an entertaining angle, English had noted the use of nicknames for MPs – a fashion especially common among Tories reliving their public school days. He asked me if I knew enough such soubriquets to support a light-hearted feature article. My list included the following:

John Boyd-Carpenter, a senior ex-minister with a peculiar hopping gait, who was known as *Spring-heeled Jack*; Sir David – later Viscount – Eccles, known as *Smarty Boots*, not only because of the sheen on his hand-made shoes but because, as Harold Macmillan observed, he was vain, bumptious and had a high-opinion of himself (so cheekily vain, in fact, that when as Minister of Works he helped arrange the Queen's coronation in 1953 he described her as his 'leading lady'); lawyer Sir David Maxwell-Fyfe – who became Lord Kilmuir – was called *Dai Bananas*, but not to his face; Hector Hughes, a puffed-up, not very competent Labour barrister known as *Necessity* Hughes, for as the old adage puts it – 'Necessity knows no law'. On the Tory benches lounged one of my favourite nicknamed characters – the *One-armed Bandit*. Having lost an arm while serving with the Welsh Guards in the Second World War, William Rees-Davies was a barrister who was himself often in trouble with the law for drunken driving and property offences. A fast-living gambler, he was suspended from the Bar a number of times for failing to appear in court. He wore with panache a stained black cloak to hide his amputation and his ravaged face reflected many late night indulgences with strong liquor and wild, wild women. English liked the list.

One of my favourite people on the *Daily Sketch* was the chief reporter Noel Botham, hearty and entertaining, who, among other things, reported on the doings of the Royal Family. One Sunday we went to a nearby pub for lunch and as we got to the bar, I could sense that he was in a state of suppressed excitement. He told me he had been asked by an equerry of Princess Margaret to retrieve some passionate love letters she had written to Robin Douglas-Home,

Charlie's brother, during a short-lived affair. The letters had been stolen from Robin's home after he had committed suicide in 1968 with an overdose of pills and alcohol. They had then been sold to the French scandal-mongering magazine *Paris Match* and Noel said he had recently been to Paris, bought back the letters on behalf of Princess Margaret and had them returned to her. At the time of her affair with Robin, the Princess was married to Lord Snowdon, formerly Anthony Armstrong-Jones, a motorbike-riding photographer well connected in society. Robin's mother was the sister of Earl Spencer and he was a cousin of a young girl named Diana who was to become the doomed Princess of Wales. In 1965, his marriage to fashion model Sandra Paul finally broke up. They had been married for six years and had one son.

Noel was sitting on a sensational story – but one he could not write. I assumed he had taken copies of the letters, but decided not to ask him. I pondered on who could have carried out the theft. Clearly it was someone who had been close to Robin, knew of the existence of the letters and where to find them. I immediately ruled out Charlie, who had too much class to commit such an act, and who would not have wanted to do anything to damage the name of his brother for whom he had such affection. Whoever had taken them was apparently in league with someone who knew the market for such material and was sufficiently unscrupulous to conduct the sale and broker a profitable deal with the French journal. Within a few years I was pretty sure I had guessed their identity.

I recalled Noel's story when in 1976 *Private Eye* reported that *'letters of an intimate nature dating from 1967 purporting to be from Princess Margaret to her 'lover' Robin Douglas-Home had come to light.*

'If bona fide, they prove that her marriage to the Earl of Snowdon was effectively over when the affair started. The gracious lady writes of her diminutive husband on March 23rd, 1967 on Kensington Palace paper:

"I am in fear of him and I don't know what lengths he won't go to, jealous as he is, to find out what I am up to and your movements, too. Our love had the passionate scent of new mown grass and lilies about it. Promise you will never give it up, that you will go on encouraging me to make the marriage a success and that given a good and safe chance I will try to come back to you one day. I daren't at the moment."'

Thanks to Michael Edwards, the bustling industrial correspondent of the Sketch, I got to know the most intelligent and successful of the trade union leaders of the 1960s and 70s – Clive Jenkins. The Welsh whiz-kid who revelled in his reputation as a champagne Socialist built up his union –the Association of Scientific, Technical and Managerial Staffs (ASTMS) – by clever organisation and mergers. Starting with the Association of Supervisory Staffs, Executives and Technicians (ASSET) he became General Secretary in 1960 and more than trebled its membership to 65,000 by 1968, when it merged with the 20,000 strong Association of Scientific Workers to become ASTMS. Mike, a close, drinking friend of the ebullient, chatty Clive, took me along to one of his famous Labour conference parties, where hundreds guzzled as corks popped. I was flattered when he recalled my reporting for *Reynolds News*. The son of a Welsh railway worker, he had been a card-carrying communist in the 1950s but by the 1980s had become a leftish Labour Party moderniser. Whenever I met him after Mike's helpful introduction I was struck by his contempt for many of the other, less clever trade union bosses – and for many Labour politicians. They in turn disliked him for his high-living style and left-wing views, accusing him of being devious and arrogant. After leaving journalism for public affairs consultancy, I continued to meet him at Labour Party and TUC conferences and watched with awe as ASTMS became the fastest growing union in the 1970s and 80s, wielding a powerful block vote at the party conference, which he would manipulate, following backstage deals and his high-pitched Welsh oratory on the rostrum. In 1987, his union became even larger and more influential when it merged with the Technical and Supervisory Staff (TASS) led by communist Ken Gill to form the Manufacturing Science and Finance Union (MSF). Through this merger, which brought the union membership to over 650,000, I got to know Gill, who had a gift for portraiture. At a conference dinner one evening he quickly drew an excellent likeness of me on the back of a menu – which I still possess. Clive Jenkins and Gill served for a time as joint secretaries of the union. Then suddenly, Clive, aged 62, decided to retire early and announced that he was leaving his wife and heading for Tasmania with a young girlfriend to do environmental work – and no doubt drink a lot of Australian bubbly.

Despite David English's inspiring leadership, our efforts at the Sketch were not putting on readers and the paper was losing money – though not as much as the *Daily Mail,* our sister journal. Faced with this serious financial problem, proprietor Lord Rothermere and his son Vere Harmsworth began to consider a drastic solution. Their plan involved converting the broadsheet Mail, circulation 1.8 million, into a tabloid and merging it with the Sketch, which at the beginning of 1971 had a circulation of about 800,000. David English would be appointed editor of the combined paper that would retain the more prestigious *Daily Mail* title. The merger would lead to huge job losses.

Unaware of this secret plan taking shape, I was delighted to learn that I would be in the group of Lobby correspondents flying out to Singapore to cover the January 1971 Commonwealth Prime Ministers' Conference. As the conference approached I knew that the Government's decision to resume arms sales to South Africa – vehemently opposed by black African Commonwealth members – would ensure that it would be bad tempered and stormy. Tanzania had threatened to withdraw from the Commonwealth and Nigeria had warned Heath that Britain could face expulsion over the issue. Behind the scenes, a major disagreement had led to a clash between the Prime Minister and the Queen. Fearing that her presence as head of the Commonwealth could be embarrassing, Heath had told Queen Elizabeth that it might be inadvisable for her to attend. This advice was badly received by Her Majesty who replied that she thought the Head of the Commonwealth should be present. Heath, equally stubborn, replied that if she went, his government would be liable to criticism from the old Commonwealth for putting her in an awkward position and from the newer members for seeking to use her politically to soften their position on disputed policies. Very reluctantly the Queen, in the end, agreed to stay away.

Heath's main opponents, Presidents Nyerere of Tanzania and Kaunda of Zambia – dubbed the *"Terrible Twins"* – flew into Singapore the day after I arrived in the exciting South-east Asian city ruled by Lee Kuan Yew, a hard-headed political wizard. His blend of realism and commercial flair had made Singapore a booming metropolis where soaring luxury hotels and well-run services enticed growing numbers of business men on the conference circuit to spend their money.

As his staff rolled out the red carpet for the incoming premiers, Lee was confident that no matter how angry they might be with Mr Heath, they would not walk out of the conference for fear of offending their host and other Asian leaders. I reported that the famed local Chinese fortune-tellers were forecasting that the Commonwealth would not be killed off by the bad tempered summit meeting. They included a Mr Tommy Eng who had predicted the fall of the Wilson government and the Kennedy family tragedies.

One *"white Commonwealth"* leader busy doing his bit behind the scenes to hold the club together was Canada's Pierre Trudeau. Sporting a fresh orchid in his buttonhole, he was exciting the interest of the ladies and photographers. Half English, half Quebecois, he had a trendy style and a handsome lived-in face. After consuming an eleven-course meal of local delicacies he was awarded the title of *"Chopstick Champ"* of the visiting statesmen. Although he was often accused of arrogance, he was a rather shy, complex man behind his confident, jokey façade. At home, as a cosmopolitan, he did his utmost to ensure that Canada was multicultural and bilingual and opposed Quebec nationalism.

As the conference bumped along, Zambia's Kenneth Kaunda told me at a Hilton Hotel breakfast that he and other African states had agreed a plan for economic counter moves against Britain to force Heath to think again about arms for South Africa. Heath, however, was undeterred by threats that British firms and investments in black Africa would suffer. He seemed more concerned that if he refused to accept South Africa's orders for arms its tough no-nonsense leader Dr Vorster would tear up the agreement under which the Royal Navy was allowed to use the strategically important Simonstown base

Then an ugly note was struck by the most extreme of the African leaders, President Milton Obote of Uganda. Having led Uganda to independence in 1962, he had turned to repression when he failed to achieve his goals, relying on the army to crush opposition. Now he hinted darkly at the conference that the lives of Britons in his country might even be in danger. Heath's team were appalled. They knew what Obote was capable of.

Then, after days of haggling, the deadlock was broken. Heath, by firmness and negotiating skill succeeded in manoeuvring the conference into agreeing to a review by an eight-nation committee of the problems of defending the trade routes round the Cape. It was not expected to report for six months and, meanwhile, Britain would not freeze arms sales to South Africa. The Commonwealth remained in place. The same could not be said for Mr Obote.

As the talks were drawing to a close the news broke that in his absence from Uganda he had been overthrown by his army chief, General Idi Amin. There was an air of rejoicing in Heath's team of Whitehall advisers. Someone recalled that at a special conference session on the arms issue attended by the Africans, Heath's policies had been described as "racialist" and he had retorted sharply: *"I wonder how many of you will be allowed to return to your own countries from this conference?"*

There can be no doubt, in fact, that British Intelligence, alarmed by Obote's flirting with the Communist bloc, had a hand in his replacement by Amin. The general, we were told by Heath's advisers, was a splendid man, a gentle giant trained by the British Army who would be a major force in helping to stop the spread of communist influence in Africa. Heath's spokesman and Press Secretary Donald Maitland, an ex-Foreign Office official, was especially forthcoming in his praise for Amin as we drank in a cool bar to escape the island's enervating, clammy heat. I have often come to question the judgement of the men at the FO, but their reaction to the Amin take-over must take the prize for a monumental misreading of a situation. Covered in medals he had awarded to himself, the General soon showed what a ruthless monster, unrivalled in Africa for mass-murder and appalling cruelty, he was. There had been a warning of his lethal brutality. In 1963, as a soldier under British command he had faced a court martial for killing fourteen members of a neighbouring tribe – but the proceedings were dropped. Once in power, his killings were on such a vast scale that the rivers and lakes around Kampala overflowed with human remains. He also turned on Uganda's Asian population, expelling these industrious people who had been responsible for most of the country's commerce and industry. Before that came to pass, Britain's High Commission in Kampala advised that the result of Amin's take-over *"could be a healthier society for Uganda. I think Amin has the wherewithal to provide a satisfactory administration..."*

Heath quickly recognised the new regime and invited him to London where he was entertained to lunch by the Queen at Buckingham Palace. He styled himself *"His Excellency President for Life, Field Marshall Al Hadji Doctor Idi Amin, VC, DSO, MC Lord of all the beasts of the earth and fishes of the sea, and conqueror of the British Empire in Africa in General and Uganda in Particular."*

After presiding over the murder of some 300,000 of his subjects in his nine-year rule he was finally overthrown and died in exile in Saudi Arabia in 2003. As a soldier he had been taught to kill by the British in Uganda border skirmishes and apparently got a taste for it.

The Amin experience should have made Britain's politicians much more wary about the type of people to whom they were prepared to hand over power in Africa. Margaret Thatcher's willingness some years later to allow a known killer in the shape of the merciless Robert Mugabe to head up the new state of Zimbabwe when, to my knowledge, her officials had evidence of a massacre that could have cost him his election victory, is proof that sadly they had not learned that lesson.

Before departing from Singapore I celebrated my forty-second birthday in the Press Club section of the famous old Raffles Hotel. Sitting under gently whirring fans and drinking gin slings with my friends I was unaware that I was entering a year of dramatic change and personal upheaval.

Back in the office of the *Daily Sketch* moves towards the merger with the Mail were gathering pace behind the scenes. My wife and I spent a weekend in Kent with my parents and I had an uneasy feeling of foreboding as we returned to London. Following an announcement of the impending marriage of the papers, David English made known that he would be interviewing staff about their future. It soon became clear that he would be taking most of the top people with him – that, in fact, the *Sketch* was virtually taking over the *Mail*. I was to discover from English, however, that, for me, there was a problem. My friend and rival Walter Terry had been moved from the Parliamentary Press Gallery when his affair with Marcia Williams had begun to become an embarrassment and had been appointed an associate editor. English was taking his associate editors from the *Sketch* and did not want Walter to continue in that job. He was offered his old one back as political editor, which he had done with such success for so many years. Walter, privately very angry, had accepted the demotion. To add to his irritation, he was given the responsibility meanwhile of telling some of his senior *Mail* colleagues that they were being made redundant. Arthur Brittenden, fired as *Mail* editor, had left the office without carrying out that unpleasant duty. Howard French, in his new role as editorial director of Associated Newspapers, wrote to most of the unwanted staff to inform them of the bad news. It became a sad joke in the office to reveal that you had a *"French letter"*. English explained to me in the nicest possible way that under the circumstances there would be no political job for me on the merged paper. He said he would do his best to help me find a new position if I needed assistance – and, in fact, he was able to head me towards a new career.

I had wept when the *News Chronicle* died. Tears had welled in my eyes as I walked the dismal streets around Kings Cross on the night *Reynolds News* had been killed off. But I could not shed a tear for the *Daily Sketch*. It had been a decent, breezy little paper but it had no soul. Its staff, frankly, would have found it difficult to state what it had stood for except survival – but not, to be fair, at any price. It had not got down into the gutter to fight it out with the *Sun*.

Within ten years three national newspapers had sunk under me – two in the most dramatic of circumstances with hundreds of journalists and technicians thrown out of work. Where could I go next? Ian Aitken wrote a wry short piece in the *Guardian* drawing attention to my plight and suggesting that I appeared to be akin to an unlucky albatross. Friends begged me jokingly not to endanger their papers by joining them. It was not that easy. There were no vacancies for a political editor in Fleet Street and I had to admit that I had not covered myself with glory at the *Sketch* for I was not suited to tabloid journalism. Perhaps I should try my hand at something new?

A few years earlier, Conrad Voss-Bark had left the BBC political team, after a messy divorce, to become a parliamentary consultant at the well-established City advertising and public relations firm of Charles Barker. He had extolled to me the civilised conditions of his new life and I had wondered whether that type of work would, in due course, suit me. Certainly the prospect of having to deal at all hours with the demands and queries of Fleet Street news desks when I was in my fifties did not appeal.

It was as though David English read my thoughts. He phoned me one day as I was working out my notice to say that a friend who ran a public relations company in Fleet Street needed someone with parliamentary experience to work on an important new account involving the City of Cardiff, which was opposed to Government proposals for local government reform. If I was interested I should phone David Wynne-Morgan at Partnerplan PR. I thanked David English and said I would. This could be just the opening I needed to test the waters of political consultancy.

Unbeknown to me at the time, English had also been offered a new job secretly – the editorship of the *Daily Express*. Max Aitken, however, had left it too late to persuade him to replace the ailing Derek Marks as Rothermere had by then produced his plans for the revamped *Daily Mail*. As English began to devote more time to the *Mail* in preparation for the merger, my old friend Lou Kirby, who had originally enticed me on to the *Sketch*, was left in his role as deputy editor to close down the paper, producing the last issue in May – wrapped around the *Mail*. A *Sketch* wake had been organised but I decided not to attend.

The announcement in March that the *Sketch* was to cease as a separate newspaper brought predictable reaction from the Government and MPs. Trade Minister John Davies, in the Commons, very much regretted the disappearance of a national newspaper. He added, however, that it was not unexpected in view of the failure of the newspaper publishers to come to grips with well-known problems.

Restrictive practices, prevalent in the industry, were largely to blame for what had happened. He saw no need for an inquiry. Harold Wilson, too, spoke of a serious situation and warned that other papers were likely to go under with consequent loss of freedom of choice.

Sir Frederic Bennett MP, the friendly contact who years before had alerted me to the imminent resignation of Sir Alec Douglas-Home as Tory leader, phoned me to express his regrets. Freddie, who had been a journalist for a time, said he would table a Commons motion that he read to me. While profoundly regretting the demise of the *Sketch*, it expressed the view that no new inquiry was needed to point to the reasons for past, present and any future erosions of the public's free choice of newspaper reading. It urged Wilson and the Labour Party to devote their energies to curtailing trade union restrictive practices and maverick strikes.

One of a number of other friends and contacts who phoned me to commiserate and to wish me well was Percy Clark, Director of Information for the Labour Party. He had succeeded John Harris in the job and was well liked by journalists and those who worked with him. Dismayed by what he saw as the damage done by far left campaigners to Labour's image and electoral prospects, he supported the party's National Agent, Reg Underhill, in drawing up a dossier on the operations of Militant Tendency. He had good judgement and was always pleasant to deal with no matter at what hour I called him to seek information. His filing system, however, was a joke. He had a natural aversion to *"bumf"* and someone who worked for him told me that when the paper in his in-tray reached a certain height he would empty it into his waster paper basket. In 1972, he married Doreen Stainforth, an efficient party executive in charge of the television sector.

Another friend who phoned was Willie Hamilton, Labour MP for Central Fife and up to that time one of the few Englishmen ever to win a Scottish seat. Holding republican views, Willie kept up an unremitting barrage of criticism of the cost of maintaining the royal family. He lived near me in Dulwich and when I met up with him on the train one night he told me he was preparing for another battle over royal upkeep. In the last column I wrote for the *Sketch* I described how *"the restless roundhead"* was girding himself up for his biggest fight yet *"against royal pomp and privilege"*. He was to describe the Queen's request to Parliament to review the Civil List as *"the most insensitive and brazen pay claim made in the last two hundred years."* He proposed that Buckingham Palace officials should be quizzed by a Commons committee on the extent of the royal fortune. As for Princess Margaret, he was to describe the Queen's sister as *"an expensive kept women"* and a *"monstrous charge on the public purse."*

I reported that a member of the previous Labour Government had told me that Willie, an able MP who had become vice chairman of the Parliamentary Labour Party, was not given a job by Wilson because of his fierce criticism of the Palace. *"When he's finished with the latest royal pay claim he will have talked himself out of a government post for ever,"* I concluded.

Willie, however, was not interested in office. He once said that his role was to be *"bloody minded"*.

We had a laugh about my column item when we next met on the Dulwich-bound train. He confessed, with his typical frankness, that he did not normally read the *Sketch* but as he knew I was writing about him he had picked up a copy in the Commons tearoom. *"Not many people did read the Sketch,"* I replied. *"That's been the trouble."*

"Well, best of luck," he said as we parted at the station. *"I'll miss you in the Lobby – but I expect you'll soon be back."*

On that last point he was wrong.

I did not return to the Commons as a lobby journalist. Instead, I was soon back in the Houses of Parliament as a parliamentary consultant or, as I preferred to be described, a lobbyist. At the age of forty-two, I began a new career that was to last for almost forty further years.

For a year or two I missed the excitement of the daily battle to try to keep ahead of rival reporters in breaking the news. But even as I was leaving Fleet Street change was in the air – due largely to Rupert Murdoch whose launch of the saucy *Sun* faced the tabloids *Mirror* and *Sketch* with a startling challenge. By February 1981, the dynamic Australian had enlarged his newspaper empire by becoming owner of *The Times* and *The Sunday Times*. This development proved fortunate for my old friend Charlie Douglas-Home. Murdoch had a high regard for Harry Evans, editor of *The Sunday Times*, and switched him to the more important editor's chair at *The Times*. In that new role, however, Evans was a disappointment. Lack of consistent leadership led to serious discontent among the staff. In March 1982, Charlie, by then deputy editor, and John Grant, the experienced managing editor, whom I later came to know and like, threatened to resign. Evans was forced to quit and Charlie became editor, winning the confidence of the staff by his firm leadership and widespread respect for his improvements to the newspaper that increased circulation. He told me that, on the whole, he enjoyed working for Murdoch. But it was not to last long. Suffering increasingly from an agonising cancer, he died in October 1985. He was forty-eight.

For about a decade after I had left Fleet Street, newspaper managements were sniffing tentatively at introducing revolutionary new technology in the form of computerised operations by which journalists could type their reports straight into the system, thus cutting out the typesetters whose irresponsible print unions had imposed a stranglehold on newspaper proprietors. With typical sharpness, columnist Bernard Levin – my friend from university days – said Fleet Street newspapers were produced *in conditions which combined a protection racket with a lunatic asylum.*"

Early in 1985, Murdoch's patience in dealing with the grasping, intransigent print unions snapped. He decided to switch his operations to a printing plant he had built some years before at Wapping in London's dreary Docklands. The move for all four of his national papers involved the introduction of the new technology with journalists and advertising staff setting words in type without the use of members of the print unions.

Rightly anticipating strikes and violent picketing he had the plant fortified and finally tasted victory in January 1987, with a financial deal with the striking newspapermen. As the pickets dispersed he could claim that he had broken the hold of the unions. Margaret Thatcher, who had defeated the striking coalminers, saw it as another victory against the militant labour movement. Other newspaper managements followed his lead. One by one they adopted the same process and moved out of the Fleet Street area to more suitable offices. It was no longer the exciting street of opportunity I had entered as a young reporter in 1956. The pubs were no longer filled with journalists. They now rely on lawyers, public relations men and tourists for their trade. I'm glad I got out when I did.

That was a sentiment I shared with Anthony Howard, with whom I had undergone similar experiences as a young man. When he died aged seventy-six in December 2010, an honoured and respected former senior figure in Fleet Street, it was revealed that he had said that if he had started his career forty years later he would not have chosen Fleet Street – only to end in wretched Wapping. In his view – as in mine – for the young man seeking opportunity, adventure and a cause to which to harness his pen, the job had become no more than 'crouching over a terminal'.

As for the ongoing love/hate relationship between politicians and the Press, by 2010 persistent probing by journalists had uncovered such blatant and widespread dishonesty in Parliament that the British public's trust in politics had hit an all-time low.

The British Social Attitudes survey published in December that year revealed that four in ten people no longer trusted politicians to put the national interest first. The majority were of the belief that MPs never told the truth. In fact, mistrust in politics was four times higher than in the mid 1980s. Ominously, the survey concluded that Britain had come to adopt a "straightforwardly cynical" attitude towards central government as a whole.

The public's damning verdict followed the spectacular scandal of the dishonest manipulation of their expenses arrangements by many MPs and peers, uncovered by an investigation carried out by the indefatigable *Daily Telegraph* in 2009.

Many of the worst offenders had been ejected from Parliament at the May 2010 general election, but as rioting students rampaged around Parliament Square in the following December over proposed changes in university fees the *Daily Telegraph* commented:

"Beyond the traditional cynicism of the under-thirties lie new demographic tensions that are partly the fault of the middle-aged politicians, especially Labour ones."

As someone who had actively supported the Labour Party for so many years of my life and had watched with dismay its intellectual and moral decline, I could not disagree with that depressing conclusion.

What is one to think of a party when one of its leading members can be described by a prominent newspaper columnist, without public challenge, as *'an integrity free zone'*? Most Labour politicians were prepared to support such an odious operator if he could keep them in power at the 2010 general election. In Labour's great old days when it was led by Clem Atlee, Mr Integrity himself, even that ruthless politician Herbert Morrison would have disowned him.

Overshadowed by the continuing expansion of the Murdoch News Corporation empire, the running battle between politicians and the media took an extraordinary tangled turn in December 2010. During the year I had watched with interest as media companies, including newspaper publishers and the BBC, had opposed a proposed bid by News Corp for BSkyB, the satellite broadcaster. They appeared to me to have good reason for arguing that News Corp, which already owned *The Times* and *Sun* newspapers and thirty-nine per cent of BSkyB, would have a disproportionate influence over the British media if it owned the other sixty-one per cent of Sky.

Cabinet Business Secretary Vince Cable had to decide by the end of January 2011 whether to refer the controversial bid to the Competition Commission. BSkyB's board had already firmly rejected News Corp's initial offer, made in the previous June. Then Mr Cable, the most senior Lib Dem minister in the Coalition after deputy Premier Nick Clegg, was caught out by the *Daily Telegraph* in an interview boasting that he had declared war on Mr Murdoch – *'and I think we're going to win.'*

Uproar! Cable was responsible for overseeing media, telecom and broadcasting companies. As he had indicated to the *Telegraph's* undercover reporters that he would try to prevent News Corp from taking over BSkyB, he had to be relieved of that responsibility. The Prime Minister announced this on December 21.

The *Daily Telegraph* had been too clever by half. As one of the newspapers opposed to the News Corp bid, it had managed to force the removal from that area of responsibility of the minister most likely to block it. The newspaper that had scored a bull's eye by exposing the great Commons expenses scandal had shot itself in the foot.

The regulator Ofcom on January 25 declared that the *News Corp* takeover 'may be expected to operate against the public interest since there may not be a sufficient plurality of persons with control of media enterprises providing news and current affairs.'

This affair had become sufficiently important to bring Rupert Murdoch, looking tired and stressed, flying into London. To his dismay, another twist in the story involving one of his newspapers threatened to damage his prospects of success: mounting public pressure for a full-scale inquiry into Scotland Yard's handling of the allegations regarding hacking into the mobile phones of politicians and celebrities by journalists on his red top *News of the World*.

On January 27, the Metropolitan Police confirmed that it had received 'highly significant' new information and was reopening the case. Critics of the Met., which in 2007 had secured the conviction of the tabloid journal's royal reporter and a private investigator on phone hacking charges, complained that its failure to investigate adequately the alleged involvement of other journalists at the paper had been shocking. From 2008 to the beginning of 2011 Scotland Yard and the Crown Prosecution Service maintained that there was not enough evidence to prosecute anyone else. Politicians who suspected their private phone messages had been hacked demanded action. There was a growing suspicion that there had been too close a link between the police and the *News of the World* and other papers, involving lush entertainment and the passing of money in brown envelopes in return for information of value to reporters.

I knew from my years on the *Daily Express* and *Daily Sketch* just how close the relationship could be between crime reporters and well-placed coppers. Such a relationship could raise embarrassing problems when the journalists were alleged to have broken the law. As rumours and accusations grew, Andy Coulson, the Prime Minister's director of communications and former editor of the *News of the World* resigned in a blaze of publicity from his key Downing Street post, confessing that the row was a distraction from his role. He had always denied any knowledge of phone hacking while he was editor but had resigned from that job in 2007, in the light of the scandal that led to the jailing of the paper's royal affairs reporter. I was one of those who believed that David Cameron had then shown bad judgement in giving him such an important post in his team. During my years in Fleet Street it had been my regular responsibility to attend the editor's daily news conferences and I found it incredible that anyone in charge could not know if information for stories had been gathered by phone hacking operations.

However, despite the hacking hullabaloo, Murdoch was to get his way over the takeover bid for British Sky Broadcasting. On March 3ʹ Culture Secretary Jeremy Hunt, who had replaced Cable as the responsible minister, announced that he would not, after all, refer the controversial bid to the Competition Commission as News

Corporation had agreed to spin off Sky News into a separate listed company. By spurning the advice of the media regulator Ofcom, the minister had, in the words of the *Daily Telegraph*, *'fuelled suspicion'* that the Cameron Government, like the previous Labour administration, would perform considerable contortions *'to oblige the most powerful media magnate on the planet'*.

As part of the deal, Murdoch would continue to hold a controlling 39.1 per cent stake in the news channel. The man who had rescued the newspaper industry from the stranglehold of the print unions had succeeded, with the help of misguided politicians, in replacing it with his own monopolistic grip. Then, on Wednesday July 6, 2011 those same politicians who for years had been prepared to overlook the misdeeds of Murdoch's minions in return for their support and hospitality turned on them in outspoken fury. What had caused this sudden sea change?

It had been revealed that an investigator working for the *News of the World* had hacked into the mobile phone of the murdered teenager Milly Dowler, deleting voice mail messages, before the police had discovered her body. The hacking scandal previously confined mostly to celebrity victims had been given a shocking and sensational new twist.

The deletion of messages had led Milly's distraught parents to believe that she could still be alive and could have erased evidence that would have assisted the police in their search for the girl.

When Murdoch had launched his down-market *Sun* in 1969 I had accused him of deliberately lowering press standards – but I never foresaw just how low those standards would fall under his leadership.

In the Commons Labour MP Chris Bryant, accusing the *News of the World* of "systematic criminality", called for an emergency debate and public inquiry. Swept along on a wave of public outrage, many MPs supported his demand and the Speaker granted a three-hour debate for the following day.

Reporting the debate for the *Daily Telegraph*, Andrew Gimson wrote:

"This was the day MPs stopped being frightened of Rupert Murdoch. Timid reticence about the misdeeds of his company, News International, gave way to total condemnation of its behaviour... There is something faintly ignoble about the way in which MPs who until a few days ago were terrified of annoying Mr Murdoch are now terrified of saying anything that might be construed as support for him."

Prime Minister David Cameron, jumping on the bandwagon, announced that he would order an independent inquiry into media ethics once police investigations had been concluded. Simultaneously, Scotland Yard announced a second police inquiry into whether the *News of the World* had made illegal payments to serving police officers.

News International, by then under intense pressure, confirmed it had uncovered emails that, it was claimed, implicated Cameron's friend Andy Coulson in the payment of officers when he edited the *News of the World*.

As more revelations involving victims of crime and bereaved relatives of war dead shocked the country, leading companies began to withdraw advertising from the biggest selling English-language newspaper in the world.

Adding to Rupert Murdoch's mounting problems, it appeared that the hacking scandal could de-rail his bid to take full control of BSkyB when Ofcom confirmed it had a duty to be satisfied that the holder of a broadcasting licence was 'fit and proper'.

Then, in a stunning surprise move designed to try to end the uproar, Murdoch, citing inhuman behaviour of some staff, announced that the *News of the World* would be shut down after its last issue on the coming Sunday. Hundreds of journalists would lose their jobs. My mind went back to the untimely death of the *News Chronicle*. I could sympathise with them. Most of them were innocent of misdeeds. But I had never considered working for '*the News of the Screws*', even though it was my dear father's favourite Sunday newspaper.

Murdoch had hoped that by brutally killing off his 168-year-old newspaper he would improve his prospects of gaining the profitable BSkyB. By Monday, however, the tricky Aussie was deploying a new tactic, seeking to delay the proposed takeover in order to allow public anger over phone hacking to subside. In another surprise move, News Corp withdrew its proposal to spin off Sky News as an independent unit, forcing Culture Secretary Jeremy Hunt to refer the bid to the Competition Commissioner, after all. Experts forecast that this could result in a lengthy inquiry lasting up to a year. The troublesome issue had been kicked into the long grass.

Meanwhile, as his former official advisor and ex *News of the World* editor Andy Coulson was arrested by police, David Cameron warned that there must be a different relationship between politicians and the media in future. Ominously, he announced that yet another independent public inquiry would be held into media ethics and standards that could lead to new laws to police the press. Conveniently, he ignored the fact that it was not a police investigation or government action that had exposed the depravity of Murdoch's newspaper empire but a determined campaign by a newspaper – *The Guardian*.

As I thought at the time, Cameron – despite warnings – had shown appalling personal judgement in employing Coulson and no other top politician in recent times had become closer to some of Murdoch's top most people. Was he now bent on another, even more serious, error of judgement by initiating a crackdown on the media in general?

A new system that would undermine the media's ability to expose wrongdoing – such as the widespread fiddling of their expenses by MPs of all the main parties uncovered by the *Daily Telegraph* – would no doubt be welcomed by many in Parliament. Newspapers warned them that it would be wrong to punish the media as a whole for the crimes of the *News of the World*. Freedom of speech must remain sacrosanct.

As battle lines were drawn for yet another clash between politicians and the press in the stormy summer of 2011, one was prompted to ask: what can now outdo this eventful chapter in the ongoing saga that was once Fleet Street's and is now the wider media's fight to get the better of politicians? The answer has already hit the headlines – 'Wikileaks'.

As *The Guardian* newspaper has noted in reporting on the official cables unloaded by the Wikileaks system of Mr Julian Assange, they "revealed wrongdoing, war crimes, corruption, hypocrisy, greed, espionage, double-dealing and the cynical exercise of power on a wondrous scale".

"Journalism at its noblest," Matthew Norman has written in *The Daily Telegraph*, "is about exposing information that the powerful would like to keep hidden, and Wikileaks has an honourable record of tackling vested interests of all political persuasions."

By 2011 politicians around the world faced the hard fact that, armed with this new source of previously closely guarded information, the media had at last got the upper-hand – at least in truly democratic states.

As for my later experiences beyond Fleet Street in that other vital element of the democratic process, the world of lobbying, I recommend, dear reader, a perusal of my already published memoirs covering that period, entitled *"People, Politics and Pressure Groups."*

EPILOGUE

Monday, 18 October 2010. Fifty years after the *News Chronicle* was swallowed up by the *Daily Mail*, I joined a group of twenty-four journalists from the famous old liberal newspaper to mark the special anniversary of that shameful event. Appropriately, we gathered for lunch in the former *Daily Mail* building in Tudor Street, between Fleet Street and the River Thames. It had been converted into a smart bar and restaurant named The Class Rooms. The invitation had been headed *'News Chronicle takes over Daily Mail.'*

I had missed few such annual reunions since the Cadbury family owners of the *Chronicle* had sold it to Lord Rothermere's very different right-wing paper in October 1960. As I entered the building on the corner of Whitefriars Street I asked myself: "What other former newspaper had ever enjoyed such loyalty and devotion from its staff?"

After a reunion held thirty years before in 1980 in the Press Club, attended by about two hundred and fifty people who had worked for the paper, a former reporter Joyce Egginton, who had travelled from the United States to attend, wrote in *The Observer*: *"The News Chronicle was so special to those who worked there that after a gap of twenty years more than enough of them showed up to bring out a new edition of the newspaper. They travelled from Singapore, New York, Geneva, Bonn, Strasbourg and Paris, and came out of retirement from villages all over England. There was ex-Chronicle staff from virtually every newspaper in Fleet Street... not only journalists came, but middle-aged men who used to be copy boys, library assistants and hall porters... Mr Laurence Cadbury was not invited."*

Cadbury, who so disgracefully failed the great newspaper and its dedicated staff, has been long since dead. Regretfully, most of those who attended the 1980 reunion had also died. Among the oldest survivors at the 2010 reunion were Douglas Brown who had been the Parliamentary Correspondent and then political columnist; Geoffrey Goodman, Labour and Industrial Correspondent; and George Vine, Bonn Correspondent. With an average age of ninety they sat at the top table with Betty Thomson, organiser of the reunions and daughter of my old friend and brilliant journalist Francis Williams. Also there sat Joyce Egginton who once again had made the journey from New York.

Geoffrey Goodman put into words what was special about the newspaper that Charles Dickens had launched. In a short speech he said that the *Chronicle* was a liberal newspaper with a small 'L' that became the voice of radical feeling in Fleet Street. He recalled how, in the 1930s, it had revealed the horrors of the fascist war machine in the Spanish Civil War and had opposed the appeasement of Nazi Germany. It was the voice of a real community brought together to preserve a journalistic ethos – the overriding importance of revealing the truth. It was a community entirely special in the history of the British Press.

Maybe we had enjoyed the best days of Fleet Street. Today, concluded Geoffrey, journalists did not get the opportunity they would have had on the *Chronicle.*

As we dispersed, some for the last time, I asked myself whether it would have been better for Fleet Street if I had accepted the invitation in October 1960 to join Granada Television instead of moving on to help kill off two more national newspapers and earn my reputation as a jinx.

BIBLIOGRAPHY

Boyd, Francis – *Richard Austen Butler*, Publishing Corp. 1956

Chisholm, Anne & Davie, Michael – *Beaverbrook, A Life*, Hutchinson 1992

Crosland, C.A.R. – *The Future of Socialism*, Jonathan Cape 1956

Crossman, Richard – *The Diaries of a Cabinet Minister*, Hamish Hamilton and Jonathan Cape

Dalton, Hugh – *Memoirs 1945-60*, Frederick Muller Limited 1962

Evans, Harold – *Downing Street Diary*, Hodder and Stoughton 1981

Fremantle, Anne – *The British Fabians*, New American Library 1960

Glenton, George & Pattinson, William – *The Last Chronicle of Bouverie Street*, George Allen & Unwin Ltd. 1963

Greenslade, Roy – *Press Gang*, Macmillan 2003

Lord Hailsham, – *A Sparrow's Flight*, Collins 1990

Haines, Joe – *Glimmers of Twilight*, Politico's Publishing 2003

Harland, Oswald – *Yorkshire North Riding*, Robert Hale Ltd. 1951

Junor, John – *Listening for a Midnight Train*, Pan Books & Chapmans 1990

Kinrade, Derek – *Alf Morris, People's Parliamentarian*, National Information Forum 2007

Randall, Mike – *The Funny Side of Fleet Street*, Bloomsbury 1988

Shawcross, William – *Murdoch*, Chatto & Windus Ltd. 1993

Wheen, Francis – *Tom Driberg*, Chatto & Windus 1990

Yeats, W.B. – *The Collected Poems*, Macmillan & Co.
Limited 1950

INDEX

340